Praise for
The Good News of God's Reign

"Carl Toney's *The Good News of God's Reign* is a beautifully produced, sure-handed guide to the New Testament writings. Accessible, engagingly written, informative, perfectly structured—this book offers everything one could want in a college-level introduction to the New Testament. Students who read this book will gain a clear understanding of the overall shape of the New Testament writings, the first-century world and contexts in which they were authored, and the major themes of these texts. Perhaps most importantly, students will encounter the central claim of the New Testament: Through the mission and work of Jesus, God is in charge."

—**David J. Downs,** PhD, Clarendon-Laing Professor in New Testament Studies, Keble College, University of Oxford

"Many course texts aimed at introducing the New Testament are written for advanced student populations and therefore have little hope of serving as a useful resource for undergraduates. Against that general trend, Carl Toney has produced an academically informed, visually attractive, and pedagogically intuitive volume designed for undergraduate students and rooted in his years of experience in effective classroom teaching. This book is an excellent classroom resource. I warmly commend it, both to professors and their students."

—**Christopher W. Skinner,** PhD, Professor of New Testament and Early Christianity, Loyola University Chicago

"This textbook does more than explain what's in the Bible—it invites readers into the glorious drama of God's reign in Christ. Carl Toney skillfully guides students through the New Testament with academic integrity and theological illumination. This is a perfect starting place for students and interested Bible readers who want to make sense of ancient texts from another time and place. Highly recommended!"

—**Nijay K. Gupta,** PhD, Professor of New Testament, Northern Seminary

"In *The Good News of God's Reign*, Carl Toney has provided an introduction to the New Testament that is both highly engaging and visually stimulating. Writing with prose that is highly accessible for undergraduate and seminary students, Toney deftly brings his readers into the world of the New Testament, its critical issues, and the story of its books, authors, and original readers. The vivid art and striking pictures compliment well the book's readable content, and they will no doubt help keep students engaged as they read. As one who has taught undergraduate students for the past 20 years, I highly commend *The Good News of God's Reign* to those teaching introductory courses on the New Testament and plan to use it in such courses of my own moving forward."

—**Adam Winn,** PhD, S. Louis and Ann W. Armstrong Professor, Samford University

"This is a quintessential textbook for undergraduates. Not only is it informative and readable but the many pictures, maps, and charts invite students to enjoy a visual feast as they read. Each chapter opens by providing the historical context behind the respective New Testament writing, and then the content of that writing is deftly handled. Instructors will appreciate that each chapter ends with relevant key terms, recommended readings, and questions to assist discussions in a classroom setting."

—**B. J. Oropeza,** PhD, Professor in the School of Theology, Azusa Pacific University and Seminary; coeditor of *Perspectives on Paul: Five Views*

"Concise, accurate, up-to-date, and above all interesting. Readers will find themselves caught up in the gospel story afresh. Carl Toney's *The Good News of God's Reign* is perfect for all those who are eager to encounter the life-changing message of the New Testament."

—**Matthew W. Bates,** PhD, Professor of New Testament, Northern Seminary, author of *Why the Gospel?*, host of *OnScript* podcast

"The concept of the 'fullness of time' is central to the proclamation of the gospel and makes it clear that, in God's economy, timing is everything. Carl Toney offers *The Good News of God's Reign* to the world at a perfect time. As the need grows for people to not only recapture the biblical story but understand how to engage it well, Toney's creative, thoughtful, and inviting approach provides an accessible entrée into the world of the New Testament. Students of the Bible will find in this book a valuable resource that will lead to a deeper understanding of the text and equip them to embody its message."

—**Abson Prédestin Joseph,** PhD, Professor of New Testament and Vice President for Academic Services, Bethel University, Indiana

"Carl Toney has produced a rich, readable, and visually stunning introduction to the New Testament. Professor Toney is consistently sensitive to the varying ways New Testament texts relate to the older biblical texts of the Jewish scriptures and to the contemporary Greco-Roman world in which they were written. He is conversant with scholarly discussions and debates without losing his readers in the weeds of those debates. Perhaps most importantly, he leads readers of the New Testament into those primary virtues that mark—or should mark—followers of Jesus: love, faith, and hope."

—**Rafael Rodríguez,** PhD, Professor of New Testament, Pittsburgh Theological Seminary; author of *Jesus Darkly: Remembering Jesus with the New Testament*

The GOOD NEWS *of* GOD'S REIGN

AN INTRODUCTION TO THE

NEW TESTAMENT

The GOOD NEWS *of* GOD'S REIGN

CARL N. TONEY

Abilene Christian University Press

THE GOOD NEWS OF GOD'S REIGN

An Introduction to the New Testament

ACU
PRESS

ISBN 978-1-68426-111-6 | LCCN 2025003708

Printed in the United States of America

LIBRARY OF CONGRESS CATALOGING-IN-PUBLICATION DATA
Names: Toney, Carl N., 1975- author.
Title: The good news of God's reign : an introduction to the New Testament / Carl N. Toney.
Description: Abilene, Texas : ACU Press, [2025] | Includes bibliographical references.
Identifiers: LCCN 2025003708 (print) | LCCN 2025003709 (ebook) | ISBN 9781684261116 (paperback) | ISBN 9781684268481 (ebook)
Subjects: LCSH: Bible. New Testament—Introductions.
Classification: LCC BS2330.3 .T66 2025 (print) | LCC BS2330.3 (ebook) | DDC 225.6/1—dc23/eng/20250331
LC record available at https://lccn.loc.gov/2025003708
LC ebook record available at https://lccn.loc.gov/2025003709

Cover design by Bruce Gore
Interior text design by Sandy Armstrong, Strong Design

For information contact: Abilene Christian University Press

ACU Box 29138 | Abilene, Texas 79699

1-877-816-4455 | www.acupressbooks.com

25 26 27 28 29 30 31 // 7 6 5 4 3 2 1

To Kip Lines and J. Blair Wilgus

CONTENTS

MAPS AND CHARTS

SIDEBARS

ACKNOWLEDGMENTS

Into the vast sea of New Testament introductions, I have now cast two volumes. The first is a graduate-level introduction, in which I revised Ralph Martin's *New Testament Foundations*. After that project was complete, I was contacted by Jason Fikes to compose a shorter introduction geared toward undergraduate students. He gave me permission to focus more on the message of the New Testament rather than following the rabbit trails of scholarly discussions. This work is the result.

Life can be funny sometimes. I've known Jason for over twenty years. I met my wife, Lisa, in my first class at Fuller Seminary. It was a Greek class, and Jason was our professor. My wife is now a pastor, and we have four kids—Zoe (named in honor of that Greek class), Gus (my favorite theologian is Augustine), Paxton (named after the city of peace: Jerusalem), and Eden (because we also took Hebrew)—and our dog, Apricot (she's the color of the fruit).

Speaking of family, I am grateful for my parents, Larry and Teena; my sister, Trisha, along with her kids, John and Kristina; and my uncles and aunts, Ray, Kristin, Linda, Gary, George, and Karen. I'm also thankful for my wife's extended family, including Bob, Lenora, Paul, Jessica, Lindsey, Andy, Jack, Charlotte, Eli, Isaac, Kristin, Jenna, Nick, Hannah, Ellie, James, Julie, Ty, and Lauren.

I could not have traveled this journey as a New Testament scholar alone. I'm indebted to mentors like Thomas Tobin, Ralph Martin, Rick Iwanaga, and Joe Grana. I'm thankful for teachers like Urban von Wahlde, Pauline Viviano, Donald Hagner, and David Scholer, who invested in me. I'm grateful for my academic friends through the years, including David Downs, David Creech, Adam Winn, Chris Spinks, Katy Lines, Matt Grant, Matt Jenson, Darian Lockett, Abson Joseph, and Brannon Hancock. Among these friends, I cannot forget J. Blair Wilgus and Kevin "Kip" Lines, two people who refuse to use their first names.

I'm thankful for my fellow faculty at Hope International University, including Kelly Dagley, Phil Towne, Curtis Holtzen, Matt Thompson, Robbie Phillips, James Yuile, Fay Ellwood, Natalie Hewitt,

Lydia Knopf, Laura Steele, Joyce Lee Yang, and Steve Edgington. I'm also thankful to Kent Anderson, whose endowment has provided me time for writing.

There have been so many friendships over the years, and I'm grateful for Erik and Camille Waage, Andy and Amy Rosdil, Ryan and Sarah Trobaugh, Gary and Nancy Fontan, Tom and Karen Babineau, Peter and Jeray Torry, John and Danice Burdett, John and Shauna Attwood, Caleb Kaltenbach, Rudy Hagood, Rob Denton, Scott Martin, Andy Janssen, Jen Bryan, Heidi Roux, Chris Hook, Shane Drake, Luke and Jenny Bayon, and Kiley Wallace. I'm also thankful for my church family, including Cynthia Fluker, Kelly Roth, Harmony Bathauer, Aaron McRae, and Woody Morwood.

Finally, I'm thankful to God for my community and for the opportunities to serve his kingdom.

ABOUT THIS BOOK

Welcome to the world of the New Testament! This book is an invitation to enter that world. The opening chapter contextualizes our journey by retracing the history of the Jewish scriptures and bridging the gap between their ending and the beginning of the New Testament in the first century. It orientates us to the main theme of the book by asking how God is in charge.

Those wishing to look more closely at the Jewish scriptures may wish to consult the counterpart of this book: *The God Who Saves: An Introduction to the Message of the Old Testament* by Glenn Pemberton. Readers may wonder why I've chosen to describe the Old Testament as the "Jewish scriptures." First, this label reminds us that these texts were written by an ancient ethnic group: the Jewish people. This can help increase our cross-cultural competence. Second, this helps us to remember that the early Christians were Jewish. Of course, part of the good news is that non-Jewish people have been invited to join the people of God. The term "Jewish scriptures" respectfully acknowledges that Christianity shares these writings with Judaism, and both recognize these writings as sacred. Third, I generally avoid the label "Hebrew scriptures" because many of the early Christians used the Greek translation of these writings. Fourth, I find the contrast between "Old" and "New" unhelpful because it can be misunderstood as diminishing the relevance and importance of these Jewish writings for Christians. Finally, the choice of "Jewish scriptures" is not meant to diminish the traditional Christian label of "Old Testament," which does have the benefit of tying the Old Testament and New Testament together.

After the opening chapter, each New Testament work is introduced by either describing the author or the audience. For Part One (Matthew, Mark, Luke, and Acts) and Part Three (non-Pauline writings including the Johannine literature), the discussion focuses on the traditional author, while Part Two (the Pauline letters) allows us to focus on the audience, including highlighting specific figures in Pauline communities. These are reconstructions consisting of a composite of biblical materials, traditional materials, and other historical sources. However, as readers will discover, there are some debates about the identities and circumstances of these people, and they will need to discern the extent that they accept or refute traditional views.

These figures help us to immerse ourselves in the sociocultural world of the New Testament. These people—both women and men from various socioeconomic and ethnic backgrounds—remind us that real people wrote the works of the New Testament to address the particular needs of real communities. As we explore these writings, we will discover that we share some of those same needs and are asking similar questions today. But we'll also discover that we have some different needs and have different questions. It is important to notice both similarities and differences between their world and ours. We will do well to remember that the New Testament was not written to us, but it was written for us. Not everything can or should apply to us, but we can learn some important teachings that can impact our lives.

After these introductions, every chapter moves on to present the themes of each New Testament work. Additionally, for the Gospels and Acts, readers are exposed to the general flow of their stories. This book drills down on the message and content of each work more than introducing broader scholarly debates (such as authorship and composition). These concerns are considered, but they are woven into the presentation of material. Further, sidebars allow readers to engage with selected critical issues and scholarly discussion. Readers interested in engaging with the wider academic discussions may wish to read my more extended New Testament introduction, coauthored with Ralph Martin: *New Testament Foundations.*

Each chapter also includes suggested readings of the biblical text. While any reader would undoubtedly benefit from reading the entire New Testament, these selected readings highlight the gist of each book. Readers may wish to read the introductory material in this book to familiarize themselves with each New Testament work before reading the biblical text. For the sake of review, each chapter includes a summary of key terms and people. Readers who are less familiar with the New Testament may benefit from becoming familiar with these concepts prior to reading the chapter. In addition, reflection questions are included to help readers recall important material. Finally, a brief selection of commentaries and recommended books are listed for those readers wishing to engage beyond this book.

In terms of arrangement, this book has sixteen chapters to allow college courses to use approximately one chapter per week. Some courses may need to combine a couple of chapters. The book is also divided into three parts. Each connects to one of the three primary Christian virtues—love, faith, and hope (1 Cor. 13:13)—and moves from Jesus to Paul to the wider church.

"Part One—The Love of God: Jesus and the Church" introduces readers to the main character of this book, Jesus, who is central to the Christian faith. As such, this book intentionally begins and ends with stories about Jesus. Mark's Gospel is explicated first because it is considered by most scholars to be the first Gospel written, while John's Gospel is found near the conclusion because it may be one of the last New Testament works written. Mark's Gospel also provides the opportunity to broadly outline the ministry of Jesus. The chapters on Matthew and Luke follow because of the similarity of their material, and these chapters highlight unique perspectives about Jesus in these Gospels. Acts, which tells the story of the growth of the early church, serves as a transition to the letters of Paul.

Part One also introduces readers to the main theme of this book: God is in charge. This theme is based on Jesus's gospel message: "The time is fulfilled and the kingdom of God has come near. Repent and believe in the gospel!" (Mark 1:15 LEB). With this proclamation, Jesus declared that God is in charge, and he invited his followers to join God's kingdom. The New Testament is written from the perspective that Jesus's life, death, and resurrection inaugurated this kingdom and provides present benefits for the church. It challenges people to submit to God's rule because of the hope in the final consummation of God's reign when Jesus returns. Those interested in unpacking Jesus's gospel further may enjoy N. T. Wright's *Simply Good News*.

"Part Two—The Faith of God: Pauline Christianity" explores the thirteen letters of Paul. Paul's letters illuminate his role as an ambassador for the kingdom of God, and they provide a window into the early churches as they lived in light of God's rule. When possible, Paul's letters are connected to the relevant portions of Acts. While the New Testament arranges Paul's letters from longest to shortest, this book has generally arranged them chronologically from his earliest to last. A sidebar is provided when there is debate about this arrangement (especially in terms of Paul's imprisonment) or Paul's authorship. Readers wishing to follow the order of the New Testament can still do so since all these letters are treated individually in each chapter.

"Part Three—The Hope of God: The Wider Church" explores the remainder of the New Testament letters, as well as works connected with John the disciple. We will learn how other Christian communities lived out the truth of God's reign. I encourage readers not to move too swiftly through these works because they are so distinct from Paul's letters. Unfortunately, works like Hebrews and James are often read through the lens of Paul. Readers will discover the unique presentation in Hebrews of Jesus as high priest and James's wonderful emphasis upon faith in action. James and Jude are intentionally paired because of their parallels with 1–2 Peter, which are noted. Finally, we return to the stories about Jesus's life and ministry with the Gospel of John. We also gain insights into how early Christians responded to this Gospel in 1–3 John. Revelation, which describes the return of Jesus and the establishment of his reign, serves a fitting end for this work that reminds us that God is in charge.

Carl N. Toney
Fullerton, California

ABBREVIATIONS

Aram.	Aramaic
AYB	Anchor Yale Bible
AYBD	*Anchor Yale Bible Dictionary*. Edited by David Noel Freedman. 6 vols. Doubleday, 1992.
BDAG	Bauer, Walter, Frederick W. Danker, William F. Arndt, and F. Wilbur Gingrich. *Greek-English Lexicon of the New Testament and Other Early Christian Literature*. 3rd ed. University of Chicago Press, 2000.
BNTC	Black's New Testament Commentaries
DJG	*Dictionary of Jesus and the Gospels.* Edited by Joel B. Green, Jeannine K. Brown, and Nicholas Perrin. 2nd ed. IVP Academic, 2013.
DPL	*Dictionary of Paul and His Letters: A Compendium of Contemporary Biblical Scholarship*. Edited by Lynn H. Cohick and Nijay K. Gupta. 2nd ed. IVP Academic, 2023.
Germ.	German
Grk.	Greek
Heb.	Hebrew
Herm.	Hermeneia
Lat.	Latin
LSJ	Liddell, Henry George, Robert Scott, Henry Stuart Jones. *A Greek-English Lexicon.* 9th ed. with revised supplement. Clarendon, 1996.
LXX	Septuagint
MT	Masoretic Text
NIB	*The New Interpreter's Bible*. Edited by Leander E. Keck. 12 vols. Abingdon, 1994–2004.
NICNT	New International Commentary on the New Testament
NIDOTTE	*New International Dictionary of Old Testament Theology and Exegesis*. Edited by Willem A. VanGemeren. 5 vols. Zondervan, 1997.
NIGTC	New International Greek Testament Commentary
RNT	Reading the New Testament
SBL	Society of Biblical Literature
SBLDS	Society of Biblical Literature Dissertation Series

SP	Sacra Pagina
Str-B	Strack, H. L., and P. Billerbeck. *Kommentar zum Neuen Testament aus Talmud und Midrasch.* 6 vols. 1922–1961.
TDNT	*Theological Dictionary of the New Testament.* Edited by Gerhard Kittel and Gerhard Friedrich. Translated by Geoffrey W. Bromiley. 10 vols. Eerdmans, 1964–1976.
WBC	Word Biblical Commentary

Abbreviations for biblical texts are from the *Chicago Manual of Style*, 18th ed.
Abbreviations for ancient texts are from the *SBL Handbook of Style*, 2nd ed.

PART ONE

THE LOVE OF GOD

Jesus and the Church

1

GREAT EXPECTATIONS

From the Jewish Scriptures to Jesus

Who's in charge? Who's really in charge? The answer seemed clear to people living in the first-century province of Judea.

The Romans.

God's Promises to Abraham

The Romans had been in charge since the days of Pompey in 63 CE (Eusebius, *Ant.* 14.4.1–5). But the Jewish scriptures tell a different story. The stories in Genesis describe how the God who made the world (Gen. 1–2) chose Israel's ancestors—Abraham and Sarah—from among all the people in the ancient world to be his people (Gen. 12:1–9). They were called out of Ur in the land of Mesopotamia to the land of Canaan. God said to them:

> Go from your country and your kindred and your father's house to the land that I will show you. I will make of you a great nation, and I will bless you and make your name great, so that you will be a blessing. I will bless those who bless you, and the one who curses you I will curse; and in you all the families of the earth shall be blessed. (Gen. 12:1b–3)

SUGGESTED READING

Genesis 1:1-3:24
Genesis 11:27-12:9
Genesis 15:1-21
Genesis 17:1-27
Genesis 49:1-33
Exodus 1:1-14:31
Exodus 20:1-24:18

God made with them a formal commitment, which was called a "**covenant**" (Heb. *berith*; Grk. *diathēkē*).[1] He promised them three things: (1) their family would grow to be a great nation with countless heirs; (2) they would be given the land of Canaan; (3) their people would become a blessing to the nations of

[1]In this book, foreign words that are italicized without any notation are Greek (Grk.). Otherwise, the language is indicated, such as Hebrew (Heb.), Aramaic (Aram.), and Latin (Lat.). The typical format is to put the Greek word first, but this chapter will occasionally put the Hebrew first when referencing the Jewish scriptures.

Abraham and Sarah Hosting Three Angels by Franco Vignazia. Church Chiesa di San Giuseppe Artigiano. Forlì, Italy. (2019)

the world. This commitment was so significant that the Jewish scriptures recorded it three times on three different occasions (Gen. 12, 15, 17).[2] The sign of this covenant was the circumcision of all Jewish males eight days after birth (Gen. 17:9–14; Lev. 12:3; cf. Luke 1:59; Acts 7:8). Strangely, while God promised that Abraham's household would be great, he only had two named heirs—Ishmael and Isaac.[3]

Isaac also had two sons—Esau and Jacob. Of these two, the Jewish people trace their ancestry to Jacob, who was renamed by God as "Israel" after he wrestled with God (Gen. 32:28). His two wives, Leah and Rachel, and two concubines, Zilpah and Bilhah, bore him one daughter, Dinah, and twelve sons. These sons' names were associated with the twelve tribes of Israel: Reuben, Simeon, Levi, Judah, Zebulun, Issachar, Dan, Gad, Asher, Naphtali, Benjamin, and Joseph. From Joseph came the two half-tribes of Ephraim and Manasseh (Gen. 29:32–30:24, 35:16–26, 49:1–28; Josh. 14:3–5).[4]

Because of God's covenants with Abraham, Isaac, and Jacob, the Jewish people viewed the world through the lens of a binary contrast between those who were Jews versus those people who were not Jews. Anyone not ethnically Jewish was called a "**Gentile**" (Heb. *goyim*; *ethnos*). However, Gentiles were welcome to join the Jewish people. Women could join via marriage, and men could join through certain rituals, such as circumcision. Those Gentiles, who followed many of the Jewish laws, were called God-fearers (e.g., Acts 13:6; Josephus, *Ag. Ap.* 2.280–86). A "proselyte" (*prosēlytos*; Heb. *ger*) was any Gentile male who was circumcised and followed the law (e.g., Acts 15:1, 15:5; Jth. 14:10; m. Pesaḥ. 8:8; b. Pesaḥ. 92a; t. Pesaḥ. 7:14; b. Šabb. 135a).

[2] For a brief introduction to the idea of "covenant," see Goldingay, "Covenant OT and NT," *NIB*, 1:767–78.

[3] Notably, according to Jewish scriptures, the heirs of both sons enjoyed God's promised blessings. This account differs from Muslim tradition, which identifies Ishmael as the child of the promise.

[4] By one count, there were thirteen tribes because Joseph's portion was split into two portions. Jewish inheritance law gave the firstborn heir a double portion. Jacob broke with this tradition by giving this to Joseph (Gen. 50).

The Leadership of Moses

Every year at "**Passover**" (Heb. *pesach*; *pascha*), Jewish families tell the greatest story ever told. This is the story of the Jewish people's deliverance from Egypt, which could be described by some as "good news" (Heb. *besrah*; *euangelion*). The Passover story began when there was a famine in the land of Canaan, which caused Jacob and his family to move to Egypt (Gen. 46–47). Jacob's family settled in the land of Goshen, where God made good on his promise to Abraham as his family grew to become a numerous nation (Exod. 1:1–7).

However, the time in Egypt did not go well for the Israelites because the Egyptians enslaved them (Exod. 1:8–14). Thankfully, God had not forgotten about his people, nor did he forget his other promises to Abraham. God raised up a great prophet and deliverer named Moses (Exod. 2–4). Through ten miraculous and mighty deeds of power, God freed the Jewish people from their oppressive Gentile ruler, the Pharaoh (Exod. 5–14). After destroying the Pharaoh and his Egyptian army in the Red Sea (Exod. 14:1–31), God led the Israelites to Mount Sinai (Exod. 16–19).

At Mount Sinai, God made the Mosaic covenant with his people. He gave them his perfect law, including the Ten Commandments (Exod. 20; Deut. 5). The first half of the commandments taught people to love God. People were commanded to: (1) remember God's deliverance from Egypt, (2) worship God alone and not make idols, (3) honor God's name, and (4) observe God's Sabbath. The last half of the commandments taught the love of neighbors. People were commanded to: (5) honor their parents, (6) not murder, (7) not commit adultery, (8) not steal, (9) not give false legal testimony, and (10) not covet.[5] God promised to bless those who obeyed his commands and to curse those who disobeyed (Deut. 27–28; 2 Chron. 7:12–22).

This modern Passover Seder plate includes (clockwise) horseradish (Heb. *maror*), egg (Heb. *beitza*), lamb shank bone (Heb. *zeroah*), onion or lettuce (Heb. *maror/chazeret*), charoset, and parsley (Heb. *karpas*). On the left is salt water and charoset. On the right is parsley (Heb. *karpas*) and a cup of wine.

Matzah bread served at a Passover Seder.

[5]There are at least three ways to divide the Ten Commandments, or more literally translated as the "ten words" (Exod. 34:28; Deut. 4:13; 10:4 LEB). The modern Jewish division (followed here) begins with remembering salvation from Egypt (an emphasis upon God's grace). Ironically, Christian divisions begin with the command to have no other gods (an emphasis upon the law).

Some rabbis calculated that there were 613 commands in the Mosaic law—365 laws to match the days of the year and 248 laws like the bones in a body (b. Mak. 23b). Some teachers summarized the law with just two commandments. According to one story (Luke 10:27), an unknown expert in the law summarized everything with "Love the LORD your God with all your heart and with all your soul and with all your strength" (Deut. 6:5 NIV) and "love your neighbor as yourself" (Lev. 19:18 NIV). Likewise, Jesus summarized the law with these two **greatest commandments** (Mark 12:29–30; Matt. 22:37–39). Linking the law to the love of God was no surprise since this command was taken directly from the beginning of the Shema, a prayer the Jewish people recited two or three times each day (Deut. 6:4–5).

Elsewhere, another writer put these commands on the lips of the sons of Jacob. Supposedly, Issachar exhorted, "Keep the law of God, my children; achieve integrity: live without malice, not tinkering with God's commands or your neighbor's affairs. *Love the Lord and your neighbor . . .*" (T. Iss. 7.6—emphasis added). Likewise, Dan urged, "Observe the Lord's commandments, then, my children, and keep his law. Avoid wrath, and hate lying. . . . Throughout all your life *love the Lord and one another* with a true heart" (T. Dan 5.3—emphasis added).

Even the famous Jewish writer Philo divided the law between conduct "*towards God* by the rules of piety and holiness, and of one's conduct *toward men* by the rules of humanity and justice" (*Spec. Laws* 2.63—emphasis added). Rabbi Hillel summarized the law this way: "What is hateful to you, do not do to your fellow human being. This is the entire law, all of it; the rest is commentary. Go and study" (b. Šabb 31a). Concerning Leviticus 19:18, Rabbi Akiva said, "This is the great general rule of the Torah" (y. Ned. 9:4, I:1a; cf. Sifra 89b).

The Jewish people were thankful for the law because it was considered to be the best expression of God's will. The law acted like a fence protecting God's people and keeping them distinct from the Gentiles. The Letter of Aristeas 139 teaches:

> In his wisdom the legislator [Moses], in a comprehensive survey of each particular part, and being endowed by God for the knowledge of universal truths, surrounded us with unbroken palisades and iron walls to prevent our mixing with any of the other peoples in any matter, being thus kept pure in body and soul, preserved from false beliefs, and worshiping the only God omnipotent over all creation.

Obedience to God's commands made the Jewish people unique among other nations. Visible marks of distinction included male circumcision, worship of God on the Sabbath, and adherence to food laws, including abstaining from Gentile foods like pork. In addition, some thought the Jewish people were given these laws and customs to discipline their souls.[6] Thus, we read in 4 Maccabees 1:34–35:

> Therefore, when we crave seafood and fowl and animals and all sorts of foods that are forbidden to us by the law, we abstain because of domination by reason. For the emotions of the appetites are restrained, checked by the temperate mind, and all the impulses of the body are bridled by reason.

[6]Hellenistic Jewish authors made a distinction between ethical commandments and other regulations. They still practiced the regulations because they symbolized and promoted virtue (Let. Aris. 143–52, 162–66; Philo, *Decalogue*; *Spec. Laws* 1–4; *Dreams* 1.93–94; Josephus, *Ant.* 1.25, 3.259–60; *Ag. Ap.* 2.164–219; Ps.-Phoc. 3, 6, 8, 14–15, 18, 22–30, 84–85, 99–101, 109, 177–86, 190–92, 198, 213–14, 220–22, 225–26; cf. 1 Cor. 9:8–11). Tobin, *Paul's Rhetoric*, 67–68.

During their time at Sinai, the Israelites also built the tabernacle, an elaborately decorated portable tent (Exod. 25–40). The tabernacle gave a place for God to dwell in their camp as they began their journey to the promised land. After they settled in the land, King Solomon built a more permanent sanctuary for God with the temple in Jerusalem (1 Kings 5–9; 2 Chron. 2–7).

God set aside the tribe of Levi to function as his priests, who would serve God in his sanctuary (Num. 1:50–54, 3:5–13). The regulations for the priesthood are found in the book of Leviticus (especially the Holiness Code in Leviticus 17–26). More specifically, God identified Aaron and his sons to function as the high priests (Exod. 28–29; Lev. 8). Inside the tabernacle and eventually the temple was the Holy of Holies, which only the high priest could enter once a year on the Day of Atonement (Lev. 16; Exod. 30:10). In this space was the Ark of the Covenant, which was said to be the footstool of God (Ps. 132:7; 1 Chron. 28:2).

Various regular sacrifices were made in the courtyard of the sanctuary, including the burnt, grain, fellowship, sin, and guilt offerings (Lev. 1–7). All year long, the priests would offer sacrifices on behalf of the people. But once a year, the high priest would offer an atoning sacrifice on the Day of Atonement, also called Yom Kippur (Lev. 16; Exod. 30:10). First, a bull was offered as a sin offering for the high priest and his house. Then, two goats were presented to God. Lots were cast to determine each goat's fate. One goat was the sin offering for the nation, and its blood was spread on the mercy seat of the ark. The other "scapegoat" had the people's sins symbolically placed upon its head by the high priest before it was sent out into the wilderness.

Additionally, the priests offered regular sacrifices to God (Exod. 29:38–46; Num. 28:1–8). It was only at the tabernacle, and later at the temple in Jerusalem, where sacrifices could be made. The priests performed daily sacrifices on behalf of the people because most people could not afford to visit God's house regularly since traveling to it was prohibitively expensive. To help pay for these regular sacrifices and the upkeep of God's sanctuary, every Jewish male paid a half-shekel tax each year (Exod. 30:13; cf. Matt. 17:34; Neh. 10:33–34; Josephus, *J.W.* 7.6.6; *Ant.* 18.9.1).

There was one pilgrimage festival that every Jew attempted to attend—the Passover and the Feast of Unleavened Bread, which lasted for seven days (Exod. 12:1–20; Num. 9:1–14; Deut. 16:1–8; Ezek. 45:21–25).[7] After the temple was built in Jerusalem, the population of the city swelled as

Tribe of Levi stained glass window by Marc Chagall. Hadassah Hospital. Jerusalem. (1962)

[7] Passover was one of the three major pilgrimage festivals, which also included the Feast of Weeks and the Feast of Booths. These festivals corresponded with the harvest seasons (Exod. 23:14–19, 34:18–26; Deut. 16:1–17).

Jewish families came to celebrate Passover. For anyone living outside the land, they might attend once in their lifetime, or they might send others to Jerusalem on their behalf.

On the Day of Preparation, the priests sacrificed one-year-old unblemished lambs for Passover during the afternoon of Nisan 14. On the evening of Nisan 15, families shared their Passover meal (Exod. 12:8–10).[8] Along with the roasted lamb, they ate bitter herbs as a reminder of the bitterness of slavery (Exod. 12:8). They consumed unleavened bread as a reminder of the sudden flight from Egypt (Exod. 12:14–20). Over time, a few other traditions were added, including drinking four cups of wine to remember both the joy of redemption and God's wrath poured upon their enemies (Exod. 6:6–7).[9] By remembering these stories during Passover, a first-century Jewish family could not help but wonder if God would deliver them from their current Gentile rulers: the Romans.

The Israelites crossed the Jordan River when they entered the promised land.

From the Wilderness to the Promised Land

Despite God's great act of delivering the Israelites from Egypt, the people did not fully trust God during their journey to the promised land (Num. 13–14). Even the great leaders Moses and Aaron had moments of failure (Num. 20:9–13). This resulted in the entire generation, which had been delivered from Egypt, wandering in the desert for forty years. But God remained with his people during this time, and his power was displayed through the great miracle worker Moses, who provided manna and quail to eat (Exod. 16:1–36; Num. 11:31–35) and fresh water to drink (Exod. 15:22–27, 17:1–7; Num. 20:1–13). When Moses died, he promised that God would send a future prophet like him (Deut. 18:15–22). And the Jewish people continued to look for this prophet (John 1:21, 1:24).

Although those delivered from Egypt failed to trust God, God remained faithful to his promises. He raised up a new leader named Joshua (Josh. 1:1–9). Joshua was Moses's protégé, and he led the twelve

[8] Jewish days begin at sunset, so evening started the day (Gen. 1:5, 1:8, 1:13, 1:19, 1:23, 1:31).

[9] Jewish communities continue to celebrate the Passover and have expanded the traditions. For example, see Scherman and Scherman, *The Illustrated Haggadah*.

tribes of Israel as they crossed the Jordan River (Josh. 3). The stories in the books of Joshua and Judges tell us how God finally made good on his promise to Abraham when the Jewish people conquered the land of Canaan. When the land was divided among the twelve tribes (Josh. 13–22), the Levites, as God's priests, didn't receive a portion because they were to serve God and the tabernacle (Josh. 14:3–5). Although the prophet Ezekiel envisioned a future where all the tribes, including Levi, received a portion of the land (Ezek. 45:1–9, 48:1–35).

Echoing these momentous events, the first-century prophet John baptized people near the Jordan River (Mark 1:1–11; Matt. 3:1–17; Luke 3:1–22; John 1:19–34). He called people out to the desert, to enter the Jordan River through baptism, and then to return to the land. He urged the Jewish people to repent for the forgiveness of their sins, and he preached a gospel that proclaimed, "God's rule [not the Romans' rule] had come" (Matt. 3:2; cf. Mark 1:4; Luke 3:3). John's preaching had the Jewish people asking if there was a new Joshua who could deliver them from their enemies and help them to reclaim their land.

An Israelite Kingdom: David the Son of God

After settling into the land, the Jewish people eventually asked God for a king. The first Jewish king was Saul (1 Sam. 9–10), but he was rejected by God because he disobeyed God (1 Sam. 13:13–14). Then God promised a shepherd from the tribe of Judah named David that he would establish his dynasty forever (1 Sam. 16:1–13). God called David and his descendants his "sons" (2 Sam. 7:14; 1 Chron. 17:13; Ps. 2:7). In fact, one of the kingly titles for the expected savior was the **son of God**. This relationship is celebrated in Psalm 2:7, when God said, "You are my son; today I have begotten you." Elsewhere, God's everlasting covenant with David is recorded:

> When your days are fulfilled and you lie down with your ancestors, I will raise up your offspring after you, who shall come forth from your body, and I will establish his kingdom. He shall build a house for my name, and I will establish the throne of his kingdom forever. I will be a father to him, and he shall be a son to me. When he commits iniquity, I will punish him with a rod such as mortals use, with blows inflicted by human beings. But I will not take my steadfast love from him, as I took it from Saul, whom I put away from before you. Your house and your kingdom shall be made sure forever before me; your throne shall be established forever. (2 Sam. 7:12–16; cf. 1 Chron. 17:11–14)

Carl N. Toney

This inscription commemorates the victory of an Aramean king over the "king of Israel" and the "king of the House of David." Tel Dan. (ninth cent. BCE)

In accordance with this promise, David's son Solomon replaced the tabernacle by building the first temple for God in Jerusalem (1 Kings 5–9;

2 Chron. 2–7). The temple was considered the center of God's presence among his people in the land. After the temple was dedicated to God, God appeared to Solomon and made him this promise:

> I have heard your prayer, and have chosen this place for myself as a house of sacrifice. When I shut up the heavens so that there is no rain, or command the locust to devour the land, or send pestilence among my people, if my people who are called by my name humble themselves, pray, seek my face, and turn from their wicked ways, then I will hear from heaven, and will forgive their sin and heal their land. Now my eyes will be open and my ears attentive to the prayer that is made in this place. For now I have chosen and consecrated this house so that my name may be there forever; my eyes and my heart will be there for all time. (2 Chron. 7:12–16)

Solomon was known far and wide for his wisdom. According to Jewish scriptures, God promised Solomon that he could have whatever he requested. Solomon asked God for divine wisdom. God was so pleased with his answer that he also blessed Solomon with wealth and power (1 Kings 3:1–15; 2 Chron. 1:1–13). Solomon's wisdom was so famous that the queen of Sheba traveled to Jerusalem to test him (1 Kings 10:1–29; 2 Chron. 9:1–28). Writings such as Song of Songs, Ecclesiastes, many portions of Proverbs, and the Wisdom of Solomon are attributed to this sage. One proverb reminds us, "The fear [or awe] of the LORD is the beginning of knowledge; fools despise wisdom and instruction" (Prov. 1:7). Yet, Solomon's wisdom was not always practiced in his own life. Solomon was known for introducing foreign gods to Israel (1 Kings 11:26–40, 12:24) and marrying foreign wives (2 Kings 11:1–13). By the first century, the Jewish people became much more cautious about non-Jews, who were stereotyped as sexually immoral and idolatrous (e.g., Rom. 1:18–31).

Unfortunately, Solomon's son Rehoboam did not inherit his father's wisdom. His oppressive rule increased the demand for forced labor, and his high taxes started a revolution that ended with the northern ten tribes of Israel forming their own nation under the leadership of Jeroboam (1 Kings 11–12; 2 Chron. 10). Only the southern two tribes of Judah and Benjamin remained loyal to the house of David. They became known as the kingdom of Judah. With Rehoboam, the nation became broken. However, the Jewish people hoped to be reunified one day under God's chosen king.

The Assyrian and Babylonian Exile

The Jewish scriptures testify to God's "covenantal faithfulness" (Heb. *hesed*) to his people, as expressed by his grace and mercy (Exod. 20:5–6). God unconditionally chose Israel. With the Mosaic law, he graciously made a covenant with the Jewish people. God told Moses:

> It was not because you were more numerous than any other people that the LORD set his heart on you and chose you—for you were the fewest of all peoples. It was because the LORD loved you and kept the oath that he swore to your ancestors, that the LORD has brought you out with a mighty hand, and redeemed you from the house of slavery, from the hand of Pharaoh king of Egypt. (Deut. 7:7–8)

These scriptures also teach the importance of responding with obedient allegiance to God and his law. Some people misunderstand this call for obedience as trying to earn salvation. Rather, a person's obedience is a

Twelve tribes of ancient Israel.

response to God's promises not a *condition* for these promises.[10] Moses described this obedience as the following:

> Know therefore that the LORD your God is God, the faithful God who maintains covenant loyalty with those who love him and keep his commandments, to a thousand generations, and who repays in their own person those who reject him. He does not delay but repays in their own person those who reject him. Therefore, observe diligently the commandment—the statutes and the ordinances—that I am commanding you today. (Deut. 7:9–11)

This obedience is also linked with faith. God's people were called to "trust in the LORD" by offering proper sacrifices (Ps. 4:5), avoiding idolatry (Ps. 3:6), doing good (Ps. 37:3), and not relying on their own wisdom (Prov. 3:5–6). Those who "trust in the LORD" are secure (Ps. 125:1; Isa. 26:4; Jer. 17:6–7) because of God's covenantal faithfulness (Ps. 32:10). The importance of faith as underlying the commands is encapsulated by Rabbi Simelai. This rabbi, like the Christian writer Paul (Rom. 1:17), reduced all the commands in the Jewish scriptures down to just one command using Habakkuk 2:4. Simelai (b. Mak. 24a) wrote, "Habakkuk further came and based them [all the commands] on one, as it is said, 'But the righteous shall live *by his faith*'" (emphasis added).

Public Domain

Icon of Elijah being taken to heaven. Nizhniy Novhorod school. (fifteenth to sixteenth cent. CE)

The stories from Jewish scriptures recount how obedience leads to God's blessings, while disobedience leads to cursing (Deut. 27–28; 2 Chron. 7:12–22). The Israelites remained God's people, but their obedience or disobedience determined whether they received blessings or curses. The cycle of sin, punishment, repentance, and deliverance is repeated over and over again in the stories from the book of Judges. In addition, the stories of the Jewish kings found in 1–2 Kings and 1–2 Chronicles demonstrate this cycle playing itself on repeat until the Jewish people were finally driven out of God's land. Repeatedly, God sent his prophets to remind Israel of God's covenant. They warned against idolatry. They called for acts of justice and mercy (Exod. 22:22; Lev. 19:15; Deut. 10:18; etc.). They warned against mistreating the poor, the widows, foreigners, and immigrants (Isa. 1:17, 10:2; Jer. 7:6, 22:3; Zech. 7:10; Mal. 3:5; etc.).

[10] The issues surrounding works, the law, faith, and grace will be further explored in our chapters on Galatians and Romans.

A lion from the Ishtar Gate, built by King Nebuchadnezzar II, who conquered Jerusalem. Istanbul Archaeology Museum. (ca. 569 BCE)

Two of the greatest prophets were the miracle workers Elijah and his disciple Elisha, who lived during the reign of one of the most wealthy and successful but idolatrous kings of Israel: Ahab (1 Kings 17–2 Kings 13). As these prophets implored people to turn back to God, they miraculously fed people, healed the sick, controlled the weather, and even raised the dead. According to tradition, Elijah didn't die. Instead, God took him up to heaven in a fiery chariot (2 Kings 2:1–12).

During the first century, people wondered if Elijah might one day return and continue his ministry of miracle-working and calling people to repentance (Mal. 4:5–6; cf. Mark 9:2–13; Matt. 17:1–13; Luke 9:28–36). Some thought that John the Baptizer could be this Elijah (Matt. 11:13–14, 17:10–12; Luke 1:16), or maybe it was Jesus of Nazareth (Mark 6:15, 8:28; Matt. 16:14; Luke 9:8, 9:19). Others continued to look for someone else who might be Elijah (Mark 15:35–36; Matt. 27:47–49).

Eventually, God had had enough of his people's disobedience, and the most drastic measure was taken. God punished his people by removing them from the land. First, the northern kingdom of Israel was conquered by the Assyrians. In 722 BCE, Sargon II deported some of the population and imported other conquered people into the land (2 Kings 17:4–6, 17:24). This mixed population left behind eventually became the Samaritans, a group of half-Jewish people who had their own version of the Jewish scriptures, the Samaritan Pentateuch. They also worshiped God at their own temple on Mount Gerizim. Resentment between these two people groups continued into the first century (Matt. 10:5; Luke 9:32–55, 10:30–37; John 4:9, 4:20).

Second, the Babylonians conquered the southern kingdom of Judah in several waves. In the final wave, the Babylonian ruler Nebuchadnezzar took the leaders into exile in 586 BCE (2 Kings 24:14–16, 25:12; Jer. 52:28–30; 2 Chron. 36:17–21). Prophets like Jeremiah bewailed the destruction of Jerusalem (e.g., Jer. 4:5–31). Isaiah spoke of the suffering of the Jewish people as the "servant of the LORD" (Isa. 42:1–4, 49:1–6, 50:4–9, 52:13–53:12). Many have understood this suffering servant to represent the nation. Others have identified this figure as the savior of the nation. Christians have identified this savior as Jesus (Matt. 8:17, 12:17–21; Luke 22:37; Acts 8:32–35; 1 Pet. 2:21–25).

Most tragically, the temple, the place where God dwelled in the land, was destroyed in 586 BCE (2 Kings 24:10–16) as God had warned Solomon (2 Chron. 7:19–22). Ezekiel spoke to the Jewish people in exile and envisioned God's presence leaving the temple and the land to join them in exile (Ezek. 10). With the loss of the temple and their displacement from the land, the Jewish people began to meet in synagogues for teaching and worship (Ezek. 11:16; Jer. 39:8).[11] Any ten Jewish men could form a synagogue, and the synagogue, instead of the temple, became the center of religious life. The Jewish people learned to speak and write Aramaic during this time as well. This dispersion of the Jews among these Gentile nations, which continued into the first century, was called the **Diaspora**.[12] However, the Jewish people continued to look forward to a time when God would regather them (e.g., Isa. 11:10–16, 27:12–13; Jer. 23:3–4, 29:14; Zech. 10:8–12).

While living among the Gentiles, questions arose about keeping a distinctive Jewish identity. During this time, the Jewish people began to emphasize kosher food laws, ritual purity, and marriage exclusively among themselves.[13] From this time of exile, faithful Israelites like Daniel and his friends avoided idolatry and didn't eat Gentile food (Dan. 1:8–17).[14] Daniel and his friends were presented as ideal Israelites who obeyed God's laws while serving their Gentile rulers. However, they also looked forward to a future when God would depose the Gentile nations, and the "son of man" would rule God's kingdom. Thus, Daniel envisioned:

> There before me was one like a son of man, coming with the clouds of heaven. He approached the Ancient of Days and was led into his presence. He was given authority, glory and sovereign power; all nations and peoples of every language worshiped him. His dominion is an everlasting dominion that will not pass away, and his kingdom is one that will never be destroyed. (Dan. 7:13–14 NIV)

Other Jewish writers became enamored with this figure. Stories attributed to Enoch (1 En. 37–71), who was taken to heaven by God (Gen. 5:21–24), recount his visions of this figure deposing the Gentile nations:

---

[11]"Synagogue" derives from a Greek word (*synagōgē*). The Hebrew expression is "house of assembly" (Heb. *beth-keneseth*). While Jewish tradition identified Moses as the founder of the synagogue (e.g., Philo, *Moses* 2.215–16; *Creation* 128; Josephus, *Ag. Ap.* 2.10–11, 175; y. Meg. 4.1, 75a; cf. Acts 15:21), archaeological evidence points to third-century Egyptian "houses of prayer" (*proseuchē*). But the concept of a synagogue may have arisen during the Babylonian exile (Jer. 39:8; Ezek. 11:16; Ezra 1:1–4).

[12]We should not make too great a distinction between Palestinian Jews and Hellenistic Jews. Hengel, *Judaism and Hellenism*.

[13]The emphasis on these identity markers is particularly argued by Dunn, *New Perspective on Paul*, 2008. See also the reframing of the law and Judaism in Sanders, *Paul and Palestinian Judaism*; and Wright, *Climax of the Covenant*.

[14]We have numerous stories of Jewish heroes during this period who kept their ethnic identity (Tob. 1:10–12; Jth. 12:2, 12:19; Add. Esth. 14:17; Jos. Asen. 7.1, 8.5; 3 Macc. 3:4).

> This Son of Man whom you have seen is the One who would remove the kings and the mighty ones from their comfortable seats and the strong ones from their thrones. He shall loosen the reins of the strong and crush the teeth of the sinners. He shall depose the kings from their thrones and kingdoms. (1 En. 46.4–5a)

In the first century, some of the Jewish people expectantly awaited this "**Son of Man**," who would be sent to save God's people. While Enoch's Son of Man was a figure of triumph who destroyed Israel's enemies, Daniel presented a humbler son of man. Daniel's vision begins with four fantastic beasts representing the four great nations—the Babylonians, Medes and Persians, Greeks, and Romans—that had oppressed the Jewish people (Dan. 7:1–7, 7:17, 7:19–26). The vision ends when God delivers his people from these beasts and gives their kingdoms to this son of man (Dan. 7:8–14, 7:18, 7:27). Within the logic of the vision, just as the beasts represent nations, so the son of man represents the nation of Israel. It is striking that the Gentile nations are represented by four vicious beasts, but Israel is represented by a human. We get competing images for this "Son of Man." Will he be a triumphant warrior as in 1 Enoch, or will he be like Daniel's figure, who represents those who suffer at the hands of the nations but then is given his reign by God?

The Persians and the Return

God also called Ezekiel the "son of man" ninety-three times (Ezek. 2:1, 2:3, 2:6, etc.). This was Ezekiel's prophetic title, and it was meant to contrast his humanity with God's divine glory. Ezekiel was a prophet who lived in exile. He provided his people hope that God's presence was with his people in exile and would return with his people to the promised land where there would be a new temple (Ezek. 40–48). Ezekiel promised that God would renew his covenant and write it on the hearts of his people (Ezek. 36:22–38; cf. Jer. 31:31–37; Heb. 8:8–13, 10:16).

The prophets also retold the exodus story during this time of exile from the land. Isaiah envisioned a time when the Jewish people would be freed from foreign captivity (Isa. 61:1–11). He spoke of their return from the wilderness of exile (Isa. 40:3). He promised a restoration of the Davidic king (Isa. 9:1–7), who would be like a righteous branch springing forth from the stump of Jesse (Isa. 11:1–9). It was during this period of exile that the Jewish people developed the expectation of the Messiah as the savior of God's people.

Mike Peel (CC BY-SA-4.0)

The Cyrus Cylinder refers to restoring sanctuaries and repatriation of deported people. (sixth cent. BCE)

Under Persian rule, the land of Judah became the province of Yehud (Ezra 5:8). Isaiah described the Persian ruler Cyrus II (550–530 BCE) as God's chosen "**Messiah**" (Heb. *mashiah*; *christos*)—literally, the "Anointed One." While the kings of Israel (e.g., 1 Sam. 15:1, 15:17; Ps. 2:2), priests (e.g., Lev. 16:32; Num. 35:25), and prophets (e.g., 1 Kings 19:16; 1 Chron. 16:22; Ps. 105:15) were anointed by

God, this was the first time "Messiah" was used as a title for a human agent of God.[15] Cyrus was considered God's agent of salvation because he allowed the Jewish people to return to the promised land (Isa. 45:1–13; cf. 2 Chron. 36:22–23). Ezra records the decree of Cyrus:

> The LORD, the God of heaven, has given me all the kingdoms of the earth, and he has charged me to build him a house at Jerusalem in Judah. Any of those among you who are of his people—may their God be with them!—are now permitted to go up to Jerusalem in Judah, and rebuild the house of the LORD, the God of Israel—he is the God who is in Jerusalem; and let all survivors, in whatever place they reside, be assisted by the people of their place with silver and gold, with goods and with animals, besides freewill offerings for the house of God in Jerusalem. (Ezra 1:2–4; cf. Ezra 6:2–5)

With this decree, some of the Jewish people returned to their land around 538 BCE with vessels from the temple under the leadership of Sheshbazzar (Ezra 1:5–11), who helped lay the foundations for the new temple (Ezra 5:16). During the reign of Darius the Great (522–486 BCE), a second wave of Israelites returned, with Zerubbabel as their governor and Joshua as their high priest around 522 BCE (Ezra 1–2; Hag. 1). Under their leadership, the people rebuilt the "second" temple, which was completed around 515 BCE (Ezra 5–6).

Later, during the reign of Artaxerxes I (465–424 BCE), Ezra the priest and scribe returned to the land, along with additional Israelite families, around 458 BCE (Ezra 7:1–10). He led significant religious

Carl N. Toney

Alexander the Great routing Persian soldiers. Istanbul Archaeology Museum. (ca. fourth cent. BCE)

[15]"Anointing" language can be divided into two groups (1) Exod. 25:69–Num. 7:88 (54x) focuses on priests, while (2) 1 Sam. 2:10–1 Kings. 5:1 focuses on kings. See the debate regarding messianic expectations between Collins, *The Scepter and the Star*; and Fitzmyer, *One Who Is to Come*.

reforms, including an emphasis on no longer intermarrying with Gentiles (Ezra 9–10). Then Nehemiah, the cupbearer of Artaxerxes I, was appointed governor of Judah, and he oversaw the rebuilding of the walls of Jerusalem around 445 BCE (Neh. 2:1–2).

But this return to the land did not mean complete freedom for God's people. If these people who returned to the land were asked, "Who is in charge?" their answer would have been the Persians. Things were certainly better for the Jewish people, but they had not regained independence.

The Greeks and the Hasmoneans

God wasn't done with his people, and a new answer to the question of "Who's in charge?" was about to be given. Alexander the Great (356–323 BCE), a Greek student of the philosopher Aristotle, reshaped the world with his conquest of the Persian Empire. In 332 BCE, the Jewish people submitted to his rule.

Alexander's grand vision was to unify the world through **Hellenization**. This involved adopting the Greek way of life, including learning the Greek language and culture (2 Macc. 4:10–17; cf. 2 Macc. 6:9, 11:24).[16] During this period, the province of Yehud became known as Judea, and the Jewish people were called Judeans. Under Alexander and his successors, the common language in the world shifted to Greek. However, people in the land of Israel continued to speak Aramaic. Outside the land, there were so many Jews who only spoke Greek that their scriptures were translated into Greek. This translation of the Hebrew Bible was called the **Septuagint** (LXX). Septuagint means "seventy" because of the tradition that there were seventy translators (Let. of Arist. 28–50, 121–27, 301–7).

When Alexander suddenly died in 323 BCE, his empire was divided into four major regions, each ruled by one of his generals or their successors who were called the *Diadochi* (lit. "successors"). Cassander was king of Macedonia. Ptolemy I Soter reigned over Egypt. Lysimachus ruled western Asia Minor. Seleucus I Nicator was sovereign over eastern Asia Minor with the eastern territories of Persia. The Jewish people became caught in the middle of the continual conflicts between two of these ruling dynasties. To the north, the Seleucids ruled over eastern Asia Minor and the east. To the south, the Ptolemies ruled in Egypt. Over the years, the Jewish people were tossed back and forth like a ball, perpetual vassals between rulers. Over and over again, the people asked the question, "Who's in charge?"

In 175 BCE, Antiochus IV "Epiphanes" ("God manifest") became the ruler of Asia Minor and ruled the Jewish people. With his ascension, events were set into motion that would lead to the great Maccabean revolt in 167 BCE (1–2 Macc.; Josephus, *Ant.* 12.258–64). Forgetting lessons from the exile, the leaders of Jerusalem decided to assimilate with the Greeks. They sought to fashion Jerusalem into a Greek "city" (*polis*). They requested permission from Antiochus IV to build a gymnasium in the city, to remove marks of circumcision from Jewish males, to stop practicing the law, and to observe Gentile customs (1 Macc. 1:11–14; 2 Macc. 4:7–17).

Even more damning, Jason, the high priest of Israel, bribed Antiochus IV to take the office of high priest from his brother Onias III. This God-ordained, lifetime office became a commodity and a means for Gentile rulers to exert their influence upon the Jewish people. Three years later, Menelaus out-bribed Jason and had Onias III assassinated. When Jason attempted to take back the office, Antiochus IV

---

[16] Hengel, *Judaism and Hellenism*; Hengel, *Jews, Greeks and Barbarians*; Barclay, *Jews in the Mediterranean Diaspora.*

While the temple's menorah had seven branches, Hanukkah's hanukkiah has nine branches, with eight candles representing the eight nights that the oil lasted, and the ninth candle being used to light the others.

returned to Jerusalem, profaned and plundered the temple, reestablished Menelaus as high priest, and set up an altar to Zeus (1 Macc. 1:20–40; 2 Macc. 5:15–27). In his fury, Antiochus IV forbade the Jewish people from practicing their laws, including circumcision, food laws, Sabbath observance, and keeping other festivals (1 Macc. 1:41–64; 2 Macc. 6:1–17). This made the people wonder if God had abandoned them.

Then in the village of Modi'in, a priest named Mattathias and his family began a rebellion in 167 BCE. Mattathias's actions were reminiscent of those zealous for God in Scripture. During the exodus, the priest Phinehas demonstrated his zeal for God when he killed an Israelite and his foreign wife to curtail God's wrath (Num. 25:7–18). During the reign of Ahab, Elijah showed his zeal when he slaughtered the prophets of Baal on Mount Carmel (1 Kings 18:16–40). Likewise, out of zealous loyalty to God, Mattathias killed a Jewish man attempting to sacrifice to Zeus.

Mattathias's actions sparked the flames of rebellion that his five sons would fan into the wildfire that drove their Greek masters from the land. The most famous of these freedom fighters was Judas "Maccabee" (r. 165–160 BCE), whose nickname meant "hammer." Under Judas, the Jewish people took back Jerusalem and purified the temple in the month of Kislev in 164 BCE (1 Macc. 4:36–61; 2 Macc. 10:1–9). In remembrance of this victory and of God miraculously supplying oil for the menorah in the temple, the Jewish people celebrate yearly the festival of Hanukkah (1 Macc. 4:36–61; 2 Macc. 10:1–9; John 10:22).

After Judas died, his brother Jonathan (r. 160–142 BCE) continued to lead the rebellion toward victory. Jonathan was appointed as both high priest and provincial governor by the Seleucids (1 Macc. 11:23–57). But peace did not last, and their Seleucid overlords captured and killed Jonathan (1 Macc. 12:39–53, 13:12–24). In response, his brother Simon (r. 142–135 BCE) continued the war against the Seleucids. He helped gain further freedoms for the Jewish people. In 140 BCE, the high priesthood was bestowed upon Simon and his descendants (1 Macc. 14:27–45; Josephus, *Ant.* 13.6.7). Finally, Simon's son, John Hyrcanus I (r. 134–104 BCE), secured the Jewish people's complete independence from the Seleucids and established the Hasmonean dynasty. This dynasty would last for sixty-six years. Because of the Maccabees, the Jewish people could finally say God was in charge and had given his people their independence.

When reflecting on these events, some people began to see people's righteous deeds and deaths as functioning like atoning sacrifices for the sins of others. There was a story about a priest named Eleazar and a mother, along with her seven sons, who died as martyrs. When Antiochus IV tried to force them to eat pork, they chose death rather than disobey God's laws. One Jewish writer described their actions as "a ransom for the sin of our nation. And through the blood of those devout ones and their death as an atoning sacrifice" (4 Macc. 17:21–22). This language sounds similar to how Christians describe Jesus's death as a "ransom" (Mark 10:45; Matt. 20:28) and an "atoning sacrifice" for sin (Rom. 3:25; Heb. 2:17; 1 John 2:2, 4:10).

Jewish Life under the Hasmoneans

After the Jewish people were free under the Hasmoneans, their religion, politics, and way of life began to develop. During this time, the Pharisee, Sadducee, and Essene sects came into existence (Josephus, *J.W.* 2.119, 164–65; *Ant.* 13.171). The Pharisees and Sadducees actively participated in court and religious life, while the Essenes withdrew from public spaces.

The **Sadducees'** power resided among the priests, scribes, and Jewish aristocracy, especially near Jerusalem. They considered the five books of Moses—Genesis, Exodus, Leviticus, Numbers, and Deuteronomy—to be the only source of religious authority. As such, they believed God blessed the righteous and punished the wicked in this life. They did not believe in the resurrection of the dead (Mark 12:18–27; Matt. 22:23–33; Luke 20:27–40). They denied the existence of angels and spirits (Acts 23:8). They also emphasized free will. Because the Sadducees saw wealth and power as direct blessings from God, they supported whoever was in political power, even if those in power were foreigners.

The **Pharisees** gained much of their support from the ordinary people, especially those in the rural population. They saw the oral tradition of Jewish elders as necessary along with the law and the prophets (Mark 7:3). They encouraged all Israelites to follow the purity regulations (Mark 7:1–23). They accepted both free will and divine providence. They believed in an afterlife that included the resurrection from the dead (Acts 23:8), a concept found only in a few places in Jewish scriptures, like in Daniel 12:2–3 and Isaiah 26:19. While the Pharisees initially favored the Hasmoneans, their opposition to Alexander Jannaeus's rule (r. 103–76 BCE) led to eight hundred of them being crucified (Josephus, *J.W.* 1.4.5–6; *Ant.*

13.14.1–2). But when his wife, Alexandra Salome (r. 76–67 BCE), became queen, she made peace with them. During Roman times, the Pharisees looked forward to a coming Messiah.

Writings to Help Us Understand the New Testament

Apocrypha (ca. 250 BCE–100 CE) means "hidden." These Jewish writings are composed in Greek, are additions to the Hebrew Bible, and are included in the Septuagint. The core list consists of Tobit, Judith, Wisdom of Solomon, Sirach (also called Ecclesiasticus or Ben Sira), Baruch, 1–2 Maccabees, Greek Daniel, and Greek Esther. This list can also include 1 Esdras (also called 3 Ezra), 2 Esdras (4 Ezra and 5 Ezra), and Psalm 151.[17]

Pseudepigrapha (ca. 250 BCE–200 CE) means "false writing." These Jewish writings typically claim to be composed by famous persons who did not actually write the work. Significant works include the Letter of Aristeas, 1 Enoch, Testaments of the Twelve Patriarchs, Jubilees, 4 Ezra, and the Psalms of Solomon.[18]

The **Dead Sea Scrolls** (ca. third cent. BCE to first cent. CE) are Jewish writings that were discovered in 1947 in caves at Qumran.[19] The oldest copies of every work from the Hebrew Bible were discovered, except for Esther. A complete copy of Isaiah was one of the original writings found. Before this, the earliest Hebrew copies were the Cairo Codex of the Prophets (ca. 895 CE), Codex Aleppo (ca. 925 CE), and the earliest complete copies of the Greek translation (third and fourth cent. CE). Other important sectarian works attributed to the Essenes include the Rule of the Community (1QS), Damascus Document (CD), and War Scroll (1QM).

Philo of Alexandria (20 BCE–50 CE) was a contemporary of Jesus and Paul. He lived in Alexandria, Egypt, and he was known for his allegorical interpretations of the Jewish scriptures and for being influenced by Middle Platonism. When interpreting the Ten Commandments (*Decalogue*), Philo understood them as producing virtue better than any Greco-Roman philosophy.

Flavius Josephus (ca. 37–100 CE) was a contemporary of Paul and provided essential historical information about the time after the Jewish scriptures were written. He gave information about Palestine during the time of the early church leading up to the first Jewish war, including the major Jewish sects of the Pharisees, Sadducees, Essenes, and Zealots. His writings include *Life*, *Jewish Antiquities*, *Jewish War*, and *Against Apion*.

Apostolic Fathers (late first cent. to early second cent. CE) are a collection of early Christian writings that slightly overlaps and generally follows the New Testament period. The works include 1–2 Clement, Letters of Ignatius, Letter of Polycarp, Martyrdom of Polycarp, Didache, Epistle of Barnabas, Epistle to Diognetus, and Shepherd of Hermes.[20]

Gnostic Writings (Nag Hammadi) (second to fourth cent. CE) are a collection of writings attributed to a Christian heretical group called the Gnostics. They held a dualistic worldview favoring the spiritual

---

[17] Most of these are found in English Bibles that include the Apocrypha.

[18] For a scholarly collection, see Charlesworth, *Old Testament Pseudepigrapha*.

[19] A helpful introduction is VanderKam, *Dead Sea Scrolls Today*. See also the translation and introductions in Wise, Abegg Jr., and Cook, *Dea Sea Scrolls*; Florentino and Tigchelaar, *Dead Sea Scrolls*.

[20] Holmes, *Apostolic Fathers*.

over the evil material world and believed salvation was obtained through secret knowledge. These writings include the Gospel of Thomas, Gospel of Truth, Treatise on the Resurrection, Apocryphon of James, Apocryphon of John, and Apocalypse of Peter.[21]

New Testament Apocrypha and Pseudepigrapha is a large and poorly defined collection of noncanonical writings attributed to or about New Testament figures. Some of these writings overlap with Gnostic writings. Important works include the Infancy Gospel of Thomas, the Protevangelium of James, the Gospel of Peter, and the Acts of Paul and Thecla.[22]

Not all Jews were happy with the temple and priesthood during these times. This led to one group, the **Essenes**, withdrawing their community to Qumran by the Dead Sea. Their collection of the Jewish scriptures and their own writings are called the Dead Sea Scrolls. They believed that their community functioned as the temple and priesthood as a replacement for the corrupt temple and priesthood in Jerusalem (1QS 8.4–6). They emphasized a lifestyle of purity and asceticism, and many were celibate. Many believe this community awaited two Messiahs—a priestly Messiah and a kingly Messiah—who would deliver God's people (1QS 9.11; cf. CD 12.23, 19.10–11, 20.1).

The Roman Republic and the Need for a Messiah

God had granted the Jewish people independence, but the conflict between Alexandra's sons, Hyrcanus II and Aristobulus II, resulted in their resubjugation. While Hyrcanus II was the elder son and rightful

Carl N. Toney

The Essenes lived at Qumran near the Dead Sea. Around 90 percent of the Dead Sea Scrolls were discovered at Qumran Cave 4.

[21] Meyer and Funk, *Nag Hammadi Scriptures*.
[22] Schneemelcher and Wilson, *New Testament Apocrypha*.

Public Domain

Pompey the Great. Venice National Archaeological Museum.

heir, Aristobulus II wanted what was not meant to be his. He gathered an army to force his older brother to give up being the high priest and king. However, Hyrcanus II found support from the Nabatean King Aretas III to help him regain the throne. Their continued fighting led to an intervention by the Roman general Pompey, who subdued the Jewish people in 63 BCE.

As part of his victory, Pompey desecrated the temple by trespassing within its courts (Josephus, *J.W.* 1.6.5–7.6; *Ant.* 14.4.4; Tacitus, *Hist.* 5.9; Appian, *Mith.* 106, 114; Florus, *Epitome of Roman History* 1.40.30; Livy, *Per.* 102; Plutarch, *Pomp.* 39). Under Pompey, Hyrcanus II retained his title as high priest (63–43 BCE); however, he was now a Roman "ethnarch" (ruler of a nation). Judea was forced to pay tribute to Rome and was placed under the authority of the Roman governor of Syria.

This Roman invasion cut the Jewish people to the core. Bewailing the state of Jerusalem and the corruption of the leadership helped to crystallize a hope for a true king who would expel the Romans and rule God's people. This savior figure would be the Messiah. This messianic hope was expressed in the Psalms of Solomon (ca. 50 BCE), with statements like: "May God cleanse Israel for the day of mercy in blessing, for the appointed day when his Messiah will reign" (Pss. Sol. 18.5).

And so the seed was planted for the expectations of a political Messiah who would rid the Jewish people from the shackles of their oppressors. He would be a revolutionary, like the Maccabees, but he would also turn the people's hearts back to God. This Messiah is further described as follows:

> And he will be a righteous king over them, taught by God.
> There will be no unrighteousness among them in his days,
> for all shall be holy,
> and their king shall be the Lord Messiah. (Pss. Sol. 17.32)

The Roman Empire and King Herod

Unfortunately, the Jewish prayers for a political Messiah were not answered. Instead, the Romans further subjugated them as Rome transitioned from a republic to an empire. Civil war erupted between Pompey and Julius Caesar. Caesar defeated Pompey with the aid of Hyrcanus II and an Idumean named Antipater. As a reward, Antipater was granted Roman citizenship and was appointed as Judea's "procurator" (*epitropos*) while Hyrcanus II remained ethnarch and high priest. Julius also granted the Jewish people several important rights, including the ability to follow the Mosaic law, gather in synagogues on the Sabbath, establish kosher markets, and financially support the Jerusalem temple.

The world of the New Testament: the provinces of the Roman Empire under Augustus.

Julius Caesar was assassinated on March 15, 44 BCE. His grand-nephew and adopted son, Octavian, waged war against his enemies and eventually his allies. He joined forces with Lepidus and Mark Antony to defeat Caesar's assassins, Brutus and Cassius, at Philippi in 42 BCE. Octavian then sidelined Lepidus and rose to power in the west, while Antony ruled in the east. Eventually, the relationship between Octavian and Antony broke down and led to war. With Octavian's victory over Antony at the Battle of Actium in 31 BCE, he secured his reign as the first Roman emperor. The senate awarded him the title "**Augustus**" (meaning "illustrious one") and credited him with bringing an age of peace, described as the ***Pax Romana*** ("Roman peace"). This peace was secured through the might of the Roman armies, which could swiftly travel on Roman roads across the Roman Empire.

Augustus was the "lord" (*kyrios*) of the empire, and his troops swore oaths of fealty to him, declaring, "Caesar is lord." After Julius died, he was given divine honors by the senate in 42 BCE. As Julius's son, Augustus was known as the "son of God." Throughout the empire, temples were erected to honor Rome as well as the

Augustus Caesar. Vatican Museums.

emperor. Much of Roman money, including the silver denarius (worth a day's wage), bore the emperor's image as well as the titles of "lord" and "son of God."

During this time, the emerging ruler of Judea was Antipater's son, **Herod the Great**. His father initially appointed Herod as the "governor" (*stratēgos*) of Galilee. When Antony ruled the east, he made Herod and Herod's brother Phasael "tetrarchs" (minor rulers) over Judea. After a short period when Herod lost control of the region, he fled to Rome. The Roman senate granted him the title of "confederate king," and he returned to Judea and established his rule in 37 BCE. To secure his reign further, Herod married the last Hasmonean princess, Mariamne. He eventually extinguished the Hasmonean legacy by killing her in 29 BCE, his mother-in-law in 28 BCE, and all the male descendants of Hyrcanus II in 25 BCE. Despite backing Cassius and Antony during the Roman civil wars, Herod was allowed to continue to reign after he submitted to Augustus in 30 BCE. Herod ruled over Judea, Samaria, Galilee, and parts of the Transjordan as client king of Rome for thirty-three years (37–4 BCE).

Public Domain

Moving from north to south, this arial view of Caesarea Maritima includes the ruins of the harbor, hippodrome, Herod's place with a swimming pool, and theater.

While Herod was a ferocious ruler, he was also a visionary leader whose building projects transformed the land of Israel. His fortress of Masada, by the Dead Sea, would eventually be the last stronghold for the first Jewish revolt against Rome (72–73 CE). He fashioned a significant seaport at Caesarea Maritima, named in honor of the emperor, where nearly fifty thousand people lived in a Greek-styled city, which included a theater, palace, hippodrome, baths, and marketplace. Most importantly, he began the expansion of the Jerusalem temple in 20 BCE. He did this to secure the Jewish people's goodwill and to fashion himself like a new King Solomon. While the sanctuary of the temple was completed after eighteen months, the entire temple compound was not completed until 63 CE. To fund these magnificent projects, Herod used various private tax collectors to collect poll taxes, land revenues, and sales taxes.

After Herod died in 4 BCE, his kingdom was divided among his three sons,

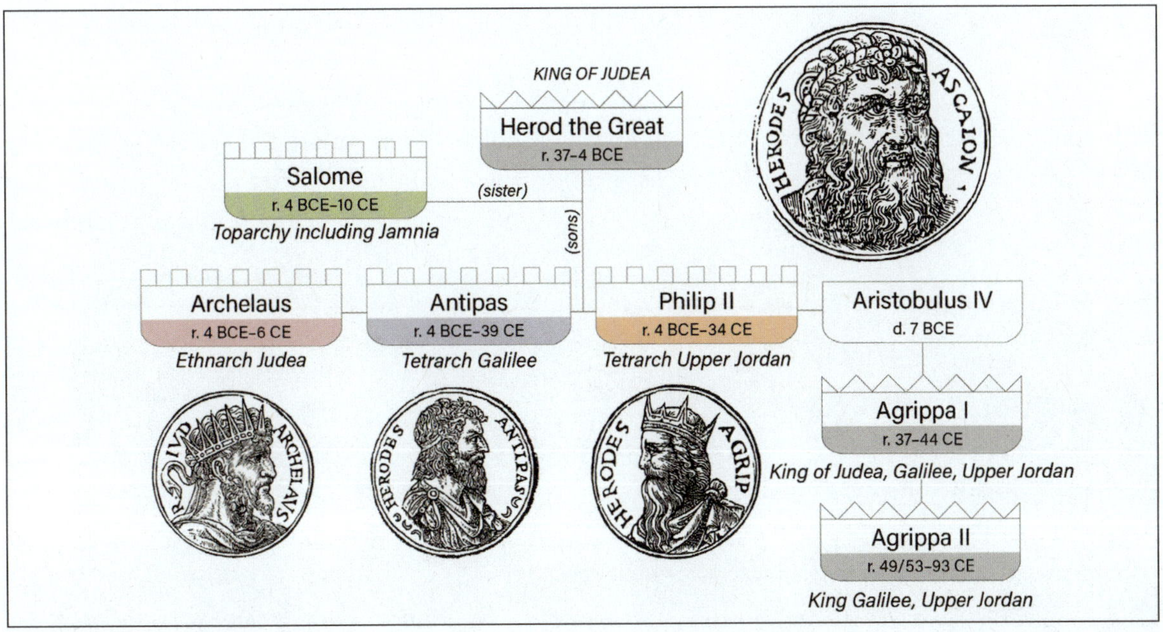

Carl N. Toney

The Herodian Dynasty.

Archelaus, Antipas, and Philip II, as well as his sister, Salome I. Antipas was granted the title of tetrarch and ruled Galilee and Perea (4 BCE–39 CE). Likewise, Philip II was given a tetrarchy over the Upper Jordan (4 BCE–34 CE). However, Archelaus was given the title of ethnarch (designating his larger territory) and was granted Judea, Samaria, and Idumea (4 BCE–6 CE).

Because of Archelaus's poor rule, he was removed from office and replaced by a Roman prefect (later called procurator). This prefect governed the province of Judea and was under the supervision of the imperial legate of Syria. During this time, Quirinius the legate of Syria conducted a census to determine the tribute Judea would owe Rome (Luke 2:1–7). Some of the most notable prefects of Judea were Pontius Pilate, Felix, and Festus. These prefects chose the seaport of Caesarea as their seat of power and would only visit Jerusalem on noteworthy occasions, such as Jewish festivals. With each visit from the Roman prefect, those in Jerusalem were reminded that Rome was truly in charge.

Eventually, the Jewish people had had enough. The Maccabees' models of zeal inspired them to be zealots for God. A group of revolutionaries, who called themselves **Zealots**, participated in the first Jewish revolt against the Romans in 66–70 CE in response to the Roman procurator Florus's abuse of power, including stealing money from the temple treasury. Unfortunately, unlike those ancient zealots, this revolt ended in the tragic destruction of Jerusalem and the temple by the future Roman emperors Vespasian and Titus in 70 CE. When this second temple was destroyed, the Jewish people could no longer offer sacrifices. As a solution, the rabbis replaced sacrifices with the study of the Jewish scriptures.

But things got worse. In 130 CE, Emperor Hadrian ordered a new city, Aelia Capitolina, to be built over the ruins of Jerusalem, with a new temple dedicated to the god Jupiter. This led to a second Jewish revolt, led by Bar Kokhba in 132–35 CE. However, the revolutionaries were crushed, and the Jewish people were banned from Jerusalem. With these losses of the city and the temple, Rome wanted the Jews to know who was in charge.

Masada was a Hasmonean fortress that King Herod fortified as a refuge in the Judean Desert by the Dead Sea. The Roman siege of Masada in the first Jewish war ended in 73 CE, after 960 rebels died from mass suicide.

But one of the radical messages of the New Testament is that the God of Abraham, Isaac, and Jacob is really in charge. In this book, we will listen to various authors who offer their insights into the significance of God being in charge. This claim that the Jewish God was in charge was shocking. During New Testament times, the Romans thought they were in charge. In the world today, various voices claim authority over our lives. Maybe we think of figures in government as being in charge. Maybe it's our parents or another relative. Perhaps an employer. Possibly our school. Or maybe we think we are the ones in charge. As we journey together through these pages surveying the New Testament, we might ask ourselves how we will respond to its message that God is in charge.

Key Terms and People

Augustus: the adopted son of Julius Caesar and founding emperor of the Roman Empire; he was known for bringing Roman peace and was called the "son of God"
Covenant: God's promise to Israel
Diaspora: the scattering of the Jewish people among the Gentile nations
Essenes: the ascetic Jewish community that lived in the desert at Qumran
Gentile: a binary classification for anyone who is not ethnically Jewish
Greatest commandments: the law is summarized with two commands—love God (Deut. 6:5) and love your neighbor (Lev. 19:18)
Hellenization: adopting the Greek way of life, including learning the Greek language and culture
Herod the Great: the king of Israel, who Matthew's Gospel reports attempted to kill the baby Jesus; he was famous for his building projects, including remodeling the Jewish temple and building a seaport at Caesarea Maritima
Messiah or Christ: the "Anointed One"—a title used to describe the savior figure who would establish God's rule; Christians identify Jesus as God's Messiah. *Messiah* is Hebrew, and *Christ* is Greek
Passover: the festival that celebrates the exodus of Israel from Egypt
***Pax Romana*:** the Roman peace that was achieved by Augustus
Pharisees: Jewish religious leaders who gained support from the populace; they were known for following the tradition of the elders, believing in the resurrection, and upholding ritual purity codes
Sadducees: Jewish religious leaders associated with the temple and Jerusalem leadership; they upheld the first five books of the Jewish scriptures, did not believe in resurrection, and understood God as rewarding and punishing people in the present life
Septuagint: (LXX) the Greek translation of the Hebrew Bible (Old Testament/Jewish scriptures)
Son of God: a title used by the Romans to describe their emperor and to ascribe to him divine honors; Jewish people also used this expression for the Davidic king (2 Sam. 7:14; 1 Chron. 17:13; Ps. 2:7)
Son of Man: based on the figure from Daniel 7:13–14, this phrase refers to the future leader of Israel; he will suffer, but God will defeat his enemies and exalt him to a heavenly enthronement
Zealots: revolutionaries associated with the first Jewish revolt

Conversation Starters

1. Why did God make a covenant with Abraham? What were the three parts, and how did God make good on his promises to Abraham throughout Jewish history? How do you think Jews in New Testament times considered these promises?
2. How is the exodus story essentially the "gospel" story of the Jewish scriptures? What is the significance of Passover?
3. What is the purpose of the Sinai covenant, and how does the law relate to the identity of the Jews? Particularly, what are the three markers of Jewish identity?
4. Why do the Jewish people celebrate Hanukkah? How does the story of the Hasmonean's rise and loss of power inform the expectations of the Jewish people in the New Testament?
5. What three Jewish groups developed during the Hasmonean period? What were their beliefs?
6. What were some of the major political developments during Roman rule? Consider the significance of Pompey, Caesar, and Augustus.
7. In terms of Jewish rule, who was Herod the Great, and what were some of his significant accomplishments? How did the political landscape change after Herod's death?
8. What are some of the foundations behind the concept of a Messiah that you learned from this chapter? Consider God's promises to David and Solomon. Can you explain the development of "anointed one" from someone who is dedicated to God to someone who is a political savior?
9. Why does this chapter continue to ask, "Who is in charge?" How do you think this question will relate to the New Testament?

FOR FURTHER READING

Burge, Gary M., Gene L. Green, and Lynn H. Cohick, eds. *The New Testament in Antiquity.* Zondervan, 2009.

deSilva, David A. *Judea under Greek and Roman Rule.* Essentials of Biblical Studies. Oxford University Press, 2024.

Ferguson, Everett. *Backgrounds of Early Christianity.* 3rd ed. Eerdmans, 2003.

Hubbard, Moyer. *Christianity in the Greco-Roman World: A Narrative Introduction.* Baker Academic, 2010.

Neufeld, Dietmar, and Richard E. DeMaris. *Understanding the Social World of the New Testament.* Routledge, 2010.

Osiek, Carolyn. *What Are They Saying about the Social Setting of the New Testament?* Paulist, 1984.

Porter, Stanley E., and Craig A. Evans, eds. *Dictionary of New Testament Background.* InterVarsity Press, 2000.

Theissen, Gerd. *The Shadow of the Galilean: The Quest for the Historical Jesus in Narrative Form.* Fortress, 2007.

VanderKam, James. *An Introduction to Early Judaism.* Eerdmans, 2001.

2

MARK MAKES HIS MARK

Where Did Our Bible Come From?

Have you ever tried to convert kilometers to miles when driving a car? Or maybe you've had to measure grams versus ounces when cooking a recipe. You could get in lots of trouble if you mixed up your measurements. Things just wouldn't work out. Being clear and consistent with measurements is essential for avoiding speeding tickets and baking cakes. Likewise, having a consistent standard for religious texts is crucial for any faith.

The collection of the sixty-six works consisting of the Old Testament and New Testament and deemed authoritative for religious practices and beliefs of Christians is called the **canon** (lit. "measuring rod").[1] As God's Word, these writings are considered trustworthy and uniquely inspired by God (2 Tim. 3:15–16; 2 Pet. 1:20–21, 3:15–16). As human words, they were written in specific sociocultural contexts by human authors.[2] The thirty-nine works of the Old Testament, or Jewish scriptures, were generally inherited from the Jewish roots of Christianity. However, the selection of the twenty-seven works in the New Testament canon was shaped by a process that took nearly four hundred years.[3]

SUGGESTED READING

Mark 1:1–16:8

There were three criteria for accepting a New Testament work as canonical. First, a work had to be old enough to trace its roots to the first generation of Christians. All the New Testament books were thought to be composed in the first century. While valuable, later Christian writings, like Justin Martyr's *Apologies*, were not included. Second, a work needed to be orthodox, meaning it aligned

[1]Note that this is the Protestant canon. Other Christian groups have slightly different canonical collections.

[2]The trustworthy nature of these writings is described by some as infallible regarding doctrine. Others promote inerrancy—that is, the Bible's original autographs are without any factual errors. This debate concerns hypothetical documents that are lost to history. It does not concern modern Bibles, which contain transmission and translation errors. See our further discussion of this issue in the chapter on 2 Timothy.

[3]The first recorded list of authoritative New Testament books included only ten works and was produced by a heretic named Marcion. An essential means of combating false teaching was determining which works Christians deemed to be authoritative writings.

The Gutenberg Bible was the first book printed using movable type. New York Public Library. (1450s)

with the teachings found in other accepted books. Thus, a work like the Gospel of Thomas, which claimed women could only be saved after becoming men, was rejected (Gos. Thom. 114). Third, a work needed to have the stamp of apostolic authority. These works needed to be written by an early Christian leader or someone connected to an early Christian leader like Paul, Peter, or James. The Didache, which was anonymous and contained many Christian teachings, including sayings similar to those found in Matthew, did not make it into the canon.

One way to think of the formation of the New Testament canon is the analogy of three snowballs rolling down a hill and forming into a snowman. The first snowball is the collection of the Gospels and Acts, which would have formed around the Gospel of Mark. The second snowball collection is the letters formed around the thirteen letters of Paul. Hebrews is also included in this collection because some people thought Paul wrote it. Paul may have been responsible for starting this collection since authors were known to keep personal copies of their letters. The third snowball is a far more unstable collection. It consists of various works that were included and excluded over time. Works that were sometimes included like the Shepherd of Hermes ended up not sticking. Other works like 2 Peter and Revelation were hotly debated but eventually were included. These three collections eventually formed our canon. The first official list resembling our modern Bible was Athanasius's Easter letter (367 CE).

The New Testament canon consists of twenty-seven distinct pieces of literature, which can be grouped into four categories according to their genre.[4] **Genre** is a means of classifying writings according to their literary style. The first four works are Gospels or biographies because they recount the life,

[4]For introductions to the nature of the Bible, see Bird, *Seven Things I Wish Every Christian Knew about the Bible*; Wright, *Scripture and the Authority of God*; Wright, *Surprised by Scripture*.

death, and resurrection of Jesus. Next, Acts of the Apostles is a historical narrative that tells the history of the early church, particularly the stories of Peter and Paul. Next, we encounter letters (sometimes called epistles) written to various churches and individuals. Within these letters, the thirteen letters of Paul are arranged from longest to shortest. Finally, closing the New Testament is Revelation, which is an apocalypse, a style of writing full of symbolic imagery.

What Is a Gospel?

With a better understanding of the composition of the New Testament, let's dive into our study of the New Testament by looking at the stories of Jesus. From the early days of the church, reading the stories about Jesus has been an essential and prominent aspect of Christian gatherings and worship. Justin Martyr wrote:

> And on the day called Sunday there is a meeting in one place of those who live in cities or the country, and the memoirs of the apostles or the writings of the prophets are read as long as time permits. (Justin Martyr, *1 Apol.* 67.3)

Flipping to the beginning of several modern translation of the New Testament, readers are greeted with the title of the first book as the "Gospel according to Matthew."[5] In fact, the first four works of the New Testament are the Gospels, and each of these was given the title "Gospel according to . . ." by the second century. But it might be surprising to learn that the Greek words for "Gospel" are rarely used in Matthew, Mark, and Luke, and they are never found in John.[6] Many would classify these **Gospels** as ancient biographies because their content focuses on the life of Jesus.[7]

Looking more closely, Matthew, Mark, and Luke can be grouped together and are called the **Synoptic Gospels** because they tell a similar story with similar content—Jesus's ministry, which began in Galilee and ended in Jerusalem—while John stands on its own. The similarity between Matthew, Mark, and Luke raises the question of which Gospel came first and the literary relationship between them. We call this question the **Synoptic Problem.**

Christ Pantocrator (lit. "Christ ruler of all") icon. Saint Catherine's Monastery, Mount Sinai (sixth cent. CE). The two different facial expressions may represent Christ being fully God and fully human.

[5] E.g., NRSV, NASB, LEB, KJV. Other translations don't use this title; they open by categorizing these works as "Gospels" (e.g., NIV, ESV).

[6] "Good news" (*euangelion*) is only used in Mark (1:1, 1:14, 1:15, 8:35, 10:29, 13:10, 14:9, [16:15]) and Matthew (4:23, 9:35, 24:14, 26:13). "To proclaim good news" (*euangelizō*) is found in a quote of Isaiah 61:1 (Matt. 11:5) and ten times in Luke (1:19, 2:10, 3:18, 4:18, 4:43, 7:22, 8:1, 9:6, 16:16, 20:1).

[7] Burridge, *What Are the Gospels?*; Talbert, *What Is a Gospel?*

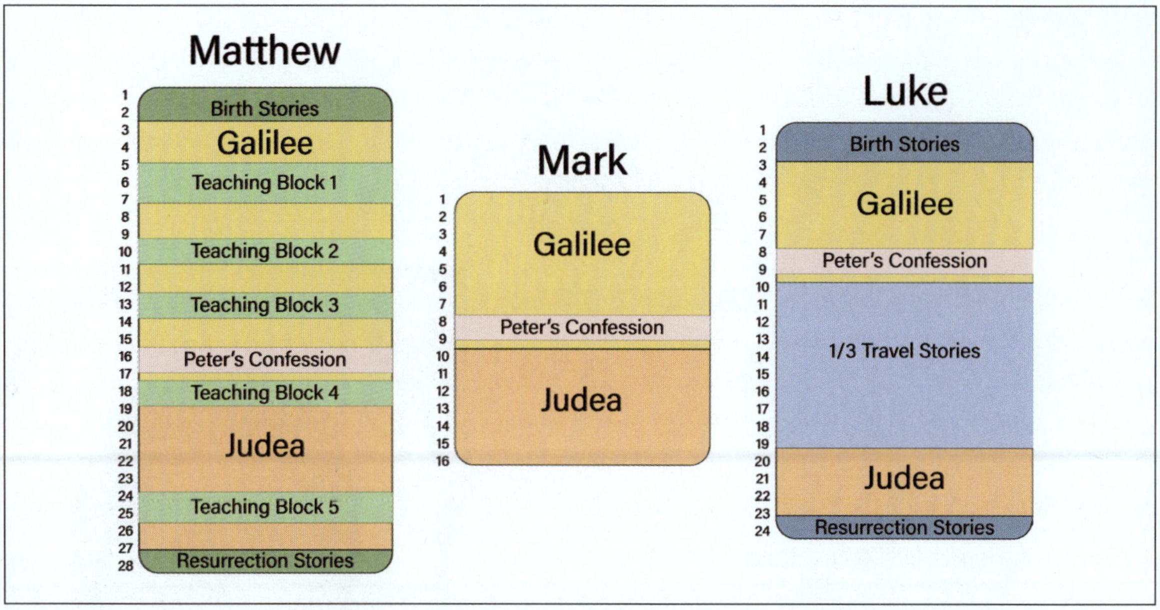

Carl N. Toney

Matthew and Luke follow Mark's outline and uniquely incorporate material into their books, with distinct birth stories and resurrection stories.

Readers may assume, based on Matthew's placement at the beginning of the New Testament, that this problem has been solved. Some early Christian thinkers (like Augustine) claimed that Matthew was the first Gospel written and that Mark then abbreviated the work.

However, when we put these three Gospels side by side, we make the surprising discovery that Mark was probably written first. Both Matthew and Luke used Mark to write their Gospels. Evidence for this dependence includes Matthew using 90 percent of Mark and Luke using 80 percent of Mark. In addition, Matthew and Luke follow Mark's outline of Jesus's life. Mark's story begins with Jesus's baptism and temptation (Mark 1:2–13; Matt. 3:1–4:11; Luke 3:1–4:13). Next, we learn about his Galilean ministry (Mark 1:14–9:50; Matt. 4:12–18:35; Luke 4:14–9:50). The story pivots when it focuses on Jesus's death after Peter's confession about Jesus's messianic identity (Mark 8:27–9:1; Matt. 16:13–28; Luke 9:18–27). Finally, the story ends with Jesus traveling to Jerusalem and being crucified, buried, and resurrected (Mark 10:1–16:8; Matt. 19:1–27:66; Luke 9:51–23:56).

Matthew and Luke also have about two hundred verses that they exclusively share with each other. Examples include the temptation of Jesus (Matt. 4:1–11; Luke 4:1–13), the beatitudes (Matt. 5:1–12; Luke 6:20–26), and the Lord's Prayer (Matt. 6:9–15; Luke 11:2–4). These common verses, which are primarily Jesus's teachings, may be material that either Matthew copied from Luke or that Luke copied from Matthew. Alternatively, it may come from a lost source that Matthew and Luke used alongside Mark. This hypothetical lost source has been reconstructed by scholars and labeled **Q**, which is an abbreviation of the German word "Quelle," meaning "source."

Matthew and Luke tend to be very different when they don't follow Mark or their shared material. Some of the clearest examples of this divergence are the birth stories, where the visitors of baby Jesus are magi (Matt. 1:1–2:23) or shepherds (Luke 1:1–2:52). Matthew and Luke both uniquely expand Mark's short description of Jesus's resurrection (Mark 16:1–8). Matthew ends with Jesus's Great Commission in Galilee (Matt. 28:1–20). Luke finishes by describing Jesus's ascension into heaven outside Jerusalem (Luke 24:1–52). Both Matthew and Luke insert unique structural features into Mark's storyline. Matthew sprinkles five teaching blocks throughout the story (Matt. 5–7, 10, 13, 18, 24–25). Luke inserts Jesus's journey from Galilee to Jerusalem, which is about one-third of the Gospel (Luke 9:51–19:27).

All this evidence supports the theory that Mark was the first Gospel written around 65–75 CE.[8] Then, Matthew and Luke wrote their Gospels around 75–85 CE.[9] Finally, John is considered the last Gospel written. John used independent sources, and his Gospel was completed sometime before 100 CE. By being placed first in the New Testament, some readers assume the Gospels were the first books written. However, the earliest Christian writings in the New Testament were letters written to small groups of Christians in various cities. There's a bit of debate about which letter gets the prize for being the earliest, but the leading contenders are Jude's letter, James's letter, and Paul's letter to either the Thessalonians or Galatians.

Four Models for the Composition of the Synoptic Gospels

Four Source Hypothesis. Mark and Q were written first. Matthew and Luke used Mark and Q separately while supplementing these with their unique material. This view is the modern scholarly consensus.[10]

Farrer-Goulder Hypothesis. Mark was written first. Then, Matthew expanded Mark, giving a Jewish emphasis. Last, Luke-Acts expanded Mark and used Matthew's material to explain God's inclusion of Gentiles.[11] This view is attractive because it shows a slow growth of material and a broadening of the audience.

Wilke Hypothesis. Mark was written first, and then Luke. Finally, Matthew used Mark's outline and reorganized material from Luke.[12] In favor of this view, many of the "primitive" versions of texts come from Luke (e.g., Matt. 6:9-13, 5:3-12; Luke 11:2-4, 6:20b-23).

Griesbach Hypothesis. Matthew was written first. Second, Luke adapted it. Third, Mark conflated Matthew and Luke when he wrote his Gospel.[13] Some early church traditions support this view.

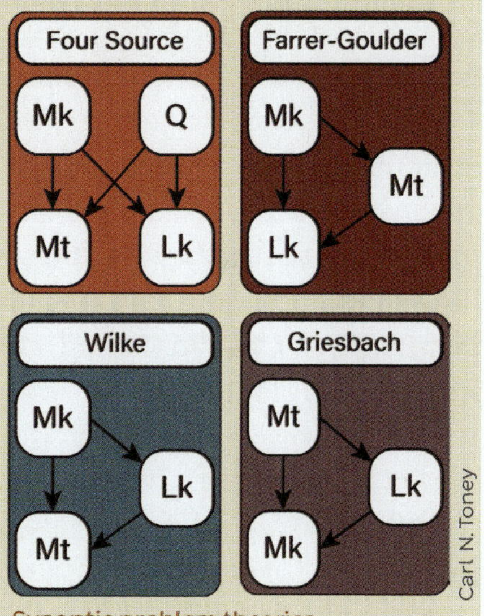

Synoptic problem theories.

[8] Mark was written sometime shortly before or after the fall of Jerusalem in 70 CE (Mark 13).

[9] We allow for a few years of the circulation of Mark before the other Gospels used the material.

[10] The theory that Matthew and Luke used Mark and Q is called the Two Source Hypothesis, which was first proposed in 1838 by Christian Weisse. Most scholars today hold to some version of the Four Source Hypothesis, proposed in 1924 by B. H. Streeter.

[11] Farrer, "On Dispensing with Q"; Goulder, "Is Q a Juggernaut?"; Goodacre, *Case against Q*. Goodacre maintains a website full of useful resources: www.markgoodacre.org/Q/.

[12] Christian Wilke made this proposal in 1838. Powell, *The Myth of the Lost Gospel*.

[13] This is named after Johann Griesbach, who made this proposal in the 1780s, but it was first proposed by Henry Owen in 1764. Farmer, *Synoptic Problem*.

Public Domain (courtesy of Getty's Open Content Program)

Mark writing his Gospel. Armenian manuscript. (1386)

Who Was Mark?

The authors of all four Gospels chose not to identify themselves, so the true identity of this Gospel writer remains a mystery. The title "Gospel according to Mark" was added sometime in the second century. Early church tradition claims that **John Mark** translated Peter's memories of Jesus while he was in Rome around 65–75 CE (Irenaeus, *Haer*. 3.1.1; Eusebius, *Hist. eccl*. 3.39.15, 6.14).

If we accept tradition, then we find some fragmentary information about John Mark from the annals of the New Testament. According to Acts 12:6–17, his mother lived in Jerusalem, and Peter went to her house after an angel released him from prison. He was also the cousin of a famous church leader named Barnabas (Acts 12:12; Col. 4:10). Barnabas was given the nickname "son of encouragement" probably for his many kind acts, including selling a family field and giving the money to the church (Acts 4:36–37).

John Mark joined Paul and Barnabas as part of the very first missionary team sent from the church of Antioch to evangelize the island of Cyprus (Acts 12:25). Unfortunately, he left the group after their first stop, which created a rift in the relationship between Paul and Barnabas because Paul thought he was a deserter (Acts 15:36–41). Eventually, Paul and Mark reconciled (Philem. 22), and Paul even called him "useful" for his ministry (2 Tim. 4:11). If church tradition is correct about Mark's authorship, then Mark's odyssey from deserter to Gospel writer shows the power of reconciliation.

While there is no way to confirm or deny the tradition of John Mark's authorship, the Gospel was written by combining a series of traditional stories and teachings of Jesus. Scholars describe each of these discrete units using the technical term **pericope**. They were written in Greek and edited together by the author. It's important to realize that all the Gospels are Greek translations of the Aramaic words of Jesus. For the most part, we don't actually have Jesus's original words. However, Mark preserves a few Aramaic phrases that may be attributed to Jesus. For example, *Talitha cum* means "Little girl, get up!" (Mark 5:41). *Abba* is translated as "Father"[14] (Mark 14:36), and *Eloi, Eloi, lema sabachthani* is "My God, my God, why have you forsaken me?" (Mark 15:34). The Gospels remind us that, from the beginning of the New Testament, the church embraced translating Jesus's teaching into the common language.[15]

---

[14]There is a popular misconception that *abba* means "daddy" (*pappas*). Instead, Mark 14:36 (and Rom. 8:15 and Gal. 4:6) translated *abba* using *patēr*, which means "father."

[15]Red-letter editions of the Bible have the tendency to prioritize the words of Jesus. But we need to be cautious. Instead, all words in the New Testament are equally authoritative as God's Word.

As the first Gospel, Mark invented the "Gospel genre" when he assembled the stories recounting the life of Jesus.[16] The Gospel genre adapted ancient biographies, which told stories of significant persons. The Gospel genre gets its name from Mark's opening line that describes the work as "The beginning of the gospel of Jesus Christ" (Mark 1:1 ASV). Both Matthew and Luke used Mark as the template for their Gospel compositions.

By the second century, other copycat works appeared, which did not enter the New Testament canon. Examples include the Infancy Gospel of James, which tells the story of Mary's birth and upbringing, her marriage to an older widower named Joseph, and Jesus's birth in a cave near Bethlehem. The Infancy Gospel of Thomas tells stories of a toddler Jesus performing miracles, like animating clay pigeons and killing children who bothered him. Another, the Gospel of Thomas, lacks any narrative structure. It focuses on the 114 hidden teachings of Jesus, ranging from the more orthodox parable of the sower and the seeds (Gos. Thom. 9) to the sexist teaching that women must become men in order to be saved (Gos. Thom. 114). The fragmentary Gospel of Peter relates stories of Jesus's resurrection, including a giant speaking cross that precedes Jesus out of the grave.

What Was Mark's Version of the Story?

The End of the Exile and the Beginning of a New Exodus

Mark's Gospel offers the shortest and most fast-paced telling of the life of Jesus in the New Testament. Mark quickly set the tone for his Gospel by opening with a mixed quotation from Malachi 3:1 and Isaiah 40:3 to describe the ministry of John the Baptist.

> See, I am sending my messenger ahead of you,
>   who will prepare your way;
> the voice of one crying out in the wilderness:
>   "Prepare the way of the Lord,
>   make his paths straight." (Mark 1:2–3)

Mark attributed this quote to Isaiah to place Jesus's story in the context of the Jewish people being in exile.

For Jesus and his contemporaries, their exile was felt through their subjugation by the foreign powers of the Roman prefect and Herodian client rulers, as well as satanic forces. Mark's imagery of exile reminded his audience that Rome was in charge. However, Mark offered a glimmer of hope that there may be "good news" (*euangelion*) on the horizon by recalling Isaiah and Malachi's prophetic promises of a return through a new exodus.

Mark dramatically set his first episode in the Judean desert by the muddy waters of the Jordan River (Mark 1:4–11). The wilderness setting evoked the forty years of wilderness wanderings that the Israelites experienced during the exodus (Num. 14:33–35, 32:13; Deut. 2:7, 8:2–4; Josh. 5:6). In these waters, a man dressed like Elijah called out for God to act and reestablish his reign. He looked like Elijah because he was the Jewish prophet associated with the end of exile (Mal. 3:1, 4:5–6; Sir. 48:1–10). This new prophet's

[16] The Gospel genre developed from the preaching of Christian missionaries. Bultmann, *History of the Synoptic Tradition*, 368–74.

Traditional site of Jesus's baptism in the Lower Jordan River.

name was John the Baptist. He called the people to repent of their sins (Mark 1:4). John knew repentance was the first step before God could begin a new exodus. John also predicted that someone more powerful would appear to lead this new exodus and baptize people with God's Spirit (Mark 1:7), fulfilling restoration promises, such as in Joel 2:28–29 and Ezekiel 36:27.

Suddenly, a man named Joshua appeared by the Jordan River, asking to be baptized. When baptized, God's Spirit descended upon him and empowered him to do miracles like Moses and prophets of Israel like Elijah and Elisha, who were anointed by God's Spirit (Mark 1:9–10). Even more astonishing, God spoke to the man, telling him, "You are my Son" (Mark 1:11), connecting this man with the Davidic dynasty of kings. He was God's Son, fulfilling God's promise to David:

> I will raise up your offspring after you, who shall come forth from your body, and I will establish his kingdom. He shall build a house for my name, and I will establish the throne of his kingdom forever. I will be a father to him, and he shall be a son to me. (2 Sam. 7:12–14; cf. 1 Chron. 17:11–13; Ps. 2:7)

This scene of Joshua entering and leaving the waters of the Jordan as God's appointed ruler recalled the story of Joshua and the Israelites first entering the promised land by crossing the Jordan River (Josh. 3–4). Of course, readers familiar with Mark's story know this Joshua by the Greek translation of his name, "Jesus" (*Iēsous*). With his immersion in the waters, anointing by God's Spirit, and God's declaration of sonship, Jesus was identified as the "Anointed One" (*Christos*). According to Mark, he was the promised Jewish Messiah (Mark 1:9–11). As the Messiah, he was expected to remind the people that God was in charge.

Images of exile and return continue to dominate Mark's narrative. Just as the Israelites spent forty years in the desert before entering the promised land, so Jesus spent forty days in the wilderness being tempted by Satan before reentering the land and beginning his messianic mission (Mark 1:12–13; Num. 14:33–35, 32:13; Deut. 2:7, 8:2–4; Josh. 5:6). Just as Joshua portioned land to the twelve tribes of Israel, Jesus chose **twelve disciples** (Mark 3:13–19, 6:7–13) to represent the symbolic restoration of the twelve tribes.

Jesus's life recapitulated several stories from the exodus. He controlled the wind and the waves (Mark 4:35–41) and walked on water (Mark 6:45–52), like the Israelites crossed the Red Sea (Exod. 14:1–31) and the Jordan River (Josh. 3–4). He fed thousands in the wilderness (Mark 6:30–44, 8:1–10), like

Herod's kingdom was divided among his heirs and a Roman prefect.

God provided manna and quail for Israel in the desert (Exod. 16:1–36; Num. 11:31–35). Jesus ascended a mountain with three of his disciples, who heard God's voice and encountered manifestations of Moses and Elijah (Mark 9:2–8), similar to Moses and his three companions ascending Mount Sinai and seeing God (Exod. 24:9–11).

Jesus's miracles recalled the signs and wonders Moses performed and those of Elijah and Elisha. Jesus purified the land of unclean spirits through his exorcisms (Mark 1:21–27, 3:11–12, 5:1–20, 7:24–30, 9:14–29; cf. Mark 6:7) and demonstrated his authority over Satan (Mark 3:22–30), just as Moses displayed God's power over Pharoah (Exod. 4:18–14:31) and Elijah proved God's supremacy over Baal (1 Kings 18:17–46). Jesus purified people through healings, like curing leprosy (Mark 1:40–45), recalling the leprosy miracles associated with Moses (Exod. 4:6–7; Num. 12:10–16) and Elisha (2 Kings 5:1–19). He made a paralyzed man walk (Mark 2:1–12) and healed a man's withered hand (Mark 3:1–6), recalling when Moses cured people with a bronze snake (Num. 21:1–9). Jesus raised the dead (Mark 5:35–43), like Elijah (1 Kings 17:17–24) and Elisha (2 Kings 4:8–37). He controlled the sea (Mark 4:35–41) and walked on water (Mark 6:45–52), just like Moses crossed the Red Sea (Exod. 14:1–31) and Elijah and Elisha crossed the Jordan River (2 Kings 2:6–8, 2:13–14). Jesus fed the five thousand and four thousand (Mark 6:30–44, 8:1–10), just as Moses provided manna and quail (Exod. 16:1–36; Num. 11:31–35) and Elijah provided flour and oil (1 Kings 17:7–16) and Elisha supplied oil for a widow (2 Kings 4:1–7) and fed a hundred people (2 Kings 4:42–44). Ultimately, during his Last Supper (Mark 14:12–26), Jesus reinterpreted the Passover

View of Capernaum from the Sea of Galilee.

Carl N. Toney

GOSPEL OF MARK

- **The Ministry of the Messiah (1:1–8:21)**
    - Baptism and Temptation of Jesus (1:1–13)
    - Jesus's Kingdom of God Ministry in Galilee (1:14–4:34)
        - Five Miracles, the Twelve Called, and Opposition Grows (1:14–3:35)
        - Kingdom Parables (4:1–34)
    - Sea of Galilee and Lessons on Boundary Crossing (4:35–8:21)
- **The Messiah's Way of the Cross (8:22–16:8)**
    - Peter's Confession, the Transfiguration, and Passion Predictions (8:22–10:52)
    - Temple Conflicts and the Olivet Discourse (11:1–13:37)
    - Last Supper, Arrest, Trial, Crucifixion, and Resurrection (14:1–16:8)

meal instituted under Moses (Exod. 12:1–20; Num. 9:1–14; Deut. 16:1–8; Ezek. 45:21–25) and identified his death as the new Passover sacrifice (Mark 14:24).

The Kingdom of God

Upon returning from the desert, Jesus began his ministry in Galilee around Capernaum, proclaiming his gospel. The word "**gospel**" (*euangelion*) is formed by the combination of "good" (*eu*) plus "message" (*angelion*), meaning "good news." For the Romans, this good news was associated with the victories of the Roman Empire, especially the Roman emperor (Philo, *Alleg. Interp.* 231; Josephus, *J.W.* 2.618; Priene Inscription). For the Jewish people, this good news was understood as a proclamation of God's reign (e.g., Isa. 52:7, 60:6; Ps. 96:2–10), salvation (Isa. 52:7; Ps. 95:1), righteousness (Ps. 40:9), and peace (Isa. 52:7).[17] Jesus's gospel message was short and simple. He announced, "The time is fulfilled and the kingdom of God has come near. Repent and believe in the gospel!" (Mark 1:15 LEB).

With this proclamation, Jesus affirmed the Jewish understanding of good news and challenged the message of the Romans. Jesus's expression "**kingdom of God**" (*basileia tou theou*) was his way of saying that God was in charge and would set the world right through his Messiah. This expression drew upon the understanding in the Jewish scriptures of the "kingdom of Yahweh"[18] (1 Chron. 28:5; 2 Chron. 13:8; cf. 1 Chron. 17:14, 29:11; Pss. 22:28, 103:19, 145:11–13; Obad. 21). With Jesus's message, the question was raised, "Who is really in charge?" The Romans appeared to be in charge by occupying the land, and the devil's minions possessed the people and land. However, the Jewish people hoped that God was really in control and would install his Davidic representative to rule (Ps. 145:83; Isa. 52:7).

Jesus's message demanded a response. He offered the forgiveness of sins apart from the sacrificial system of the temple (Mark 2:5–10, 11:25; cf. Mark 1:4–5). He called those who followed him to "repent"

[17] Friedrich, "εὐαγγελίζομαι," *TDNT*, 2:715–17. See Guelich, *Mark 1–8:26*, 13; Bowman, "Term 'Gospel' and Its Cognates," 54–67.
[18] In English Bibles, Yahweh is the name of Israel's God, and it is often translated as Lord.

(*metanoeō*), meaning to "change one's mind." Jesus was asking his followers to change their minds by abandoning their own perspectives and embracing God's perspective about themselves and the world. This kind of change would transform their character and result in new behaviors. Put another way, Jesus was not just asking them to turn away from their past errors; a more helpful model is to see this as them turning toward God.[19] This was reflected by his challenge to "believe" (*pisteuō*), which may be better translated as showing "allegiance" or "loyalty" to God's kingdom.

Jesus provided a framework to describe people's responses to his gospel message when he told the parable of the sower and the seeds (Mark 4:3–20). **Parables** were short, fictional stories that conveyed a moral theme, and they were sometimes accompanied by an explanation. Jesus's parables were based on the ordinary circumstances of a first-century Galilean and often used agrarian images. In this parable, the soil represented people and their responses to the gospel message. The hard soil symbolized those allowing Satan to steal the message from them. The rocky soil typified those whose could not endure trouble and persecution. The thorny soil characterized people who allowed wealth and the cares of the world to distract them. The fertile soil illustrated those disciples who faithfully served the kingdom of God. Those encountering Jesus in Mark's Gospel are concrete examples of these responses. Positively, the disciples and those benefitting from Jesus's miracles demonstrated the blessings of the kingdom. Negatively, Judas, demons, and the religious and political leaders revealed what opposition to the kingdom looked like.

From his contemporaries' perspective, Jesus was expected to inaugurate the kingdom of God. Jesus challenged the reigns of the spiritual and civic authorities during his ministry. He conquered the satanic kingdom by casting out demons (Mark 3:20–30). He protested the Roman occupation of the land by destroying a "legion" of demons and pigs (Mark 5:1–20). He challenged the culpability of the temple establishment by predicting the temple's destruction during his Olivet discourse (Mark 13:1–37).

Because Jesus's opponents understood that Jesus's kingdom message challenged the Roman authorities, they attempted to trap him by asking about paying taxes. Jesus's response sounded like he was affirming the Roman government when he said, "Give to the emperor the things that are the emperor's,

A denarius, worth one day's wage, depicts Tiberius as the son of the divine Augustus.

[19] Behm, "μετανοέω, μετάνοια," *TDNT*, 4:1002–1003.

The remains of a fourth-century synagogue in Capernaum are likely built upon the synagogue where Jesus drove out an impure spirit.

and to God the things that are God's" (Mark 12:17). However, Jesus's answer was actually subversive. When Jesus asked for a Roman denarius, he highlighted the image of the emperor on the coin and the inscription declaring him to be the "son of God." Both the image and inscription violated the Jewish commands against worshiping other gods and idolatry (Exod. 20:3–6; Deut. 5:7–10). The emperor's image was contrasted with the Jewish idea that people bear the image of God (Gen. 1:26–27). In light of this, Jesus was telling his audience to give back the idolatrous coin of the empire and to submit themselves to God's rule because each person bears the image of God, the mark of God's ownership.

Because religion and politics were not distinct in those days, Jesus's disciples saw him as their political Messiah, as seen in Peter's confession (Mark 8:27–30). They hoped Jesus would lead a rebellion to overthrow Roman rule. However, Jesus rejected reproducing human systems of power and called his disciples servants (Mark 9:33–37). He also revealed that his messianic mission did not involve leading a rebellion against Rome. Instead, it would end with his death at the hands of the Romans. Yet his death was part of God's plan to instigate the reign of God (Mark 8:34–9:1, 9:30–31, 10:32–34), and his resurrection would lead to his heavenly reign as the agent of God's rule (Mark 13:24–27).

Shhh . . . Jesus Is the Messiah

Not only did Jesus proclaim a gospel, but Jesus was also the one proclaimed as God's Messiah (Mark 1:1). However, a notable feature of Mark's Gospel is how often Jesus's messianic identity is hidden.[20] From his first miracle of exorcising a demon in the synagogue in Capernaum, Jesus silenced the demons when

[20]This was first observed in 1901 by Wrede, *Messianic Secret.*

Carl N. Toney

Two fish and five loaves from a restaurant near the Sea of Galilee are similar to what Jesus would have fed the five thousand and four thousand.

they revealed his identity (Mark 1:21–28, 1:32–34, 3:7–12). Those healed were commanded to say nothing (Mark 1:40–45, 5:35–43, 7:31–37, 8:22–26). Jesus's parabolic teaching intentionally concealed its meaning from the public (Mark 4:10–12), while the disciples were given private instructions (Mark 4:10–20, 4:34–41, 6:45–52, 8:14–21, 8:31–33, 9:30–32, 10:32–34). Even at Jesus's baptism, the Father only spoke to Jesus (Mark 1:9–11).

Jesus's concealment of his messianic identity may have reflected his desire to avoid overt political claims or to prevent a violent revolution.[21] His motivation for silencing demons was revealed when the religious leaders accused him of performing miracles by the power of Satan (also known as Beelzebul, Mark 3:22–30). These religious leaders accused Jesus of being a false prophet who used miracles to validate his teaching, which they believed was promoting disobedience to the law, such as breaking the Sabbath (Mark 2:23–3:6). In response to this charge of being filled by a demon, Jesus declared his miraculous activity was done by the power of God's Spirit that filled him at his baptism (Mark 1:9–11, 3:28–30). In addition, Jesus silenced demons because he recognized they were trying to co-opt Jesus's mission with their so-called confessions.

However, we should be careful not to overemphasize this theme of secrecy. Despite Jesus's instructions to remain silent, people would obviously notice a cleansed leper, a dead girl living, or a blind man seeing. Numerous miracles made Jesus a public spectacle (Mark 1:28, 1:32–34), including feeding thousands of people (Mark 6:30–43, 8:1–10).

Looking at the flow of Mark's story, Jesus initially concealed his messianic identity during the beginning of his ministry (Mark 1–8). Then, **Peter's confession** of Jesus as the Messiah was the turning point of the story (Mark 8:27–30). Afterward, Jesus clearly revealed his messianic identity during the second half of the Gospel (Mark 9–16). Glimmers of recognition are seen by unlikely characters, like the woman who anointed Jesus at Bethany (Mark 14:3–9) and the Roman centurion at the cross (Mark 15:39). Some of these glimpses also encouraged a future Gentile mission (Mark 7:24–30, 13:9–10, 14:9, 15:38–39). Jesus's messiahship was finally publicly recognized during his triumphal entry into Jerusalem (Mark 11:1–10).

The struggle to understand Jesus's messianic identity was reflected by Peter's confession, "You are the Messiah" (Mark 8:29), which contrasted with the high priest's question, "Are you the Messiah" (Mark 14:61)? Notably, the statement and question use identical words in Greek (*sy ei ho christos*). Unfortunately, English translations obscure this. In response to both of these men, Jesus affirmed his

[21] Aune, "The Problem of the Messianic Secret," 1–31.

messiahship with his favorite title, "Son of Man" (Mark 8:31, 14:62). For Peter, this question and answer led to a deeper faith and commitment to follow Jesus. Sadly, for the high priest, this question and Jesus's response resulted in his rejection of Jesus.

Jesus's self-understanding of his messiahship is reflected by his use of "Son of Man" (*ho hyios tou anthropou*). This was an allusion to Daniel's "son of man" (Aram. *bar ʾenash*; Heb. *ben ʾadam*, Dan. 7:13). In Daniel 7:1–8, there were various beasts representing the Gentile nations who ruled and oppressed Israel (some understand Rome to be the last beast). In contrast to these animals, a human-looking figure, identified as the son of man, represented Israel (Dan. 7:9–14). Notably, Daniel's son of man did not conquer the nations or seize power for himself. Instead, God defeated his enemies and gave him a heavenly dominion. Like Daniel's son of man, Jesus conceived his messiahship as being the Son of Man who represented Israel. As the Son of Man, Jesus would suffer at the hands of both Roman and satanic powers when he died on the cross. Also, like Daniel's son of man, God would vindicate Jesus and defeat his enemies, and God would exalt him to rule the kingdom of God (Mark 13:24–27).

Carl N. Toney

Model of the Jerusalem temple. Israel Museum.

The Way of the Cross

The cruel shadow of the Roman cross lurks behind the early pages of Mark's Gospel.[22] After Jesus's first miracle of exorcising a demon in a synagogue, Jesus's fame spread quickly throughout Galilee (Mark 1:21–28). This led to the next two miracle stories of healing Peter's mother-in-law (Mark 1:29–34) and cleansing a leper (Mark 1:40–45). When the scribes began to investigate, Jesus spurred their ire by linking his healing of a paralyzed man with his ability to forgive the man's sins (Mark 2:5, 2:8–11), which they deemed as blasphemy (Mark 2:6–7). The religious leaders further indicted him for calling the toll/tax collector Levi as his disciple and for sharing meals with other toll/tax collectors and sinners (Mark 2:16). The last straw came when Jesus deliberately healed a man with a withered hand on the Sabbath (Mark 3:1–6). This led to the Pharisees plotting with the Herodians to destroy Jesus (Mark 3:6).

It is only after Peter's confession (Mark 8:22–30) that the cross moves to dominate the last part of Mark's narrative. As Jesus affirmed his messianic identity, he predicted his death three times (Mark 8:31, 9:31, 10:33–34).[23] The final portion of Mark, called the **passion narrative**, focuses on Jesus's last days in Jerusalem and his confrontations with the Jewish and Roman leadership over his messiahship (Mark 11–16).[24] When Jesus entered Jerusalem on a donkey, the people hailed him as their long-awaited Messiah (Mark 11:1–10). Riding on a donkey recalled Solomon riding into the city for his coronation (1 Kings 1:33, 1:38) and contrasted Roman rulers entering cities in triumphal processions. With this action, Jesus reminded the people that God was in charge and that he was God's messianic representative.

Carl N. Toney

An inscription naming Pontius Pilate was discovered in the theater at Caesarea Maritima. Israel Museum.

When Jesus entered the temple as God's representative, he pronounced judgment against it. Symbolically, Jesus predicted the destruction of the temple just as Jeremiah did before the exile of Israel (Jer. 7:1–15, 26:1–24). Jesus performed a prophetic sign by associating the temple with a cursed fig tree (Mark 11:12–14, 11:20–25). He also enacted the destruction of the temple by overthrowing money changers' tables and disrupting sacrifices (Mark 11:15–19).[25] He denounced the religious leadership as "robbers" (*lēstai*, Mark 11:17; quoting Jer. 7:11) for committing injustice against the poor and widows (Mark 12:38–44; cf. Jer. 7:5–7, 7:13). When he left the temple, he prophesized its destruction at the hands of the Romans (Mark 13:14–21). He linked

[22] According to Marxsen (*Mark the Evangelist*, 31), Mark wrote his Gospel backward, beginning with the cross.

[23] On these passion predictions, see Fuller, *The Mission and Achievement of Jesus*, 55–64.

[24] "The gospels [are] passion narratives with extended introductions." Kähler, *So-Called Historical Jesus*, 80.

[25] Sanders, *Jesus and Judaism*, 61–76. See critique by Evans, "Jesus' Actions in the Temple," 237–70.

this destruction as a sign of his heavenly exaltation as the Son of Man (Mark 13:24–26; Dan. 7:13–14).[26]

Jesus's last day of ministry began in the evening with a Passover meal (Mark 14:12–26). Since Jewish days were marked from sunset to sunset, the same day ended with his crucifixion. Traditionally, this meal consisted of sharing a Passover lamb, eating unleavened bread and bitter herbs, and drinking four cups of wine (Exod. 12:1–20; Num 9:1–14; Deut. 16:1–8; Ezek. 45:21–25). Each year, Jewish families made a pilgrimage to Jerusalem to eat this meal to remember the exodus from Egypt. For this meal, Jesus gathered with his disciples, who were his new family. He transformed the meal into a recollection of his sacrificial death and resurrection by identifying the unleavened bread with his body and the wine with his blood (Mark 14:22–25; Matt. 26:26–29; Luke 22:14–23; 1 Cor. 11:23–26). This Last Supper, also called the **Lord's Supper** or Eucharist, continues to be celebrated by his followers to this day.

After the meal, Jesus and his disciples traveled across the Kidron Valley to the Mount of Olives to spend the evening in the Garden of Gethsemane ("Gethsemane" means "olive press"). In the garden, Jesus was arrested and taken before the Sanhedrin. The **Sanhedrin** was the highest court in Israel, consisting of seventy-one members and led by the high priest (Josephus, *Ant.* 14.167–80; *Life* 62). Jesus's prediction of the destruction of the temple (Mark 11:15–19, 13:1–2) was twisted into the false accusation that he wanted to destroy the temple (Mark 14:56–59; cf. Jer. 26:7–24).[27] With this scene, Mark reminded his audience that the destruction of the temple was a sign of Jesus's exaltation as the Son of Man when Jesus repeated

Carl N. Toney

A 4.3-inch nail in the right heel bone affixing a man to a cross. Israel Museum.

[26] France (*Mark*, 500–502) argues that Mark 13:32–37 describes Jesus's second coming. Wright (*Jesus and the Victory of God*, 339–68) argues that Mark 13 only describes Jesus's enthronement and the temple's destruction.

[27] These scenes recall Jeremiah's predictions of the temple's destruction and the Jerusalem leader's desire to kill him (esp. Jer. 7:1–15, 26:1–15).

the phrase "coming on the clouds" (Mark 14:62; cf. Dan. 7:13) from Mark 13:26. In the narrative, the high priest understood Jesus's allusion to Daniel as a claim that he would be exalted to heaven by God and that the temple would be destroyed. He decried Jesus's words as blasphemy (Mark 14:64).

Next, Jesus appeared before **Pontius Pilate**. Pilate was the ruler of the Roman province of Judea, and his job was to maintain Roman peace. The Roman prefect repeatedly declared Jesus's innocence (Mark 15:10, 15:14).[28] However, he ultimately (and cruelly) executed Jesus between two "insurrectionists" (*lēstai*, Mark 15:27). The charge of claiming to be the "King of the Jews" was placed on Jesus's cross (Mark 15:26). In recounting Jesus's death, Mark noted the political charges of Jesus's stance against the temple and the accusation of insurrection as a would-be Jewish king. But he also included an apologetic of Jesus's innocence through Pilate's statements of his innocence.

So, why did Jesus have to die? To this question, Mark presents a tapestry of answers. At the historical level, Jesus's actions against the temple and the religious leadership led them to seek his execution (Mark 11:18). Pilate decided to kill Jesus as an act of cruelty to show the Jewish people the fate of any challengers to Roman rule.

Spiritually, Jesus's death may be understood as fulfilling God's will (Mark 14:36, 14:49). As one betrayed (Mark 14:44–45), deserted (Mark 14:50), denied (Mark 14:66–72), and forsaken (Mark 15:33–34), Jesus's death may also be a model of suffering and vindication. The cross illustrated a life of self-denial, service, and sacrifice (Mark 8:34–38). Jesus's death was also linked to repentance and the forgiveness of sins (Mark 1:4–5, 2:5–10; cf. Mark 1:15, 6:12). Others point to Jesus's "ransom" (*lytron*) saying (Mark 10:45) as describing his death as purchasing human freedom like God "redeemed" (*lytroō*) Israel from Egyptian enslavement (Exod. 6:6, 15:13 LXX; cf. Matt. 20:28).[29] During Jesus's final meal with his disciples, he identified himself as a Passover sacrifice (Mark 14:1, 14:12) that established a new covenant (Mark 14:24). Jesus's death is certainly a significant focus of Mark's Gospel, and perhaps the reason for Jesus's death was a mixture of these reasons.

Jesus Is for Losers

A final surprising feature of Mark is how poorly the disciples appear.[30] From the beginning, the disciples misunderstood Jesus's ministry (Mark 1:35–39, 4:13, 4:40–41, 4:52, 7:18, 8:14–21, 8:33, 9:10, 9:32). Despite seeing Jesus's miracles, they lacked faith when Jesus stilled the storm (Mark 4:40). They could not consistently perform their own miracles (Mark 6:30–43, 9:14–29). Jesus called Peter "Satan" (Mark 8:33). Peter denied Jesus (Mark 14:54, 14:66–72), and Judas betrayed Jesus (Mark 14:43–52). Jesus rebuked the disciples for seeking power and status (Mark 9:33–37, 10:35–45). He chastised them for barring children from seeing him (Mark 10:13–16). In their final hours with Jesus, they fell asleep in the Garden of Gethsemane (Mark 14:32–42) and ran away when he was arrested (Mark 14:27, 14:43, 14:50–52). The male disciples

---

[28] On using "prefect" (Lat. *praefectus*) as Pilate's title, see Philo, *Legat*; *L'année épigraphique* 1963, no. 104. Hall, "Procurator," *AYBD*, 5:473–74.

[29] Ransom imagery could come from prisoners of war (e.g., Josephus, *Ant.* 14, 371) or manumission of slaves (POxy 1.48–49, 4.722). In the Jewish scriptures, Israel is redeemed from Egyptian enslavement (e.g., Exod. 6:6, 15:13; Deut. 7:8 LXX) and Babylonian exile (e.g., Isa. 51:11, 52:3, 62:12; Jer. 27:34 LXX). There is a host of terms in the "ransoming" family: "ransom" (*lytron*, Mark 10:45; Matt. 20:28); "redemption" (*apolytrōsis*, Luke 21:28; Rom. 3:34, 8:23; 1 Cor. 1:30; Eph. 1:7, 1:14, 4:30; Col. 1:14; Heb. 9:15); "to ransom" (*lytroō*, Luke 24:21; Titus 2:14; 1 Pet. 1:18; cf. Luke 24:21; Titus 2:14); "redemption" (*lytrōsis*, Luke 1:68, 2:38; Heb. 9:12); "ransom" (*antilytron*, 1 Tim. 2:6).

[30] Weeden, *Mark—Traditions in Conflict.*

The Church of the Holy Sepulchre is one of the traditional sites of Jesus's crucifixion and burial. Tombs discovered in the church illustrate the type of tomb in which Jesus may have been buried.

were absent at the cross (Mark 15:40–41) and did not visit Jesus's grave (Mark 16:1–8). In the final scene of the Gospel, even the women present at the cross (Mark 15:40–41) fled the tomb in fear (Mark 16:8).

However, the disciples also exhibited some positive characteristics. Peter, Andrew, James, and John left their jobs as fishermen and immediately responded to Jesus's calling (Mark 1:16–20). Jesus chose the twelve because he wanted them (Mark 3:13–19). The disciples were Jesus's true family because they did God's will (Mark 3:31–35). Jesus shared the meaning of parables with them (Mark 4:10–12). Jesus empowered them to perform miracles and carry out his mission (Mark 6:6–13). After Peter's confession (Mark 8:27–30), Jesus revealed to them that his messianic mission involved dying on the cross (Mark 8:31–34, 9:30–32, 10:32–34). Peter, James, and John witnessed Jesus's **transfiguration**—the event where Jesus radiated with glory, Moses and Elijah appeared, and God spoke from heaven identifying Jesus as his Son (Mark 9:2–8). The disciples helped organize his triumphal entry into Jerusalem (Mark 11:1–11). Jesus shared the meaning of his upcoming death during his final Passover meal (Mark 14:12–25). Mary Magdalene, Mary the mother of James, and Salome were present at the cross (Mark 15:40–41). Joseph of Arimathea buried Jesus (Mark 15:43–46), and the women visited the empty tomb (Mark 16:1–8).

The disciples were complex characters who experienced both successes and failures. In the story, they act as foils to Jesus. Initially, there is a greater emphasis on their positive features, so the audience identifies with them. As the story progresses, they increasingly mess up. Their misunderstandings and failures created opportunities to teach the true nature of Jesus and how to be a genuine disciple. Authentic disciples submit to God's rule (Mark 1:14–15). They are servants of all (Mark 9:35), take up their crosses (Mark 8:34–35), confess Jesus (Mark 8:38), and look for his return (Mark 13:35 37). Discipleship is established by the call and faithfulness of Jesus, not the merits or abilities of his followers.

Discipleship involves following a road of misunderstanding and rejection, just as Jesus's life ended with his sacrificial death. The disciples were bound to the Son of Man, whom God vindicated after his suffering and death. Anyone who follows Jesus can also expect to suffer for his sake (Mark 8:34–38, 10:38–45). To be a disciple is not easy, and the promised suffering is a potential stumbling block for would-be disciples who might have false notions of a revolutionary Messiah. The call of discipleship was particularly relevant to Mark's church in Rome, which faced persecution under Nero in the mid-sixties (including the deaths of Peter and Paul).[31] While Jesus's opponents always led him to the cross, his disciples were called to follow him to the cross.

Correcting Copying Mistakes and the Ending of Mark

There are thousands of copies of the Bible, which we call manuscripts. When scribes copied the Bible, they sometimes made mistakes. Before translating the Bible, scholars compare these copies to determine the original words and correct mistakes. This process is called textual criticism. Scholars use several criteria to reconstruct the original texts. They favor older, more reliable copies, look for inconsistencies in teaching and language, compare the number of copies that agree, and look for explanations about why differences were introduced.

Thankfully, most mistakes are minor—missing or adding a few words, misspellings, and attempts to make the Greek make more sense. However, we have a few cases where the changes are more pronounced. Three of the most noticed are the longer ending of Mark (Mark 16:9–20), the woman caught in adultery (John 7:53–8:11),[32] and the ending of the Lord's Prayer (Matt. 6:13).[33] Of these, we will explore this process using the ending of Mark as a test case.

Most English Bibles provide a footnote indicating that Mark may have ended with Mark 16:8. They also include the shorter ending of Mark, which says, "And all that had been commanded them they told briefly to those around Peter. And afterwards Jesus himself sent out through them, from east to west, the sacred and imperishable proclamation of eternal salvation." They also include the longer ending of Mark, which is Mark 16:9–20.

We can quickly eliminate the shorter ending because it is found as the ending in only one manuscript, and it is placed between Mark 16:8 and Mark 16:9 in other manuscripts. The real debate is between the longer ending (Mark 16:9–20) and ending with Mark 16:8.

[31] Lane, *Mark*, 12–17; Rawlinson, *St. Mark*, xvii.

[32] While this story is included in many manuscripts, it is omitted in the earliest copies of John, placed after 7:36 and 7:44, or put after 21:25. The story is also included after Luke 21:38.

[33] "For the kingdom and the power and the glory are yours forever. Amen" is omitted in many early manuscripts and may be based on 1 Chronicles 29:11–13.

Those who favor the inclusion of Mark 16:9–20 note that it is present in most ancient manuscripts. We also have an outside witness named Tatian, who was aware of it as early as 170 CE. They highlight the awkward ending at Mark 16:8, which in Greek says, "They were afraid for," and they note that "for" (*gar*) is the last word in Mark. They also emphasize that deleting these verses removes Jesus's post-resurrection appearances. Thus, they surmise that there must have been some damage to the scroll. Subsequent copyists either used the damaged scroll that ended with Mark 16:8 or added the shorter ending to complete the text.

However, it is more likely that Mark intended to end with Mark 16:8, and that subsequent, well-intentioned, copyists added Mark 16:9–20 using stories from the other Gospels. First, it is highly improbable that one damaged copy would produce so many manuscripts. It is also unlikely that copyists would not have access to an undamaged copy of Mark to complete the ending since early Christians were proliferative copyists.[34] Instead, it makes more sense for a copyist to have been dissatisfied with Mark's ending in Mark 16:8 and wished to expand it—either with the shorter or longer ending. In addition, the absence of Jesus's resurrection appearances in Mark helps explain why Matthew and Luke have distinct resurrection stories. Finally, the so-called awkward placement of "for" (in "they were afraid for" [*ephobounto gar*]), as the last word in Mark, reflects correct Greek grammar because "for" (*gar*) is usually the second word in its clause.[35]

Why end at Mark 16:8? It may be that Mark was never completed by its original author for unknown reasons.[36] Others understand the "fear" (*phobeō*) to be a positive reaction of reverence or awe to Jesus's resurrection.[37] However, the negative connotations of fear match Mark's negative portrayals of the disciples.[38] While the women initially responded in fear, the audience knows that they eventually overcame their fear and told the story. Rhetorically, the sudden ending and the ambiguous language of "for they were afraid" (NIV) asks the audience to respond to the angel's message. What kind of disciples would they be? Would they believe in the resurrection? Would they respond in fear that leads to silence? Or in awe that led to obedience and to continue the Gospel story?

Key Terms and People

Canon: the collection of the sixty-six works deemed authoritative for Christian practices and beliefs
Genre: a term used to distinguish different styles of writing
Gospel: "good news"; for the Romans, this good news was associated with the victories of the Roman Empire; for Jews and Jesus, this good news was understood as a proclamation that God was in charge
Gospels: the genre classification for writings that recount the life, death, and resurrection of Jesus

[34] Taylor, *Gospels: A Short Introduction*, 50.
[35] BDAG, 189.
[36] Rawlinson, *St. Mark*, 270.
[37] Stonehouse, *Witness of Matthew and Mark*, 107.
[38] Dibelius, *From Tradition to Gospel*, 230.

John Mark: cousin of Barnabas and fellow missionary with Paul; tradition considers him to be the author of Mark's Gospel, using the recollections of Peter
Kingdom of God: a Jewish expression meaning "God's reign"; Jesus's gospel message called for people to submit to God's rule
Lord's Supper: also called the Last Supper and Eucharist; the final Passover meal Jesus shared with his disciples, where the bread and wine recall Jesus's death and resurrection; churches continue to celebrate this meal.
Parables: short, fictional stories Jesus told to convey a moral theme
Passion narrative: Jesus's last days in Jerusalem resulting in his death and resurrection
Pericope: any discrete unit of Scripture
Peter's confession: Peter identified Jesus as the Messiah, the turning point in Mark's Gospel
Pontius Pilate: the Roman ruler of the province of Judea, and the man responsible for crucifying Jesus as an enemy of Rome
Q or Quelle: the material shared only by both Matthew and Luke; this may be a unique, lost source
Sanhedrin: the highest court in Israel consisted of seventy-one members, led by the high priest
Synoptic Gospels: the three Gospels—Matthew, Mark, and Luke—share similar content and outline Jesus's ministry moving from Galilee to Jerusalem
Synoptic problem: determining which Synoptic Gospel was written first and their literary relationship
Transfiguration: an event found in the Synoptics where Jesus radiates with glory, Moses and Elijah appear, and God speaks from heaven identifying Jesus as his Son
Twelve disciples: the core male disciples of Jesus represented the twelve tribes of Israel

Conversation Starters

1. What were the three criteria for accepting a work as part of the New Testament canon? Which criterion do you think was most important?
2. How would you describe the relationship between the four Gospels? Which Gospel do you think was written first? Why?
3. Who do you think is the author of Mark's Gospel? Does knowing the authorship help your understanding of the work?
4. What are some of the images of exile in Mark's Gospel? Why were the people in exile? How did Jesus help end exile? How does this motif of exile and deliverance fit into the history of Israel in Chapter One?
5. Can you explain the significant parts of Jesus's gospel message of "The time is fulfilled and the kingdom of God has come near. Repent and believe in the gospel" (Mark 1:15 LEB)? How does this message help answer the question from Chapter One of "Who's in charge?"
6. How did Jesus understand himself to be the Messiah? Why did he seem to hide his messiahship?
7. How did Peter's confession of Jesus function as a hinge in Mark's Gospel?

8. Why do you think the disciples had trouble understanding Jesus's identity and ministry? How did the disciples help model what it means to be a disciple of Jesus?
9. Why did Jesus have to die according to Mark? How was Jesus's crucifixion political? What was the connection between Jesus's death and the destruction of the temple?

FOR FURTHER READING

On Scripture

Bird, Michael. *7 Things I Wish Every Christian Knew*. Zondervan, 2021.

Fee, Gordon D., and Douglas K. Stuart. *How to Read the Bible for All Its Worth*. 4th rev. ed. Zondervan, 2014.

McGehee, Michael. *The Bible Doesn't Have to Be Hard to Read*. Smyth & Helwys, 2001.

Wright, N. T. *Scripture and the Authority of God: How to Read the Bible Today*. Rev. and exp ed. HarperOne, 2011.

———. *Surprised by Scripture: Engaging Contemporary Issues*. HarperOne, 2014.

Gospel Overview

American Bible Society. *Synopsis of the Four Gospels: Revised Standard Version*. Rev. ed. American Bible Society, 2010.

Fisk, Bruce. *A Hitchhiker's Guide to Jesus: Reading the Gospels on the Ground*. Baker Academic, 2011.

Green, Joel, Jeannine Brown, and Nicholas Perrin, eds. *Dictionary of Jesus and the Gospels*. 2nd ed. IVP Academic, 2013.

Perkins, Pheme. *Introduction to the Synoptic Gospels*. Eerdmans, 2007.

Porter, Stanley, and Bryan Dyer. *The Synoptic Problem: Four Views*. Baker Academic, 2016.

Stanton, Graham. *The Gospels and Jesus*. 2nd ed. Oxford Bible Series. Oxford University Press, 2002.

Gospel of Mark

Beavis, Mary Ann. *Mark*. Paideia. Baker Academic, 2011.

Collins, Adela Yarbro. *Mark: A Commentary on the Gospel of Mark*. Herm. Fortress, 2007.

Dowd, Sharyn. *Reading Mark: A Literary and Theological Commentary on the Second Gospel*. RNT. Smyth & Helwys, 2000.

Hooker, Morna. *The Gospel according to Saint Mark*. BNTC 2. Hendrickson, 1991.

Moore, Stephen, and Janice Capel Anderson, eds. *Mark and Method: New Approaches in Biblical Studies*. Fortress, 2008.

Rhoads, David M., Joanna Dewey, and Donald Michie. *Mark as Story: An Introduction to the Narrative of a Gospel*. Fortress, 1999.

Tan, Kim Huat. *Mark*. New Covenant Commentary Series. Lutterworth, 2016.

Wright, N. T. *Mark for Everyone*. Society for Promoting Christian Knowledge, 2004.

3

MATTHEW'S STORY

Who Was Matthew?

We now turn to our second story about the life and ministry of Jesus. Because this Gospel never directly identifies its author, it is technically anonymous. However, the title "Gospel according to Matthew" found in many Bibles introduces readers to the church tradition that this work was written by the disciple Matthew. Papias was the earliest witness to this authorship, and he wrote:

> Matthew for his part compiled the sayings in the Hebrew dialect, and everyone interpreted them as he was able. (Eusebius, *Hist. eccl.* 3.39.16; cf. *Hist. eccl.* 5.10.3, 6.25.3–4)

Some argue that the First Gospel reinforces this tradition by changing the name of "Levi" (Mark 2:13–17; Luke 5:27–32) to "Matthew" in the story of his calling (Matt. 9:9–13). **Matthew** was one the twelve core disciples of Jesus (Matt. 10:1–4; Mark 3:13–19; Luke 6:12–16). He lived in Capernaum, like other disciples who were close to Jesus: the fishermen Peter, Andrew, James, and John. Capernaum was located on the northern shore of the Sea of Galilee, and it became the center of Jesus's Galilean ministry.

Matthew was a former "toll (or tax) collector" (*telōnēs*). He collected tolls levied on the transportation of goods, including agricultural production and fishing. Toll collecting was part of the more extensive system of taxation under Herod Antipas, which included the temple tax and tithes for priests and festivals (Exod. 30:13; cf. Matt. 17:34; Josephus, *J.W.* 7.6.6; *Ant.* 18.9.1). Matthew's old job reminded everyone that Rome and its client rulers were in charge. Because of the link with Rome, tax collecting was often slurred by associating it with sinners (Matt. 9:10–11), drunks and gluttons (Matt. 11:19), prostitutes (Matt. 21:31–32), and Gentiles (Matt. 18:17).

SUGGESTED READING

Matthew 1:1-10:4
Matthew 16:13-17:9
Matthew 18:1-19:2
Matthew 21:1-24:2
Matthew 25:1-28:20

As one of the three Synoptic Gospels, Matthew's Gospel edits and expands upon Mark's basic story. Matthew followed Mark's outline, charting Jesus's ministry from Galilee to Jerusalem (Matt. 4:12–20:34; Mark 1:12–10:52) and Jesus's final days in Jerusalem (Matt. 21:1–27:61; Mark 11:1–15:47).

Since Irenaeus, each of the four Gospel writers has been associated with the four living creatures from Ezekiel 1:10 and Revelation 4:7. This thirteenth-century fresco from the Museé de Cluny in Paris follows Jerome's schema (clockwise): Matthew is a human; John is an eagle; Luke is an ox; and Mark is a lion.

He also included Peter's confession of Jesus's messiahship as its pivotal juncture (Matt. 16:13–28; Mark 8:27–9:1). He shortened many of Mark's stories to create space in his scroll for his own accounts. Within Mark's framework, Matthew inserted five teaching blocks (Matt. 5–7, 10, 13, 18, 24–25).[1] Matthew added unique stories of Jesus's birth at the beginning (Matt. 1:1–2:23) and expanded Mark's ending with his own resurrection stories (Matt. 28:1–20).

However, Matthew's extensive use of Mark's Greek text raises questions about Papias's statement about Matthew compiling the "sayings in the Hebrew dialect." These sayings cannot be most of the content of the First Gospel adapted from Mark. Instead, they may be the parts of Matthew that focused on the teachings of Jesus, which he added to Mark's story.[2] In light of Matthew's use of Mark, it is likely that Matthew's Gospel was written around 75–85 CE.

[1]This teaching material may be sayings gathered from Q. Alternatively, they may be from Matthew's source. Less likely, Matthew gathered the dispersed sayings in Luke and expanded them. Matthew may also be divided into thirds by the phrase "from that time on Jesus began" (*apo tote ērxato ho Iēsous*, Matt. 4:17, 16:21).

[2]Primitive versions of Matthew may be testified by Jerome. At least one or more Aramaic Gospels were known to the early church (e.g., Gospel of the Ebionites, Gospel of the Nazoraeans; cf. Eusebius, *Hist. eccl.* 3.27; Irenaeus, *Haer.* 1.22). Moule, *Birth of the New Testament*, 186. These "sayings" may be the basis of the Q material. Or if Mark was his only source, then they may be the collection of materials that Matthew added to Mark.

In terms of his audience, Matthew is full of Jewish concerns, such as obeying both the moral and ceremonial aspects of the law (see below). His Gospel reflects a community that was not distinct from Judaism and was in conflict with local Jewish synagogues. This conflict was reflected by Jesus's debates with the religious leaders, particularly the scribes and Pharisees. Matthew aimed to help his community understand how following Jesus truly fulfilled God's covenantal promises to the Jewish people. Most likely, Matthew was writing to Jewish Christians living in Antioch, one of the centers of early Christianity (Acts 11:19–30).[3]

What Was Matthew's Version of the Story?

Jesus's Messianic Identity

Each story about the life and ministry of Jesus offers a slightly different perspective on who Jesus was and what he came to accomplish. How a story begins tells a lot about an author's purpose. While Matthew, Mark, and Luke tell a similar story, they each start in a different place. Mark opens with the ministry of John the Baptist to introduce the themes of exile and Jesus bringing a new exodus (Mark 1:2–11). Matthew begins with Jesus's genealogy and birth (Matt. 1:1–2:23).

The very first line of Matthew declares that he was writing a record about the "origins" (*genesis*) of Jesus, the long-awaited Jewish Messiah (Matt. 1:1). By explicitly using the Greek word *genesis*, Matthew ties Jesus's origin story into the first book of the Bible: Genesis. Genesis recounts the origins of the world (Gen. 1–11) and the origins of the nation of Israel (Gen. 12–50). Matthew relates the origins of the Messiah and the origins of the church. Matthew wanted his audience to know that the coming of Jesus marked a new beginning for humanity because the long-awaited Messiah had come. And this new Messiah reminded people that God was in charge.

But why should people believe that Jesus was the Messiah?

Public Domain

Distinctive genealogies are prominent in Matthew and Luke. This *Tree of Jesse* in stained glass from the old Notre Dame church portrays Jesus's genealogy and was inspired by Isaiah 11:1-9.

[3]As a Jewish Christian, see Bacon, *Studies in Matthew*. Matthew's reliance upon the Septuagint demonstrates a greater familiarity with Greek. See the discussions in Stendahl, *School of St. Matthew*; Gundry, *Use of the Old Testament*.

Matthew's first proof of Jesus's messianic credentials is that he is the "**son of Abraham**" (Matt. 1:1). Matthew portrays Jesus, the son of Abraham, as an ideal descendant of Abraham. Jesus is compared to Abraham's son Isaac. Just as God asked Abraham to sacrifice his son Isaac (cf. Gen. 22), now the heavenly Father's Son will willingly offer himself as a sacrifice (Matt. 26:36–46). In addition, Jesus, like Isaac, was also the heir of God's covenantal promises to Israel (Gen. 12, 15, 17).

God fulfilled his covenantal promises to Israel through Jesus the son of Abraham. First, God's promise that Abraham's descendants would inherit the land (Gen. 12:7) was connected to Jesus's gospel announcement that the kingdom of God was at hand (Matt. 4:17). To fulfill this promise, Jesus went through the land and extended God's rule by liberating people from demonic forces (e.g., Matt. 8:23–27, 8:28–34, 9:32–34) and diseases (e.g., Matt. 8:1–4, 9:2–7, 9:18–26). Second, God's promise for Israel to become a great nation (Gen. 12:2) was fulfilled by Jesus calling the twelve disciples to join him in his Jewish mission (Matt. 10:1–4) but also extended beyond a nationalistic understanding to include all people. Third, God's promise for Israel to be a blessing to all people (Gen. 12:2–3) was seen in Jesus's miraculous activity, such as helping Gentiles like the centurion's servant (Matt. 8:5–13) and the Canaanite woman's daughter (Matt. 15:21–28). This culminated in Jesus's call to "make disciples of all nations [*ethnoi*]" (Matt. 28:18–20).

The second proof of Jesus's messiahship was being identified as the "**son of David**" (Matt. 1:1). The title "son of David" was tied to the Davidic king (2 Sam. 7:14; 1 Chron. 17:13; Ps. 2:7). Matthew, in particular, wanted readers to understand Jesus's messianic identity in light of being the son of David (Matt. 1:1, 9:27, 12:23, 15:22, 21:9, 21:15). Those who aligned themselves with Jesus called him the son of David. For example, near the beginning and end of his Galilean ministry, blind men called out to Jesus as the son of David (Matt. 9:27, 20:30–31). The Canaanite woman also affirmed this identity while seeking his help (Matt. 15:22). The crowds declared him to be the son of David during his ministry (Matt. 12:13) and at his triumphal entry (Matt. 21:9), as did the children when he arrived to judge the temple (Matt. 21:15). In contrast, the religious leaders rejected this identification of Jesus (Matt. 12:23–24) and accused him of being a false prophet empowered by Beelzebul (Matt. 12:22–32).

At the end of his ministry, Jesus linked his messianic identity with his role as the son of David (Matt. 22:41–46) by citing Psalm 110:1:

> The Lord said to my Lord,
> "Sit at my right hand,
>   until I put your enemies under your feet." (Matt. 22:44)

As we will see throughout this book, **Psalm 110** was an important psalm for early Christians to affirm Jesus's lordship and messianic identity (Mark 12:36; Luke 20:42; Acts 2:29–35, 13:23–39; Heb. 1:3, 1:13, 10:12–13). We also find allusions to this psalm in Acts 5:31, 7:55–56; Romans 8:34; 1 Corinthians 15:25; Ephesians 1:20; Colossians 3:1; Hebrews 12:2; and 1 Peter 3:22.

Reflecting his Jewish concerns, Matthew portrayed Jesus as fulfilling the Jewish hopes of the restoration of the Davidic throne (Pss. 89:1–4, 110; Isa. 11:1–5; Jer. 23:5). While some Jewish writers expressed this hope with a desire for the Messiah to overthrow the Gentiles (Pss. Sol. 17.21–25), Matthew

King Herod plays a prominent role in Matthew's account of Jesus's birth. This sarcophagus, which may have held the body of King Herod, was discovered at the Herodium, the king's burial site. Israel Museum.

demonstrated how Jesus's Jewish mission would ultimately include the Gentiles under God's rule (Matt. 28:18–20).

A New Beginning: Stories Surrounding Jesus's Birth

To flesh out Jesus being both the son of Abraham and the son of David, Matthew devoted the very beginning of his Gospel to Jesus's family tree (Matt. 1:2–17). Jesus's genealogy echoes the genealogical language that defines the structure of Genesis, where each major section is introduced by "these are the generations" (Heb. *ʾelleh toledot,* Gen. 2:4, 5:1, 6:9, 10:1, 11:10, 11:27, 25:12, 25:19, 36:1, 36:9, 37:1).

Jesus's genealogy, which may strike modern readers as dull, proves his messianic credentials.[4] Matthew tied Jesus's story into the much larger story of the history of Israel. He organized Jesus's family tree into three sets of approximately fourteen generations (Matt. 1:17): from Abraham to King David (Matt. 1:2–6a), from King David to the Babylonian exile (Matt. 1:6b–11), and from the exile to the birth of Jesus the Messiah (Matt. 1:12–16). The choice of fourteen is influenced by the numeric value of the letters of David's name in Hebrew, which adds up to fourteen (Heb. *dwd*).[5]

With the genealogy complete, Matthew moves on to tell stories surrounding Jesus's birth (Matt. 1:18–2:23).[6] These stories were told primarily from Joseph's perspective. In the first story, we meet Joseph the carpenter (Matt. 1:18–24; cf. Matt. 13:55). He discovered that his teenage fiancé was pregnant

[4]Johnson, *Biblical Genealogies*, 223–25.

[5]Fourteen is the sum of the value of the Hebrew letters (*d* = 4; *w* = 6; *d* = 4). An alternate spelling of David's name, *dywd*, adds up to a different number. Hagner, *Matthew*, 1:5–7.

[6]For an exploration of the birth stories and other traditions surrounding Jesus's birth, see Toney, *Ruining Christmas*.

(Matt. 1:18). As an "upstanding" (*dikaios*) man, he decided to break off the engagement quietly because he was not the father (Matt. 1:19). But an angel of the Lord appeared in a dream to tell him that this baby was a miracle from the Holy Spirit (Matt. 1:20). He was also told to name the child "Jesus" (Matt. 1:21). In Jewish culture, naming was part of the formal means of adoption. By naming Jesus, Joseph grafted Jesus into his Davidic family tree, making the genealogy meaningful. The angel also declared that Jesus's purpose was to "save his people from their sins" (Matt. 1:21). Finally, Matthew claims these events fulfilled the prophetic words found in Isaiah 7:14:

> "Look, the virgin shall conceive and bear a son,
> and they shall name him Emmanuel,"
> which means, "God is with us." (Matt. 1:23)

This is the first of numerous "fulfillment" (*plēroō*) citations found in Matthew (Matt. 1:22, 2:5–6, 2:15, 2:17–18, 2:23, 3:3, 4:14–16, 8:17, 12:17–21, 13:14–15, 13:35, 21:4, 27:9). For Matthew, fulfillment was not some simple, straightforward correspondence between a prediction and the historical event. Instead, Matthew understood fulfillment as Jesus reliving the stories of Israel.

To help us understand how Matthew used fulfillment citations, let's look at the context of his quote from Isaiah 7:14. The Israelite king, Ahaz, had been under the threat of two enemy nations (Isa. 7:1–2). Isaiah predicted that when God showed up, he would save Ahaz from his enemies (Isa. 7:3–9). God also promised to judge Ahaz for his evil deeds (Isa. 7:17). The prophet Isaiah told the king that the sign of God's presence would be a child born to a "virgin" (Heb. *ʿalmah*, Isa. 7:14). According to Jewish thought, this virgin would be a young, unmarried woman, who gave birth to a child during the reign of Ahaz (Isa. 7:10–16).[7]

Matthew takes Isaiah's prophecy and supersizes it. Instead of a virgin conceiving after having sexual relations (and no longer being a virgin), Matthew claims that Mary will conceive and give birth while *remaining* a "virgin" (*parthenos*). For Matthew, Jesus's birth to the virgin Mary was an even greater sign of God's presence. For as much buildup as there was to Jesus's birth, a reader could easily miss the actual event. Matthew simply reports, "She had borne a son; and he named him Jesus" (Matt. 1:25).

After Jesus's birth, Matthew tells the story of the magi (Matt. 2:1–12). The **magi** were astrologers from the east who followed a star to Jesus (Num. 24:17) and bore gifts for the newly born king (Isa. 60:1–4).[8] These magi affirmed Jesus's messiahship and contrasted figures from Israel's past. They juxtaposed the Egyptian magicians who opposed Moses (Exod. 7–8) and Balaam who attempted to curse Israel (Num. 22–24). Matthew's non-Jewish visitors fulfilled the Jewish visions of a time when Israel's exile would end and the Gentile nations would stream into Israel, bearing gifts like gold and frankincense

[7]The Greek *parthenos* narrowly means "virgin," similar to the Hebrew *betulah*. However, Isaiah uses a broader term (Heb. *ʿalmah*) that can mean "virgin" or "young woman of marriageable age," since those were considered similar categories. Arguably, it is most accurate to translate Isaiah 7:14 as "young woman" and to translate Matthew 1:22 as "virgin" in light of the meaning of the Hebrew and Greek words, but this makes the parallels difficult for English readers to see.

[8]According to tradition, their names were Melchior, Caspar, and Balthazar (*Excerpta Latina Barbari* 51b; ca. 500 CE). Powell, "The Magi as Kings: An Adventure in Reader-Response Criticism," 459–80; Powell, "The Magi as Wise Men: Re-Examining a Basic Supposition," 1–20.

Carl N. Toney

Modern-day Bethlehem is famous for handcrafted olive wood nativity sets. This set depicts Matthew's magi alongside Luke's shepherds visiting the baby Jesus.

(Isa. 60:1–4; cf. Isa. 2:1–5, 66:18–20; Mic. 4:1–4; Zech. 14:16; Pss. Sol. 17.31; 1 En. 53.1).[9] Their presence also signaled the inclusion of Gentiles within the church and foreshadowed Jesus's commissioning his disciples to share the good news with the whole world (Matt. 28:18–20).

Unfortunately, the hapless magi enlisted the help of the current king, Herod the Great, to find this newly birthed child. But Herod had different plans for this baby, whom he viewed as a potential usurper. To save the child, an angel appeared to Joseph again, and the family entered their own Egyptian exile (Matt. 2:13–15). When Herod's plot to kill Jesus was thwarted, he slaughtered all the children under two in Bethlehem (Matt. 2:16–17), recalling Pharoah's killing of the Jewish children (Exod. 1:15–21). After Herod died, Jesus's family performed their own exodus from Egypt by returning to Israel, where Jesus would be raised in Galilee (Matt. 2:19–23).

The Son of God

After telling the stories of Jesus's origins (Matt. 1–2), Matthew finally takes up Mark's narrative with the adult Jesus being baptized by John the Baptist in the desert (Matt 3:1–17). During his baptism, a heavenly voice declared Jesus to be the Son of God (Matt. 3:17). Later, God declared Jesus to be his Son during the

[9] Davies and Allison, *Matthew*, 1:250–53.

transfiguration (Matt. 17:5). These declarations of Jesus's sonship reflect God calling the Davidic king his son (2 Sam. 7:14; 1 Chron. 17:13; Ps. 2:7). "Son of God" was one of the titles for the Davidic Messiah, God's appointed ruler, which Peter confessed (Matt. 16:13–16), the high priest and his opponents denied (Matt. 26:63–66, 27:40, 27:43), and the centurion professed during Jesus's crucifixion (Matt. 27:54).

For a Greco-Roman audience, "son of God" was also a title associated with the Roman emperor since the time of Augustus. The political implications of Jesus being the Davidic Messiah and Son of God (in contrast to the emperor) run as an undercurrent throughout the Gospel. People needed to decide who was really in charge. This political element was brought to the forefront by the titulus of the cross that bore the charge of insurrection by labeling Jesus as the "King of the Jews" (Matt. 27:37). With a note of irony, the crucifixion correctly identified Jesus and established his reign.

Following Jesus's baptism, Matthew expands upon Mark's brief summary of Jesus's wilderness temptation (Matt. 4:1–11; Mark 1:13). Both authors emphasize Jesus's recapitulation of the wilderness wanderings of Israel during the exodus. While Israel wandered for forty years, Jesus remained in the desert for forty days (Num. 14:33–35, 32:13; Deut. 2:7, 8:2–4; Josh. 5:6). Matthew strengthens the parallel by describing the devil's three temptations of Jesus. While the Israelites failed to obey God in the wilderness, Jesus remained loyal. Jesus rejected the devil by quoting from Jewish scriptures (Deut. 8:3, 6:13, 6:16). Jesus continued gaining victory over the devil and his forces when he reentered the promised land and exorcised demons during his ministry.

After his baptism and temptation, Jesus began his public ministry. Similar to Mark 1:14–15, Jesus proclaimed, "Repent, for the kingdom of heaven has come near" (Matt. 4:17), but Matthew made a

Jesus spent forty days in the Judean wilderness.

Single-story houses in Capernaum were built using basalt rocks with roofs made of wood and thatch. Multiple-family homes were clustered together with communal courtyards. According to the Synoptic Gospels, Capernaum was the center of Jesus's Galilean ministry.

few changes. First, he linked Jesus's announcement with John the Baptist, who was the first person to proclaim this message (Matt. 3:2). Matthew also replaced the "kingdom of God" with his unique expression, "**kingdom of heaven**," to describe God's reign (33x; e.g., Matt. 3:2, 4:17, 5:3, 5:20, 7:21).[10] This replacement of "God" with "heaven" is sometimes explained as "heaven" being a circumlocution for "God" to reflect the Jewish respect for the name of God. More likely, this replacement emphasizes the heavenly origins, domain, and source of God's rule. Jesus's message and ministry contrasted God's heavenly rule with the earthly domain of the devil and the Gentile nations (Matt. 4:8, 12:25–26, 25:7; cf. Dan. 2–7).[11]

While Jesus preached that God was in charge, Matthew was careful to show that Jesus did not overtly challenge Rome or its representatives. For example, Matthew omitted the word "legion" from Mark's story of Jesus healing the Gadarene demoniacs since a legion was a group of Roman soldiers (Matt. 8:28–9:1; Mark 5:1–20; Luke 8:26–39). Also, Jesus told his disciples to go an additional mile if conscripted by Roman soldiers (Matt. 5:41). Instead of seeking to overthrow the enemies of Israel, Jesus taught his disciples to love their enemies (Matt. 5:43–48) and to turn the other cheek (Matt. 5:39). Jesus's nonviolent approach and love for enemies were rooted in his understanding that God was the sole agent of justice. He knew that God would vindicate and exalt those who submitted to his reign.

A New Teacher

Matthew clustered Jesus's teaching into five blocks that define the structure of the Gospel (Matt. 5–7, 10, 13, 18, 24–25). He emphasized that Jesus was a teacher like two of the most well-known teachers in

[10] For more on the kingdom of God/kingdom of heaven expression, see Green, "Kingdom of God/Heaven," *DJG* 468–81.
[11] Pennington, *Heaven and Earth*.

the Jewish scriptures. Like Solomon, the famous son of David (cf. Kings 3:1–15; 1 Chron. 1:2–13), Jesus dispensed wisdom, including proverbs (e.g., Matt. 6:24, 7:6, 10:16, 12:33).[12] He was also like Moses, who gave the law on Mount Sinai (Exod. 19–24). During his first extensive collection of teaching, Jesus sat on a mountain and offered his interpretation of the law in the **Sermon on the Mount** (Matt. 5–7). These teachings are placed right after Jesus called his first disciples—Peter, Andrew, James, and John (Matt. 4:18–22; cf. Mark 1:16–20)—to signify these were core instructions for his disciples to follow. Some of Jesus's most memorable teachings are found in this sermon, such as the beatitudes (Matt. 5:3–12), Jesus's call to love one's enemies (Matt. 5:43–48), and the Lord's Prayer (Matt. 6:9–13).

Reflecting a Jewish Christian audience, Jesus opened his sermon by commanding his followers to obey the law entirely. Jesus said,

> Do not think that I have come to abolish the law or the prophets; I have come not to abolish but to fulfill. For truly I tell you, until heaven and earth pass away, not one letter, not one stroke of a letter, will pass from the law until all is accomplished. (Matt. 5:17–18)

As a good Jew, Jesus believed the law was good and all of it should be obeyed. Throughout the Gospel, we witness Jesus's concern to obey the law. He commanded the cleansed leper to show himself to a priest and to offer the appropriate sacrifice after being healed (Matt. 8:4; Lev. 14:1–32). Jesus paid the temple tax (Matt. 17:24–27; Exod. 30:13–16). He upheld the command to tithe while challenging the Pharisees

The traditional site of Mount Sinai (7,497 ft.).

[12]Witherington, *Matthew*, 7–8, 16–21.

GOSPEL OF MATTHEW

- The Messiah's Origins (1:1–4:16)
  - Genealogy from Abraham to David to Exile to Jesus (1:1–17)
  - Birth Stories including the Visit of the Magi (1:18–2:23)
  - Baptism, Temptation, and Galilean Ministry Begins (3:1–4:16)
- The Galilean Ministry (4:17–16:20)
  - Calling First Disciples and the Sermon on the Mount—Teaching 1 (4:17–7:29)
  - Ten Miracles, the Twelve Called, and Missional Instructions—Teaching 2 (8:1–11:1)
  - Opposition to Jesus and Kingdom Parables—Teaching 3 (11:2–13:53)
  - Rejecting the Messiah and Peter's Confession (13:54–16:20)
- The Messiah Revealed through His Death and Resurrection (16:21–28:20)
  - Transfiguration, Passion Predictions, and Community Guidelines—Teaching 4 (16:21–19:2)
  - Judean Ministry, Temple Conflicts, and the Olivet Discourse—Teaching 5 (19:3–26:2)
  - Last Supper, Arrest, Trial, and Crucifixion (26:3–27:66)
  - Resurrection and Great Commission in Galilee (28:1–20)

to also be just, merciful, and faithful (Matt. 23:23; Deut. 14:22–29; Mic. 6:8). When his disciples appeared to violate the Sabbath by eating grain in a field (Matt. 12:1–2; Exod. 20:8–11), Jesus used their actions to engage with broader Jewish debates concerning proper obedience to the law (Matt. 12:3–8). He healed on the Sabbath to illustrate the principle of obeying the weightier laws of justice and mercy (Matt. 12:9–17).

In Matthew, Jesus did not reduce expectations for obedience to the law. Instead, Jesus raised the bar. He called his disciples to "Be perfect, therefore, as your heavenly Father is perfect" (Matt. 5:48).[13] His disciples needed to have a righteousness that exceeded that of the scribes and Pharisees (Matt. 5:20). Interestingly, Matthew uses "righteous" language more than any other Gospel.[14] For Matthew, righteousness was the moral conduct that God prescribed in the law. Characters exhibit this righteousness throughout the story. Joseph was a "righteous man" because of his treatment of Mary (Matt. 1:19). John the Baptist called people to repent of their sins as a "way of righteousness" (Matt. 21:32). Jesus "fulfill[ed] all righteousness" when he submitted to God's will in his baptism (Matt. 3:15).

Jesus gave examples of interpreting the law and following its moral standards with his "I say to you" statements (Matt. 5:21–30; cf. 1QS 9:9–19). Jesus expected external actions to match the inner motivations

---

[13] Barth, "Matthew's Understanding of the Law," 101.

[14] Matthew uses "righteousness" (*dikaiosynē*) seven times (Matt. 3:15, 5:6, 5:10, 5:20, 6:1, 6:33, 21:32) and "righteous" (*dikaios*) seventeen times (Matt. 1:19, 5:45, 9:13, 10:41, etc.). "Righteousness" (*dikaiosynē*) is used once in Luke (Luke 1:75) and twice in John (John 16:8, 16:10), and never in Mark. "Righteous" (*dikaios*) is used eleven times in Luke (Luke 1:6, 1:17, 2:25, 5:32, etc.), three times in John (John 5:30, 7:24, 17:25), and twice in Mark (Mark 2:17, 6:20).

Carl N. Toney

The Church of the Beatitudes was built on the traditional site where Jesus delivered his Sermon on the Mount.

of the heart (Matt. 23:3, 23:13, 23:26–27). The command not to murder was linked to avoiding anger (Matt. 5:21–26; Exod. 20:13; Deut. 5:17). The command not to commit adultery was linked to refraining from lust (Matt. 5:27–30; Exod. 20:14; Deut. 5:18). Jesus distilled the entire law to love God (Deut. 6:5) and love your neighbor (Lev. 19:18), which he deemed as the **greatest commands** (Matt. 5:43, 19:19, 22:37–39; Mark 12:29–30). Jesus passed his authority to interpret the law on to his disciples (Matt. 16:19), and other New Testament writers appealed to Jesus's teaching that loving one's neighbor (Lev. 19:18) summarized a believer's duty toward others (Rom. 13:9; Gal. 5:14; James 2:8).[15]

However, Jesus's teachings also put him at odds with the religious leaders. The crowds recognized that Jesus "taught them as one having authority, and not as their scribes" (Matt. 7:29). Throughout his ministry, Jesus and the religious leaders disagreed over how to interpret the law, such as associating with toll collectors and sinners (Matt. 9:11), fasting (Matt. 9:14), handwashing (Matt. 15:1–9), Sabbath practices (Matt. 12:1–13), and divorce (Matt. 19:3–9). During his final days in Jerusalem, Jesus engaged in a series of debates in the temple (Matt. 21:23–22:46), which began by questioning his authority (Matt. 21:23). In the end, he silenced his opponents (Matt. 22:46) and denounced the scribes and Pharisees for their hypocritical teaching (Matt. 23:1–36).

---

[15] See Chapter One.

The Gathering of Disciples

Throughout the First Gospel, Jesus called people to "follow me" (Matt. 1:17, 4:19; cf. 8:22, 9:9, 10:38, 16:24, 19:21, 19:28). Those who heeded his call joined a community of disciples (Matt. 4:20, 4:22, 8:23, 9:9, 9:27, 20:34, 27:55). But what was this early community called? There were a variety of terms used to describe first-century Christ followers. In Acts, Christ followers were called the "Way" (e.g., Acts 9:2, 19:9, 19:23) and eventually nicknamed "Christians" by the people of Antioch (Acts 11:26; cf. Acts 26:28; 1 Pet. 4:16). Some non-Christian writers used religious terms to describe Christ followers, such as "band, company" (*thiasos*; Lat. *collegia*).

Matthew is the only Gospel to describe Christ followers by using the word "church" (*ekklēsia*; Matt. 16:18, 18:17). However, this English translation is misleading because the English word "church" comes from a different word that means "those belonging to the Lord" (*kyriakos*; cf. 1 Cor. 11:20; Rev. 1:10). Instead, ***ekklēsia*** is better translated as a "gathering" or "assembly." The term, composed of two words, "out of" (*ek*) and "called" (*kaleō*), literally means "called-out ones." It originally referred to the ruling assembly of Greek city-states that were "called out" for meetings.

But for Matthew, this term goes beyond its Greek origins, and its meaning is reflected by its use in the Greek translation of the Hebrew Bible. The translators of the Septuagint used *ekklēsia* to translate the "assembly" (Heb. *qahal*) of Israel (e.g., Josh. 9:8; Judg. 20:2). Notably, the first uses of "assembly" are found in Deuteronomy, where Moses ratified God's covenant with the assembly of Israel (Deut. 4:10, 9:10, 18:16, 23:1, 23:3, 23:8, 31:30). Solomon also dedicated the temple with the assembly of Israel (3 Kgdm. 8:14, 8:22, 8:55, 8:65; 2 Chron. 6:3, 6:12, 6:13, 7:8). Matthew drew upon this Jewish background to claim followers of Jesus were the true "assembly" of Israel.

Matthew's first use of "church" (*ekklēsia*) is found during Peter's confession about Jesus's messiahship at Caesarea Philippi (Matt. 16:13–20). This passage is an example of how Peter is given prominence in Matthew's narrative as a representative of the other disciples (Matt. 4:18, 10:2–4, 14:22–36, 16:21–28,

Sea of Galilee.

Carl N. Toney

26:69–75). In this exchange, Matthew includes Jesus changing Peter's name from "Simon" (*Simōn*, meaning "[the Lord] has heard") to "Peter" (*Petros*, meaning "rock"). This new name of "Peter" (*Petros*) sets up the wordplay that Jesus would build his "assembly" upon this "rock" (*petra*).

Some argue that the "rock" was Peter's confession. However, the wordplay suggests Jesus was speaking about Peter, who represented all the disciples, as the foundation of the church. This is like other New Testament works that describe the apostles and prophets as the foundation of the church (Rom. 15:20; Eph. 2:20). To be clear, this is not a proof text for papal authority. This also does not deny Jesus as the church's foundation (1 Cor. 3:11) or cornerstone (Matt. 21:42; Eph. 2:20; cf. Ps. 118:22; Isa. 8:14, 28:16). These images of Jesus, the apostles, and prophets as the foundation of the church are meant to be complementary. Jesus also gave Peter the keys to "bind" and "loose" (Matt. 16:19). This expression identified Peter and the disciples' ability to interpret the law authoritatively, like Jesus (cf. Matt. 23:4; b. Šabb. 4a). Jesus's words were meant to assure Matthew's community that Jesus extended his authority to the early apostolic leadership of the church as they rightly confessed his messianic identity.

"Church" (*ekklēsia*) occurs a second time in Matthew 18:17 during Jesus's teaching about community conflicts (Matt. 18:1–19:2). Peter was, once again, the spokesperson for the disciples (Matt. 16:16, 18:21). This passage is the middle of Jesus's three teachings about discipleship (Matt. 10:5–11:1, 18:1–19:2, 24:1–26:2). When dealing with others, Jesus reminded his disciples of the importance of

Carl N. Toney

Pan's Grotto at Caesarea Philippi.

humility (Matt. 18:1–5). He also warned them to avoid causing others to sin (Matt. 18:6–9). If a community member sinned, Jesus provided a pathway for restoration (Matt. 18:10–20). Jesus used "bind" and "loose" language for the authority of the assembly to discern matters between members (Matt. 18:18). He also assured them of his presence among them during their gatherings in his name (Matt. 18:20). Jesus also highlighted the importance of forgiveness among community members (Matt. 18:21–35).

Carl N. Toney

Jesus and his disciples would have used Herodian-style dishware for meals. Israel Museum.

As an early Jewish movement, Matthew's "assembly" was based on the model of a Jewish synagogue. "**Synagogue**" (*synagōgē*) means "gathering together." Traditionally, Jewish synagogues consisted of at least ten males who met together to study God's law. Early Jewish Christians, like the ones in Matthew's community, began to describe themselves as an "assembly" (*ekklēsia*) to distinguish their gatherings from other synagogues. Because those in Matthew's assemblies believed Jesus was the Messiah, conflicts arose with other local synagogues. As followers of Jesus, Matthew's "assemblies" believed they represented the true "assembly" of Israel.

A New Ending Makes a New Beginning

Matthew's ending allowed him to revisit and reinforce his distinct purposes. This is revealed by comparing Matthew's ending with Mark's. Matthew followed Mark's story of Jesus's last days in Jerusalem (although he added details and rearranged some of the chronology).[16]

Like Mark's account, Jesus entered Jerusalem with his triumphal entry (Matt. 21:1–11). Matthew adds the crowds hailing Jesus as a prophet from Nazareth and as the messianic son of David (Matt. 21:9, 21:11). Because Jesus was the son of David, Matthew highlights how Jesus's triumph paralleled Solomon's ride into Jerusalem on a donkey (1 Kings 1:33, 1:38). After Jesus drove out those buying and selling in the temple, children identified Jesus as the son of David (Matt. 21:15). Just as Solomon built the temple, Jesus, as the new Solomon, showed his authority in the temple by driving out the money changers. However, Jesus's temple action also symbolized the future destruction of the temple, like the prophet Jeremiah (Matt. 21:12–22; Jer. 7:1–15, 26:1–15).[17]

Matthew continues to follow Mark's outline by describing Jesus's debates with the religious leaders in the temple about his authority (Matt. 21:23–27), paying taxes to the emperor (Matt. 22:15–22), the resurrection (Matt. 22:23–33), the greatest command (Matt. 22:34–40), and the identity of David's son (Matt. 22:41–46). Matthew adds several parables (Matt. 21:28–22:14), a lengthy denouncement of the scribes and Pharisees (Matt. 23:1–36), and a lament for Jerusalem (Matt. 23:37–39). After these

---

[16] For example, Mark 11:12 records the temple act occurring the day after his triumphal entry, while Matthew 21:12 records this event on the same day. In Matthew 21:18–19, the fig tree is cursed after the temple act but prior in Mark 11:12–14.

[17] See the discussion in Mark about the temple act being a sign of destruction, not a cleansing.

Raising of the Cross by Sebastiano Mazzoni. Ca' Rezzonico In Venice. (1611-78)

public controversies, Matthew expands Mark's account of Jesus speaking to his disciples about the destruction of the temple, his exaltation as the Son of Man, and the time of final judgment in his Olivet discourse (Matt. 24–25).

Continuing to follow Mark, Matthew recounts how the religious leaders began their final plot against Jesus while he shared his last Passover meal with his disciples (Matt. 26:1–35). Then, Jesus was arrested in the Garden of Gethsemane (Matt. 26:36–56) and was brought before Caiaphas and the Sanhedrin (Matt. 26:57–68). The religious leaders examined Jesus disbelieving his claim to be the messianic Son of Man (Matt. 26:64) and deemed him worthy of death (Matt. 26:57–68). They took him to Pilate, who ordered his crucifixion while cruelly proclaiming his innocence (Matt. 27:1–31).

Although Jesus's male disciples deserted him, his mother and some female disciples witnessed his death (Matt. 27:32–56). As Jesus died, the religious leaders taunted Jesus for claiming to be the king of Israel and God's Son (Matt. 27:42–43), while the centurion who oversaw Jesus's death affirmed Jesus as the Son of God (Matt. 27:54). When Jesus died, Matthew reported along with Mark that the temple veil was torn (Matt. 27:51). Matthew added some details, including an earthquake (Matt. 27:51), and he claimed that past holy persons were resurrected, possibly to represent Jesus's conquest over death (Matt. 27:52–53). Like Mark, Matthew described Joseph of Arimathea collecting Jesus's body and burying him in a tomb (Matt. 27:57–61). Matthew added an apologetic note that the Pharisees requested the tomb be sealed along with guards so the disciples could not steal the body (Matt. 27:62–66).

Matthew undergirded the faith of his community by adding stories about the resurrected Jesus. In contrast, Mark ended his Gospel with an element of mystery surrounding Jesus's resurrection. In Mark 16:1–8, Jesus did not appear, and the women fled the tomb in fear. Mark's audience must choose to believe or disbelieve the angel's message without further proof. Matthew added Jesus's appearance to the women as they were leaving the tomb (Matt. 28:8–9), and he told them not to be afraid (Matt. 28:10). Matthew added further witnesses of Jesus's resurrection with the guards who watched the sealed tomb (Matt. 27:62–66, 28:4, 28:11–15). Matthew concluded with Jesus meeting the eleven remaining disciples on a mountain in Galilee (Matt. 28:16–20). Matthew noted that when they saw him, "they worshiped him; but some doubted" (Matt. 28:17).

Matthew's language of worship (Matt. 28:9, 28:17) recalls other moments in the Gospel when Jesus received worship, beginning with the magi (Matt. 2:11) and continuing through his ministry (Matt. 8:2, 9:18, 14:33, 15:25, 20:20). Because only God should be worshiped (Matt. 4:10; cf. Deut. 6:13), Matthew's choice to make Jesus the object of worship heightened Jesus's divine association.[18] During his birth, Jesus was linked with the manifestation of God's presence when he was described as "Emmanuel . . . God is with us" (Matt. 1:23). Now at the end of the Gospel, Jesus was worshiped, and he associated himself with the Father and Holy Spirit (Matt. 28:19) with the **Great Commission**. Jesus said,

> All authority in heaven and on earth has been given to me. Therefore go and make disciples of all nations, baptizing them in the name of the Father and of the Son and of the Holy Spirit, and teaching them to obey everything that I have commanded you. And surely I am with you always, to the very end of the age. (Matt. 28:18–20)

These words reinforce themes from Matthew, including Jesus's God-given authority (Matt. 28:17), his call to obey his interpretation of the law (Matt. 28:20), and the promise of his embodiment of God's presence with his people (Matt. 28:20).

Carl N. Toney

The Garden Tomb is another traditional location of Jesus's burial.

[18] On the significance of the worship of Jesus, particularly for Christology, see Bauckham, *Jesus and the God of Israel*; Hurtado, *Lord Jesus Christ*; Dunn, *Worship Jesus?*

Jesus's command to make disciples of all "nations" (*ethnoi*) reveals a nascent interest outside of Israel. Matthew's Gospel has a clear Jewish focus with Jesus's mission to restore Israel (Matt. 10:5–15). It also traces a trajectory for including Gentiles under God's rule because the Jewish people (i.e., Matthew's community) were called to fulfill their role as a light to the nations. This embrace of non-Jewish communities aligned with the expectations of Jewish prophets, who saw a day when Gentiles would stream to Israel (e.g., Isa. 60:1–14). This continuity between Israel's past and the new people of God, consisting of Jews and Gentiles, is a significant theme of this Gospel.

We find Gentiles being included with the Jewish people throughout the Gospel. In the birth stories, Gentile women are part of Jesus's genealogy (Tamar, Rahab, Ruth; Matt. 1:3, 1:5). The Gentile magi honored Jesus's birth (Matt. 2:1–12). Foreshadowing this wider outreach, Jesus's ministry began in "Galilee of the Gentiles" (Matt. 4:15, citing Isa. 9:1–2). Jesus proclaimed justice and gave hope to Gentiles (Matt. 12:18, 12:21, citing Isa. 42:1–4). He healed Gentiles, such as the centurion's servant (Matt. 8:5–13) and the Gadarene demoniacs (Matt. 8:28–34). On the surface, Jesus's exchange with the Canaanite woman may seem to reveal racial prejudice when he called her a "dog." However, this apparent prejudice was challenged and overcame when Jesus healed her daughter because of her "great faith" (Matt. 15:28). Jesus also envisioned a time when Gentiles would be included in God's kingdom (Matt. 13:38, 21:43). Finally, Matthew ended his Gospel by removing the limited scope of the disciples' mission to Israel (Matt. 10:5–15) with this climactic charge to make disciples of all nations (Matt. 28:18–20).

These Gentiles joined the people of God through their baptism "in the name of the Father and of the Son and of the Holy Spirit" (Matt. 28:19). This baptism was an adaptation of Jewish baptismal practices. It recalled Jesus's baptism in the Jordan, which marked a new exodus (Matt. 3:13–17). The close association of the Father, Son, and Spirit is similar to several other passages in the New Testament (Matt. 28:18–20; 2 Cor. 13:13; Eph. 4:4–6; 1 Pet. 1:2; cf. 1 Cor. 6:11, 12:4–6; 2 Cor. 1:21–22; Gal. 3:11–14, 4:4–5; 2 Thess. 2:13–14; 1 Pet. 1:3–5; Jude 20–21). These passages are the basis for the doctrine of the **Trinity**, which describes God as one essence comprised of three distinct persons—the Father, Son, and Holy Spirit.

The doctrine of the Trinity is one of the major points of contention between Judaism and Christianity. Judaism is a monotheistic religion, meaning Jews believe in one God called Yahweh. Christians also claim to be monotheists, but they believe this one God consists of three persons—the Father, Jesus, and the Holy Spirit. Analogies for the Trinity are imperfect. However, some conceive of the Trinity like one triangle with three sides or one clover with three leaves. Matthew's Gospel ends with the bold claim that his community consisted of disciples of Jesus, the Father, and the Holy Spirit. This community was charged to go into the world, making disciples, and letting everyone know that God is in charge.

Key Terms and People

***Ekklēsia*:** the Greek word meaning "gathering," usually translated as "church"; Matthew is the only Gospel to use this term

Great Commission: the final command of Jesus in Matthew's Gospel is to make disciples of all nations

Greatest commands: Jesus summarizes the law with the commands to love God (Deut. 6:5) and love one's neighbor (Lev. 19:18)
Joseph: carpenter and adoptive father of Jesus; Matthew relates the birth story from his perspective
Kingdom of heaven: Matthew's unique expression for the kingdom of God highlights the domain of God's reign in contrast to the earthly rule of Gentile nations and Satan
Magi: according to Matthew's Gospel, these astrologers visited Jesus after his birth
Matthew: a former toll/tax collector and disciple of Jesus, whom tradition identifies as writing the First Gospel
Psalm 110: an important psalm New Testament writers use to affirm Jesus's messianic identity and exalted lordship
Sermon on the Mount: the most famous collection of Jesus's teachings, which includes the beatitudes and Lord's Prayer, where Jesus is presented as a new Moses providing a new interpretation of the law
Son of Abraham: a title applied to Jesus to show how God fulfills his promises to Abraham through Jesus
Son of David: a messianic title to describe future ruler of Israel, who would be from the line of David
Synagogue: a Jewish word meaning "gathering"; traditionally, Jewish synagogues comprised at least ten males who gathered to study God's Word
Trinity: the Christian doctrine describes God as one essence comprised of three persons—the Father, Son, and Holy Spirit

Conversation Starters

1. What do we know about the disciple Matthew? How much of the First Gospel do you think he wrote?
2. What are some different ways Matthew tells the story of Jesus from Mark? What do we learn by observing these different ways of telling the story?
3. Why does Matthew describe Jesus as the son of Abraham and the son of David?
4. How does Matthew use the language of "fulfillment"? How does this help us understand Jesus being born from the virgin Mary?
5. What section of the Sermon on the Mount did you find most meaningful? Were there any difficult parts? What does it mean for Jesus to be like a new Moses?
6. What does Matthew mean by *ekklēsia*? How is Matthew's community similar and different from Jewish synagogues?
7. In what ways is Matthew's ending similar and different from Mark's? What do we learn from Matthew's changes to Mark?
8. Why does Matthew end with the Great Commission? How does this concern for reaching Gentiles fit with a Gospel geared toward Jewish Christians?
9. How do you understand the relationship between the Father, Jesus, and the Holy Spirit?

FOR FURTHER READING

Bauckham, Richard. *Jesus and the God of Israel*. Eerdmans, 2008.

Brown, Jeannine K. *Matthew*. Teach the Text Commentary Series. Baker Books, 2015.

France, R. T. *Matthew: An Introduction and Commentary*. Tyndale New Testament Commentaries 1. InterVarsity Press, 1985.

———. *Matthew: Evangelist and Teacher*. Wipf & Stock, 2004.

González, Justo L. *Three Months with Matthew*. Three Months. Abingdon, 2002.

Keener, Craig S. *The Gospel of Matthew: A Socio-Rhetorical Commentary*. Rev. ed. Eerdmans, 2009.

Reid, Barbara. *The Gospel According to Matthew*. New Collegeville Bible Commentary 1. Liturgical Press, 2005.

Taylor, Barbara Brown. *The Seeds of Heaven: Sermons on the Gospel of Matthew*. Westminster John Knox, 2004.

Toney, Carl N. *Ruining Christmas—Rediscovering Jesus*. Wipf & Stock, 2021.

Witherington, Ben, III. *Matthew*. Smyth & Helwys Bible Commentary. Smyth & Helwys, 2006.

4

LOOKING AT LUKE

Who Was Luke?

We now turn to a third perspective on Jesus's life written by a man named **Luke**, who according to tradition was a doctor and a traveling companion of Paul (Irenaeus, *Haer.* 3.1.1, 3.14.1; ca. 185 CE). He was thought to have written the Gospel story from Paul's perspective sometime around 75–85 CE (Tertullian, *Marc.* 4.2.2, 4.5, 4.5.3; ca. 155–220 CE). He may have been from the city of Antioch, where the non-Jewish church began and believers were first called Christians (Eusebius, *Hist. eccl.* 3.4.2; cf. Acts 11:20, 11:26). He never married or had children, and he was martyred at eighty-four (Anti-Marcionite Prologue to Luke, ca. 160–180 CE).

Support for this traditional authorship includes the so-called "we" sections found in Acts, where the narrator appears to include himself in the story (Acts 16:10–17, 20:5–15, 21:1–18, 27:1–29, 28:1–16).[1] From Paul's writings, we discover that Luke did minister (Philem. 24) and travel with him (2 Tim. 4:11), and he was a physician (Col. 4:14). It was his connection to Paul that gave Luke the apostolic authority to share these traditions about Jesus. Like Paul's writings, Luke's Gospel emphasizes how God's promises were fulfilled for the Jewish people and now included non-Jews. Being a physician also provided him with the education necessary for writing the Third Gospel, which reflects some of the best Greek of the New Testament.[2]

SUGGESTED READING

Luke 1:1-6:16
Luke 9:1-62
Luke 10:25-11:23
Luke 15:1-16:31
Luke 17:11-19:10
Luke 19:28-24:53

Luke's Gospel is unique because it is really the first volume of a two-volume story. The second volume is the Acts of the Apostles, which gives an account of the growth of the early church. Both volumes are linked by similar formal introductions dedicated to Theophilus (Luke 1:1–4;

---

[1] A copyist added "we" to Acts 11:28. For arguments linking the "we" to Luke, see Fitzmyer, *Acts*, 50; Ramsay, *Luke the Physician*, 26. However, the "we" may a be stylistic device; see Dupont, *Sources of the Acts*.

[2] Hobart found over four hundred medical terms paralleling the medical writings of Hippocrates, Aretaeus, Dioscorides, and Galen. However, Cadbury finds these terms outside of medical writings. Hobart, *The Medical Language of St. Luke*; Cadbury, *Style and Literary Method of Luke*, 39–72.

Acts 1:1–5), whose name means "God-lover," and he was likely the patron sponsoring the writing.[3] Both works share a common vocabulary, literary style, and themes.

From the introduction of the Gospel of Luke, we learn that the author was a second- or third-generation Christian who gathered earlier traditions about Jesus (Luke 1:1–2). These early traditions included using Mark as the basic outline for the work. Like Matthew, Luke's Gospel includes distinct stories about Jesus's birth (Luke 1:1–2:52) and his resurrection (Luke 24:1–53). Luke is known for having the largest collection of Jesus's parables, including the parables of the good Samaritan (Luke 10:30–37), the prodigal son (Luke 15:11–32), and the dishonest manager (Luke 16:1–15). While Matthew collected Jesus's teachings in five sermons, Luke spread them out.[4] One of the most distinctive structural features of Luke is a travel narrative that takes up about one-third of the story (Luke 9:51–19:27). Finally, Luke and Acts are the only places in the New Testament that provide the accounts of Jesus's **ascension** into heaven (Luke 24:50–53; Acts 1:6–11).

Public Domain

Luke writing his Gospel. Medieval and Renaissance Manuscripts. New York Public Library. (1315)

Luke's Gospel also claims to provide an orderly account of Jesus's life. But "orderly" does not mean chronological sequence. For example, the Gospel relates John's imprisonment (Luke 3:20) before he baptized Jesus (Luke 3:21–21).[5] Rather, like the works of other ancient historians (e.g., Thucydides, *Histories*; Lucian, *How to Write History*), Luke's Gospel recounts Jesus's life in an order that highlights the significance of the story. Let's now turn to this third account of Jesus's life and its significance for all of humanity.

What Was Luke's Version of the Story?

God Keeps His Promises to Israel

Like Matthew, the Gospel of Luke attaches stories about Jesus's birth to the beginning of Mark. However, surprisingly, Luke did not start with Jesus's birth. Instead, he built narrative momentum by directing his reader's attention to the birth of John the Baptist (Luke 1:5–25). Luke used the stories of John to create a good-to-great comparison between John and Jesus and to align their ministries with God's promises. For Luke, it was important to

[3] Origen (*Hom. Luc.* 1.6) allegorically interpreted the name to mean the work was written for everyone who loved God.

[4] Either Luke copied these sayings from Q, or these sayings are from Matthew, which Luke shortened, as he did with Mark's material. It is less probable that Matthew gathered these sayings that are spread through Luke.

[5] Fitzmyer, *Luke*, 1:298–99; Marshall, *Luke*, 53–76.

Carl N. Toney

Filipino mosaic depicting Gabriel telling Mary she would birth Jesus. Church of the Annunciation in Nazareth.

demonstrate that God kept his covenantal promises to Israel—promises to save and promises to judge. Luke portrayed God as faithful to his people, even as he extended those promises to include Gentiles.

With these opening stories, miracles and angels are in the air. Luke used the temple and one of its priests to announce the coming of Jesus's precursor, John the Baptist (Luke 1:5–25, 1:57–80). John was born to the elderly priest Zechariah and his wife Elizabeth, who had been unable to have children (Luke 1:7). The angel Gabriel appeared to Zechariah, who was serving in the temple and foretold John's birth (Luke 1:8–20). Because Zechariah laughed and did not believe the angel, he was struck mute until John was born (Luke 1:20). This story reminds readers of other miraculous births in the Jewish scriptures. Most notable is Isaac's miraculous birth to the one-hundred-year-old Abraham and ninety-year-old Sarah (Gen. 21:1–7). They also had struggled to believe the angelic promise about their son Isaac and responded in laughter (Gen. 17:17, 18:12–15).[6]

The stories of John the Baptist are full of references to God's promises being fulfilled. Gabriel told Zechariah that his son would "turn many of the people of Israel to the Lord their God" (Luke 1:16). After being born, John was marked by the covenantal sign of circumcision (Luke 1:59). Zechariah predicted that John would be the forerunner of the savior for the "house of David" to fulfill "promises to our ancestors" and God's "holy covenant" (Luke 1:67–79). John fulfilled this in his baptismal ministry and his proclamation of

[6] Reicke, *Luke*, 58.

Carl N. Toney

This is a stone manger from Megiddo. Luke 2:7 describes Mary wrapping Jesus in swaddling clothes and laying in a manger.

the promise from Isaiah 40:3–5 of the restoration of Israel from exile (Luke 3:4–6) and warning of the potential for judgment (Luke 3:7–9).

Interwoven with the stories of John's birth are stories surrounding the birth of Jesus (Luke 1:26–38, 1:39–56, 2:1–40). Gabriel made his second appearance (Luke 1:26–38), this time to Mary, and he promised an even greater miracle than opening the womb of an elderly woman. Gabriel told the twelve- to fifteen-year-old **Mary** that she would have a child while remaining a virgin (Luke 1:34). This would be accomplished by the Holy Spirit (Luke 1:35). Gabriel told Mary to name her child "Jesus" (Luke 1:31), just as he told Zechariah to name his son "John" (Luke 1:13).

As a reminder that God was in charge with Jesus as his representative, Jesus was to be called the Son of God (Luke 1:35). We are told that he would be given the Davidic throne forever (Luke 1:34). As a sign, Mary was told that her relative Elizabeth was also pregnant (Luke 1:36). Readers learn that Jesus and John were related. When Mary visited Elizabeth (Luke 1:39–45), Elizabeth's baby was filled with the Holy Spirit and leapt in her womb (Luke 1:41).

Sometime after this visit, Mary and Joseph were forced to travel from Galilee to Bethlehem for Quirinius's Roman census (Luke 2:1).[7] This census was for taxation. Luke used this as an opportunity to mention the Roman emperor, Augustus Caesar. After Jesus was born (Luke 2:1–7), angels announced Jesus's birth to **shepherds**, who were told to visit the baby (Luke 2:8–20). Luke's story differs from Matthew's, which includes the magi's visit (Matt. 2:1–12). The angelic announcement of the good news of peace is meant to contrast Jesus's humble birth with Emperor Augustus, who was known for bringing the "Roman peace" (Lat. *Pax Romana*) to the empire. These signs surrounding Jesus's birth challenged the notion that Rome was in charge because a new leader had been born.

These stories about Jesus's birth and childhood are full of references to God keeping his promises to Israel. Gabriel told Mary that Jesus would be given the throne of David and that "he will reign over the house of Jacob forever" (Luke 1:33). Mary's song of praise (Luke 1:46–55) highlights how God "has helped

[7]Luke ties Jesus's birth to Quirinius's census, which occurred in 6 CE when Judea became a Roman province. However, Matthew places Jesus's birth during the reign of Herod the Great, who died by 4 BCE. Some propose that either Matthew or Luke got their dates wrong, or this is an unknown census. Another proposal translates this verse, "This census took place before [*prōtē*] Quirinius was governor of Syria."

his servant Israel, in remembrance of his mercy, according to the promise he made to our ancestors, to Abraham and his descendant's forever" (Luke 1:54–55). As a baby, Jesus was marked by the covenantal sign of circumcision (Luke 2:22–24, 2:39). In the temple, the stories of Simeon and Anna waiting to see the baby Jesus (Luke 2:25–38) highlighted the hope of the restoration of Israel (Luke 2:25, 2:38).

After Jesus's dedication in the temple, Jesus was taken to Nazareth. He "grew and became strong, filled with wisdom; and the favor [*charis*] of God was upon him" (Luke 2:40). Then Luke tells the story of the twelve-year-old Jesus attending a Passover celebration, a festival that remembers the exodus (Luke 2:41–52). Interestingly, Luke is the only Gospel to share a story from Jesus's childhood. During this festival, Jesus spoke for the first time in Luke's story. Identifying God as his true Father, Jesus said, "It was necessary [*dei*] to be in my Father's house" (Luke 2:49 CEB). This is the first occurrence of "it was necessary," an expression used by Luke to reinforce Jesus's actions fulfilling God's plans (Luke 2:49, 4:43, 9:5, 9:22, 13:33, 17:25, 22:37, 24:7, 24:44).

At his baptism, the Holy Spirit anointed Jesus for prophetic ministry (Luke 3:21–22). Through the rest of the Gospel, Jesus is portrayed as a prophet fulfilling God's promises to his people. Jesus began his ministry by claiming to fulfill the prophecy of Israel's restoration after reading from Isaiah 61:1–2. Later, Jesus chose twelve disciples as a prophetic sign representing the restoration of Israel's twelve tribes

GOSPEL OF LUKE

- Prologue Addressed to Theophilus (1:1–4)
- Jesus's Childhood and Preparation for Ministry (1:5–4:13)
  - Birth Stories and the Childhood of John and Jesus (1:5–2:52)
  - Baptism, Genealogy from Jesus to Adam, and the Temptation (3:1–4:13)
- Galilean Ministry (4:14–9:50)
  - Inaugural Nazareth Sermon (4:14–30)
  - Miracles and Teaching throughout Galilee (4:31–9:17)
  - Peter's Confession, Transfiguration, and Discipleship Teaching (9:18–50)
- Travel to Jerusalem (9:51–19:27)
  - First Part of the Journey (9:51–13:21)
  - Second Part of the Journey (13:22–17:10)
  - Third Part of the Journey (17:11–19:27)
- Jerusalem Ministry (19:28–24:53)
  - Temple Conflicts and the Olivet Discourse (19:28–21:38)
  - Last Supper, Arrest, Trials, and Crucifixion (22:1–23:56)
  - Resurrection and Ascension (24:1–53)

Church of the Nativity in Bethlehem. The low door of the church is designed to make all visitors bow upon entry.

(Luke 6:12–16; cf. Luke 22:30). Miracles like the feeding of the five thousand[8] portrayed Jesus as a miracle worker like Israel's greatest prophets of Moses (cf. Deut. 18:15) and Elijah (cf. Mal. 4:5). Jesus's disciples recognized him as a "prophet mighty in deed and word" (Luke 24:19; cf. Luke 7:16), but his enemies rejected his prophetic status (Luke 7:39; cf. Luke 4:24, 13:33), attributing his miracles to the power of Beelzebul (Luke 11:14–23). After his death, Jesus's disciples reflected upon their crushed hope that Jesus would fulfill God's promises to redeem Israel (Luke 24:21). In response, the resurrected Jesus appeared and encouraged them from Scripture how it was "necessary that the Messiah should suffer these things and then enter into his glory" in order to fulfill God's promises to Israel (Luke 24:26).[9]

Good News for Non-Jews

God's ability to keep his promises to Israel is foundational for understanding how these promises were extended to non-Jews. If God had abandoned his promises to Israel and made new promises to non-Jews, then God would be fickle and untrustworthy. Luke adds stories to expand Israel's promises to include non-Jews. Notably, Jesus's genealogy is not found in the birth stories (Luke 3:23–38). Instead, it is placed between Jesus's baptism (Luke 3:21–22) and temptation (Luke 4:1–12). While Matthew traced Jesus's lineage to the founder of Israel, Abraham (Matt. 1:1), Luke traced Jesus's ancestry to Adam, the

[8]Unlike Mark and Matthew, Luke does not relate the feeding of the four thousand. This reflects his editorial tendency to simplify Mark and eliminate double stories.

[9]Fitzmyer, *Luke*, 1:179–80.

first human (Luke 3:38). For Luke, Jesus is connected to all of humanity via Adam, and his ministry is for all people.

When baby Jesus was brought to the temple to be dedicated, Simeon prophesized that he would be "a light for revelation to the Gentiles" (Luke 2:32). When John the Baptist proclaimed the end of Israel's exile (Luke 3:4–5; Isa. 40:3–4), Luke extends the quotation to include "all flesh shall see the salvation of God" (Luke 3:6; cf. Isa. 40:5).[10] In his inaugural sermon in Nazareth, Jesus quoted from a text announcing the end of exile (Isa. 61:1–2), but he omitted the line concerning God's vengeance against the Gentiles.[11] Jesus also noted how the ministries of Elijah and Elisha were models for his inclusion of Gentiles and explained Jewish hard-heartedness (Luke 4:24–27).[12] However, what may be surprising to readers of Luke is that this programmatic sermon did not align with most of Jesus's ministry, which focused on the Jewish people. Regardless, the Gospel ends with Jesus commanding his disciples to proclaim his name among the Gentiles as a fulfillment of Scripture (Luke 24:44–46). With these kinds of appeals to the Jewish scriptures, Luke indicates that the mission to the Gentiles was part of the eternal will of God.[13]

For Luke, Jesus's mission focused on the Jewish people because God must first restore Israel before their promises could be extended to Gentiles. There are, however, occasional stories that foreshadow this Gentile mission. Sometimes this is cryptic, such as when Jesus appointed seventy or seventy-two

Carl N. Toney

The Magdala Synagogue is an example of a synagogue from the time of Jesus.

[10] Dupont, "Salvation of the Gentiles," 11–33.

[11] Wilson, *Gentile Mission in Luke-Acts*, 40–41; Jeremias, *Jesus' Promise to the Nations*, 44–46; Martin, "Salvation and Discipleship in the Gospel of Luke," 214–30.

[12] Creed, *St. Luke*, 66; Tannehill, "The Mission of Jesus According to Luke," 51–75, esp. 59.

[13] Wilson, *Gentile Mission in Luke-Acts*, 244.

disciples for a mission (Luke 10:1). This number alludes to the number of nations listed in Genesis 10:1–32.[14] At other times, it is more obvious. Jesus exorcized demons from the non-Jewish Gerasene demoniac (Luke 8:26–39; Mark 5:1–20; Matt. 8:28–9:1). He healed the servant of a Roman centurion (Luke 7:1–10; Matt. 8:5–13). He healed a Samaritan leper (Luke 17:11–19). Luke also omits problematic stories about Gentiles such as Jesus calling the Canaanite women a "dog" (Mark 7:24–30; Matt. 15:21–28).

Non-Jews are presented as models for godly behavior. When the Gerasene demoniac was healed and wished to follow Jesus, Jesus commissioned him to preach among the Gentile cities (Luke 8:38–39). The Jewish leadership described the centurion (Luke 7:1–10) as "worthy of having you do this for him, for he loves our people, and it is he who built our synagogue for us" (Luke 7:4–5). The Samaritan leper was the only person to return and thank Jesus for being healed (Luke 17:11–19). The good Samaritan is presented as a model for loving one's neighbor (Luke 10:30–37; cf. Lev. 19:18). At the cross, the Roman centurion declared Jesus to be innocent (Luke 23:47).[15] While Jesus's ministry did not actively focus upon Gentiles, these stories laid the groundwork for the full-blown inclusion of Gentiles in the promises of God as narrated in Acts.

Carl N. Toney

A stone chair found in Chorazin's synagogue. Sitting on "Moses's seat" may refer to the authority for interpreting the Mosaic law.

Including the Marginalized

Not only did Jesus's inclusion cross ethnic lines, but he also crossed social and gender boundaries. Luke shows God's covenantal concerns for justice and care for the poor by including Jesus's outreach to the poor (e.g., Deut. 15:7, 15:11; 1 Sam. 2:8; Pss. 12:5, 34:6; Prov. 14:31). Luke understood that poverty was the result of injustice. The poor had too little because others had too much or had exploited them (Prov. 22:16). This concern for the poor was highlighted in the ministry of John the Baptist. He urged his audience to share their food and clothes with those in need (Luke 3:11). He told toll collectors not to over-collect (Luke 3:13). He challenged soldiers not to extort money (Luke 3:14).

Jesus's first sermon in Nazareth proclaimed that his gospel was for the poor (Luke 4:18–19). His mission to the poor was tied to themes of God's promises to Israel through his citation of Isaiah 61:1–2. His ministry of healing and exorcisms provided for the material needs of the poor and outcasts (Luke 7:21–22). Jesus healed

[14] Wilson, 45–47.

[15] These positive stories of centurions in Luke look forward to Cornelius in Acts 10–11. Matson, *Household Conversion Narratives*.

destitute lepers (Luke 5:12–16, 17:11–19), marginalized demoniacs (Luke 8:26–39), and blind beggars (Luke 18:35–43). He fed the hungry by providing food for five thousand people (Luke 9:10–17).

Jesus challenged his disciples to choose between serving God or possessions (Luke 16:13). Exemplifying this choice, the rich ruler was told by Jesus to sell everything (Luke 18:18–27), while the disciples were praised for leaving their homes to follow Jesus (Luke 18:28–30). One parable tells of a poor man named Lazarus who was blessed in the afterlife while a rich man suffered punishment (Luke 16:19–31). The parable of the rich fool described the dangers of wealth (Luke 12:13–21),[16] and the faithful were called to divest themselves of material possessions (Luke 12:33, 14:33). The former tax collector Zacchaeus was an example of a wealthy person who gave his money to the poor and those he exploited (Luke 19:1–9). The disciples were told to use their wealth for the kingdom of God rather than for their own benefits (Luke 14:13, 16:1–13). In the future, the poor were promised to be blessed by God (Luke 6:20, 14:21, 16:22). There was a call to emulate the poor, such as being persistent in prayer like the widow before a judge (Luke 18:1–8). Likewise, a poor widow's generosity in giving her last coins is praised (Luke 21:1–4), unlike the scribes who devoured widows' homes (Luke 20:45–47).

Luke's inclusivity also crossed gender boundaries. By pairing stories of men and women, he showed that God's covenantal promises were for both sexes. In the birth narratives, he paired the songs of Mary and Zechariah (Luke 1:46–56, 1:67–80) and the elderly Simeon and Anna (Luke 2:22–38). He joined the parable of the woman's lost coin with the men who lost a sheep and lost a son (Luke 15:1–32). Throughout the Third Gospel, Jesus healed both men and women. For example, his first miracle of healing the male demoniac (Luke 4:31–37) was paired with healing Peter's mother-in-law (Luke 4:38–39). Likewise, Jesus performed miracles for both the hemorrhaging woman and Jairus (Luke 8:40–56). Also, Jesus raised from the dead both Jairus's daughter (Luke 8:49–56) and a widow's son (Luke 7:11–17). Similarly, he healed both a paralyzed woman (Luke 13:10–17) and a paralyzed man (Luke 5:17–26).

Luke also elevated the honor and status of women. In the birth stories, Luke gave a significant role to John's mother, Elizabeth, whose shame of infertility was overturned (Luke 1:5–45, 1:57–66). Likewise, Jesus's mother, Mary, was central to Jesus's birth story (Luke 1:26–38, 2:1–52). In fact, he highlighted the critical role of mothers throughout his Gospel (Luke 1:42, 7:28, 11:27–28, 23:28–31). Peter's mother-in-law regained her honor and showed hospitality to Jesus after her healing (Luke 4:38–39). The hemorrhaging woman was restored—physically and socially (Luke 8:43–48).

Significant women are named, such as Mary and Martha (Luke 10:38–42) and the female patrons of Jesus: Susanna, Mary Magdalene, and Joanna the wife of Herod's steward (Luke 8:2). It was only the women disciples who remained faithful to Jesus and witnessed his crucifixion (Luke 23:27, 23:49) and burial (Luke 23:55). Mary Magdalene, Joanna, and Mary the mother of James were the first witnesses of his resurrection (Luke 24:5, 24:10, 24:22, 24:24). In these stories of the female disciples, they are presented as examples worthy of imitation. When God is in charge, he elevates the status of the marginalized.

---

[16] Rindge, *Rich Fool.*

The Bible and History

The prologue of Luke's Gospel presents itself as a carefully researched account of the life of Jesus (Luke 1:1–4).[17] Yet, Luke was not a modern historian, and these stories were written to promote the Christian faith. They do not claim to be any sort of objective history. When we place the four Gospels side-by-side, we discover remarkable similarities, but we also discover some differences.

Some of the most notable differences include dating Jesus's birth during the end of Herod's reign (Matt. 2:1–15) or the beginning of Quirinius's governorship (Luke 2:1–5). Jesus's temple act is placed at the end of Jesus's ministry (Mark 11:15–19; Matt. 21:12–17; Luke 19:45–48) or the beginning (John 2:13–25). The crucifixion occurs on the Passover (Mark 14:12; Matt. 26:17–19; Luke 22:7) or on the Day of Preparation (John 19:14). Minor differences include the order of Jesus's three temptations (Matt. 4:1–11; Luke 4:1–13), Jesus healing one (Mark 10:46–52; Luke 18:35–43) or two blind men (Matt. 20:28–24), and resurrection details, like one (Mark 16:5–7) or two angels inside the tomb (Luke 24:4–9; John 20:11–13) or one angel sitting on the stone entrance (Matt. 28:2–7).

Scholars provide a variety of explanations that either harmonize or enhance these differences. During the Enlightenment, scholars began to question the historical reliability of the Gospels and asked what actually happened. They embarked upon what is now called the quest for the "historical Jesus," in distinction from the "Christ of faith."[18] They used a mixture of criteria to determine the historical reliability of the Gospel accounts, including the following:

1. The criterion of embarrassment deemed stories that appear embarrassing to the early church are historical (e.g., the sinless Jesus's received John's baptism for the forgiveness of sins, Mark 1:4–11).
2. Material that is dissimilar from either early Christianity or Judaism (e.g., Jesus's rejection of fasting, Mark 2:18–22)
3. Stories verified by multiple, independent sources (e.g., Jesus's Last Supper words, Mark 14:22–25; 1 Cor. 11:23–26; John 6:51–58). This could also include sources like Josephus.
4. Material that explained Jesus's rejection and execution (e.g., the temple act, Mark 11:15–19).
5. The criterion of coherence lets scholars include materials that flesh out Jesus's life based on other accepted materials.

Nowadays, scholars are increasingly skeptical of theories that attempt to discern "facts" from these stories. Newer theories attempt to explain the Gospel stories, such as through social memory theory, asking what is plausible for the community to remember and convey.[19]

In the midst of these discussions, we should remember that the existence of Jesus of Nazareth as a historical figure, who was crucified, is not disputed. Several non-Christian authors wrote about

[17] Luke's historical prologue is like other writings from this period (e.g., Josephus, *J.W.* 1.1; *Ant.* 1.1; cf. *Ag. Ap.* 1.1, 2.1). Cadbury, "Preface of Luke," 490–91.

[18] Albert Schweitzer chronicled this "quest," attributing the beginning to Gotthold Ephraim Lessing, who published the work of Hermann Samuel Reimarus in 1778.

[19] LeDonne, *Historical Jesus: What Can We Know and How Can We Know It?*; Keith and LeDonne, *Jesus, Criteria, and the Demise of Authenticity*; Allison, *Constructing Jesus: Memory, Imagination, History*; Crossley and Keith, *The Next Quest for the Historical Jesus*.

Jesus and the early Christians. Tacitus (*Ann.* 15.44) said, "Their name comes from Christ, who during the reign of Tiberius, had been executed by the procurator Pontius Pilate" (56–120 CE). Pliny the Younger (*Ep.* 10.96) noted that Christians worshiped "Christ as a god" (61–113 CE). The lengthiest treatment is by Josephus, who wrote:

> At this time there appeared Jesus, a wise man. . . . For he was a doer of startling deeds, a teacher of people who receive the truth with pleasure. And he gained a following both among many Jews and among many of Greek origin. . . . And when Pilate, because of an accusation made by the leading men among us, condemned him to the cross, those who had loved him previously did not cease to do so. . . . And up until this very day the tribe of Christians (named after him) has not died out. (*Ant.* 18.3.3).[20]

The Power of God's Spirit

Prophesies like Joel 2:28–29 and Ezekiel 36:27 link the fulfillment of God's promises to Israel with the coming of the **Holy Spirit**.[21] According to Jewish tradition, the prophetic Spirit ceased with Haggai, Zechariah, and Malachi, so the reappearance of the Holy Spirit in Luke's Gospel marked the commencement of a new age.[22] In the opening scenes of the Gospel, Luke stresses the prophetic activity of the Spirit. **John the Baptist** was filled with the Holy Spirit from before his birth (Luke 1:15). As a child, John grew strong in the Spirit (Luke 1:80). His ministry would be characterized by the prophetic spirit of Elijah (Luke 1:17). In addition, various characters like Elizabeth (Luke 1:41), Zechariah (Luke 1:67), and Simeon (Luke 2:25–27) were filled with the Holy Spirit and prophesied.

While John was filled by and grew in the Spirit, Jesus was conceived by the power of the Holy Spirit (Luke 1:35). At his baptism, Jesus was anointed by the Holy Spirit (Luke 3:22–23). After this moment, Jesus was filled by the Spirit and led into the desert (Luke 4:1). He returned by the power of the Spirit to begin his ministry (Luke 4:14). Jesus tied his empowerment by the Spirit with his messianic vocation to proclaim the gospel when he opened the Isaiah scroll and read, "The Spirit of the Lord is upon me" (Luke 4:18, citing Isa. 61:1–2).

Baptism of Christ by David Zelenka. (2005)

While Jesus's relationship with the Spirit was distinct, Luke also highlighted similarities with

[20] Josephus's text contains Christian additions marked by the ellipses. This text is based on the reconstruction by Meier, *A Marginal Jew*, 1:61.

[21] The Spirit is a significant theme in Luke (17x) versus Matthew (12x) and Mark (6x).

[22] For the Spirit's role in prophecy, see Lampe, "Holy Spirit in the Writings of St. Luke," 159–200. For the Spirit in the New Testament, see Barrett, *Holy Spirit and the Gospel Tradition*, 123; Marshall, *Luke: Historian and Theologian*, 91.

the Spirit's presence and empowerment among Christ followers.[23] Jesus promised his disciples that the Father would give them the Holy Spirit (Luke 11:13). He told them that the Holy Spirit would give his persecuted disciples words to say (Luke 12:12) and warned his enemies not to blaspheme the Holy Spirit (Luke 12:10). At the end of the Gospel, Jesus told his disciples that he would "send [them] what [his] Father has promised" and spoke of being "clothed with power from high" (Luke 24:49). With this promise, Jesus linked his baptism by the Holy Spirit (Luke 3:22–23) with the disciples' upcoming baptism by the Holy Spirit at Pentecost (Acts 2:1–4). While Jesus in his lifetime was the unique bearer of the "power of the Spirit," after his ascension, Jesus became the dispenser of the Spirit.[24]

Luke also connected prayer with the activity of the Spirit. Jesus prayed at crucial points in his ministry, such as his baptism (Luke 3:21), Peter's confession (Luke 9:18), and the transfiguration (Luke 9:28–29). After times of miracle-working, Jesus withdrew from the crowds to pray (Luke 5:16). Before choosing his twelve disciples, he prayed all night (Luke 6:12). Jesus taught his disciples the Lord's Prayer (Luke 11:2–4) and called them to be persistent in prayer (Luke 11:5–13). Before his arrest, Jesus went off to pray with his disciples (Luke 22:39–46). Luke's insistence on prayer is distinctive to the Third Gospel and "the means by which the dynamic energy of the Spirit is apprehended."[25] Both prayer and the Holy Spirit remain essential features for the advancement of Christianity in Acts (e.g., Acts 10:23, 10:30, 13:3–4).

Carl N. Toney

Herodian road in Jerusalem.

[23] Schweizer, "πνεύμα," *TDNT*, 6:404–15, esp. 405.

[24] Grundmann, "δύναμαι, δυνατός, κτλ," *TDNT*, 2:301; Barrett, *Holy Spirit and the Gospel Tradition*, 71, 101; Conzelmann, *Theology of Saint Luke*, 180.

[25] Lampe, "Holy Spirit in the Writings of St. Luke," 169.

Fishing boat (27 ft. x 7.5 ft.) discovered in the Sea of Galilee. (first cent. CE)

Carl N. Toney

Discipleship as a Journey

One of the most distinctive features of Luke is Jesus's journey between Galilee and Jerusalem, which takes up about one-third of the Gospel (Luke 9:51–19:27). This section lacks a clear structure. It is neither thematically structured nor geographically organized (Jesus did not travel directly from north to south.) The disciples appear more often in this travel narrative than anywhere else in the Gospel. They received instructions (Luke 10:23, 11:1, 12:1, 12:22, 16:1, 17:1, 17:5, 17:22, 18:15, 18:31) and had more active roles (e.g., Luke 10:1–20). This travel narrative aims to illustrate that discipleship takes the form of a journey.

This section contains essential teaching about discipleship, including the love commands (Luke 10:25–28) and the Lord's Prayer (Luke 11:2–4). It contains significant teachings on wealth, such as the stories of the rich young ruler (Luke 18:18–30) and Zacchaeus (Luke 19:1–10). It includes memorable parables like the good Samaritan (Luke 10:29–37), the prodigal son (Luke 15:11–32), and the rich man and Lazarus (Luke 16:19–31). It recounts important miracles like cleansing the ten lepers (Luke 17:11–19) and healing the blind man (Luke 18:35–43).

Jesus defined discipleship as following him (Luke 5:27, 9:23, 9:59, 18:22), and the way of discipleship includes self-denial and cross-bearing (Luke 9:23–24, 14:25–27). Jesus called his first disciples—Peter, James, and John—to leave their fishing business in order to follow him and become fishers of people (Luke 5:1–11). Levi the toll collector was also called to leave his profession (Luke 9:27–32). But not everyone heeded Jesus's call (Luke 9:57–62, 18:18–30).[26] We also see the connection between teaching and traveling during Jesus's post-resurrection appearance when he taught on the road to Emmaus (Luke 24:13–35). The link between travel and discipleship is made explicit in Acts, where Luke called the early community of disciples "the Way" (*hē hodos*, Acts 9:2, 19:9, 19:23, 22:4, 24:14, 24:22; cf. Isa. 40:3).[27]

One mark of discipleship is "repentance" (*metanoia*; lit. "changing one's mind"), which is an important concept in Luke and the key to Jesus's message (e.g., Luke 5:32, 10:13, 11:32, 13:3–5, 15:7, 15:10).[28] Luke links repentance and forgiveness of sins so that repentance involves turning away from "sin" (*hamartia*, Luke 5:31–32, 24:46–49).[29] Luke stresses that repentance must include concrete responses of turning toward God and reorientating oneself to the plans of God, who demands allegiance in all things.[30] For example, John the Baptist linked repentance to acts of justice (Luke 3:7–14). Also, Jesus highlighted how the prodigal son's repentance involved returning to his father's house (Luke 15:17–21).

Related to repentance is "belief" or "faith" (*pistis*, *pisteuō*). Belief led to actions that resulted in salvation (Luke 5:20, 7:9, 7:47–50, 8:48, 17:19, 18:42).[31] The faith of the paralytic's friends spurred them to bring him to Jesus for healing (Luke 5:20). The centurion's belief in the authoritative word of Jesus led to his servant's healing (Luke 7:9). The sinful woman's faith led her to anoint Jesus (Luke 7:47–50). The hemorrhaging woman's faith led to her touching Jesus to be healed (Luke 8:48). The Samaritan leper's

---

[26] Brown, *Apostasy and Perseverance*, 82.

[27] On the Jewish background of the "Way," see Fitzmyer, *Acts*, 423–25.

[28] Luke (noun 5x, verb 9x) and Acts (noun 6x, verb 5x) use the terms for "repentance" more frequently than Matthew (noun 2x, verb 5x) or Mark (noun 1x, verb 2x).

[29] Fitzmyer, *Luke*, 1:237.

[30] Green, *Theology of the Gospel of Luke*, 108.

[31] Bock, "Luke, Gospel of," *DJG*, 506.

Before his crucifixion, Jesus prayed with his disciples in the Garden of Gethsemane, located on the Mount of Olives.

faith made him well (Luke 17:19). Because of his faith, the blind man cried out for healing (Luke 18:42). Disciples who follow Jesus begin their journey with repentance and faith.

Jesus's Crucifixion, Resurrection, and Ascension

Luke concluded his Gospel with Jesus's crucifixion. Like Mark, Matthew, and John, the Third Gospel also attributes Jesus's death to the decision of the Roman ruler of Judea, Pontius Pilate (Luke 23:13–25; Mark 15:6–15; Matt. 27:15-26; John 18:38–19:16). In addition, Luke includes **Herod Antipas**, the ruler of Galilee, as participating in the trial of Jesus (Luke 23:6–12).[32] Because Jesus was from Galilee, Pilate attempted to shift the responsibility for Jesus's fate to Herod. Earlier in the story, Herod had wanted to kill Jesus (Luke 13:31), and he executed John the Baptist (Mark 6:14–29; Matt. 14:1–12; Luke 9:7–9). However, Herod wisely deferred Pilate's offer and sent Jesus back to Pilate (Luke 23:11).

For Luke, Jesus's death was a necessary part of God's plan for salvation (Luke 9:22, 9:44, 24:7, 24:26, 24:44). Luke distinctly emphasized the concept of salvation in his Gospel.[33] Jesus's role as **savior** is

[32]Hoehner, *Herod Antipas*; Jensen, *Herod Antipas in Galilee*.

[33]Luke used the verb "to save" (*sōzō*) more than any other New Testament writer. Only Luke called Jesus "Savior" (*sōtēr*, Luke 1:47, 2:11; cf. Isa. 45:21). Luke is the only Synoptic Gospel to use "salvation" (*sōtēria*, Luke 1:69, 1:71, 1:77, 19:9; *sōtērion*, Luke 2:30, 3:6).

contrasted with the Roman emperor. Like the emperor, Jesus was called a savior who brought peace (Luke 2:9–14). However, Jesus's peace was not achieved through the violence of the Roman armies but through his death on the cross. Like the emperor, Jesus was portrayed as a benefactor (Luke 22:24–30; cf. Acts 10:38). However, Jesus's role as a benefactor upended human systems of obligation by demanding the forgiveness of enemies and making everyone obligated to God. Further, Jesus surpassed the emperor because his peace and benefits continued after his death through the community of his disciples.[34]

From a Jewish perspective, Jesus who was the savior was linked with Yahweh who was the only source of salvation (e.g., 2 Sam. 22:3; Ps. 17:18–19; Isa. 59:16). As God's agent of salvation, Jesus acted like the judges of Israel, who brought deliverance to God's people (e.g., Judg. 3:9, 3:15; Neh. 9:27; cf. Isa. 19:20). In the Jewish scriptures, salvation was epitomized in the exodus story (e.g., Exod. 14:13), and Jesus brought a new exodus for all people. Jesus recalled the exodus during the Last Supper, which was a Passover meal. Using this meal, Jesus reframed the exodus story. Jesus told his disciples that his sacrifice replaced the Passover lamb,[35] and his death established a new covenant (Luke 22:19b–20).[36] Finally, the post-resurrected Jesus framed his suffering, dying, and rising as necessary acts of "the Messiah" (Luke 24:46).

Public Domain

Christ Crucified by Diego Velázquez. Museo Nacional del Prado, Madrid. (1599-1660)

Like the other Gospels, Luke's story ends with the resurrection of Jesus. With the resurrection, Jesus's disciples made their declaration of loyalty that Jesus is "the **Lord**" (*ho kyrios*) who had risen (Luke 24:34). This declaration of Jesus as "Lord" made a claim about Jesus's exaltation and heavenly rule, in contrast to the Greco-Roman claim that Caesar was "Lord." It was a proclamation that Jesus was in charge. The title of "Lord" (*kyrios*) also connected Jesus to God, following the Jewish practice of identifying God as Lord (e.g., Luke 1:6, 9) and the practice of substituting the name of God, Yahweh, with Lord (e.g., Luke 1:46, 1:68, 1:76).

Luke is the only Gospel to record the ascension of Jesus (Luke 24:50–53; Acts 1:6–11). However, the ascension is assumed in other

[34] Danker, *Benefactor*. See the later discussion on patronage in Chapter Five.
[35] Bock, *Proclamation from Prophecy and Pattern*.
[36] There is debate about the textual certainty of these verses.

places in the New Testament (John 6:62, 20:17; Eph. 4:8–10; 1 Tim. 3:16). In Mark's Gospel, Jesus just disappears (Mark 16:1–8). In Matthew, his last words are spoken on a mountain (Matt. 28:18–20). In John, Jesus continues to reappear to his disciples in various situations, including by the Sea of Galilee (John 21:1–25).

Carl N. Toney

One of the traditional sites of Jesus's ascension.

For Luke, the **ascension** illuminates Jesus's death. Jesus must die so that he can ascend and be exalted to rule in heaven (Luke 24:26, 24:46; cf. Acts 3:18, 17:3, 26:23). The ascension is the climax of the Third Gospel and serves as the launching point for Acts. It serves as a turning point in salvation history. While Jesus was "Lord" and "Messiah" from his birth (Luke 2:11), the resurrection (Luke 24:34) and ascension (Luke 24:51) made visible and concrete Jesus's exalted status, where he became the object of worship (Luke 24:52).[37] In Acts, these titles reflect Jesus's exalted rule from the right hand of God. Peter's speech in Acts 2:14–39 linked Jesus's lordship to his exaltation with Psalm 110:1 and his messiahship with Psalm 16:10 (Acts 2:36). Luke's Gospel ends on a note of triumph, where the disciples were full of joy and praising God because Jesus had taken his rightful place in heaven, and the audience knew that God really was in charge (Luke 24:50–53).

Key Terms and People

Ascension: the pivotal event narrated only in Luke-Acts, illustrating Jesus's exalted rule
Herod Antipas: son of Herod the Great and ruler of Galilee, who was responsible for beheading John the Baptist
Holy Spirit: God's Spirit anointed and empowered Jesus for his messianic ministry; the Spirit is promised to fill and empower his disciples after his ascension
John the Baptist: cousin of Jesus and the prophetic forerunner of Jesus who baptized Jesus in the Jordan River as a sign of the new exodus
Lord: title of Jesus that associates Jesus with Yahweh and emphasizes Jesus exalted and heavenly rule, in contrast to the Roman emperor, who was the lord of the empire

[37] Giles, "Ascension," *DJG*, 46–50, esp. 50. Parsons, *Departure of Jesus*; Franklin, *Christ the Lord.*

Luke: doctor and traveling companion of Paul and traditional author of Luke-Acts
Mary: the mother of Jesus, who was a virgin; Luke tells the birth story from her perspective; according to the Gospel of John, Jesus entrusted her care to the beloved disciple after his death
Savior: the title of Jesus that conveys his role as God's agent of salvation
Shepherds: those people who Luke reports visit the baby Jesus

Conversation Starters

1. Who was Luke? What did he mean by an "orderly" account?
2. What do we know about John the Baptist and his parents? Why does Luke begin with stories about John the Baptist before sharing stories about the birth of Jesus?
3. What kinds of promises does God make to Israel? How does God keep these promises? How does Jesus, as God's ultimate prophet, demonstrate that God is faithful to keep these promises?
4. In what ways did Luke have a particular interest in including Gentiles? How does Luke's genealogy show this broader interest? Are there other stories in Luke that demonstrate the inclusion of Gentiles in God's promises?
5. Why did Luke think it was essential to include the marginalized? How were the poor elevated in the Gospel? What was the status of women?
6. How was Jesus being filled by the Holy Spirit similar but also unique to how the disciples were filled? What did Jesus and the disciples do when filled by the Spirit? How did this filling fit with expectations in the Jewish scriptures?
7. Why is following Jesus a major metaphor for discipleship in Luke? What does Jesus expect of his disciples?
8. Why do you think Luke is the only Gospel to include the ascension of Jesus?

FOR FURTHER READING

Chen, Diane. *Luke*. New Covenant Commentary. Cascade, 2017.
Dicken, Frank. *Reading Luke*. Cascade Companions. Cascade, 2023.
Fitzmyer, Joseph. *The Gospel According to Luke*. 2 vols. AYB 28-28A. Yale University Press, 2008.
González, Justo. *Luke*. Belief. Westminster John Knox, 2010.
Johnson, Luke Timothy. *The Gospel of Luke*. SP 3. Liturgical Press, 1991.
Kraybill, Donald. *The Upside-down Kingdom*. Herald Press, 2011.
Levine, Amy-Jill, and Ben Witherington III. *The Gospel of Luke*. New Cambridge Bible Commentary. Cambridge University Press, 2018.
Lieu, Judith M. *The Gospel of Luke*. Epworth Commentaries. Wipf & Stock, 2012.
Ringe, Sharon. *Luke*. Westminster Bible Companion. Westminster John Knox, 1995.
Wright, Catherine J. *Spiritual Practices of Jesus: Learning Simplicity, Humility, and Prayer with Luke's Earliest Readers*. IVP Academic, 2020.

5

THE STORY OF THE EARLY CHURCH IN ACTS

Who Wrote Acts?

In the last chapter, we learned that tradition identifies the anonymous author of the Third Gospel and Acts as Luke. This is supported by internal evidence from both documents. Both works were written around 75–85 CE, possibly in Rome. The similar prologues dedicated to Theophilus bind these two works together (Luke 1:1–4; Acts 1:1–2). Theophilus was Luke's patron who provided financial support for writing the two-volume work of Luke-Acts.

The patron-client relationship was foundational to Roman society and created a network of "favor" (*charis*) and "loyalty" (*pistis*) among people (Seneca, *Ben.* 1.4.2). Patrons were those in Roman society with financial resources and higher social status who could provide goods and resources to clients lacking those resources. Ideally, these gifts were given for the benefit of the client and were not motivated by self-interest (Aristotle, *Eth. nic.* 1385a35–b3; Seneca, *Ben.* 3.15.4). In exchange for these benefits, clients gave their loyalty, honor, and service to increase the reputations of their patrons. In this system, it was important to find clients known for expressing the appropriate gratitude for gifts (Isocrates, *Dem.* 29).

One of the words used to describe the patron's favor was "grace" (*charis*), and the client's appropriate response of loyalty was sometimes called "faith" (*pistis*, Seneca, *Ben.* 3.14.2). The greater the "gift" (*charis*) required the greater response of "loyalty" (*pistis*). Failing to properly honor the gift dishonored the patron and could result in the patron's wrath (Aristotle, *Rhet.* 2.2.8). The use of "grace" and "faith" in the New Testament should be understood within this patron-client context.[1] God, as the patron of all humanity, offers the ultimate, priceless gift or grace of a renewed relationship with him through his Son. Jesus mediates this favor,

SUGGESTED READING

Acts 1:1-17:9
Acts 17:15-18:23
Acts 19:1-20:16
Acts 21:17-23:11
Acts 23:31-25:12
Acts 27:1-28:31

[1]For more on patronage, see deSilva, *Honor, Patronage, Kinship, & Purity*; Bates, *Gospel Allegiance*; McKnight, *King Jesus Gospel*.

secured from God through his life, death, and resurrection. Unlike the Roman system, no person was worthy of this benefit, but God still generously bestowed it. Those who accept God's "gift" or "grace" (*charis*) are called to respond by "faith" or "loyalty" (*pistis*).

Jesus's sacrifice on the cross upended the Roman system of favors and loyalty. A Christian's loyalty to God supersedes all obligations to others. A believer no longer sees his or her resources as his or her own. Rather, they are God's. Because of God's priceless gift, those believers with wealth and resources in the early Christian communities were willing to share their resources with others without expecting any personal benefit (2 Cor. 9:8–10). In this way, God received honor through the actions of believers.

Christian patrons were following the example of the generosity of Jesus (2 Cor. 8:9–14). They shared their resources as a means of expressing loyalty to God. Throughout this introduction to the New Testament, you'll encounter several patrons of the early church, including Phoebe (Rom. 16:1–2), Chloe (1 Cor. 1:11), and Nympha (Col. 4:15). Often, patrons provided homes for house churches (Rom. 16:23; 1 Cor. 16:19; Col. 4:15) or sponsored missionary activities (Philem. 22; 2 John 5–8). Jesus and his disciples had several women as patrons of his public ministry, including Mary Magdalene, Joanna, and Susanna (Luke 8:2–3).

We owe a debt of gratitude for Theophilus's patronage, which provided the means for Luke to write his two-volume account of Jesus and the early church. Theophilus's generosity was a reflection of God's generosity, and reading these works are meant to bring honor to his patron, God the Father, as well as his Son, the Lord Jesus Christ.

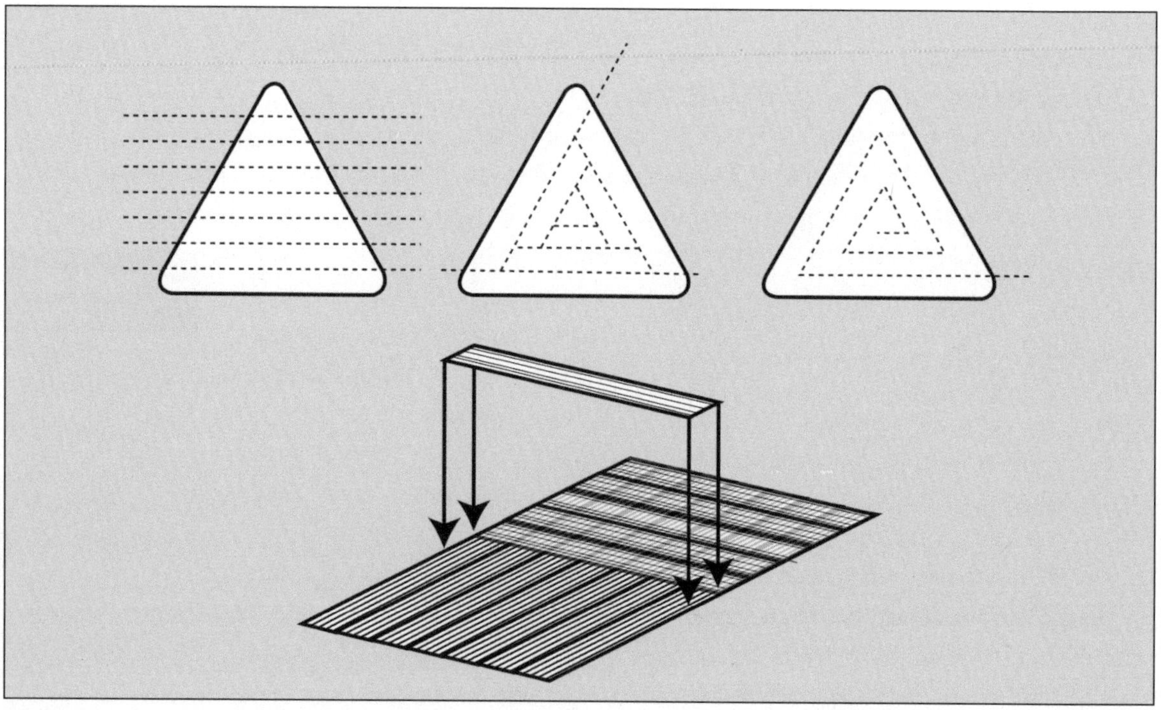

The New Testament originally was written on scrolls made by hammering alternating layers of the stems from the papyrus plant.

What Was Acts All About?

The Origin Story of the Church

The author of Luke-Acts provided a sizable contribution to the New Testament, writing about one-third of its material.[2] In terms of genre, the Third Gospel is similar to ancient biographies, and Acts is written like ancient history.[3] But we should not confuse these ancient styles with their modern equivalents. Luke did not delve into the feelings or psychology of his subject in his biography. Nor does Luke's claim of an orderly account necessitate chronological order. Instead, he approached his subject thematically.

Without Acts, we would not have a clear record of the history of the growth of the early church from Jerusalem to across the Roman Empire. Rather, we would have to rely upon the episodic data from Paul's letters. Many readers consider Jesus's final words in Acts as an outline of the work:

> But you will receive power when the Holy Spirit has come upon you; and you will be my witnesses in Jerusalem, in all Judea and Samaria, and to the ends of the earth. (Acts 1:8)

Carl N. Toney

One of the keys to the expansion of the early church was the extensive network of Roman roads, like this road in Berea.

Thus, Acts focuses first on the apostles' activities in Jerusalem (Acts 1–7). Then, the gospel spread to Judea and Samaria because of persecution (Acts 8–12). Finally, the gospel spread to the ends of the earth through the missionary activities of Paul (Acts 13–28).

Two figures dominate the pages of Acts. In the first part, Peter led the church in its expansion from Jerusalem to Judea and Samaria (Acts 1–12). He was responsible for the pivotal conversion of the Gentile family of **Cornelius** and his household (Acts 10:1–11:18). In the second part, Paul is brought to the fore (Acts 13–28). He is first introduced by his Jewish name, Saul, and he was a persecutor of the church (Acts 7:58–8:3). However, on the Damascus Road, he was dramatically called by Jesus to become the apostle to the Jews and Gentiles (Acts 9:1–19; cf. Acts 22:6–16, 26:12–18). This calling led to his missionary journeys

[2] The New Testament can be divided into three main bodies of work, each consisting of roughly one-third of the material. These "thirds" are associated with three men. Luke is credited with writing Luke-Acts. Paul is the named author of thirteen letters. John of Zebedee is associated with the Fourth Gospel, 1-3 John, and Revelation. This rough breakdown should be taken with a grain of salt since significant materials are omitted (Matthew, Mark, Hebrews, James, 1-2 Peter, and Jude).

[3] Josephus also pairs a biography (*Life*) with history (*Jewish Wars*; *Antiquities*) that begin with historical prologues (*J.W.* 1.1; *Ant.* 1.1). See Lucian, *How to Write History.*

throughout Asia Minor, Macedonia, and Greece (Acts 13:1–14:28, 15:36–21:16). His missionary travels ended after his arrest in Judea (Acts 21:17–26:32), but his arrest resulted in him carrying the gospel to Rome (Acts 27–28). When we look at Paul's letters, we will connect many of them with his story in Acts.[4]

Acts is also known for its numerous speeches. However, readers should not assume these are verbatim records of what was spoken. Otherwise, most of these "speeches" would be under five minutes! Instead, they were opportunities for Luke to use his characters to convey his main themes, and he was following the conventions of ancient historians (Thucydides, *Histories* 1.22.1; Pliny the Younger, *Ep.* 1.16; Lucian, *How to Write History* 58).[5]

Notable speeches include Peter's speech at Pentecost (Acts 2:14–39), which led to three thousand people becoming Christians (Acts 2:41). Later, Peter defended the freedom of Gentile Christians at the Jerusalem Council in light of his experience with Cornelius (Acts 15:7–11). **Stephen**, the first martyr, recounted the salvation history of Israel as he was being stoned (Acts 7:2–53). On his first missionary journey, Paul gave his first speech in Pisidian Antioch, offering salvation to his fellow Jews (Acts 13:16–41).[6] Paul was also known for his "Mars Hill" speech before the Gentile philosophers at the Areopagus in Athens, which is sometimes seen as a model for apologetics (Acts 17:16–34).[7] After his arrest, Paul gave several defense speeches before Jewish (Acts 23:1–11) and Roman leadership (Acts 24:10–21, 26:1–32).

Foundation: The Resurrection and Exaltation of Jesus

Acts begins where the Third Gospel ends. The Gospel concludes with Jesus's disciples confessing the resurrected Jesus to be the Lord (Luke 24:34), followed by Jesus's ascension into heaven (Luke 24:50–53). Acts programmatically begins with a similar ascension story (Acts 1:6–11). This emphasis upon Jesus's ascension is especially striking since Luke and Acts are the only New Testament works to narrate this scene. Jesus's departure was not meant to emphasize his absence from his disciples. Instead, it signified his heavenly exaltation and rule.

Despite appearances, Jesus remains a central figure in Acts. While Jesus sat enthroned in heaven, ruling as God's agent, he remained present on earth through the preaching of the gospel (Acts 4:30, 13:26), the work of the Holy Spirit (Acts 16:7), his disciples exorcising demons (Acts 16:18), and his embodiment in the lives of his followers (Acts 9:5).[8] As a character, Jesus regularly appeared in the story, providing direct revelation and guidance (Acts 1:1–11, 9:3–6, 9:10–16, 16:7, 18:9–10, 22:7–8, 22:10, 22:18–21, 23:11, 26:14). Invoking power in the "name" of Jesus is particularly important for Acts (Acts 2:21, 3:6, 4:12, 6:18, 10:43). His disciples prayed in the "name" of Jesus (e.g., Acts 4:24–31). Sins were forgiven (Acts 10:43), and people were saved through Jesus's "name" (Acts 4:12, 16:31). Jesus's disciples experienced his presence during the Lord's Supper held in his "name" (Acts 2:46, 20:7, 20:11, 27:35; cf. Matt. 18:20; John 20:19–29).

---

[4]For parallels between Acts and Paul's letters, see Fitzmyer, *Acts*, 134–35. Also see Vielhauer, "On the 'Paulinism' of Acts," 33–50; Toney, "Paul in Acts," 242–53. However, there is much debate about the relationship between Paul's letters and Acts.

[5]Fitzmyer, *Acts*, 103–9. See also, Bruce, *Speeches in the Acts*; Talbert, *Reading Acts*, 29–30. There are twenty-eight speeches in Acts, including ten by Paul, eight by Peter, and one by Jesus.

[6]For the parallels between the lives of Jesus, Peter, and Paul, see Toney, "Paul in Acts," 239–61.

[7]Apologetics is popularly understood as the defense of the Christian faith.

[8]MacRae, "Whom in Heaven Must Receive Until the Time," 151–65.

Ascension of Jesus by John Singleton Copley. Museum of Fine Arts, Boston. (1775)

ACTS

- The Gospel Is Preached in Jerusalem (1:1–8:3)
  - Prologue Addressed to Theophilus (1:1–3)
  - Jesus's Ascension and Commission of the Disciples (1:4–11)
  - The Twelve Restored and Pentecost (1:12–2:47)
  - Peter and John's Miracles and Sanhedrin Trials (3:1–5:42)
  - The Persecution of Believers Begins with Stephen's Martyrdom (6:1–8:3)
- The Gospel Message Extends to Judea and Samaria (8:4–12:25)
  - Philip's Mission to Samaria and the First Gentile Convert (8:4–40)
  - Saul's Encounter with Christ on the Damascus Road (9:1–30)
  - Peter and the Conversion of Cornelius's Household (9:31–11:18)
  - The Beginning of the Church in Antioch (11:19–30)
  - Agrippa I Kills James and Arrests Peter (12:1–25)
- The Gospel Is Proclaimed to the Ends of the Earth (13:1–28:31)
  - Paul's First Mission (13:1–14:28)
  - Jerusalem Council (15:1–35)
  - Paul's Second Mission (15:36–18:22)
  - Paul's Third Mission (18:23–21:16)
  - Paul's Imprisonment and Trip to Rome (21:17–28:31)

In Acts, Jesus moves to the center of the proclamation of the gospel (e.g., Acts 5:42, 8:5, 8:35, 9:20, 11:20, 17:3, 28:31). In the Third Gospel, Jesus proclaimed the gospel as the coming kingdom of God (Luke 4:43). Acts equates Jesus's life, death, resurrection, and ascension with this gospel of God's reign (Acts 8:12, 19:8, 20:25, 28:23, 28:31).[9] Salvation involved Jesus establishing a new covenant between God and humanity (Acts 3:19–23; cf. Acts 7:37; Deut. 18:15–16). Like Luke's Gospel, Acts connects salvation with God as a benefactor (Acts 10:38; cf. Acts 4:8).[10] As a benefactor, God provides present benefits, including the forgiveness of sins and the power of the Holy Spirit (Acts 2:11). He also provides future benefits, including eternal life (Acts 13:48) and deliverance from final judgment (Acts 2:19–21).

Acts uniquely emphasizes Jesus's resurrection and exaltation over his suffering and death for bringing salvation. Acts 2:34–35 quotes Psalm 110:1 to interpret Jesus's ascension as proof that God exalted Jesus both as "Lord and Messiah" (Acts 2:36). Acts provides regular reminders of Jesus's rule, calling him "Lord Jesus" (e.g., Acts 1:21, 4:33, 8:16, 9:17, 15:11, 28:31) and "Lord" (e.g., Acts 1:6, 9:1, 11:16, 22:10, 23:11, 26:15). Jesus was the rightful Lord who poured out the Spirit upon his people (Acts 2:34–35; cf.

[9] Franklin, *Christ the Lord*, 29–47.
[10] Danker, *Jesus and the New Age*, 28–46, 82–89.

Luke 3:16). Although Jesus's authority was felt in the present, it was incomplete, and believers faced opposition while spreading the gospel. However, Acts looks forward to a future when Jesus's rule will be complete (Acts 3:20–21).[11]

The Power of the Holy Spirit

Readers of Acts cannot help but notice all the activity of the Holy Spirit throughout the work. Some readers have suggested the work should be called "The Acts of the Holy Spirit."[12] By the power of the Holy Spirit, the church spread from Jerusalem to Rome (Acts 2:33, 3:13–16, 5:31–32, 7:55, 7:56, 7:59, 10:40–45, 13:2–4, 19:21, 20:22–23, 21:11). Early believers were guided by the Holy Spirit (Acts 8:29, 8:39, 10:19, 11:12, 13:2–4, 16:6–7, 19:21, 20:22–23, 20:28).[13] The Spirit was with the church because of Jesus's heavenly exaltation (Acts 1:8, 2:33). In fact, the Spirit conveyed Jesus's presence so much that it was called the "Spirit of Jesus" (Acts 16:7).[14]

Public Domain (Getty Images)

This book of benedictions from Regensburg, Germany, illustrates the apostles receiving the Holy Spirit at Pentecost. At left center in the top row is Peter, gray and balding. Paul, anachronistically, sits at the right center in the top row. (ca. 1030-40)

Just as Jesus's ministry began after he was baptized by the Holy Spirit (Luke 3:21–22), the disciples' mission began after their baptism by the Spirit (Acts 2:1–13, 9:17–18). The coming of the Holy Spirit at **Pentecost** demonstrated God's presence with the early believers as he renewed his covenant (Joel 2:28–32; cf. Ezek. 36:26–27; Jer. 31:31–34). Pentecost, which occurred fifty days after the Passover, was a Jewish harvest festival (Acts 2:1; cf. Exod. 23:16, 34:22; Deut. 16:9–10; 2 Chron. 8:1). Pentecost was also linked with the giving of the law on Mount Sinai (Exod. 19–20; Jub. 1:1, 6:17–19, 14:20, 22:1–16).[15] Acts portrays Pentecost as a new Sinai where God was present with his people to renew his covenant. Just as God's presence was manifested by the burning bush and the pillar of fire in the exodus (Exod. 19:18), the "tongues of fire" among the disciples portray God's presence with the Spirit's coming (Acts 2:3). Similarly, the "wind" (*pneuma*) entering the house (Acts 2:2) echoes the creative "wind" or "Spirit" (Heb. *ruah*) of God in Genesis 1:2.

---

[11] Marshall, *Luke: Historian and Theologian*, 77–102, 157–95.

[12] Ehrhardt, "Construction and Purpose of the Acts," 55. There are sixty-two occurrences of "spirit" (*pneuma*) in Acts.

[13] But God also directed his people through prophets (Acts 11:28, 21:11), angels (Acts 5:19, 8:26, 10:3, 10:7, 10:22, 11:13, 12:7-10, 12:23, 27:23-24), and visions (Acts 10:3, 10:11–19, 11:5–10, 16:9–10).

[14] Reicke, "Risen Lord and His Church," 157–69.

[15] Fitzmyer, *Acts*, 234.

Peter declared that the pouring out of God's Spirit at Pentecost fulfilled the prophecy of Joel 2:28–32. This scene also echoed Ezekiel 36:26–27, where God promised to put his Spirit within his people so that they would obey his commands. Similarly, Jeremiah 31:31–34 spoke of a new covenant where God would write the law on his people's hearts. Giving the law was also connected to speech and flame by Philo (*Decalogue* 33), who wrote, "Then from the midst of the fire that streamed from heaven there sounded forth to their utter amazement a voice, for the flame became articulate speech in the language familiar to the audience, and so clearly and distinctly were the words formed by it that they seemed to see rather than hear them."

With the story of Pentecost, Acts portrays the Spirit's transfer from Jesus to his disciples as it did from Moses to Joshua (Deut. 34:9) and from Elijah to Elisha (2 Kings 9–14).[16] The disciples' baptism fulfilled the promises made by John the Baptist (Acts 1:5; Luke 3:16) and Jesus (Acts 2:23; Luke 11:13). Just as the Holy Spirit filled and anointed Jesus for ministry, his disciples were filled and anointed (Acts 2:1–13, 9:17–18; Luke 3:21–22, 4:1, 4:14). Just as the Spirit empowered Jesus to perform miracles, the disciples performed miracles, such as healing paralytics (Acts 5:17–26, 14:8–18; Luke 5:17–26), curing the sick and demon-possessed (Acts 5:13–14, 16:16–18, 28:7–10, 19:11–17; Luke 4:31–40, 8:43–48), and raising people from the dead (Acts 9:36, 20:7–12; Luke 7:11–17, 8:40–56). Just as the Spirit inspired Jesus's words, the disciples' speech was guided by the Spirit (Acts 1:8, 4:31, 6:10, etc.; Luke 4:18, 10:21).

Pentecost set the pattern for demonstrating God's activity among believers in Acts (Acts 2:1–13). Disciples joined the believing community through the public confession of Jesus as Lord and water baptism (Acts 5:12, 5:36, 8:36–38, 10:44–48, 16:13–15, 16:33).[17] Baptism was sometimes (Acts 2:38, 9:17–18, 10:47–48, 19:2–6) but not always (Acts 8:16) linked to the reception of the Holy Spirit. The presence of the Spirit was occasionally demonstrated by speaking in "**tongues**" (*glōssai*). In Acts, speaking in tongues involved speaking in a foreign language (Acts 2:6, 2:11).[18] Speaking in tongues confirmed God's activity at critical moments in Acts where the gospel spread among the Samaritans (Acts 8:14–17), Gentiles (Acts 10:44–48), and Paul's ministry (Acts 19:1–7).

Finally, we should highlight some of the contributions of Acts to our understanding of the Holy Spirit. While Jesus's anointing by the Holy Spirit in Luke was unique and part of his identity as God's Son, in Acts the presence of the Spirit joined the disciples to the family of God's Son. The Holy Spirit was personal as it spoke (Acts 10:19), called (Acts 13:2), was lied to (Acts 5:3), and was tested (Acts 5:9). The emphasis in Acts upon the Spirit conveying the presence of Christ is very similar to John 20:19–23. Although, we should also note that John recounts the initial coming of the Holy Spirit differently from Acts by having Jesus give the Holy Spirit directly to the disciples while they were in an upper room. The emphasis in Acts upon the Spirit's role in empowering the disciples for prophetic witness and works (Acts 1:8) is distinct from Paul's emphasis upon the moral aspect of the Spirit's presence (e.g., Gal. 5:22–23; Rom. 8:1–4). In addition, the understanding in Acts of "tongues" as a foreign language

[16] Stronstad, *Charismatic Theology*.

[17] Luke's theology of baptism is less developed than other New Testament writings (e.g., Rom. 6:1–14; 1 Pet. 3:18–22). Beasley-Murray, *Baptism in the New Testament*, 93–122.

[18] Barrett, *Acts*, 1:109.

(Acts 2:6, 2:11) is different from the spiritual gift of heavenly speech that required an interpreter, as found in Paul's letters (1 Cor. 13:1, 14:2, 14:9, 14:23).

A Community of Fellowship

The coming of the Holy Spirit forged the early Christians into a community. Nineteen times, Acts describes followers of Jesus as the "church" (*ekklēsia*, Acts 5:11, 8:1, 8:3, 9:31, 11:22, 12:1, 12:5, etc.)—that is, an assembly regularly meeting together. Luke presented the Jerusalem church as an idealized model of "fellowship" (***koinōnia***) that grounded its identity in the exalted Messiah and Lord. According to Aristotle (*Eth. nic.* 8.9.1), fellowship was essential to true friendship. In Acts 2:42, the believers' fellowship included listening to the apostles' teaching (cf. Acts 6:1–7, 11:1–18, 15:30–35, 20:7–12, 20:17–35), community prayer (cf. Acts 1:24, 4:24–30, 6:4, 12:5, 20:36), and the breaking of bread together (cf. Acts 2:46, 20:7, 20:11). This breaking of bread echoed Jesus's practice of table fellowship and alluded to celebrating the Lord's Supper. These shared meals also created a common household of faith.[19] Elsewhere, we learn that Christians sang and chanted hymns and songs during their fellowship gatherings (Col. 3:16; Eph. 5:19).

Another characteristic of this idealized community was members selling their possessions and caring for the poor (Acts 2:44–45, 4:32–37). This aligns with the portrayal in the Third Gospel of wealthy disciples caring for Jesus and the poor, and Jesus calling would-be disciples to sell everything (Luke 18:22–25). The selling of possessions in Acts was voluntary, even as generosity remained a theme, as seen by the collection for the Jerusalem church (Acts 11:27–30) and Paul's almsgiving (Acts 24:17). Through these acts of generosity, the early believing community fulfilled Greco-Roman ideals of friendship and the ideals in Jewish scriptures of covenantal obedience (Deut. 15:4–5).[20]

In Acts, as the early Christian movement traveled outside Jerusalem, believers were described as followers of "**the Way**" (*ho hodos*, Acts 9:2, 18:25–26, 19:9, 19:23, 24:4, 24:14, 24:22). In the eyes of other Jews, they were "Nazoraeans" (Acts 24:5). Acts presents these early Jewish believers as a "sect" (*hairesis*) of Judaism, not as a new religious movement (Acts 24:5, 24:14, 28:22). As a sect, they were part of Judaism, like other Jewish groups, such as the Sadducees and Pharisees (Acts 5:17, 15:5; cf. Josephus, *Ant.* 13.171; *Life* 10, 12, 191). In Acts, Paul made it a point that he shared similar views on the resurrection as the Pharisees (Acts 23:6–7), and some believers still identified themselves as Pharisees (Acts 15:5). Further, the disciples

According to Acts, followers of Jesus received the nickname "Christians" by people from Antioch (Acts 11:26). By the second century, early Christians used the symbol of the *Ichthys* (ΙΧΘΥΣ), which means "fish" and is an acronym in Greek for "Jesus Christ God's Son Savior" (Ἰησοῦς Χρῖστός Θεοῦ Υἱός Σωτήρ).

---

[19] Marshall, *Last Supper and Lord's Supper*; Lietzmann, *Mass and Lord's Supper*; Matson, "Eating and Drinking Whatever They Provide," 371–89; Esler, *Community and Gospel in Luke-Acts*, 84.

[20] Johnson, *Sharing Possessions*.

Acts records numerous voyages. Sailors favored staying near the coast whenever possible. This image of the Mediterranean coast illustrates the kinds of shorelines encountered by Paul and his companions.

still gathered in the temple (Acts 2:46, 3:1–26, 5:20–26, 5:42). James and the Jerusalem leadership commented that Jewish Christians were "zealous" for the Jewish law (Acts 21:20). Even Paul demonstrated obedience to the law by circumcising his Jewish disciple Timothy (Acts 16:3–4), fulfilling a Jewish vow (Acts 18:18), and participating in the rites of purification, including attempting to make a sacrifice in the temple (Acts 21:23–26).[21] Acts portrays Jewish believers remaining within the community of Israel by adhering to the ethnic markers of circumcision (Acts 11:2, 16:3), food laws (Acts 10:14), and the Jewish calendar (Acts 15:21, 20:16).

However, these early Jewish believers distinguished themselves from other Jewish sects by their assertion that Jesus of Nazareth was the Messiah who came, died, resurrected, and ascended as Lord (Acts 2:22–36, 28:31). Their missionary faith also made them different from other Jewish sects. Unlike the Pharisees and Sadducees, they actively sought adherents to join them (Acts 2:38–39, 3:17, 3:19, 3:26).[22] As this Jewish Christian movement went beyond Israel, it gained more Gentiles and became increasingly distinct from Judaism. Eventually, the residents of Antioch (who were known for giving nicknames) recognized this distinction and called them "**Christians**" (*Christianoi*, Acts 11:26; cf. Acts 26:28).[23]

Inclusion of Outsiders

In the Roman Empire, society had a clear social stratification that favored the wealthy and those with social power. However, Acts presents a concern for the poor and those without social status. In Acts, the ideal church sold possessions and cared for the poor (Acts 2:43–47). Joseph (whom we know by his nickname, **Barnabas**, which means "son of encouragement"), is praised for his generosity (Acts 4:32–37). In contrast, God killed Ananias and Sapphira for attempting to gain status through their false generosity (Acts 5:1–11). Leaders were appointed to help distribute food to widows (Acts 6:1–6).

[21] Paul's writings confirm his Jewish orthodoxy (Rom. 3:1–2; 1 Cor. 9:19–23; 2 Cor. 11:22; Phil. 3:4–6). However, Paul critiques the law as a means of salvation (13:38–39; cf. Phil. 3:7–11).

[22] Sevenster, *Roots of Pagan Anti-Semitism*, 201–18. But there is debate about how to understand Matthew 23:15.

[23] "Christian" is only used once outside Acts (1 Pet. 4:16).

When the people of Jerusalem experienced a famine, the Antioch church provided famine relief (Acts 11:29–30). Demonstrating his piety, Paul brought alms for the poor to the temple before his arrest (Acts 24:17).[24] Miracles also demonstrated God's care for the poor, like Peter's first miracle of healing a crippled beggar (Acts 3:1–10). Peter also raised from the dead Tabitha/Dorcas, who devoted herself to charity (Acts 9:36–43).[25]

Although part of a patriarchal society, the early church was also a place that elevated the status of women. Mary and other women prayed in the upper room along with the male disciples before Pentecost (Acts 1:14). Peter proclaimed that God's Spirit was poured out upon both women and men, fulfilling Joel's prophecy (Acts 2:17–18). Both women and men were part of the persecuted (Acts 8:3, 9:2, 22:4) but growing church (Acts 5:14, 8:12). In Pisidian Antioch, leading women and men turned against Paul and Barnabas (Acts 13:5), but Paul also converted leading women in Thessalonica (Acts 17:4) and Berea (Acts 17:12). Philip's four daughters, who were prophets (Acts 21:9), are mentioned alongside the prophet Agabus (Acts 21:10–11). Prominent women in the church are named, such as John Mark's mother, Mary, and her servant Rhoda (Acts 12:12–17), and Tabitha (also known as Dorcas, Acts 9:36–43).[26] Lydia was a patron of the church in Philippi (Acts 16:11–15). Priscilla (also known as Prisca) and Aquila were leaders in the church in Corinth (Acts 18:1–28; cf. Rom. 16:3). Thus, Acts portrays the church, as the new people of God, beginning to reverse the values of their society through concern for the poor and by including women.

God's Faithfulness to Israel

Acts opens with the disciples raising Jewish ethnocentric interests when they asked Jesus about restoring the "kingdom to Israel" (Acts 1:6). Their first action after Jesus's ascension was to symbolically restore the twelve tribes with their choice of Mattathias as the twelfth apostle (Acts 1:12–26). The first portion of Acts reflects their Jewish concerns, as it records the primary focus of the early church on its mission to Israel (Acts 1–7).

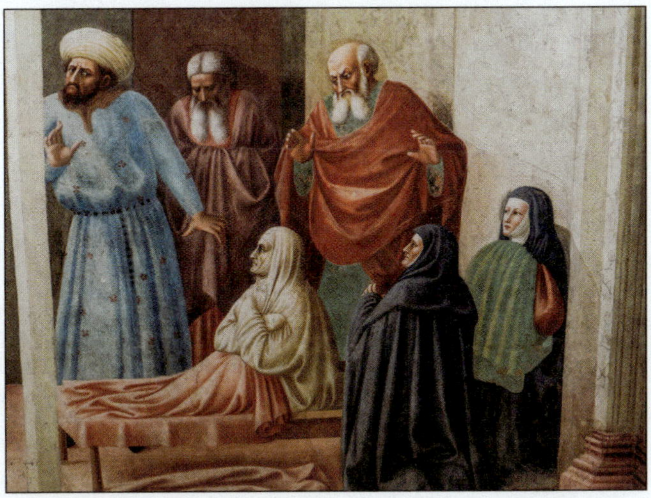

Detail from *Healing of the Cripple and Raising of Tabitha* by Masolino da Panicale. Church of Santa Maria del Carmine. Florence, Italy. (1425)

Peter with his speech at Pentecost aimed to share the gospel with his fellow Jews (Acts 2:14–36). He described the Spirit's coming as fulfilling Joel 2:28–32. Jesus's resurrection fulfilled Psalm 16:8–11. His ascension fulfilled Psalm 110:1. Acts highlights the growth of the church in Jerusalem by noting the conversion of thousands of Jews (Acts 2:41, 4:4; cf. Acts 2:47, 5:14, 6:1, 6:7, 21:20). Traditional opponents are described as becoming believers with comments like "a great many of the

---

[24] Downs, "Paul's Collection and the Book of Acts Revisited," 50–70.

[25] Reimer, *Women in the Acts of the Apostles.*

[26] Negatively, Sapphira (Acts 5:1–11).

Carl N. Toney

Facing the temple mount, Jews are buried on the Mount of Olives in anticipation of their final resurrection when the Messiah returns.

priests became obedient to the faith" (Acts 6:7) and "some of the believers who belonged to the sect of the Pharisees" (Acts 15:5). Stories of Jewish conversions are sprinkled through Acts (e.g., Acts 13:43, 14:1, 16:1, 17:1–4, 28:14–15). Acts concludes with Paul expressing the "hope of Israel" (Acts 28:20) among Jews in Rome who believed his message (Acts 28:24).

The early Jerusalem church concentrated its mission on national, ethnic Israel. They hoped to win over their fellow Jews by calling them to acknowledge past failures. They trusted God's promise of national forgiveness in response to this repentance. By restoring Israel, they believed that the salvation of the Gentiles would come about. Israel would be the messenger to the nations when its true vocation as God's servant was restored (Isa. 1:21–31, 4:2–6). This expectation is reflected in passages describing Jerusalem as the focal point of salvation where the Gentile nations come in the end time to seek the God of Israel (Isa. 2:2–4, 25:6, 49:6; Jer. 3:17; Zech. 8:20–23; cf. Tob. 14:6–7).[27]

However, God had other plans.

A Place for Gentiles

While the activities of the Jerusalem church still appear at significant moments in the last two-thirds of Acts (Acts 12:1–25, 15:1–29, 21:17–23:22), the narrative focuses upon the mission among the Gentiles.

[27] Gerhardsson, *Memory and Manuscript*, 214, 275-76; Munck, *Paul and the Salvation of Mankind*, 303-4; Jeremias, "Gentile World in the Thought of Jesus," 18-28.

Jesus responded to the disciples' question about the restoration of the "kingdom of Israel" (Acts 1:6) with his vision for a mission "to the ends of the earth" that included Gentiles (Acts 1:8).

The inclusion of Gentiles began with the persecution of the church in the wake of the murder of Stephen (Acts 7:1–8:3). Initially, Philip shared the gospel with the Samaritans, who were traditional enemies of Israel (Acts 8:4–25). The gospel also expanded into Africa through Philip's evangelization of an Ethiopian (Acts 8:26–40). This African was the first Gentile convert in Acts. In addition, he was a eunuch, a person usually excluded from the Israelite assembly (Deut. 23:2; Lev. 21:17–21; but see Isa. 56:3–4). His story challenged prejudice and spoke to the availability of the gospel to all people of all ethnicities.

Even more surprising, an identified persecutor of the church, Saul (Acts 8:1, 8:3), joined the Christian movement after encountering the resurrected Jesus on the **Damascus Road** (Acts 9:1–19, 22:1–21, 26:2–23).[28] Jesus called Saul to share the gospel among the Gentiles (Acts 9:15). Shortly after this event, we read about the conversion of the Roman centurion Cornelius and his household (Acts 10:34–48, 11:1–18, 15:7–11). Both the stories of Saul's call and the conversion of Cornelius's family were so significant for the Gentile mission that they are repeated three times. Following these stories, the Gentile church established itself in Antioch (Acts 11:19–25). These events marked the transition toward emphasizing the inclusion of the Gentiles on equal footing as part of the promises of God.

Public Domain

The Conversion of Saint Paul by Luca Giordano. Museum of Fine Arts in Nancy in Napels (1690). The motif of Saul falling off a horse was introduced around the twelfth century.

[28] There is a debate about whether Paul received a prophetic call or was converted. Hedrick, "Paul's Conversion/Call," 415–32; Talbert, *Reading Acts*, 83–90; Gaventa, *From Darkness to Light*. On the importance of his call, see Kim, *Origin of Paul's Gospel*. Conversion stories are about one-fourth of Acts. Matson, *Household Conversion Narratives*, 11, 15.

According to Acts, Paul took three missionary journeys and one final trip to Rome.

The majority of the last portion of Acts is dominated by Saul's missionary journeys among the Gentiles (Acts 13:1–14:28, 15:31–21:16). During a time of worship, the Holy Spirit prompted the Antioch church to send Barnabas and Saul on their first missionary journey (Acts 13:1–3). They took Barnabas's cousin John Mark and traveled to Cyprus (Acts 11:20). Several significant events occurred during this journey. First, in Cyprus, Saul moved to the head of the emerging missionary movement after converting the proconsul Sergius Paulus (Acts 13:4–12). Second, readers learn that Saul's Greek name was Paul (Acts 13:9), and Acts shifts to using this name for the apostle.[29] Third, John Mark left the team (Acts 13:13) as the mission expanded into Asia Minor (modern-day Turkey) in the cities of Pisidian Antioch, Iconium, Lystra, and Derbe (Acts 13:14–14:28). Fourth, Paul gave his first sermon to the Jews of Pisidian Antioch (Acts 13:16–41), which paralleled Peter's first speech at Pentecost (Acts 2:14–39). Fifth, Paul faced Jewish opposition (Acts 13:50), which plagued his ministry and ultimately led to his arrest in Jerusalem (Acts 22:27–36). Sixth, the pattern of Paul's missionary activity was established when he began sharing the gospel with his fellow Jews before moving on to the Gentiles (Acts 13:46).

The programmatic **Jerusalem Council** occurred between Paul's first two missionary journeys (Acts 15:1–31). The influx of Gentiles from the success of Paul and Barnabas's initial mission raised questions regarding how Gentiles should be included in the promises of God. The Pharisees, representing Jewish Christians, expected Gentiles to follow the traditional conversion pathway through circumcision and following the law (Acts 15:1, 15:5). This was not meant as a works-based requirement. Instead, the logic was that Jesus was a Jewish Messiah, so one must join the Jewish people to enjoy the benefits of salvation. However, after hearing the testimony of Peter, Paul, and Barnabas, the council decided that Gentiles did not need to become Jews first. Rather, they must avoid offensive practices that kept Jews

[29] However, whenever Paul recounts his Damascus Road encounter, he reverts to using Saul (Acts 22:6–16, 26:12–18).

from associating with Gentiles, including eating idol food, engaging in sexual immorality, eating strangled meat, and consuming blood (Acts 15:20, 23–29; cf. Acts 21:25).[30]

After the council recognized that the gospel should not be bound to ethnic identity, Paul returned to his missionary activities among the Gentiles. Unfortunately, Paul and Barnabas split up because of a disagreement over allowing John Mark to rejoin the team (Acts 15:36–39). Paul recruited Silas to accompany him as he revisited the churches in Asia Minor (Acts 15:40–16:5). In Lystra, Timothy joined the team (Acts 16:3). After traveling to the northern part of the Galatian province (Acts 16:6), Paul's mission expanded into Macedonia and Greece. His team shared the gospel in Philippi, Thessalonica, and Berea (Acts 16:7–17:15). In Athens, Paul shared the gospel at Mars Hill. His audience of Stoic and Epicurean philosophers rejected the gospel when he began to speak about the resurrection of Jesus (Acts 17:32–34). Because the Stoics believed that salvation involved a release from the cycle of rebirth, and because the Epicureans did not believe in an afterlife, Paul's resurrection message was not good news. Ultimately, Paul's team stayed in Corinth for eighteen months after the proconsul Gallio declared their religious practices to be legal (Acts 18:1–18). Finally, Paul returned to Antioch and Jerusalem (Acts 18:19–23).

On his final missionary journey, Paul spent about three years (Acts 20:31) in Ephesus (Acts 9:1–41).[31] Paul used Ephesus as a home base for upbuilding churches in Asia Minor, Macedonia, and Greece, as well as for dealing with problems in Corinth (Acts 20:1–6). After a successful work among the Gentiles, Paul returned to Jerusalem (Acts 21:15–25). This influx of Gentiles continued to bother the Jerusalem

Carl N. Toney

Stadium and coastline at Caesarea Maritima where Paul was imprisoned for two years.

[30]These obligations are like the Noahic covenant (Gen. 9:1–4; cf. Lev. 17:13; b. Sanh. 58b). They also fit with Jewish stereotypes of Gentiles as sexually immoral idolaters (e.g., Let. Aris. 152; Josephus, *Ag. Ap.* 2.199; Philo, *On Abraham* 135–36).

[31]Acts provides a range of dates for Paul's time in Ephesus from two and a quarter (Acts 19:8–10) to three years (Acts 20:31). For the sake of simplicity, this time will be described as "about three years."

church, especially James. They were concerned by a rumor that Paul was telling Jewish Christians to stop following the law (Acts 21:20–21). To prove his orthodoxy, Paul was asked to sponsor a purification ceremony in the temple (Acts 21:22–26). Ironically, while Paul attempted to show his obedience to the law, he was arrested because of a rumor started by his Jewish opponents from Asia Minor that he was violating the law by bringing a Gentile into the temple (Acts 21:27–31).

The last portion of Acts focuses on Paul's arrest (Acts 21:26–22:30). Unlike modern times, imprisonment was not usually used as punishment. Instead, it was intended to secure a person until trial, to coerce a confession, or to confine the guilty until their punishment. Military authorities administered the prison system. Often, prisoners were deprived of food and sleep, crowded in confined spaces with poor ventilation and sanitation, and subject to violence from other prisoners.[32]

Paul's arrest allowed him to share the gospel with the Sanhedrin and several Roman prefects while imprisoned in Jerusalem and Caesarea for two years (Acts 23:1–26:32). Like the Athenian philosophers, the Sanhedrin rejected Paul's gospel when he spoke about the resurrection of Jesus (Acts 23:1–10).[33] The Roman prefects were not interested in Paul's release, so Paul decided to appeal to Nero Caesar for justice. This resulted in Paul being sent to Rome and remaining for two years under house arrest (Acts 27:1–28:31). With Paul's arrival in the capital of the empire, Acts portrays Jesus's commission as being fulfilled (Acts 1:8). His disciples had carried the gospel from Jerusalem to Judea and Samaria and to the ends of the earth.

Racism and the Church

Racism, meaning prejudice against others based on race or ethnicity, is not a new problem. Like any sin, racism can include individual, communal, institutional, and spiritual dynamics. Some consider racism a sin of commission (acting inappropriately) as well as omission (failing to act). Others add that racism can be intentional but may also result from unintentional blind spots. Modern solutions have included highlighting the unity of humanity (sometimes described as being "colorblind"), celebrating multicultural diversity, challenging power structures, and calling for gospel-centered justice, reconciliation, and mutual accountability.[34]

The early church struggled with racism and lived in a world with racial prejudice. The Greeks called those who could not speak their language "barbarians" because they were considered uncultured and their words sounded like "bar-bar" gibberish (e.g., 1 Cor. 14:11). Roman prejudice against Jews included accusations of atheism (meaning the Jews did not worship the Roman gods), hating other races (because of laws that separated Jews from Gentiles), promoting vices through their teaching, and not providing any positive contribution to society (Josephus, *Ag. Ap.* 2.145–48).[35]

---

[32] Rapske, *The Book of Acts and Paul in Roman Custody.*

[33] The Sadducees did not believe in resurrection, and the Pharisees only believed in a final resurrection, so Jesus's resurrection did not fit either of their systems.

[34] Yancey, *Beyond Racial Gridlock: Embracing Mutual Responsibility*, 19–87, 138–50. A helpful book for addressing racism is McPherson, *The Third Option.* See also McCaulley, *Reading While Black.*

[35] Even Jewish origins were slandered. According to Josephus (*Ag. Ap.* 1.227–87, 288–303, 304–20), the Egyptians Manetho, Chaeremon, and Lysimachus claimed the Jewish people were lepers banished from Egypt.

Jewish prejudice was expressed by categorizing anyone who was not a Jew as a "Gentile" (*ethnos*; Heb. *goyim*, e.g., Ps. 2:1; Lev. 26:33; Isa. 11:10; Matt. 5:47, 18:17). Gentiles were considered idolatrous, sexually immoral, and impure sinners (Acts 10:28, 15:20, 15:29; 1 Cor. 6:9–11). The early church adopted the categories of Jews and Gentiles (e.g., Rom. 2:14; 1 Cor. 1:23, 5:1). But the gospel was also intended to bring about racial reconciliation (Rom. 1:16–17; 1 Cor. 1:22–24) and to fulfill the hope of bringing salvation to all nations (e.g., Pss. 22:7, 22:67; Isa. 49:6, 56:6–8, 60:1–3, 66:18–23; Jer. 16:19–21; Zech. 2:11; Mal. 1:11).

Despite Jesus's command to make disciples of the nations (Matt. 28:19–20) and his charge to take the gospel to the ends of the earth (Acts 1:8), the early Jewish church struggled with how to include non-Jews. However, Acts also provides a glimmer of what it looks like to include Gentiles. Acts attributes Philip as being responsible for converting the first Gentile, an African eunuch (Acts 8:26–40). Peter converted the first Gentile family of Cornelius after receiving a vision from God (Acts 10, 11, 15). Antioch was the first church established in a Gentile city (Acts 11:19–30). Paul, Barnabas, and Silas were the first missionaries to share the gospel among the Gentiles (Acts 12–14, 16–22).

Carl N. Toney

Inscriptions such as this forbade Gentiles from entering the temple beyond the court of the Gentiles. Israel Museum.

With the influx of non-Jews into the early church, questions were raised about how to include the Gentiles as part of God's people. One approach required Gentiles to join Judaism through circumcision and observing the law (cf. Acts 15:1–2, 15:5). In response, the Jerusalem Council only required Gentiles to avoid idolatry and sexual immorality (Acts 15:20, 15:28–29). Ultimately, the church adopted Paul's position, which allowed observant Jews to follow the law, while Gentiles (and some Jews) were free from observing the law, because their salvation and common identity were found in Christ (1 Cor. 12:13; Gal. 3:28; Col. 3:11). Paul used several metaphors for this "diverse-unity," including branches in an olive tree (Rom. 11:17–24), one body with many parts (Rom. 12:5; 1 Cor. 12:12–31; Eph. 1:23, 4:4, 4:12–16; Col. 1:18), and one temple built with various stones (Eph. 2:20–22).

The book of Revelation concludes the New Testament by casting a vision of hope for diversity and racial harmony in God's kingdom, where a heavenly multitude from "from every nation, from all tribes and peoples and languages, stand before the throne and before the Lamb" worshiping God (Rev. 7:9). The work ends with a new heaven and earth, with people from all nations walking in the light of God's glory (Rev. 21:24–26).

Carl N. Toney

Parthenon in Athens. Paul's travels sharing the gospel included engaging with the Stoic and Epicurean philosophers of Athens.

A Community for Everyone

Acts aims to portray the salvation of both Jews and Gentiles. Certainly, in the opening chapters of Acts, many Jews accepted the gospel (Acts 1–7). However, by the end of the story, salvation seems to have moved from the Jews to the Gentiles. Before his death, Stephen foresaw the Jewish rejection of the gospel during his martyrdom (Acts 7:2–53). Stories of the Jewish opposition to the gospel are regularly featured in the last two-thirds of Acts (e.g., Acts 13:50, 14:19, 17:13). Paul's missionary pattern of witnessing to the Jews first and then the Gentiles can be understood as a response to Jewish rejection and persecution (Acts 13:13–52, 18:6–7, 28:25–28). Finally, Acts ends with Paul describing Israel as never understanding and salvation being given to the Gentiles (Acts 28:25–28).

However, the Jewish rejection of the gospel in Acts is not nearly as bleak as we may perceive. First, the stories of Jewish rejection must be balanced by similar stories of Gentiles rejecting the gospel (e.g., Acts 14:19, 17:32). More importantly, there are consistent stories of Jewish acceptance of the gospel (e.g., Acts 13:43, 14:1, 16:1, 17:1–4). Second, Paul's missionary pattern should be understood in light of his Damascus Road calling to be a witness to both Jews and Gentiles (Acts 9:15, 22:15, 26:17).[36] His mission to both Jews and Gentiles aligned with the hope of Israel to regather those Jews spread

[36] Interpreters debate whether to understand Paul's Damascus Road experiences as a "call" (a commissioned apostle), "conversion" (an opponent turned ally), or "conquest" (an overpowered enemy). Talbert, *Reading Acts*, 83–90.

among the Gentile nations (e.g., Isa. 11:10–16, 27:12–13; Jer. 23:3–4, 29:14; Zech. 10:8–12). Third, Paul's final words in Acts 28:25–28 are a quote from Isaiah 6:9–10. They were not a blanket statement about the rejection of Israel. Rather, Paul evoked Isaiah as a prophetic warning and an evangelistic appeal to change.[37]

In Acts, the church grew from a sect of Judaism to a global movement where God's promises included both Jews and Gentiles (e.g., Acts 9:15–16, 26:16–18, 28:20, 28:28). By the end of the story, Acts presents a church that consists of a mixture of Jews and Gentiles. Acts emphasizes how the gospel crosses racial, social, and gender boundaries. Acts makes significant steps toward dismantling racism, classism, and sexism with targeted stories that highlight the inclusion of Gentiles, the poor, and women in the promises of God. No longer was salvation linked with ethnicity or prejudice. For Luke-Acts, God's promises are available for everyone who wishes to acknowledge the exalted reign of Christ. Acts ends with Paul boldly proclaiming in the heart of the Roman Empire Jesus's gospel of the kingdom of God and the lordship of Jesus the Messiah (Acts 28:31).

Key Terms and People

Barnabas: the nickname of Joseph, a leader of the early church and Paul's traveling companion on his first missionary journey
Christian: the name of Christ followers, given by the people of Antioch
Cornelius: the Gentile convert whom God used to convince Peter and the Jerusalem Council to accept the salvation of Gentiles
Damascus Road: where Paul was changed from being a persecutor to being a disciple of Jesus
Jerusalem Council: this meeting determined that Gentiles could follow Jesus without practicing the law
Koinōnia: means "fellowship" and was the essence of true friendship; early Christian gatherings were known for teaching, reading scriptures, communal prayer, communal meals, sharing possessions, and singing hymns
Pentecost: the event in Acts when the Holy Spirit was poured out on God's people for the first time
Stephen: the first Christian martyr
The Way: the name in Acts for the early Christian movement
Tongues: Spirit-inspired language; it is a foreign language in Acts and heavenly speech requiring an interpreter in Paul's writings

Conversation Starters

1. Who are some of the major characters that appear in Acts? What do their stories teach us?
2. Why is Jesus's resurrection and exaltation so important in Acts, especially in terms of salvation?
3. What is the significance of Pentecost? What is the role of the Holy Spirit in Acts?

---

[37] Johnson, *Acts*, 473–76.

4. What are some characteristics of Luke's ideal Christian community? What is the significance of fellowship and sharing of possessions?
5. How is Christianity presented as both a sect of Judaism but also as a distinct movement?
6. How does Acts portray God being faithful to keep his promises to Israel both in terms of salvation and judgment?
7. How are Gentiles included in the promises to Israel? Why is this faithfulness to Israel important for God's promises to Gentiles?
8. What lessons can we learn from the inclusion of outsiders in Acts? How does the gospel message present solutions to racism, classism, and sexism?

FOR FURTHER READING

Alexander, Loveday. *Acts*. The Daily Bible Commentary 5. Hendrickson, 2007.

Fernando, Ajith. *Acts*. NIV Application Commentary. Zondervan, 1998.

Fitzmyer, Joseph. *The Acts of the Apostles: A New Translation with Introduction and Commentary*. AYB 31. Yale University Press, 2008.

Gaventa, Beverly. *The Acts of the Apostles*. Abingdon New Testament Commentaries. Abingdon, 2003.

Gupta, Nijay K. *Strange Religion: How the First Christians Were Weird, Dangerous, and Compelling*. Brazos, 2024.

Jennings, Willie James. *Acts*. Belief. Westminster John Knox, 2017.

Johnson, Luke Timothy. *Sharing Possessions: What Faith Demands*. 2nd ed. Eerdmans, 2011.

———. *The Acts of the Apostles*. SP 5. Liturgical Press, 2006.

Longenecker, Bruce. *The Lost Letters of Pergamum: A Story from the New Testament World*. Baker Academic, 2003.

Talbert, Charles. *Reading Acts: A Literary and Theological Commentary on the Acts of the Apostles*. Rev. ed. RNT. Smyth & Helwys, 2005.

Websites for Exploring the Roman Empire

Barrett, David. *BibleMapper: Premier Digital Bible Map Resources*. https://biblemapper.com.

Rasmussen, Carl. *Holy Land Photos*. https://holylandphotos.org.

Scheidel, Walter, and Elijah Meeks. *The Stanford Geospatial Network Model for the Roman World*. https://orbis.stanford.edu.

PART TWO

THE FAITH OF GOD

Pauline Christianity

6

PAUL BEGINS TO WRITE

1-2 Thessalonians

An Introduction to Paul

After Jesus, Paul is the second most influential figure in Christianity. He is attributed to writing thirteen of the twenty-seven works of the New Testament. This material accounts for nearly one-third of the New Testament. So, what do we know about Paul?

"**Paul**" (*Paulos*; Lat. *Paullus*) was his Roman family name (Lat. *cognomen*), and it means "small." Roman citizens had a three-part name (Lat. *tria nomina*), which included a personal name given by their parents (Lat. *praenomen*), a clan name (Lat. *nomen*), and the name of the family branch within the clan (Lat. *cognomen*). He was also known by his Jewish name, "Saul" (*Saulos*; Heb. *sha'ul*), which means "asked of God" (Acts 13:9). He was named after the most famous person in his tribe of Benjamin, the first king of Israel, King Saul (1 Sam. 9:1–31:13; 1 Chron. 9:35–10:14).

SUGGESTED READING

Acts 17:1-15
1 Thessalonians
2 Thessalonians

Despite the rumors, God did not change his name from Saul to Paul on the Damascus Road (Acts 9:1–19, 22:1–21, 26:2–23). In fact, Acts continues to use his Jewish name, Saul, after this experience (Acts 7:58–13:9). The shift from Saul to Paul occurred after he took over the leadership of the Gentile mission and worked among Greek speakers (Acts 13:9). One reason that he may have preferred to use Paul among Greek speakers was because the Hebrew name sounded similar to the Greek word *saulos*, which referred to the "loose, wanton gait of courtesans." Others have speculated that Paul took his name from his first Gentile convert, Sergius Paulus, the proconsul of Cyprus (Acts 13:7, 13:12).[1] He used his Roman name, Paul, in his letters because he was addressing an audience that spoke Greek.

Paul was born in Tarsus to a wealthy Jewish family that gained Roman citizenship (Acts 16:37–38, 21:39, 22:3, 22:25–29).[2] His hometown was famous for being the birthplace of Zeno, the father of Stoicism.

[1] LSJ, 1586

[2] For chronologies of Paul's life, see Murphy-O'Connor, *Paul*, 1–31; Riesner, *Paul's Early Period*, 1–32, 318–26.

Image of Paul from a mosaic in the Basilica of San Vitale. Ravena, Italy.

In his writings, he often engaged with the contemporary version of this philosophy, especially when speaking about topics related to "virtue" (*aretē*), "conscience" (*syneidēsis*), and "desire" (*epithymia*).[3] The Stoics believed that a good life was guided by "reason" (*logos*), which helped a person overcome "passion" (*pathos*) and "desire" (*epithymia*) to live a virtuous life. However, Paul taught that a life guided by the Holy Spirit overcomes these things and produces Christian virtue (Gal. 5:16–26).

His Tarsus citizenship was not cheap. It required that his family maintain capital of at least five hundred drachmae (about $29,000; see Dio Chrysostom, *Or.* 34.23).[4] However, since becoming a Christ follower, he lived a much humbler life, working with his own hands as a "tentmaker" (*skēnopoios*, Acts 18:3, 20:34–35). Paul traveled through the Roman Empire making and repairing leather tents. This trade gave him great mobility and independence so that he could share the gospel.[5]

Paul's Roman citizenship proved useful in his travels. When he entered a new city, the population often became suspicious of his "new" eastern Jewish religion. At times, he was brought before local magistrates and accused of civic unrest, misanthropy, and disloyalty to the empire (e.g., Gal. 1:17; 2 Cor. 11:21–33). Sometimes, he convinced Roman rulers like Sergius Paulus in Cyprus (Acts 13:4–12) and Gallio in Corinth (Acts 18:12–17) that his beliefs merely reflected a sect of Judaism, which meant that he was promoting a legal religion. (All religions were required to get legal sanctions from the Roman Empire, and new religions were often looked on with suspicion.) At other times, like in Philippi, Paul couldn't convince the civic leaders of the legality for Christians to practice their beliefs. So, as a leader, he was beaten and thrown in jail. Only his Roman citizenship saved him (Acts 16:16–40).

He was raised as a devout Jew and was educated under the great rabbi Gamaliel (Acts 22:3; Phil. 3:5; cf. Acts 5:34). As the son of a Pharisee, Paul practiced the law like the Pharisees (Acts 23:6; cf. Acts 26:5; Phil. 3:5). However, everything changed for him on the Damascus Road (Acts 9:1–19, 22:1–21, 26:2–23). Paul received his apostolic calling from Jesus (1 Cor. 9:1, 15:8–10; 2 Cor. 4:6; Gal. 1:15–16; Phil. 3:4–10).[6] While he had been an enemy of Christ who had persecuted the church, he was now led as a prisoner

---

[3] Sevenster, *Paul and Seneca*, 152–56; Engberg-Pedersen, *Paul & the Stoics*; Malherbe, *Paul and the Popular Philosophers*; deSilva, "Paul and the Stoa," 563–64. Paul doesn't use the word "virtue" (*aretē*), but he does compose virtue lists (e.g., Gal. 5:22–23). More will be said about Paul's promotion of Christian virtues below under 1–2 Thessalonians, as well as the chapters on Galatians and 1 Corinthians.

[4] A Greek drachma was equivalent to a Roman denarius, which was one day's wage. Assuming a federal government standard rate of $7.25 per hour, this would be the equivalent of $58 per day.

[5] Hock, *Tentmaking and Apostleship*; Barnett, "Tentmaking," 925–27.

[6] On the debate among framing Paul's Damascus Road experience as a "call," "conversion," or "conquest," see Talbert, *Reading Acts*, 83–90.

of Christ in his triumphal procession throughout the Roman Empire as he shared the gospel (1 Cor 15:8–10; 2 Cor 2:14–17). Some people mistakenly think that Paul converted from one religion, Judaism, to a new religion, Christianity. However, Paul understood that Christ came to fulfill the Jewish hopes (Gal. 3:15–29; Rom. 15:8–9).[7]

Others mistakenly think that Paul realized that he was not good enough to earn his salvation from God through good deeds.[8] They think that Paul rejected a legalistic law in favor of grace. However, if you read Paul's writings carefully, you'll discover that he considered himself blameless and righteous according to the Mosaic law (Phil. 3:4–6; 2 Cor. 11:22). In fact, Paul thought the law was good and that the law was the best expression of God's will (e.g., Rom. 2:25, 3:1–2, 9:4–5, 14:5–6).

Instead, on the Damascus Road, Paul was confronted with a harder reality.[9] He had thought he was purging the heresy of Christ followers from his beloved Judaism (Phil. 3:6). His persecution of

Carl N. Toney

This street and shops in Pompeii illustrate the urban environment of Paul's travels.

[7]Stendahl, "Paul and the Introspective Conscience of the West," 78–96.

[8]This view is based on misunderstanding the "I" of Romans 7:7–25 as Paul. The statement "I was once alive apart from the law" (Rom. 7:9) could not have been Paul since a Jewish person always had the law in their life. Instead, Paul personified Gentile converts to Judaism with his "I" language. Alternatively, this could be written in the persona of Adam and Eve. Tobin, *Paul's Rhetoric*, 225–45.

[9]For the significance of the Damascus Road, see Kim, *Origin of Paul's Gospel*.

Christians was done out of zealous loyalty to God. However, in truth, he was the one standing under God's judgment because he had rejected the Messiah, Jesus. He encountered the resurrected Jesus on the Damascus Road and swore loyalty to him. In his letters, Paul expressed this loyalty by calling himself a "slave" (*doulos*) of Jesus (Rom. 1:1; Phil. 1:1; cf. James 1:1; 2 Pet. 1:1; Jude 1), and he declared Jesus to be his "Lord" or "Master" (*kyrios*, Rom. 1:7, 5:1; 1 Cor. 1:2; 2 Cor. 1:2; etc.).[10]

Paul considered himself an "**apostle**" (*apostolos*; lit. "sent one") to the Gentiles (Rom. 11:13; cf. 1 Tim. 2:7, 4:17), and his primary mission was among the "nations" (*ethnos*, Gal. 2:8–9). As an apostle, he received his commission from the resurrected Lord Jesus Christ to share the gospel (Rom. 1:1–5; 1 Cor. 1:1, 9:1–27; etc.). However, he still had an underlying heart for his own people. In fact, his Gentile mission aimed to "arouse my own people to envy and save some of them" (Rom. 11:14 NIV). In this way, he wished for "all Israel [to] be saved" (Rom. 11:26).

Some people thought Paul was inconsistent with his stance on the law (Gal. 5:11–12; cf. 1 Cor 9:19–23). Paul considered everyone free from the works of law (Gal. 2:14–21), and he fought against demanding that Gentile Christians follow these works (Gal. 5:1–10; cf. 1 Cor 9:21). However, he made allowances for Jewish Christians to practice the law, including circumcision, food laws, and observing the Sabbath (Rom. 14:1–15:13; Gal. 5:11–12). At times, Paul continued following the law as a witness to his fellow Jews (1 Cor. 9:20). In fact, Paul was arrested in the temple, where he was paying for sacrifices for the Nazarite vows of some Jewish Christians (Acts 21:23–24; cf. Num. 6:1–21). Ultimately, Paul believed that a Christ follower's actions were motivated by service to the lordship of Jesus Christ because he envisioned people under God's reign (Rom. 14:7–12), and he summarized the whole law with the command to love one's neighbor (Gal. 5:14; Rom. 13:10; Lev. 19:18).[11]

Letter Writing

After traveling throughout the Roman Empire and establishing new churches in major city centers, Paul discovered the need to maintain communication and to disciple his communities. Thus, he began to write letters.[12]

Letter writing was truly a remarkable technological achievement. While only 10 percent of the population knew how to read and write, most people had access to a "**scribe**" (Lat. *amanuensis*) or someone who could read or write for them.[13] Sometimes Paul would write his own letters (possibly Philem. 19), but other times he would use a scribe like Tertius (Rom. 16:22; cf. 1 Cor. 16:21; Gal. 6:11; 2 Thess. 3:17). The scribe would take shorthand notes as Paul dictated his thoughts. Then, the scribe would go back and complete his ideas, which Paul proofread before sending out a final copy (e.g., Jer. 36:4, 36:18). Paul's use of scribes helps to explain variations in the writing style between Paul's letters.

Following typical letter-writing practices, Paul kept a copy of each letter. This may have inspired the creation of the core of his letter collection that made its way into the New Testament.[14] While Paul

[10] The word "slave" (*doulos*) signifies that God was acting through the human agent, and "in this sense, 'slave' remains limited to a few people who are entrusted by God with special tasks in and for the church." Beare, *Philippians*, 51.

[11] Toney, *Paul's Inclusive Ethic*, 2, 54–56, 72–74, 194–95.

[12] For the process and cost of letter writing, see Richards, *First-Century Letter Writing*.

[13] Hezser, *Jewish Literacy in Roman Palestine*.

[14] Richards, *First-Century Letter Writing*, 156–61, 214–15.

AN OUTLINE OF PAUL'S LIFE

ca. 4 BCE	Birth of Jesus in Bethlehem
ca. 5 to 10 CE	Birth of Paul in Tarsus
30 or 33 CE	Crucifixion of Jesus
33-34 CE	**Damascus Road call (Gal. 1:15-16; Acts 9:1-22; etc.)**
33-36 CE	Paul in Arabia and Damascus (Gal. 1:17; 2 Cor. 11:32-33)
37 CE	Two-week visit to Jerusalem (Gal. 1:18-20; Acts 9:26-30)
37-46 CE	Barnabas brings Paul to Antioch (Gal. 1:21-22; Acts 9:30, 11:27-30)
46-47 CE	Visit to Jerusalem for famine relief (Acts 11:27-30, 12:25; Gal. 2:1-10?)
47-48 CE	**First mission: Cyprus and South Galatia (Acts 13:49-14:28)**
48 CE	Peter and the crisis in Antioch (Gal. 2:11-21) *Galatians?*
48-49 CE	**Jerusalem Council (Acts 15:1-30; *Gal 2:1-10?)**
49-51 CE	**Second mission: South and North Galatia, Asia Minor, Macedonia, Greece (Acts 15:36-18:22)**
49 CE	Claudius expels Jews from Rome (Acts 18:1-2)
50-51 CE	Corinth (eighteen months) and Gallio (Acts 18:1-18) *1 Thessalonians {*2 Thessalonians?}*
51-57 CE	**Third mission: North Galatia, Asia Minor, Macedonia, Greece (Acts 18:23-21:16)**
51-54 CE	Ephesus: center of Paul's mission (2.25-3 years) (Acts 19:1-41) **Galatians?*
Summer 53 CE	Paul is imprisoned in Ephesus (1 Cor. 15:32; 2 Cor. 1:8-11; Phil. 1:13)? **Philippians? *Philemon? {*Colossians? Ephesians?}*
Winter 54 CE	Paul is released and remains in Ephesus *1 Corinthians {Titus? 1 Timothy?}*
Fall 55 CE	Travels through Macedonia to Corinth (Acts 20:1-2) *2 Corinthians*
56-57 CE	Corinth (three months) (Acts 20:3) *Romans*
58-59 CE	**Temple arrest and imprisonment in Jerusalem and Caesarea (Acts 21:17-26:32)** *Philippians? Philemon? {Colossians? Ephesians?}*
60-62 CE	**Voyage to Rome and house arrest (Acts 27:1-28:31)** Traditional: *Philippians? Philemon? {Colossians? Ephesians?}*
62-64 CE	Option 1: Paul remains confined until execution {**2 Timothy?*} Option 2: Paul released; fourth mission to Spain until arrested again Traditional: {*1 Timothy? Titus? 2 Timothy?*}
64 CE or later	**Execution under Nero** Paul's disciples write: {*2 Thessalonians? Colossians? Ephesians? 1 Timothy? Titus? 2 Timothy?*}

? Indicates alternative dates | * Indicates dates chosen in this book | {} Indicates disputed authorship

The Apostle Paul by Rembrandt van Rijn. National Gallery of Art. Washington, DC. (c. 1657)

dispatched numerous letters, the early church collected only thirteen, which they deemed as inspired and worthy of study. One author even called Paul's writing "Scriptures" (2 Pet. 3:15–16). Paul's thirteen letters were arranged from longest to shortest in the New Testament. However, Paul's collection of thirteen letters does not compare to one of the greatest letter writers of all time, Marcus Tullius Cicero (ca. 106–43 BCE), who left behind 931 letters!

When Paul wrote, he didn't usually do it alone. Letter writing was a communal process for Paul. Often, he cowrote with others, such as Sosthenes (1 Cor. 1:1), Timothy (2 Cor. 1:1; Phil. 1:1; Col. 1:1; Philem. 1), and Silvanus (1 Thess. 1:1; 2 Thess. 1:1). Sometimes, out of authenticity concerns, Paul included a signature with his letters (1 Cor. 16:21; Gal. 6:11; Col. 4:18; 2 Thess. 3:17; Philem. 19). Sometimes, his greetings were from one church gathering to another (Gal. 1:1). With just a few strokes of a reed pen on a piece of papyrus or velum leather, Paul could convey his personal presence to people thousands of miles away.

Personal Presence

Paul was one of many people to think that letters were a useful tool to convey his presence. The great statesman and philosopher Cicero (*Fam.* 2.4.1, 12.30.1) considered a letter the means to speak with an absent friend and described a letter as a surrogate for actual dialogue. Likewise, Demetrius (*Eloc.* 223), who wrote an instructional manual on letter writing, regarded a letter as one side of a conversation. However, letter writing was not cheap. It could cost one to twenty denarii to produce a letter (or about one hundred to several thousand dollars)![15]

Like other authors, Paul entrusted his letters to letter carriers who were instructed to convey his tone, posture, and expressions to his audience. In this way, Paul's letters reflected his personality (Cicero, *Fam.* 16.16.2; Seneca, *Ep.* 40.1; Demetrius, *Eloc.* 227). Throughout his travels, Paul used a variety of letter carriers, such as Phoebe (Rom. 16:1–2) and Tychicus (Col. 4:7; cf. Eph. 6:21; 2 Tim. 4:12; Titus 3:12). When his letters were read, it was like a virtual reality experience, where his audience felt like he was standing there in their midst, directly addressing them. Although sometimes, his writings did a better job of conveying his presence and ideas. Some complained that "His letters are weighty and strong, but his bodily presence is weak, and his speech contemptible" (2 Cor. 10:10).

Public Domain

Reed stylus and ink well for writing from Tebtynis, Egypt. Museo Egizio. Turin, Italy. (first or second cent. CE)

Rhetoric

Paul didn't just write words on a page. His goal was to use the power of persuasion to convince his audience of his intentions.[16] Paul made

[15] These costs are based on the table of estimated costs in Richards, *First-Century Letter Writing*, 169, and it assumes the current federal minimum wage of $7.25 per hour.

[16] Introductions to rhetoric include Kennedy, *New Testament Interpretation through Rhetorical Criticism*; Witherington, *New Testament Rhetoric.*

Public Domain

St. Paul Preaching in Athens by Raphael. Victoria and Albert Museum, London. (1515)

rhetorical appeals using the three standard forms of argumentation set out by the great philosopher Aristotle in his *Art of Rhetoric*. Sometimes Paul used "logic" (*logos*), and other times he made "emotional" (*pathos*) appeals. At different times, he made appeals based on his "character" (*ethos*).

As Paul constructed his arguments, he had a rich rhetorical toolbox based on the examples of great rhetoricians like Aristotle, Cicero, and Quintilian.[17] Paul modeled some of his letters on the three common kinds of speeches, including (1) law-court speeches that had the purpose of accusing or defending, (2) deliberative speeches that functioned to persuade or dissuade, and (3) epideictic speeches that offered praise or blame (Aristotle, *Rhet.* 1.4–15).

One of the clearest examples of Paul writing his letters like a speech is the letter to the Galatians. Like any good speech, Galatians 1:6–10 begins with an "introduction" (*prooimion*; Lat. *exordium*) in order to secure the audience's goodwill and interest. Second, there is a "narration" (*diēgēsis*; Lat. *narratio*) of the points of dispute in Galatians 1:11–2:14. This leads to the "proposition" (*prothesis*; Lat. *propositio*, *partitio*, or *divisio*) or thesis statement in Galatians 2:14–21, which is the main idea that needed to be proven. This leads to the main body of the speech in Galatians 3:1–4:30, which consists of "proofs" (*pistis*; Lat. *probatio* or *confirmatio*) that are the arguments used to defend the thesis. A "refutation" (Lat. *refutatio*) of the opponent's arguments was sometimes included, but in Galatians, Paul replaced this with an "ethical exhortation" (Lat. *paraenesis*) in Galatians 5:1–6:10. Finally, the "conclusion" (*epilogos*; Lat. *peroratio*) in Galatians 6:11–18 summarizes the argument and makes a final emotional appeal to the audience.[18]

Epistle Form

All of Paul's writings begin with a letter's standard naming of the author and recipients. His opening greeting of "grace and peace" (e.g., Rom. 1:7; 1 Cor. 1:3; 2 Cor. 1:2) is a combination of the Jewish salutation of "peace" (*eirēnē*; Heb. *shalom*, Judg. 19:20; Num. 6:26) with "grace" (*charis*), an adaptation of the similar sounding Greek word for "greetings" (*charein*, Acts 15:23, 23:26; James 1:1). Paul was not alone in using this combined greeting. Other New Testament writers and other Jewish authors followed this practice (1 Pet. 1:2; 2 Pet. 1:2; with variants in 2 John 3; Jude 2; 2 Bar. 78.3).[19]

---

[17] Ancient rhetorical handbooks: Aristotle's *Art of Rhetoric*, Cicero's *On the Orator* and *On Rhetorical Invention*, Quintilian's *Institutes of Oratory* and *Rhetoric for Herennius*.

[18] See the influential study of Betz, *Galatians*, 14–25. For a series that interprets Paul's letters in light of Rhetoric, see the Socio-Rhetorical Commentaries by Ben Witherington III and David deSilva.

[19] "Thus speaks Baruch, the son of Neriah, to the brothers who were carried away in captivity: Grace and peace be with you" (2 Bar. 78.3).

Fresco of Greek dramatist Meander reading a scroll. Pompeii. (first cent. CE)

Carl N. Toney

Authorship and Pseudonymous Writings

For many of the New Testament works, we rely upon traditions to identify authorship. None of the Gospels specifically name their authors. However, tradition links Mark as Peter's scribe. Luke's "we" passages have been interpreted as being Luke, the traveling companion of Paul. Matthew was a former toll collector and apostle. John's "beloved disciple" was John of Zebedee.

Other works in the New Testament are also ambiguous. Hebrews does not name its author but is linked by tradition with Paul. The unnamed author of 1 John is linked with the elder in 2–3 John, who was thought to be John of Zebedee. Additionally, John of Patmos in Revelation is thought to be this same John.

More difficulty arises when a work names the author but scholars dispute its authorship based on thematic and stylistic differences. This is especially true when evaluating the thirteen letters of Paul and the two letters of Peter. It is also the case with the letters of James and Jude, which tradition has linked to the brothers of Jesus. When a literary work claims authorship by one person but was written by another, it is called a pseudonymous (lit. "false name") writing or **pseudepigraphy** (lit. "false writing").

Paul's writings can be divided according to scholars' views of his authorship. Seven letters are considered undisputed (Romans, 1–2 Corinthians, Galatians, Philippians, 1 Thessalonians, and Philemon), three are disputed (Ephesians, Colossians, and 2 Thessalonians), and three are thought not to be written by Paul and are called "Deutero-Pauline" (1–2 Timothy, Titus). Many scholars also consider 2 Peter not to be written by Peter.

Because the early church rejected many pseudonymous writings due to their false claims of authorship (e.g., Gospel of Thomas, Infancy Gospel of James), people argue that all the writings of the New Testament must have been written by the named author. Others have used the pseudonymous classification to lessen the authority of certain New Testament works by claiming the later church corrupted the teachings from the apostolic age. However, these are false dichotomies. All twenty-seven New Testament works are authoritative for Christians because they are in the Christian canon, so labeling a writing as pseudonymous should not diminish the canonical authority of the work. It is equally troubling to create a false privilege between primitive Christian material and later writings. If we follow this logic, then the earlier writings of Paul would have greater value than the later Gospel stories of Jesus.

Stylistic differences can be explained by an author using different scribes. Thematic differences may be attributed to different circumstances or the development of an author's thoughts. Another solution is to approach the concept of New Testament authorship that moves away from notions of individual authors toward the concept of "schools." We have a school of Paul, a school of Peter, a school of James, and a school of John. Each "school" is based on a community of disciples who were responsible for gathering and communicating their leader's teachings (e.g., John 21:24). A similar model is found in the prophetic schools, such as Isaiah and Jeremiah (e.g., Jer. 36:4, 36:18). A school could publish a work bearing its teacher's name, and it would draw upon its teacher's tradition and authority. As you read this book, we will briefly discuss the debates about authorship, and you will have to make your own decisions. These debates should not detract from the message and authority of each work.

When you read Paul's letters, it can be helpful to notice the typical pattern for letter writing in the New Testament.[20] Letters usually begin with an opening that includes greetings (e.g., Rom. 1:1–7; Phil. 1:1–2; Gal. 1:1–3; cf. 1 Pet. 1:1–2; 2 John 1–3). Next, many letters include a prayer of thanksgiving to secure the audience's goodwill (e.g., Rom. 1:8–15; Phil. 1:3–11; cf. 1 Pet. 1:3–12; 2 John 4). Then, letters may include a thesis statement at the beginning of the body of the letter (e.g., Rom. 1:16–17; Gal. 2:15–21; cf. 1 Pet. 1:6–9; 2 John 5–6). The body of the letter is where the main content is found, and the author provides evidence and arguments that include both theoretical and practical matters. Some people subdivide the body of the letter into the exposition (e.g., Rom. 1:16–11:36; Gal. 2:15–4:31) and exhortation (e.g., Rom. 12–15; Gal. 5:1–6:10). Finally, the letter's closing wraps everything up with some final greetings (e.g., Rom. 16; Gal. 6:11–18; cf. 1 Pet. 5:12–14; 2 John 12–13).

Carl N. Toney

Agora (central public space) and odeon (small theater) in Thessalonica. (second cent. CE)

While Paul followed the typical pattern of a New Testament letter, it can be useful to notice when he broke the pattern. For example, Romans 16 includes a lengthy closing greeting that name-dropped all sorts of people in the city so that the church could follow up with any of these people as character references. Interestingly, 1–2 Thessalonians and Galatians also break the pattern of having a thanksgiving. In 1–2 Thessalonians, Paul poured forth double thanksgivings because he was keenly interested in encouraging a discouraged congregation (1 Thess. 1:2–10, 2:13–16; 2 Thess. 1:3–12, 2:13–15). However, Galatians omits any words of thanksgiving; instead, Paul vented his frustration with them (Gal. 1:6–10).

Now that you know the basic patterns for writing letters, you should be able to follow the arguments of Paul and other New Testament letter writers with greater ease. And, if you're really lucky, when you close your eyes, you can imagine Paul's presence as he speaks to you from these pages.

1-2 Thessalonians

The Story So Far

Thessalonica was known as "the mother of all Macedonia" (Antiper, *Anthologia Palantia* 4.428), and it was in the northern portion of modern-day Greece. The city had a population of around sixty-five thousand to one hundred thousand people (Strabo, *Geogr.* 7 frag. 21; Lucian, *Asin.* 46.2). It was an important

[20] For an introduction to ancient letters, see Malherbe, *Ancient Epistolary Theorists*; Klauck, *Ancient Letters and the New Testament*, 183–206. Ancient handbooks that classified letters include Demetrius, *De elocutione* (ca. second cent. BCE to first cent. CE), Pseudo-Libanius, *Epistolary Styles* (ca. fourth to sixth cent. CE), and Bologna Papyrus 5 (third or fourth cent. CE).

center of trade, possessing one of the best harbors on the Aegean Sea and located on the major east–west trade route called the **Via Egnatia** (built around 130 BCE; Strabo, *Geogr.* 7.7.4). It is not a surprise that Paul choose to stop here and share his gospel because of how quickly it could disseminate throughout the region.

Thessalonica was an old city. It was founded in 316–315 BCE by the Greek general Cassander. He named the city after his wife, Thessaloniki, who was the stepsister of Alexander the Great. When the Romans took charge in 146 BCE, they recognized the importance of the city and made it the capital of the province of Macedonia. They granted it the privilege of being a "free city," which included minting their own coins, possessing tax exemptions, and having an independent government that included a Greek-style "council" (*boulē*), "assembly" (*dēmos*), and five or six "magistrates" (*politarchai*).

The Thessalonians expressed their loyalty to the empire with temples dedicated to Augustus and the goddess Roma. Other religious cults included those that worshiped Dionysius, the Egyptian gods Isis and Serapis, and Cabrius, a kingly figure who was murdered, divinized, and expected to return. Despite Roman rule, the Thessalonians maintained their Greek culture and identity with only a small percentage of people speaking Latin.

When Paul, Silas, and Timothy first arrived in the city, they stayed at Jason's house, and he helped them connect with the local synagogue (Acts 17:1–9).[21] This visit was part of Paul's second missionary journey. The church in Antioch sent Paul and Silas to share the gospel with Jews and Gentiles throughout the Roman Empire (Acts 15:36–41). Timothy joined the team in Lystra (Acts 16:1–5).

Carl N. Toney

Neapolis (modern-day Kavala) was the seaport Paul arrived at in Macedonia before going to Philippi and Thessalonica.

[21] Correlating the movements of Paul, Silas, and Timothy in Acts with 1–2 Thessalonians has some challenges. According to Acts 17:14–16 and 18:5, Paul was alone in Athens and Timothy joined him in Corinth. According to 1 Thessalonians 3:1–6, Timothy was sent from Athens back to Thessalonica. Here we are reminded that neither Paul's letters nor Acts provide a complete account of his travels. Bruce, *1 & 2 Thessalonians*, 60–61.

Order and Authenticity of the Thessalonian Letters

If you read 1–2 Thessalonians in one sitting, you may notice how similar these letters are in their structure and teaching. These are Paul's only letters with double thanksgivings, and both address a church struggling with their expectations about Christ's imminent return. It may also be surprising to read two letters written together in a very short span of time.

In light of these kinds of observations, some scholars speculate that a disciple of Paul wrote 2 Thessalonians using 1 Thessalonians as a model. They argue that the teaching about Christ's return changes in the letters, reflecting a later period (1 Thess. 4:13–5:11; 2 Thess. 2:1–12). However, this shift is exaggerated, and we see a greater difference in letters accepted as being written by Paul (2 Cor. 5:1–10; Phil. 1:22–26). They also consider the moralistic teaching to be different from Paul's other letters (2 Thess. 1:5–10, 2:12). But we should not expect all of Paul's letters to be the same since they addressed specific historical situations. Some scholars also argue that the "signature" in 2 Thessalonian 3:17 is a sign of a pseudonymous author, but including a signature actually aligns with Paul's other letters (1 Cor. 16:21; Gal. 6:11; Col. 4:18; Philem. 19).

In addition, some scholars reverse the order of the letters, suggesting that 2 Thessalonians was written first. This is because in 2 Thessalonians believers were being persecuted (e.g., 2 Thess. 1:4–7), but 1 Thessalonians appears to treat this as a past event (e.g., 1 Thess. 2:14). However, if we keep the canonical order, then this change reflects the intermittent nature of their persecution. Others argue that the command for believers to work "as we directed you" (1 Thess. 4:11) refers to his commands to work in his other letter (2 Thess. 3:11–12). But the expression "as we directed you" does not need to refer to a previous letter and could refer to directions given while Paul was with the community. Others cite Paul's claim to repeatedly try to visit (1 Thess. 2:17–18) as making more sense in a second letter. But this is an unnecessary assumption because Paul's travel plans were known to change (2 Cor.1:15–17). The strongest argument in favor of the canonical order is that 2 Thessalonians speaks about a previous letter (2 Thess. 2:2, 2:15, 3:17), and the similar themes represent Paul clarifying topics from his first letter of 1 Thessalonians.

Originally, this missionary team had intended to stay in Asia Minor (modern-day Turkey). Then, in Troas, Paul had a vision to expand his mission to the province of Macedonia (Acts 16:6–10). Paul's first stop in Macedonia was Philippi, where he and Silas were thrown in jail for their strange and foreign teaching (Acts 16:11–40). However, Paul was not discouraged and continued to share the gospel with other Macedonian cities, leading him to Thessalonica (Acts 17:1–9). For about three weeks, Paul presented his case that Jesus was the Jewish Messiah. This resulted in forming a core community of Christ followers, who were a mixture of Jews and Gentile proselytes. Paul also gained influence over a few leading women in the community (Acts 17:4).

Unfortunately, other Jews from the city became upset and brought charges against Paul for being disloyal to the empire and causing civil disobedience. They claimed Paul was teaching that Rome was not in charge and was proclaiming "another king named Jesus" (Acts 17:7). After Paul's arrest, Jason posted a bond to free Paul, and the community sent Paul away (Acts 17:8–9; 1 Thess. 2:17–18). This unrest prevented him from returning to the city, despite his wishes. The Jews in Thessalonica were so impassioned against Paul's message that they chased him completely out of the province of Macedonia (Acts 17:13). The Thessalonian believers were never able to quell the rumors of civic unrest, and opposition from the city continued.

What These Letters Are All About

We now turn to what may be the earliest letter that Paul wrote to churches.[22] Paul sent his first letter around 50 CE from Corinth after Timothy reported their discouraging situation (1 Thess. 3:1–10; Acts 18:5).[23] Paul responded to several issues for which the Thessalonians sought guidance, including showing proper love for others (1 Thess. 4:9), worries about those who recently died (1 Thess. 4:13), speculations about Jesus's return (1 Thess. 5:1), complaints against idleness in the community (1 Thess. 5:12), and concerns about Paul's apostolic authority (1 Thess. 2:4–8).

In his first letter, Paul rejoiced over their steadfastness under trials (1 Thess. 3:6). He encouraged them to strengthen their faith by dispelling doubts (1 Thess. 4:11–12, 4:13, 5:1, 5:14). He also defended himself

Carl N. Toney

Twenty-four Roman bathtubs in Thessalonica. (second cent. CE)

[22] Some consider Galatians to be Paul's first letter. See the next chapter for a discussion on that letter's dating.
[23] Malherbe, *Thessalonians*, 71–74, 350.

1 THESSALONIANS

- Letter's Greeting (1:1)
- First Thanksgiving and Prayer (1:2–10)
- Paul's Apostolic Ministry (2:1–3:13)
    - Model of Paul's Ministry in Thessalonica (2:1–12)
    - Second Thanksgiving (2:13–16)
    - Paul's Desire to Visit and Timothy's Report (2:17–3:10)
    - Second Prayer (3:11–13)
- Community Conduct (4:1–5:24)
    - A Life Pleasing to God including Loving One Another (4:1–12)
    - Assurance of the Lord's Return (4:13–5:11)
    - Final Exhortations (5:12–22)
    - Third Prayer (5:23–24)
- Letter's Conclusion (5:25–28)

against those maligning his motives and character (1 Thess. 2:1–12). He wanted to provide hope by assuring them of Jesus's triumphal return and reign in God's kingdom (1 Thess. 4:13–5:11). Overall, he exhorted the Thessalonians to "encourage one another and build up [*oikodomeite*] each other" (1 Thess. 5:11).

To the surprise and joy of the Thessalonians, they received a second letter only a few months later. In his second letter, Paul continued to charge them, "Do not be weary in doing what is right" (2 Thess. 3:13). Again, he encouraged them to place their hope in Christ's return (2 Thess. 2:1–17). He further addressed the problem of idleness in the community (2 Thess. 3:6, 3:11) and defended his apostolic authority (2 Thess. 3:8–10).

Suffering and hope. The **four cardinal virtues** taught by the Greco-Roman philosophers were "prudence" (*phronēsis*), "temperance" (*sōphrosynē*), "fortitude" (*andreios*), and "righteousness" (*dikaiosynē*). Of these four, Paul often talked about "righteousness" (*dikaiosynē*) in his other letters (e.g., Rom. 1:17, 3:21, 4:3; 1 Cor. 1:30; 2 Cor. 5:21; etc.). But in these letters, Paul focused upon the **three theological virtues** of "faith" (*pistis*), "hope" (*elpis*), and "love" (*agapē*) (1 Thess. 1:3, 5:8; 2 Thess. 1:3–4, 2:16, 3:2–5; cf. 1 Cor. 13:13; Rom. 5:1–5; Gal. 5:5–6; Eph. 1:15, 4:2–6; Col. 1:4–8; 1 Tim. 1:1–5; Heb. 6:10, 10:22).[24] He opened his first letter by praising the Thessalonians for living out these virtues:

> We always give thanks to God for all of you and mention you in our prayers, constantly remembering before our God and Father your work of *faith* and labor of *love* and steadfastness of *hope* in our Lord Jesus Christ. (1 Thess. 1:2–3—emphasis added)

[24] See Augustine (*Enchir.*) and Aquinas (*Summa Theologica* I-II, q. 57, 62) versus Plato (*Resp.* 4.426–35).

Public Domain

Cardinal and Theological Virtues by Raphael. The women represent three of the cardinal virtues: fortitude (left), prudence (center), and temperance (right). The fourth virtue, justice (not shown), is on the ceiling. Three cherubs (*putti*) are the theological virtues—love (harvesting acorns), hope (holding a torch), and faith (pointing to heaven). Apostolic Palace, Vatican City. (1511)

And he closed his letter by urging them to protect themselves with these virtues:

> But since we belong to the day, let us be sober, and put on the breastplate of *faith* and *love*, and for a helmet the *hope* of salvation. (1 Thess. 5:8—emphasis added)

In truth, the Thessalonians excelled in faith and love (1 Thess. 1:8, 3:12, 4:9–10; 2 Thess. 1:3–4). Their faith motivated them to trust God and turn from idols (1 Thess. 1:8–9). They abounded in love for each other because they followed Jesus's teaching to "love one another" (1 Thess. 4:9; cf. Lev. 19:18). However, they struggled with hope (1 Thess. 4:13, 4:18; 2 Thess. 2:16–17), and much of these letters taught about proper Christian hope.

The Thessalonians' hope had waivered because they had faced so much suffering, particularly as they grieved the unexpected deaths of other Christians in their community. They faced persecution, and some members died (1 Thess. 4:13). Believers wondered if they were dying because the community had somehow been unfaithful to God and lost their reward. Conversely, they wondered if God was being unfaithful. They asked if a believer died before Christ's return, would that believer lose her or his reward?

In response, Paul encouraged them by reminding them that he also suffered at the hands of the Roman officials in Philippi, but God delivered him (1 Thess. 2:1–2). Further, he asked the believers to recall how he labored and suffered when he was with them for the sake of the gospel (1 Thess. 2:9–10). Paul reminded the Thessalonians that if God could deliver him from suffering, then God could deliver them. He also promised that because God was in charge, he would ultimately judge those afflicting them (2 Thess. 1:5–12) and reward them for their faithfulness (2 Thess. 2:14).

Jesus is coming back! The Thessalonian church faced various issues connected to their understanding of the end of the world. The fancy name for studying events related to the "last things" is **eschatology**. Another related term is **apocalyptic**, meaning "unveiling," which is an outlook that reveals the underlying spiritual reality that controls and transforms the material world.

Paul wanted the Thessalonians to look at their circumstances from God's perspective. From Paul's initial preaching, the Thessalonians had expected Jesus's imminent return and deliverance from their struggles. Jesus's second coming is sometimes called the **parousia**, a Greek word that means "presence," or "coming." Like many early Christians, the Thessalonians believed Jesus would return in their lifetime to establish God's reign.

Paul corrected their assumptions with his description of Jesus's return. In his first letter, he used the language of being "caught up" (*harpazō*), which means to "snatch, seize, or take away suddenly." The Latin equivalent is *raptus*, and this passage has been understood by some Christians as describing a

The Arch of Titus in Rome commemorates the conquest of Jerusalem in 70 CE, portraying Titus in a triumphal procession. (first cent. CE)

Carl N. Toney

heavenly **rapture**.[25] However, this passage is understood by others as describing Jesus's return to earth at his second coming. Paul described Jesus's return using imagery drawn from a Greco-Roman triumph, a parade celebrating the victory of a general, public official, or ruler over a conquered enemy, sickness, or famine. Paul described Jesus's return as follows:

> For this we declare to you by the word of the Lord, that we who are alive, who are left until the coming of the Lord [*parousian tou kyriou*], will by no means precede those who have died. For the Lord [*kyrios*] himself, with a cry of command, with the archangel's call and with the sound of God's trumpet [*salpingi*], will descend from heaven, and the dead in Christ will rise first. Then we who are alive, who are left, will be caught up [*harpagēsometha*] in the clouds together with them to meet [*apantēsin*] the Lord [*kyriou*] in the air; and so we will be with the Lord [*kyriō*] forever. Therefore encourage one another with these words. (1 Thess. 4:15–18)

Paul used an image that would be familiar to the Thessalonians. He described Christ's return as being like a victory parade of a triumphant ruler or official. The triumphal procession began when the victorious ruler or official would "come" (*parousia*) to a city. Likewise, Paul looked forward to a time when Jesus would "come" to the earth (1 Thess. 4:15). The announcement of victory was called "good news" (*euangelion*). Similarly, Paul and Timothy had announced the "good news" about Jesus's victory to the Thessalonians (1 Thess. 1:5, 2:2, 2:4, 2:8, 2:9, 3:2).

2 THESSALONIANS

- Letter's Greeting (1:1–2)
- First Thanksgiving and Prayer (1:3–12)
- Paul's Apostolic Message (2:1–17)
  - The Lord's Return and the Lawless One (2:1–12)
  - Second Thanksgiving and Prayer (2:13–17)
- Community Conduct (3:1–16)
  - Pray for Paul's Apostolic Ministry (3:1–5)
  - Warning against Idleness (3:6–13)
  - Dealing with Disobedient Members (3:14–15)
  - Third Prayer (3:16)
- Letter's Conclusion (3:17–18)

[25] The verb "caught up" (*harpazō*) is used to describe Paul's ascent into heaven (2 Cor. 12:2, 12:4). Revelation does not describe a "rapture." Christians who understand the rapture as believers being taken to heaven must make assumptions about where it fits into Revelation. Some believe this event occurs before the great tribulation, while others think it occurs during the middle or at the end of the tribulation.

Carl N. Toney

According to some traditions, the Messiah will enter Jerusalem through the eastern gate of the temple mount (Ezek. 44:1-3). The present gate was sealed around 1187 and was rebuilt by Sultan Suleiman around 1541.

During a triumph, the greeting committee of the city would go outside the city gates to "meet" (*apantēsis*) and escort the victory procession back inside (e.g., Cicero, *Att.* 8.16.2, 16.11.6). Similarly, the Thessalonians were told that they would "meet" Jesus as a triumphal ruler who had returned to this world, and they would escort him back to the earth in his victory procession (1 Thess. 4:17).[26] A Roman triumph also included a trumpeting herald, so Jesus's return would include a "trumpet" (*salpinx*) announcing his return (1 Thess. 4:16). In these ways, Paul used the imagery of a triumphal procession to encourage the Thessalonians that when Jesus returned in triumph, they would be caught up with him as he came to the earth in victory. Thus, Jesus's return as "Lord" (*kyrios*) would be like a giant parade!

Further, in his second letter, Paul encouraged his audience that when Christ returned, he would bring God's reign and justice to the world (2 Thess. 1:5–12). While the righteous currently suffered, Christ would return with angels in vengeance (2 Thess. 1:7–8; cf. 1 Thess. 4:1–5:11) and would punish those who afflicted believers with eternal destruction and separation from the presence of God (2 Thess. 1:9). In addition, Christ's "coming" (*parousia*, 2 Thess. 2:1), also called the "day of the Lord" (2 Thess. 2:2; cf. Amos 5:18–20), would not occur until the "man of lawlessness" (2 Thess. 2:3) appeared and was judged by God (2 Thess. 2:3–12).

The identity of this "lawless man" is unclear. Some speculate that he was a Roman emperor, such as Caligula (37–41 CE), Nero (54–68 CE), or Domitian (81–96 CE), who persecuted either the church or the Jewish people. Others have tried to connect this to John's antichrist (1 John 2:18, 2:22, 4:3; 2 John 7), the beast of Revelation (Rev. 11:7, 13:1–18), or Daniel's abomination desolation (Dan. 9:27; cf. Mark 13:14; Matt. 24:15). Most likely, this image was probably the personification of evil forces working against God (2 Thess. 2:9–10, 3:2). Until Jesus returned to finally destroy this evil (2 Thess. 2:8), God acted as a "restrainer" (2 Thess. 2:6–7) who holds back evil in this world until the gospel has been shared (2 Thess. 3:3–5).[27]

---

[26]This interpretation is reflected as early as Chrysostom, *Homilies on 1 Thessalonians* 8.

[27]The "restrainer" may also be Satan (2 Thess. 3:3), Apollyon (Rev. 9:11), Michael (Jude 9; Rev. 12:7), the church or a Christian leader (Mark 13:10), or the Roman Empire (Rev. 13:1–7).

Overall, Paul encouraged the Thessalonians to make sure that their future hope impacted their present lives. This future hope should not lead to a life of idleness (1 Thess. 4:11–12, 5:14; 2 Thess. 3:6–13). The reason that believers live different, moral lives now is because of their confidence in the future of God's reign. Believers live in the present according to the reality of their future. Thus, Paul called the Thessalonians to moral living by abstaining from sexual immorality (1 Thess. 4:3–7) and not growing weary in "doing what is right" (2 Thess. 3:13).

The Thessalonian letters challenge readers to consider what we believe about the future. Are our futures controlled by ourselves, others, society, or God? Do we let our beliefs about the future impact our present? Do we believe the message of these letters that God is in charge? And if God controls our future, are we willing to trust God with our present lives?

Key Terms and People

Apostle: "sent one" in Greek; refers to those God commissioned to share the gospel; it more specifically applies to Paul and anyone in the early church, including the twelve disciples who received their commission from Jesus
Apocalyptic: means "unveiling" and reveals the heavenly reality controlling and transforming the material world
Eschatology: the study of the last things
Four Greco-Roman virtues: prudence, temperance, fortitude, and righteousness
Parousia: Jesus's second coming
Paul: the Greek name of the apostle to the Gentiles whose Hebrew name was Saul
Pseudepigraphy: when a work is written by an anonymous author but attributed to a well-known figure (lit. "false writing")
Rapture: the event when Jesus returns to earth to gather believers during his second coming
Scribe: someone who composed a letter on behalf of the author, such as Tertius
Three theological virtues: faith, hope, and love
Via Egnatia: the major east–west trade route through Asia

Conversation Starters

1. If you were to write a biography about Paul, what would you include? What were some of the most significant events in his life? What did Paul think about the law? How did he understand his apostleship?
2. Why did Paul write letters? What were some standard features in Paul's letters? How did Paul try to persuade people of his ideas?
3. What are your thoughts and reactions to pseudepigraphy? Do the New Testament works need to be written by the named author? Does using a scribe or school help us understand how a work was written?

4. What are the three Christian virtues? How are they similar to or different from Greco-Roman virtues? How did Paul encourage Christian virtue in these letters?
5. Why were the Thessalonians so worried about the future? How did Paul encourage them? How do our views about the future impact our living in the present?
6. What was Paul's understanding of Jesus's return that he presented in these letters? How does Jesus's return contribute to our understanding that God is in charge?

FOR FURTHER READING

Paul

Barclay, John. *Paul and the Gift*. Eerdmans, 2015.

Dunn, James D. G. *The Theology of Paul the Apostle*. Eerdmans, 1998.

Hock, Ronald F. *The Social Context of Paul's Ministry: Tentmaking and Apostleship*. Fortress, 1980.

McKnight, Scot, Lynn H. Cohick, and Nijay K. Gupta, eds. *Dictionary of Paul and His Letters: A Compendium of Contemporary Biblical Scholarship*. 2nd ed. IVP Academic, 2023.

Johnson, Luke Timothy. *The Canonical Paul*. 2 vols. Eerdmans, 2020–2021.

Morgan, Teresa. *Roman Faith and Christian Faith:* Pistis *and* Fides *in the Early Roman Empire and Early Churches*. Oxford University Press, 2017.

Murphy-O'Connor, Jerome. *Paul: A Critical Life*. Clarendon, 1996.

Richards, E. Randolph. *Paul and First-Century Letter Writing: Secretaries, Composition, and Collection*. InterVarsity Press, 2004.

1-2 Thessalonians

Bridges, Linda McKinnish. *1 & 2 Thessalonians*. Smyth & Helwys Bible Commentary. Smyth & Helwys, 2008.

Fee, Gordon D. *The First and Second Letters to the Thessalonians*. NICNT. Eerdmans, 2009.

Gaventa, Beverly. *First and Second Thessalonians*. Interpretation. Westminster John Knox, 1998.

Gupta, Nijay K. *1–2 Thessalonians*. New Covenant Commentary. Eugene, Cascade, 2016.

Malherbe, Abraham J. *The Letters to the Thessalonians: A New Translation with Introduction and Commentary*. AYB 32B. Yale University Press, 2008.

Witherington, Ben, III. *1 and 2 Thessalonians: A Socio-Rhetorical Commentary*. Eerdmans, 2006.

7

LETTERS FROM PAUL

Galatians and Philippians

Galatians

The Story So Far

Paul called his audience foolish "Galatians" (*Galatai*, Gal. 3:1; cf. Gal. 1:2), but their identity is a bit of a mystery. This label of "Galatians" originally referred to an ethnic group of Celts who left Gaul in the fourth century BCE and settled in northern Asia Minor in the region around Ancyra shortly after 280 BCE. However, since 25 BCE, this label referred to the much larger area of the Roman province of Galatia when Emperor Augustus added regions in the south. It now included Phrygia Galatica (with the towns of Antioch and Iconium) and Lycaonia Galatica (with the villages of Lystra and Derbe). This enlarged province (in the heart of modern Turkey) extended from Pontus on the Black Sea in the north to Pamphylia on the Mediterranean Sea in the south (Pliny, *Nat.* 5.147; cf. Acts 16:6, 18:23; 1 Pet. 1:1).

SUGGESTED READING

Acts 13:13–14:23
Acts 16:1–5
Acts 16:6
Acts 18:23
Galatians
Acts 16:8–40
Philippians

Some readers identify the Galatians as churches in the southern portion of the Roman province.[1] Acts 13:13–14:23 gives detailed stories of Paul and Barnabas's travels in the cities of Pisidian Antioch, Iconium, Lystra, and Derbe in the southern regions of the province of Galatia. During the first round of these travels, Paul was stoned to death in Lystra, but he was revived by God (Acts 14:19–20). This region is also where Timothy came from, and he joined Paul and Silas when they passed through these cities a second time (Acts 16:1–5).

[1] Ramsay, *Galatians*; Ramsay, *Church in the Roman Empire*. In favor of the southern view, Barnabas (Gal. 2:1) helped establish the southern churches in Acts 13–14, and he did not go to the north. Paul's language of being received like an angel (Gal. 4:14) could be similar to these cities hailing them as Zeus and Hermes (Acts 14:11–18).

The Relationship between Paul's Letters and Acts

A challenge that sometimes comes when reading biblical passages about similar events is determining what actually happened. We encounter this challenge when reading parallel passages about Jesus's life in the Gospels. We also face this challenge when relating the material in Paul's letters with Acts. In order for us to explore this complexity, let's compare Paul's letter to the Galatians with Luke's account of Paul's travels in Acts. This comparison is important for determining the date of composition of Galatians. Comparing the evidence from these two sources is like putting together a picture by combining two similar but different puzzles because each is missing a few pieces. One problem is that Galatians mentions two separate trips to Jerusalem (Gal. 1:18–20, 2:1–10), but Acts describes three (Acts 9:26–30, 11:27–30, 15:1–30). We will do our best to create a picture, but it won't be complete or perfect.

According to Galatians, Paul made his first visit to Jerusalem to meet with Peter and James (Gal. 1:18–20). Then Paul departed to the regions of Syria and Cilicia (Gal. 1:21). This first trip occurred three years after Paul's Damascus Road experience when Jesus appeared to him and gave a "calling" from God to proclaim the gospel to the Gentiles (Gal. 1:15–16). This first visit matches Luke's description of Paul's initial visit to Jerusalem (Acts 9:26–30) and his time in Tarsus and Antioch (Acts 11:25–26). So far, so good. The pieces of the puzzles are matching nicely.

However, things become more complex when matching the next visit to Jerusalem. According to Galatians, Paul returned to Jerusalem fourteen years later with Barnabas and Titus (Gal. 2:1–10). This is where things get complicated because Paul's language here is vague. Did he mean fourteen years after his Damascus experience (Gal. 2:1), or did he also add the three years prior to his first visit to Jerusalem (Gal. 1:18), which makes seventeen years? During this second trip to Jerusalem, Titus, who was a Gentile, was brought before the apostles to settle the question of whether a Gentile needed to be circumcised (Gal. 2:3). Thankfully, Paul and the Jerusalem leaders came to an agreement that Gentiles did not need to be circumcised (Gal. 2:4–5). They also decided Paul's ministry would focus on the Gentiles, while Peter and James would focus on the Jews (Gal. 2:7–9). Last, they asked Paul to remember the poor (Gal. 2:10).

© V. Korostyshevskiy / Adobe Stock

The Dying Gaul, formerly known as *The Dying Gladiator*, is an ancient Roman marble copy of a lost bronze Hellenistic sculpture depicting a wounded Galatian. It was commissioned some time between 230 and 220 BC by Attalus I of Pergamon. Capitoline Museums, Rome.

Following the chronology of Acts, we assume that Paul's second visit to Jerusalem in Galatians (Gal. 2:1–10) corresponds with the account in Acts of Paul and Barnabas's second journey to provide famine relief (Acts 11:27–30). Unfortunately, the purposes of these two trips do not match. In Acts 11:27–30, the objective was famine relief, while in Galatians the aim was to discuss Paul's Gentile mission and Gentile freedom from circumcision (Gal. 2:1–10). Instead, the purpose of Paul's visit in Galatians (Gal. 2:1–10) matches Paul's third journey to Jerusalem for the Jerusalem Council (Acts 15:1–30). If this letter was written after the Jerusalem Council, then Paul was upset that his Jewish Christian opponents had violated the decision of the council.

We are left with a choice. We either strictly follow the chronology of Acts and assume this was Paul's second journey to Jerusalem. Or Paul omitted his second trip to Jerusalem in Acts and talked about his first and third trips to Jerusalem. Usually, those who favor the chronology of Acts also identify the Galatians as the churches from Paul's first missionary journey (Acts 13–14). Most who argue that this letter was written after the Jerusalem Council favor the northern group (Acts 16:6, 18:23). However, it is possible to date the letter after the Jerusalem Council and to identify the Galatians with the southern group. Of these two views, we favor dating the letter after the Jerusalem Council.

Alternatively, Paul could have used the term to describe the ethnic Galatians, and he was writing to the churches in the north.[2] Acts only briefly mentions Paul and Silas's travels among the northern regions to establish churches (Acts 16:6, 18:23). Peter attested to the success of this mission when he addressed these churches in his first letter to encourage them during a time of suffering (1 Pet. 1:1–2).

Map of North and South Galatia.

What happened in Galatia that prompted this letter? Apparently, Jewish Christians coming from Jerusalem infiltrated this newly formed community. These Jewish Christians proclaimed their version of the gospel grounded in their understanding of God's grace. Like Paul, they believed that Jesus had died for people's sins. They believed that salvation was a gift to be received, not something to be earned. So far, so good.

But they disagreed with Paul concerning who could be saved. From their perspective, only Jews could be saved by God's grace. Their logic was that if Jesus was the Jewish Messiah, then he came to save only the Jewish people. To receive the free gift of salvation, a person must first become a Jew. These Jewish Christians followed the standard practices of the day by insisting that Gentile Christians be circumcised to join the Jewish community. In addition, the Galatians were attracted to the opponents' message because they appreciated the clear moral guidelines that Mosaic law provided versus Paul's nebulous advice of being guided by the Holy Spirit.[3] Needless to say, all of this upset Paul, who wrote them a letter from Ephesus around April or May 53 CE (Acts 19:1–41).

[2] In response to Ramsey, see Lightfoot, *Galatians*, 1–35. The traditional view favors the north. Both Acts and Galatians use the term "Galatians" to refer to the ethnic group in the north. Acts distinguishes "Phrygia and Galatia" (Acts 16:6) from the cities of Derbe and Lystra (Acts 16:1–5). Paul describes the church using the ethnic term (*Galatai*) in Galatians 3:1. Mentioning Barnabas does not mean that he visited the city since he didn't visit Corinth, but he is mentioned in 1 Corinthians 9:6. Paul's illness (Gal. 4:13) differs from his miracle working in Acts 14. This primarily Gentile church also fits better in the north. Murphy-O'Connor, *Paul*, 183–84.

[3] Martyn, *Galatians*, 18–19, 117–36, 302–6; Murphy-O'Connor, *Paul*, 196–99; Tobin, *Paul's Rhetoric*, 62–63; Toney, *Paul's Inclusive Ethic*, 72–74.

What This Letter Is About

Paul's apostolic authority. Paul was mad. While his other letters usually opened with a prayer of thanksgiving, this letter did not. Instead, in frustration, Paul vented, "I am astonished that you are so quickly deserting the one who called you in the grace of Christ and are turning to a different gospel" (Gal. 1:6). Paul wrote to defend his apostleship and to remind the Galatians of his gospel, which he "received through a revelation of Jesus Christ" (Gal. 1:12).

Apostles Peter and Paul by Andrey Mironov. (2021)

GALATIANS

- Letter's Greeting (1:1–5)
- Rebuking the Galatians (1:6–10)
- Paul's Call and His Conflict with Peter at Antioch (1:11–2:14)
- All Are Justified by Faith in Jesus Christ (2:15–21)
- Arguments and Evidence (3:1–4:31)
    - The Galatians Received the Spirit by Faith (3:1–5)
    - Abraham's Example of Being Justified by Faith (3:6–14)
    - Christ Is Abraham's True Heir (3:15–18)
    - The Purpose of the Law (3:19–25)
    - Baptism into Christ Makes Believers Heirs of Abraham (3:26–4:11)
    - Paul's Personal Appeal (4:12–20)
    - Allegory of Sarah and Hagar (4:21–31)
- Exhortations regarding Freedom and the Holy Spirit (5:1–6:10)
- Letter's Conclusion (6:11–18)

On the one hand, Paul downplayed the apostolic authority of the Jerusalem church while noting they acknowledged his ministry among the Gentiles (Gal. 2:6, 2:9). On the other hand, he elevated his own apostolic identity by describing his divine commission on the Damascus Road to share the gospel with Gentiles (Gal. 1:1, 1:11–12, 1:16–17, 2:8). This letter provides a rare autobiographical account of Paul's transformation from a persecutor of the church to a proclaimer of the gospel (Gal. 1:13–24). He became the apostle to the Gentiles (Gal. 2:1–14) and a staunch defender of Gentile freedom (Gal. 2:15–21).

According to Paul, the leaders of the Jerusalem church had agreed that Gentiles were free from the Jewish obligations to the law, especially circumcision and food laws (Gal. 2:1–10). Acts 15:1–30 describes this agreement as the Jerusalem Council. However, Paul felt the Jewish leadership broke this agreement during Peter's time in Antioch (Gal. 2:11–14). While in Antioch, Peter initially followed the agreement by eating with the Gentiles. But after people came from James, Peter withdrew from fellowship and was compelling the Gentiles "to live like Jews" (Gal. 2:14). Paul recalled his rebuke of Peter in this letter (Gal. 2:15–21).

Paul wrote Galatians because he was witnessing history repeat itself. He was upset that the Jewish Christian opponents in Galatia were ignoring the terms set out by the Jerusalem Council (Gal. 2:1–10; Acts 15:1–30). Just as Paul had to rebuke Peter and Jewish Christians in Antioch, now Paul rebuked a new group of Jewish Christians attempting to infiltrate the Galatian church. His rebuke included the main purpose of Galatians: "that a person is justified not by the works of the law but through faith in Jesus Christ" (Gal. 2:16). Paul's frustration over fighting about an issue that was supposed to be resolved

Public Domain

One of the oldest copies of the Ten Commandments (Deut. 5:1-6:1). Dead Sea Scrolls (4Q41). Israel Antiquities Authority. (ca. 30-1 BCE)

comes out in his harsh language: "You foolish Galatians! Who has bewitched you?" (Gal. 3:1) and "I wish those who unsettle you would castrate themselves!" (Gal. 5:12).

Paul and the law. Central to this dispute was an understanding of the law. Paul and his opponents had different perspectives about the law and the works of the law. In Paul's writings, "law" (*nomos*) has a variety of meanings, depending upon the context. Broadly speaking, "law" can mean "principle," "order," or "rule" (Rom. 3:27, 7:21, 7:23, 8:2). When speaking about Gentiles, Paul sometimes referred to a universal moral law (Rom. 2:14–15, 2:26–27).

When connected to Jewish scriptures, Paul's understanding of law derived from the Jewish concept of **Torah**.[4] Torah is more than law or rule; it means "instruction" or "teaching." "Law" can refer to all of the Jewish scriptures (Rom. 3:19; 1 Cor. 14:21), the Pentateuch (Rom. 3:21), or a particular book or verse referenced (e.g., Genesis in Gal. 4:21; Psalms in Rom. 3:19; Isaiah in 1 Cor. 14:21).[5] Most frequently, Paul referred to the Mosaic law (e.g., Gal. 3:17, 5:3; Rom. 2:14, 2:17–18, 5:13–14; 1 Cor. 9:8–9; 2 Cor. 3:1–18).[6] This law is exemplified by the Ten Commandments (Rom. 2:20–24, 7:2, 7:7–12, 13:8–9) and summarized by the command to love one's neighbor (Gal. 5:14; Rom. 13:9–10). The Mosaic law separated Jews from Gentiles (Gal. 2:15; Rom. 2:1; 1 Cor. 9:20–21).

When there are statements about earning salvation through "works" (*erga*, e.g., Rom. 3:27–28, 4:2, 11:16) and the "works of the law" (*erga nomou*, e.g., Gal. 2:21, 2:16, 3:10), some understand following the Mosaic "law" (*nomos*) as opposing God's "grace" (*charis*). The logic is that since nobody can completely follow the law, earning salvation through good works is impossible. Everyone sins, falls short, and comes under the curse of the law (Gal. 3:10). This may be taken further as an argument against using good works to curry God's favor so that Paul was making a statement against legalism (e.g., Gal. 2:15–21; Rom. 10:3; Phil. 3:9). From this perspective, Paul's opponents were promoting legalism and using the law to earn their salvation.

[4] Paul uses a variety of terms for the Jewish law, such as "commandment" (*entolē*, e.g., Rom. 7:8–13, 13:9) and "writing" (*graphē*, e.g., Rom. 9:17, 10:11). The Hebrew Bible also uses a variety of terms besides "Torah" (Heb. *torah*), including "statute, decree" (Heb. *hoq*), "judgment, legal decision" (Heb. *mishpat*), "word" (Heb. *davar*), and "commandment" (Heb. *mitzvah*).

[5] Westerholm, "Torah, Nomos, and Law: A Question of Meaning," 327–36.

[6] Older views incorrectly saw the presence of the article indicating the Mosaic law, and those without the article referred to the law in a general sense (e.g., Slaten, "Qualitative Use of Νόμος," 213–18). However, see Paul's use in Romans 7:7 (cf. Rom. 2:17–27, 5:13–14; Gal. 3:10–13).

What Was Paul's Understanding of the Role of the Mosaic Law?

Many readers of Paul understand him through the lens offered by the medieval theologian Thomas Aquinas (*Summa Theologica* I-II, q. 99–108). When looking at the Mosaic law, Aquinas distinguished between the permanent moral laws and the temporary judicial and ceremonial laws. According to Aquinas, believers continued to follow moral laws because these were part of the natural order of the world and revealed God's will. However, believers were not obligated to follow the judicial laws because these pertained to the nation of Israel. Nor did they need to follow the ceremonial laws, which included laws related to the temple system since Christ's work annulled them.

During the Protestant Reformation, Martin Luther (*Smalclad Articles* 2) determined that the law had two negative functions—to reveal and restrain sin. For Luther, only God's grace could save people, and the "works of the law" described people's failed attempts to earn their salvation. Another reformer, John Calvin (*Inst.* 2.7.6–12), agreed with Luther's analysis of the two negative functions of the law, but he added an important positive third use of the law: that it could provide moral guidance.

Presentation of the Blessed Virgin. Detail of the high priest wearing a breastplate, ephod, blue robe, woven tunic, turban, and sash. Church of the Immaculate Conception. Ballymote, Ireland.

More recently, E. P. Sanders helped begin a scholarly movement labeled the "New Perspective."[7] He argued that Mosaic law was a divinely initiated covenant and was freely given. The Jewish people did not do anything to enter this covenant. Following the law was a response to this gracious covenant. It was not a means to gain God's favor or to stay in the covenant. God did not demand perfect obedience, and the law prescribed a system for forgiveness and atonement for those who repented. Sanders's positive understanding of the law is called "covenantal nomism."

J. D. G. Dunn further refined Sanders's arguments.[8] Dunn contended that observing the law made Israel distinct as God's chosen people. Circumcision, Jewish dietary restrictions, Sabbath keeping, and other conduct prescribed by the law served as boundary markers between Jews and non-Jews. These were the "works of the law" that Paul stood against. However, God's ultimate intention was to extend salvation beyond Israel to the entire world, and the Mosaic law served as a temporary means of protecting Israel until the fulfillment of God's promises in Christ.

[7] Sanders, *Paul and Palestinian Judaism*; Sanders, *Paul, the Law*. For a rebuttal of Sanders, see Westerholm, *Perspectives Old and New on Paul: The "Lutheran" Paul and His Critics*.

[8] Dunn, *New Perspective on Paul*, 2008.

However, we need to reconsider Paul's understanding of the law.[9] Like many of his fellow Jews, Paul considered the law good because it was the best expression of God's will (Rom. 3:2, 7:12; Phil. 4:6). The Letter of Aristeas described the law positively as a protective fence (Let. Aris. 139). The author of 4 Maccabees viewed the law as a means to help people master their desires (4 Macc. 1:34–35). Many first-century Jews believed they were part of a covenant of grace, and obedience to the law was simply the proper response to God's covenant (Josephus, *Ant.* 8.111).[10]

Paul often spoke positively about the law. The law was holy (Rom. 7:12), spiritual (Rom. 7:14), and good (Rom. 7:16; cf. 1 Tim. 1:8). These statements counter the narrative that Paul had a crisis of faith because he could not follow the law (based on a misunderstanding of Romans 7:7–25, which was rhetorically referring to the struggles of a Gentile convert).[11] Instead, Paul considered himself blameless and righteous, according to the law (Phil. 3:6). What was Paul's problem with the law? Paul discovered that the law was good but insufficient for salvation. This is because Christ, not the law, was the only means to obtain salvation for the whole world (Phil. 3:9–11).

However, relying upon the **works of the law** for salvation was bad. These works of the law referred to the Jewish identity markers, including (but not limited to) circumcision (Gal. 5:2–3, 6:12–13), dietary laws (Gal. 2:11–12), and observance of special days like the Sabbath (Gal. 4:10). These identity markers functioned to separate Jews from Gentiles (Gal. 2:12). In speaking against the "works of the law" (Gal. 3:10), Paul wrote against Jewish particularism, which attempted to ground salvation in their covenantal identity and to restrict salvation to the Jewish people (Gal. 2:14). Paul was against enforcing these identity markers upon non-Jews since they were temporal, extrinsic, unnecessary, and even harmful demarcations of who was in and who was out of God's covenant (Gal. 2:14, 5:6, 6:13).[12]

Paul broadened the recipients of salvation to include Gentiles through belief in Jesus (Gal. 5:6, 6:13). Being baptized into Christ meant there were neither Jews nor Gentiles (Gal. 3:27–29). Paul emphasized that salvation was based on the faithful work of Christ, who was the one true heir of the Abrahamic promises (Gal. 3:16). All people—both Jews and Gentiles—were adopted because of Christ (Gal. 3:29, 4:5). This fulfilled God's promise to Abraham (Gal. 3:15–18, 3:29) and brought freedom for true heirs (Gal. 4:21–31).

Faith in/of Jesus. According to Paul, "A person is not justified by the works of the law, but by faith in Jesus Christ. So we, too, have put our faith in Christ Jesus that we may be justified by faith [*ek pisteōs*] in Christ and not by the works of the law" (Gal. 2:16 NIV). Paul adapted the language of "by faith" (*ek pisteōs*) from Habakkuk 2:4, which he cites in Galatians 3:11, "the righteous will live by faith."[13]

Paul wrote that people are "justified *ek pisteōs Christou*" (Gal. 2:16, 2:20). Traditionally, this Greek expression is translated as "justified by **faith in Christ**" (as reflected in most translations), in reference

9 Dunn, "New Perspective on Paul," 1983, 95–122.

10 First-century Jews had a variety of beliefs about the role of the law. Some groups did connect salvation with obeying the law (e.g., 4 Ezra; 1 En. 1–5; Jub. 4.22–24, 30.21–24, 36.10).

11 The "I" in Romans 7:7–25 likely represents a Gentile convert. A Jew could never say they were alive apart from the law (Rom. 7:9). Or, this could represent Adam and Eve. Paul spoke in the first person as a speech in character. See Tobin, *Paul's Rhetoric*, 225–45.

12 Dunn, "Yet Once More," 215.

13 Campbell, "Romans 1:17—A Crux Interpretum," 265–85; Watson, "By Faith (of Christ)," 147–63; Dunn, *Romans*, 1:44–46. We will look more closely at this verse in our chapter on Romans.

Public Domain

Death of Jesus on the Cross. Convent of the Santísima Trinidad. Santiago, Chile. (1732)

to a believer's faith.[14] However, it is possible to understand this as justified by the **faith(fulness) of Christ** (as seen in the King James Version and New English Translation), in reference to Jesus's personal faith.[15] In this case, Paul was saying something new. He was describing the object of people's belief: Jesus's faithfulness. Jesus's faithfulness may be understood as his faithful obedience to God, including his crucifixion. Or it may be his faithfulness to save humanity from sin. The debate concerning whose faith—a believer's or Jesus's—extends to the other times Paul used this expression (Gal. 2:16, 2:20, 3:22; Phil. 3:9; Rom. 3:22, 3:26; cf. Eph. 3:12).[16]

---

[14] Jesus never "believes" (*pisteuō*), nor is he described as "faithful" (*pistos*), so we should not expect the noun to be used to describe Jesus's faith. Instead, it is "faith in Jesus." Dunn, "Once More," 733–44; Porter and Pitts, "Πίστις with a Preposition and Genitive Modifier," 33–53; Tobin, *Paul's Rhetoric*, 132–34.

[15] In support of "Christ's faith," all of Paul's uses of the noun "faith" (*pistis*) refer to the "faith" or "faithfulness" of the individual. Notably, Paul uses the same expression to describe Abraham's faith (Rom. 4:16). Hays, *The Faith of Christ*; Hooker, "Πίστις Χριστοῦ," 321–42.

[16] Some have argued that Paul was intentionally ambiguous and may have encapsulated both ideas. Others propose a "third view" of "Christ-faith" as an event, gospel message, or sphere of salvation. Sprinkle, "Πίστις Χριστοῦ as an Eschatological Event," 165–84. See also Grasso, "Linguistic Analysis of πίστις Χριστοῦ," 108–44.

While this debate may not be easily or quickly resolved, one benefit from the discussion has been a renewed emphasis on God's faithfulness, as demonstrated through Jesus (Gal. 3:10–14). Regardless of one's understanding of faith in Christ, Paul clearly called Christ followers "to believe" (Gal. 2:16). But Paul also placed a great deal of emphasis upon God's faithfulness to humanity by keeping his promises (Gal. 3:15–18, 3:23–29). In fact, Paul most often spoke of the object of faith as either God (e.g., Gal. 3:6; Rom. 4:3, 4:5, 4:17) or the gospel (e.g., Rom. 6:8, 10:9; 1 Cor. 15:11). God can keep his promises through the work of Christ, and believers benefit from this work through participating "in Christ" (e.g., Gal. 2:17, 2:20, 3:28). With these verses, Paul rooted salvation in the faithful work of God that humans respond with faith. In addition, considering the patronage system's understanding of "grace" and "faith," we can further understand this faith as people responding to the grace of God with "allegiance" to God.[17]

Right relationships. For anyone growing up in the church, it may be a surprise that Paul's "justification" language is limited to mainly three letters—Galatians, Philippians, and Romans.[18] Galatians 2:16 is the first time that Paul developed this concept. So, what is justification?

First, we need to note that "righteousness" and "justification" are English translations of words from the same Greek word family, meaning these concepts overlap.[19] The wider Greco-Roman world saw justification through the lens of law and politics (Plato, *Resp.* 1–4; Aristotle, *Eth. nic.* 5.1129b; Cicero, *Leg.* 2.13).[20] "Righteousness" (*dikaiosynē*) also included an ethical dimension since it was one of the four cardinal Greco-Roman virtues.[21] From a Jewish perspective, "righteousness" (Heb. *tsedeq, tsedaqah*) was the type of conduct expected by the requirements of a particular relationship. This relationship was defined by the Jewish people's covenantal relationship with God, as expressed in the Torah. To reflect these legal, ethical, and relational qualities, a more satisfactory translation of **righteousness** may be "right relationship."[22] In the past, the Mosaic law provided the means of establishing and maintaining this right covenantal relationship. However, with Christ, God enlarged this covenant to include Gentiles.

American Numismatic Society, Public Domain

The reverse side of a Roman denarius issued by Nerva and depicting the goddess Justice, one of the virtues associated with the emperors since Augustus. (ca. 96 CE)

In Galatians, Paul argued that people are put in a right relationship by trusting in Christ's work on the cross, not the works of the law. This right relationship may be with God

[17] See Chapter Five. This will also be explored further in our chapter on Romans.

[18] In 1–2 Thessalonians, it is a Greco-Roman virtue (1 Thess. 2:10) and reflects God's ability to judge correctly (2 Thess. 1:5–6). It is less frequent in 1–2 Corinthians, Ephesians, and the Pastorals. It is absent in Colossians and Philemon.

[19] The family includes the nouns (*dikaiosynē, dikē*), the adjective (*dikaios*), and the verb (*dikaioō*). For a historical survey of Paul's understanding of "righteousness," see Irons, *Righteousness of God*, 9–60.

[20] "Justice" is personified by the goddess Dike, daughter of Zeus (Hesiod, *Op.* 256; cf. Acts 28:4).

[21] See the discussion of virtues in our chapter on 1–2 Thessalonians.

[22] Dunn, *Galatians*, 134–35. See similar ideas in Wright, who sees four layers: right behavior, law court, covenant, and eschatological cosmic rectification. Wright, *Paul and the Faithfulness of God*, 796–804.

(what we may call piety) or with other people (what we may call justice). Further, we should be wary of reducing this righteousness to merely an individual or personal quality. Paul's language is much grander; God puts the entire fallen cosmos (not just individuals) in a right relationship under Christ's lordship, reflecting the reign of God (cf. Rom. 8:18–30).[23] These right relationships compel the church to move outward from itself to its mission to impact society as a whole because God is in charge.

Freedom! Paul wrote, "For freedom Christ has set us free" (Gal. 5:1; cf. Gal. 5:13). He reminded his Gentile audience that Christ freed them (Gal. 4:4–7) from their false gods (Gal. 4:8–9) and the "elemental spirits of the world" (*ta stoicheia tou kosmou*, Gal. 4:3; cf. Col. 2:8, 2:20). Greco-Roman religion was polytheistic and included an adaptation of the Olympian gods (Homer, *Il.*, *Od.*; Hesiod, *Theog.*; Virgil, *Aen.*) as well as the veneration of local deities that were appeased through public sacrifices and rituals. People also believed they were held in the grip of spiritual beings that tormented humanity. These elemental spirits may be the four basic substances of the world—earth, water, air, and fire (2 Pet. 3:10, 3:12; Wisd. of Sol. 7:17)—that were sometimes divinized (Philo, *Contempl. Life* 3; *Decalogue* 53–55), or the heavenly bodies, like the stars, that influenced humanity (Wisd. of Sol. 13:2–3; T. Sol. 8:2–4; Diogenes Laertius 6.102; Corpus Hermeticum 13.12).[24]

Paul's opponents promised that obedience to the law freed people from these false gods and elemental spirits. They also told the Galatians that the clear guidelines of the law freed people from sin. Both promises appealed to the Galatians. However, Paul argued that obeying the law jeopardized the Galatians' freedom (Gal. 5:1–12). Being bound to obey the commands of the law was not true freedom. Instead, those who followed Paul's gospel were freed from the "elemental spirits of the world" because they were placed under God's authoritative rule.

Further, God's people (both Jews and Gentiles) were marked off by being "in Christ" (Gal. 3:28). Paul expressed this unity of Jewish and Gentile believers when he wrote, "There is no longer Jew or Greek, there is no longer slave or free, there is no longer male and female; for all of you are one in Christ Jesus" (Gal. 3:28). Similarly, he said, "in Christ Jesus neither circumcision nor uncircumcision counts for anything" (Gal. 5:6).

Being "in Christ" and having the presence of God's Spirit is what provides freedom from the vices of the "Flesh" (*sarx*, Gal. 5:13–23). But what did Paul mean by the "Flesh," and how is it contrasted with the "Spirit" (*pneuma*)? Greco-Roman thinkers contrasted people's material bodies with their immaterial spirits. Paul rejected this dualism that somehow divided people between their body and spirit. Instead, Paul used language of the "Flesh" to represent the realm of humanity and living according to human standards. Living like a base human was acting according to the Flesh, and this generated evil "desire" (*epithymia*) and "passion" (*pathēma*, Gal. 5:16, 5:24).[25] The "Spirit" is shorthand for the Holy Spirit, which is God's active presence in the world. For Paul, living according to the Spirit meant submitting to God's rule.

---

[23] Bultmann, "Theology of the New Testament," 1:270–329; Käsemann, "Righteousness of God," 168–82.

[24] Dunn, *Galatians*, 213. Elsewhere, Hebrews 5:12 uses "elements" to describe the fundamentals of religion.

[25] "Flesh" can also refer to living as a human (Gal. 2:20) and can allude to circumcision (cf. Gal. 5:2–6, 5:11–12).

Dove of the Holy Spirit by Gian Lorenzo Bernini. St. Peter's Basilica, Vatican City. (1660)

Paul contrasted the vices of humans living according to the Flesh (Gal. 5:19–21) with the virtues of God's Spirit (Gal. 5:22–23). Paul's vice-virtue catalog fit with the conventional morality of the time (e.g., Plato, *Gorg.* 525a; Aristotle, *Eth. nic.* 2.7.2–15; Epictetus, *Diatr.* 2.8.23; 1QS 3.25–4.11). While the law could help curb sinful passions, it could not change someone. Paul argued that the Galatians' reception of the Spirit freed people from sin, changed them, and empowered them to do God's will (Gal. 3:1–5, 3:14, 4:6).

Because the law was an external means of correcting behavior, it could not bring about lasting ethical change. Instead, the indwelling of God's Spirit brings a lasting inner change (like righting the inner compass of humanity). It allows God to be in charge of the believer. This freedom is expressed through the command to love one's neighbor (Gal. 5:14; cf. Lev. 19:18), which is also called the "law of Christ" (Gal. 6:2). True faith in Christ alone puts the sinner in a right relationship with God, who forgives their sins (Gal. 2:16–21). True freedom in the Spirit releases a moral dynamic unknown by external codes, philosophical pursuits, or religious institutions (Gal. 4:10).[26] Paul promised that God's Spirit brings real, lasting change. Believers, under God's rule, are transformed from the inside out.

Philippians

The Story Continues

Philippi was located on the main east–west trade route called the Via Egnatia. It was located eight miles inland from Neapolis in the Roman province of Macedonia (modern Kavala in northern Greece), the seaport of the city. The town used to be called the "Krenides" (meaning "spring") because of the

Carl N. Toney

Paul's Macedonian Call. Church of Saint Nicholas. Kavala, Greece.

[26] Dunn, "New Perspective on Paul," 95–122.

PHILIPPIANS

- Letter's Greeting (1:1–2)
- Thanksgiving and Prayer (1:3–11)
- Examples of Having the Mind of Christ and Calls to Imitate (1:12–4:9)
    - Paul's Suffering and a Call to Imitate (1:12–2:4)
    - Christ Gave Up His Privilege and a Call to Imitate (2:5–18)
    - The Service of Timothy and Epaphroditus and a Call to Beware of Opponents (2:19–3:4a)
    - Paul Gave Up His Privilege and Call to Imitate (3:4b–4:1)
    - Euodia and Syntyche to Have the Mind of Christ and a Call to Practice Virtues (4:2–9)
- Closing Thanksgiving (4:10–20)
- Letter's Conclusion (4:21–23)

abundant number of streams in the area. Then it was called "Philip's city" when the town was renamed after Philip II of Macedon (the father of Alexander the Great), who captured it from the Thracians around 360 BCE. The rich gold mines in the region ended up helping Philip II expand and secure his reign (Strabo, *Geogr. 7 frag.* 34, 42–43).

In 168 BCE, the city came under Roman rule. In 42 BCE, a decisive battle occurred near the town where the forces of Octavian (also known as Augustus) and Antony defeated Brutus and Cassius (Horace, *Carm.* 2.7.9–12). After the battle, Octavian's veteran soldiers were given land to settle. The city grew again after a further intake of soldiers after the defeat of Antony and Cleopatra at the Battle of Actium by Octavian in 31 BCE.

With the influx of soldiers, Philippi became a Roman colony called *Colonia Julia Augusta Philippensis* (Lat.) in honor of Augustus's daughter. Philippi was the urban center for the surrounding land that covered more than seven hundred square miles, including nearby Neapolis, Oisyme, and Apollonia (Strabo, *Geogr. 7 frag.* 41). Most of the inhabitants lived in agricultural settlements, including the veterans who had estates with enslaved people working in the countryside.

Because Philippi was a city full of former soldiers, the most important religion was the imperial cult, which venerated the Roman Empire and the emperor. Inscriptions mentioned priests of the deified emperor and his genius (e.g., Julius, Augustus, Claudia), and monuments were erected for the emperor's gifts of peace and victory.

As a Roman colony, the city followed Roman laws (Lat. *Ius Italicum*) for local affairs. In addition, the city was exempt from Roman tribute and taxation (Acts 16:12). This privilege "by which the whole legal position of the colonists in respect of ownership, transfer of land, payment of taxes, local administration, and law, became the same as if they were upon Italian soil; as, in fact, by a legal fiction, they were."[27] These Roman laws were central to the conflict between Paul and the civic leaders when he visited the city.

Paul and Silas came to Philippi on their second missionary journey (Acts 16:11–40). Originally, they had no intentions of visiting the city. Their missionary travels began by revisiting many of the churches in Asia Minor that Paul had established during his first trip. However, as Paul and Silas ventured further west, Paul felt the Holy Spirit guiding his mission in new directions (Acts 16:6–8). While in Troas, Paul had a mystical experience: a vision of a man from Macedonia beckoning Paul to share his gospel with the Philippians (Acts 16:9–10).

When Paul arrived in Philippi, he found the local Jewish population meeting outside the city near a river (Acts 16:13, 16:16). They met outside town because the Philippians' intolerance of the Jewish people meant they were not allowed to worship in the city. Among them was a "God-fearing" (*sebomenē ton theon*) Gentile woman named Lydia, who was a seller of purple cloth (Acts 16:14). She was likely a former slave who had moved to Philippi from her hometown of Thyatira, which was known for producing wool and purple dyes (Homer, *Il.* 4.141–42; cf. Rev. 2:18–29). Purple was associated with luxury, and the dye was made from both the more economical madder root and the more expensive murex sea snails.[28] The use of her personal name, along with her trade, suggests she enjoyed high social status among freed persons and merchants.[29] When Lydia heard Paul and Silas's message, she and her whole household were baptized, giving them the modern reputation as Paul's first European converts (Acts 16:15). Paul and

Carl N. Toney

Roman forum in Philippi.

[27] Cadbury, *Beginnings of Christianity*, 4:190.

[28] Graves, "What Is the Madder with Lydia's Purple?," 3–29.

[29] Because her husband was not named, she was likely widowed, single, or divorced. Others argue that Lydia was a slave or freedwoman and had a lower status since she practiced an unpleasant trade, and immigrants would have had limited opportunities. Litwak, "Lydia, Lydians," *NIB*, 3:736.

Carl N. Toney

Gladiator relief in Philippi.

Silas stayed with Lydia during their time in the city. Her hospitality was one reason that Paul considered those part of the church in Philippi to be his friends.

One day while traveling to a place of prayer, Paul cast a demon out of a slave girl (Acts 16:16–18). Because she was a source of revenue for her owners, they took Paul and Silas before the magistrates and accused them of disturbing the peace and introducing a foreign religion (Acts 16:19–21). The antisemitic flavor and suspicion of these charges probably reflected Claudius's recent expulsion of Jewish Christians in Rome for causing civic disturbances (49 CE; Acts 18:2).

Paul and Silas were beaten with rods, flogged, and thrown into prison (Acts 16:22–24). Despite an earthquake breaking open the cells, Paul and Silas remained in prison. Their actions converted the jailer and his family (Acts 16:25–34). The next day, they were quickly released because of their Roman citizenship, which exposed their dishonorable treatment by the magistrates (Acts 16:35–38). While the magistrates apologized, they still required Paul and Silas to leave the city (Acts 16:39–40). After this, the nascent church remained on shaky footing with the local people and government. This episode was the first documented formal conflict between Christians and the Roman authorities.

After Paul and Silas left, animosity against the infant Christian church continued (Phil. 1:28–30, 2:15). While Paul was staying in Ephesus (Acts 19:1–41), he began to share correspondences with the church. First, the church learned that Paul had been imprisoned (Phil. 1:7, 1:12–18), so they sent Epaphroditus to share their common trials and to bless Paul with a gift (Phil. 4:18; cf. Phil. 2:25, 4:14). Unfortunately, the church received news that Epaphroditus became ill (Phil. 2:26–27), and he learned that they were concerned for him (Phil. 2:26). Finally, Paul sent him back to Philippi with this letter in the summer of 53 CE (Phil. 2:25, 2:28–30), where he encouraged them to remain steadfast during their trials (Phil. 1:27, 2:16, 4:1).[30]

But this letter was not the end of the story having to do with the church and with Paul. According to Acts 20:1–6, after his three-year stay in Ephesus, Paul returned to Philippi as part of his mission to encourage believers in Macedonia and Greece. Because Paul was dealing with the Corinthian crisis (1 Cor. 16:5), this visit was not pleasant (2 Cor. 7:5; cf. 2 Cor. 2:13). However, the positive relations with the Macedonian churches and their generous support helped maintain Paul throughout this bleak time (2 Cor. 8:1–15).

[30] For the cause of Paul's imprisonment, see Murphy-O'Connor, *Paul*, 184. Some reduce this to three trips. First, news reached the Philippians of Paul's imprisonment. Second, while Epaphroditus was sent to Paul, news of his illness reached the Philippians, and the Philippians consoled him. Third, Epaphroditus was sent with the letter.

Paul's Imprisonment

Five out of Paul's thirteen letters were written from prison: Ephesians, Philippians, Colossians, Philemon, and 2 Timothy. The first four letters are sometimes called the **Prison epistles**, or Captivity letters. (2 Timothy is linked with the "Pastorals"). From Acts, we learn about Paul's brief imprisonment in Philippi (Acts 16:23–40), his two-year imprisonment in Caesarea (Acts 21:32–26:32), and his final Roman imprisonment (Acts 28:30–31). Because 2 Timothy appears to have been written prior to Paul's death, this letter would have been written from Rome. However, we are unsure of the location where Paul wrote Ephesians, Philippians, Colossians, and Philemon.

The traditional view is that Ephesians, Philippians, Colossians, and Philemon were written during Paul's Roman imprisonment as recorded in Acts 28:30–31 (Eusebius, *Hist. eccl.* 2.22.1, 3.15.1; ca. 60–62 CE). An alternative view proposes these letters were written in Caesarea (Acts 21:32–26:32; ca. 58–59 CE).[31] In favor of either location, potential "developments" in Paul's thoughts may reflect the end of his ministry. In these letters, Paul presented high views of Christ (e.g., Christ's divinity in Phil. 2:6–11 and Col. 1:15–20), more formal views of church structure (e.g., bishops and deacons in Phil. 1:1), and patriarchal household codes (Col. 3:18–4:1; Eph. 5:21–6:9). In addition, the reference in Philippians to the imperial guard (Phil. 1:13) and Caesar's household (Phil. 4:22) may point to Rome or Caesarea.

Rome, Philippi, Ephesus, and Caesarea are locations of Paul's imprisonments.

[31]First proposed in 1799 by H. E. G. Paulus of Jena.

A third option favors an unnamed imprisonment in Ephesus (ca. 53 CE) as the location for the composition of Philippians, Colossians, and Philemon.[32] In support of this view, we have early traditions of an Ephesian imprisonment (Marcionite Prologues; Acts of Paul). Paul's letters also describe multiple imprisonments not recorded in Acts (2 Cor. 6:5, 11:23; Rom. 16:7; cf. 1 Clem. 5.6). We also find allusions to an Ephesian imprisonment, including Paul fighting with "wild animals" in Ephesus (1 Cor. 15:32) and experiencing hardships and a death sentence in the province of Asia (2 Cor. 1:8–9, 2:4:7–12; cf. Phil. 1:19–20).

Several factors may favor an Ephesian imprisonment, especially for Philippians and Philemon. (If Colossians was written at the same time as Philemon, then it could also have been written from Ephesus.) In light of the multiple travel accounts recorded in Philippians and Philemon, the proximity of Ephesus to Philippi (five hundred miles) and Colossae (one hundred miles) was more reasonable than the great distance of these cities from Rome to Philippi (1,200 miles) and Colossae (1,800 miles) or from Caesarea to Philippi (1,250 miles) and Colossae (850 miles).[33] Based on distance, the multiple journeys recorded in Philippians fit better with Ephesus. Likewise, Philemon's description of a slave fleeing from Colossae to Ephesus is easier to imagine than a slave fleeing to Rome. It is even more difficult to imagine that Onesimus could have evaded capture in Caesarea.

The presence of Timothy with Paul (Phil. 1:1; Philem. 1; Col. 1:1) also fits an Ephesian imprisonment (Acts 19:22). An earlier Ephesian imprisonment also aligns Paul's future plans to travel west (Rom. 15:23–24, 15:28) and with his desire to visit Philippi (Phil. 2:24) and Colossae (Philem. 22) after leaving Ephesus (Acts 20:1–6). This earlier Ephesian imprisonment would also explain Paul's failure to mention the Jerusalem collection in Philippians, a letter that praises their generosity.[34] While the traditional view that Paul wrote these letters from Rome is commendable, an Ephesian imprisonment also offers a plausible location for Philippians, Philemon, and Colossians.[35]

The Philippians' reputation for generosity and sincerity was later recorded by Polycarp (*Phil.* 11.3), who recalled, "[Paul] boasts about you in all the churches." Similarly, the Marcionite prologue to this letter says, "[The Philippians] persevered in faith after they had accepted the word of truth and they did not receive false prophets." Most likely, it was the Philippian's generosity toward Paul (Phil. 2:25; cf. 2 Cor. 8:1–5, 8:8) that inspired him to take up a collection for the Jerusalem church (1 Cor. 16:1–4; 2 Cor. 8:1–9:15; Rom. 15:14–32). The Jerusalem collection was designed to relieve poverty, to engender solidarity between Jewish and Gentile believers, and to fulfill prophecies of the Gentiles bringing gifts in the last days (2 Cor. 8:13–14, 9:12; Rom. 15:26–27; Isa. 2:1–5, 60:5–14, 66:18–20; cf. Mic. 4:1–4; Zech. 14:16).

[32] First proposed in 1900 by Heinrich Lisco.

[33] All numbers are rounded. The following days of travel were calculated by using https://orbis.stanford.edu. From Ephesus to Philippi: twenty-seven days by land (500 miles); six days by land and sea (430 miles). From Ephesus to Colossae: six days by land (100 miles). From Rome to Philippi: seventy days by land (1,200 miles); eighteen days by land and sea (1,600 miles). From Rome to Colossae: ninety-seven days by land (1,800 miles); twenty-one days by land and sea (1,400 miles). From Caesarea to Philippi: sixty-nine days by land (1,250 miles) and seventeen days by land and sea (1,300 miles). From Caesarea to Colossae: forty-seven days by land (850 miles) and sixteen days by land and sea (675 miles).

[34] See the discussion of the collection in the chapter on 2 Corinthians.

[35] Issues of Pauline authorship will be explored under each letter. Ephesians could also be written during an Ephesian imprisonment if "to the Ephesians" is not original to the letter.

What Philippians Is All About

Let's be friends. The Philippians' friendship with Paul was reflected by Paul addressing them as siblings (Phil. 1:12, 1:14, 2:25, 3:1, 3:13, 3:17, 4:1, 4:8, 4:21) unlike his usual address to churches as children (e.g., 1 Thess. 2:7, 2:11; Gal. 4:19–20; 1 Cor. 1:14–15, 7:14; 2 Cor. 6:13, 12:14–17).[36] Paul expressed his affection and longing to be with the church (Phil. 1:7–8, 4:1). Because of this relationship, Paul wrote the Philippians a letter of friendship. According to Demetrius (*Eloc.* 225, 229, 231–32), letters of friendship were meant to help maintain friendships.

Like other letters of friendship, Philippians includes a pattern of emulation. Paul presented examples like Timothy (Phil. 2:19–24), Epaphroditus (Phil. 2:25–30), and himself (Phil. 1:12–25, 2:17–18, 3:3–17). In contrast to these positive models, Paul urged the Philippians not to imitate those who preached the gospel out of selfish motives (Phil. 1:15–18), those who promoted following the law (Phil. 3:3–6), or the bickering of Euodia and Syntyche (Phil. 4:2–3). Most importantly, the Philippians were called to imitate Christ's humility, whose lordship called them to follow his premier paradigm (Phil. 2:6–11).[37]

Because of their friendship, Paul was disturbed to hear about the disunity within the church (Phil. 2:2–4, 2:14, 4:2). As a cure, Paul highlighted their "fellowship" (*koinōnia*) with each other (Phil. 1:5, 2:1, 3:10, 4:15) because "fellowship is the essence of friendship" (Aristotle, *Eth. nic.* 8.9.1). Likewise, this unity and fellowship was expressed by having the single mind of Christ (Phil. 2:2, 2:5, 4:2).[38]

In addition, Paul used the language of friendship and mutuality throughout the letter (e.g., Phil. 1:27–2:18, 4:2–3).[39] He stressed the importance of equality and agreement (Phil. 1:27–2:4, 4:2). Reciprocity (Phil. 1:7, 1:30, 2:17–18, 4:14), including giving and receiving, was important for friendship (Phil. 4:10–20). Paul was grateful for the financial gift that he received (e.g., Phil. 1:3, 1:5, 2:25, 4:10, 4:14–20).[40] Paul considered them to be partners in the gospel (Phil. 1:5) who shared in God's grace (Phil. 1:7). They shared common experiences of suffering (Phil. 1:29–30) and

Public Domain

This fresco from the dyer's shop (Lat. *fullonica*) in Pompeii depicts a man on the left brushing wool and a man on the right whitening fabric. The owl represents Athena, protector of wool merchants.

[36] On friendship, see Saller, *Personal Patronage under the Early Empire*, 1–22; Fitzgerald, *Friendship, Flattery, and Frankness*; Konstan, *Friendship in the Classical World*.

[37] Humility, not selfish ambition or "low self-esteem," puts others first (Phil. 2:3–4).

[38] Cousar, *Galatians, Philippians, and 1 Thessalonians*, 118.

[39] Paul's emphasis upon mutuality is reflected by his frequent use of words with the prefixes "with" (*syn-*), like "co-assist" (*syzygos*, Phil. 4:3), "co-help" (*syllambanō*, Phil. 4:3), "co-worker" (*synergōn*, Phil. 4:3), "co-struggle" (*synathleō*, Phil. 1:27, 4:3) "co-rejoice" (*sygchairō*, Phil. 2:17, 2:18), "co-sharers" (*sygkoinōnos*, Phil. 1:7), and "co-soul" (*sympsychos*, Phil. 2:2).

[40] O'Brien, "Thanksgiving and the Gospel in Paul," 151–52.

distress (Phil. 4:14). But they also shared their citizenship in heaven, had a common hope (Phil. 3:20), and possessed a mutual joy (Phil. 2:2, 2:17–18, 4:1).

Along with patronage, friendship was considered a fundamental social institution that held the Greco-Roman world together. Patronage defined hierarchical relationships, and friendship defined relationships between equals. True friendship was based on common virtues (Phil. 4:8–9). Aristotle (*Eth. nic.* 8.1.4) wrote that friendship was "the bond of the state; lawgivers seem to set more store by it than they do by justice, for to promote concord, which seems akin to friendship, is their chief aim, while faction, which is enmity, is what they are most anxious to banish. And if men are friends, there is no need of justice between them." For Paul, this Greco-Roman ideal of friendship was transformed by the presence of Christ into a three-way reciprocal relationship between Paul, the Philippians, and Christ."[41]

Redemptive suffering. Unfortunately, suffering is part of the human condition. Followers of Jesus do not get to avoid suffering. Paul reminded the Philippians how he suffered when imprisoned in Philippi (Phil. 1:27–30; cf. Acts 16:16–40). He again suffered as a prisoner (Phil. 1:17). The Philippians shared a similar life of suffering (Phil. 1:29, 3:10), as they lived in an evil society (Phil. 2:15). Their suffering was

Carl N. Toney

The Philippian jail where Paul may have been imprisoned.

[41]Cousar, *Galatians, Philippians, and 1 Thessalonians*, 119; Fee, *Philippians*, 12–14.

not a sign of God's displeasure, nor was Paul's suffering a sign of his failed apostleship or a false gospel (Phil. 1:12–18). Instead, suffering occurred because God permitted it (Phil. 1:27–30). More importantly, it was an opportunity to imitate Christ's suffering and vindication (Phil. 2:6–11).

Paul's opponents had a different view of suffering. They claimed that the Christian life should be free from hardship, strife, and loss because believers should already experience the power of Christ's resurrection on earth (Phil. 3:10–16; cf. Phil. 3:21). As Jewish Christians, their appeal included the importance of membership within the "true" Israel, which was secured through circumcision (Phil. 3:2–3).[42] For the Philippians, this assurance of salvation and the simplicity and clarity of following a clear set of rules was appealing.

In response, Paul argued that believers currently suffered but that their bodies would be transformed when Christ returned (Phil. 3:10–11, 3:20–21). He contrasted his opponents' Jewish credentials with his own (Phil. 3:4–6). While he was blameless according to the law, this was insufficient because salvation for everyone was found through Christ. These things were now "rubbish" (*skybalon*, Phil. 3:7) because of the work of Christ.[43] With fiery language, Paul called these Jewish Christians "enemies of the cross of Christ" (Phil. 3:18) and "dogs" (Phil. 3:2).[44] He equated their desire for circumcision as a shameful (Phil. 3:19) mutilation of the flesh (Phil. 3:2). He belittled their kosher diet writing, "Their god is the belly" (Phil. 3:19).

Paul's view of suffering derived from his end-time expectations. While believers (including Paul and the Philippians) shared in Christ's sufferings, they could endure because their future goal was exaltation and a heavenly dwelling under God's rule (Phil. 3:10–14, 3:21). This hope transformed their current suffering from something shameful into a privilege (Phil. 1:29). In response to present suffering, Paul encouraged the Philippians to stand firm (Phil. 1:27, 4:1) and bear witness to Christ (Phil. 2:15).

For Paul, suffering was redeemable when it leads to sharing the gospel (Phil. 1:12–18). Christian suffering follows the model of Christ's suffering (Phil. 2:6–11). This allows believers to participate in Christ's suffering in the present (Phil. 3:10), which will lead to participation in his resurrection in the future (Phil. 3:11). Christian suffering is also transformative, and Paul expressed this hope when he wrote, "I am confident of this, that the one who began a good work among you will bring it to completion by the day of Jesus Christ" (Phil. 1:6).

Joy and the mind of Christ. In response to their suffering, Paul called the Philippians to have a joyful mindset. Sixteen times Paul emphasized "joy" and "rejoicing" (*chara*, *chairō*, *synchairō*, Phil. 1:4, 1:18, 1:25, 2:2, 2:17–18, 2:28–29, 3:1, 3:17–18, 4:1, 4:4, 4:10). Because "joy" (*chara*) should be consistent and not dependent upon circumstances (Phil. 4:10–14), Paul exhorted the Philippians to rejoice (Phil. 3:1, 4:4). Joy offers strength amid suffering (Phil. 2:17–18).

Joy does not abandon emotions but instead is grounded in the hope found in Christ. Present joy is experienced through hope created by the mutual encouragement of other believers through their actions,

---

[42] Hawthorne and Martin, *Philippians*, liv-lv; Jewett, "Agitators and the Galatian Congregation," 198–212.

[43] *Skybalon* has a variety of meanings, including dung/feces, spoilt food, scraps/leftovers from a meal, trash/refuse, a half-eaten corpse, or filth-like lumps of manure (Lang, "σκύβαλον," *TDNT*, 7:445–47).

[44] Calling his opponents "dogs" (*kynai*) may allude to the "Cynics" (*Kynikos*), whose name derived from "dog" (*kyōn*) because of crude public behavior.

Game carved into a street at Philippi.

prayers, and support (Phil. 1:4, 3:1, 4:4, 4:10). Their future hope included the assurance of their heavenly citizenship (Phil. 3:20) and the expectation that Jesus would return soon and reign (Phil. 4:5). This hope transformed their present sufferings into joy through Christ (Phil. 4:4–5).

Paul considered the key to **joy** to be a mind guided by Christ (Phil. 2:1–5). Paul's emphasis upon a proper mindset was reflected in his ten uses of the term "to think" (*phroneō*, Phil. 1:7, 2:2 [2x], 2:5, 3:15 [2x], 3:19, 4:2, 4:10 [2x]). Unlike today, "happiness" (*eudaimonia*) in the ancient world was not a feeling. Instead, philosophers argued that a happy life occurred when "reason" (*logos*) controlled a person's passions and desires (e.g., Aristotle, *Eth. nic.* 2.6.1106b; Plato, *Meno* 88c). Rather than reason being the key to having a good life, Paul argued that having the same mindset as Christ led to a virtuous life. A mindset of Christ reveals virtuous qualities, such as selflessness, humility, love, and generosity (Phil. 2:6–11). A heavenly mindset is a sign of maturity and brings assurance (Phil. 3:15), while an earthly mindset causes destruction (Phil. 3:19). In sum, joy is found when a person thinks and acts like Christ.

A hymn to Christ. Did you know that early Christians sang (or at least chanted)? Jesus and the disciples sang psalms during the Lord's Supper (Mark 14:26). Elsewhere, Paul described Christians gathering to sing hymns (1 Cor. 14:26; Eph. 5:19; Col. 3:16). Pliny the Younger (*Ep.* 10.96; ca. 112–13 CE) told us that Christians sang hymns to Christ "as a god." When Paul and Silas were in jail in Philippi, they sang hymns (Acts 16:25). What did this songbook look like? One viable option is the book of Psalms. It is also possible that the New Testament contains early hymns, which functioned as confessions of faith.[45]

One of these early hymns may be the "Christ hymn" in Philippians 2:6–11. Paul introduced this hymn because he wanted his audience to have the same mind as Christ (Phil. 2:5), and he concluded by exhorting believers to obedience (Phil. 2:12–18) by "work[ing] out your salvation with fear and trembling" (Phil. 2:12). A helpful image of the purpose of this hymn is the "way of Christ as a yardstick or standard for the life of Christians."[46] Paul described Christ as Lord of the Philippians, who should be obeyed by his servants, who were called to conform to his attitude of humility and unselfishness.

Spatially, the hymn contains a U-movement (heaven-earth-heaven). It begins with Jesus's heavenly existence (Phil. 2:6). Jesus was understood as **preexistent**—that is, he existed in heaven before becoming human. Christ's divinity is described as being in God's "form" (*morphē*).[47] Next, Jesus moved down to his earthly humiliation and death (Phil. 2:7–8). The concept of the divine Jesus becoming a human is

[45] Johannes Weiss (1899) first noticed the poetic nature of these verses. Some scholars argue that Paul was quoting and modifying a pre-existing document. For an in-depth study, see Martin, *A Hymn of Christ Philippians 2:5–11 in Recent Interpretation & in the Setting of Early Christian Worship.*

[46] This is the subheading for these verses in the 1982 *Deutsche Bibel.*

[47] Fee, *Philippians*, 204.

called the **incarnation**, and this is one of several key passages that expounds on this (John 1:1–18; Rom. 1:3–4; Col. 1:15–20; Heb. 1:1–14). In the process of becoming human, Jesus "emptied" (*kenoō*) himself of his divine attributes. This emptying is called **kenosis**. Christ's willingness to give up his equality with God contrasts with Adam's failed attempt to become like God (Gen. 3:1–7). The language of Christ humbling himself also draws upon the servant passages of Isaiah, including Isaiah 52:13–53:12. Finally, God raised Jesus back up to heaven with his divine exaltation and rule over everything in heaven and earth (Phil. 2:9–11). This exaltation drew upon the messianic motifs of Christ's lordship from Psalm 110:1 and the Son of Man from Daniel 7:13–14.

Discussions surrounding the identity of Jesus fall under the broad category of **Christology**, which refers to the study of Christ. Early church debates about the nature of Jesus would not be resolved until the councils of Nicea (325 CE), which affirmed the Trinity, and Chalcedon (451 CE), which affirmed Jesus's two natures (he is fully divine and human)—formally called the **hypostatic union**. Paul, however, was not interested in these later doctrinal debates. Paul used this hymn to challenge the fear and outlook of meaninglessness in the broader Greco-Roman culture. He asserted that God was in charge and that life had meaning.[48] In addition, Christ was presented as the ultimate ethical example of sacrifice

Carl N. Toney

Philippi Theater.

[48] Dunn, *Christology in the Making*, 114–21.

and service for the Philippians to follow (Phil. 2:5; cf. Phil. 1:7, 2:2, 3:15, 3:19, 4:2, 4:10). Paul asked the Philippians to consider what Jesus would do. They followed his example because Jesus was now in charge since he has been exalted above every name "and every tongue should confess that Jesus Christ is Lord" (Phil. 2:11).

Key Terms and People

Christology: the study of Jesus

Faith in/of Jesus: this expression may be understood as either a believer's faith in Jesus's death and resurrection or the faithfulness of Jesus either to God or to humanity through his death and resurrection

Hypostatic union: the belief that Jesus is fully God and fully human

Incarnation: the belief that God became a human when Jesus was born

Joy: when a person thinks and acts like Christ

Kenosis: the belief that Jesus temporarily put aside some of his divine attributes when he became human

Preexistence: Jesus existed as God prior to becoming human

Prison epistles: the letters Paul wrote from prison (Philippians, Ephesians, Colossians, Philemon)

Righteousness: understood as the right relationship between God and people, as well as between people based on God's covenantal promises

Torah/law: the Jewish understanding of the law, encapsulated by the word *Torah*, is "instruction" or "teaching"; the law can refer to the Jewish scriptures, the Pentateuch (Genesis to Deuteronomy), a particular book, a specific commandment, or a general principle; the law is good, and salvation has always been a free gift from God

Works of the law: the works of the law are either (1) attempting to earn salvation through "good works" or (2) Jewish identity markers like food laws, circumcision, and Sabbath observance that separated Jews from Gentiles

Conversation Starters

1. Do you think Paul was writing to the Galatians in the north (Acts 16:6, 18:23) or those in the south (Acts 13:13–14:23)?
2. Why was Paul so mad at the Galatians? What do you think of Paul's opponents' message that since Jesus was a Jew, he only saved the Jewish people?
3. How would Paul describe the law? Do you agree or disagree with the idea that Paul thought the law was good?
4. Do you think Paul was talking about having faith in Christ or the faithfulness of Christ?
5. What is the relationship between righteousness and justification? How do you understand these terms?
6. Why was freedom so important for Paul? How does the Holy Spirit help bring freedom?

7. Where do you think Paul wrote his various Prison epistles?
8. What did friendship look like between Paul and the Philippians?
9. What did you learn about Jesus from the Christ hymn?
10. How is Christian suffering different from the usual suffering in life? How do Christians find joy in suffering? How is Christ a model for people who suffer?

FOR FURTHER READING

Galatians

Betz, Hans Dieter. *Galatians: A Commentary on Paul's Letter to the Churches in Galatia*. Herm. Fortress, 1979.

Cousar, Charles B. *Reading Galatians, Philippians, and 1 Thessalonians: A Literary and Theological Commentary*. RNT. Smyth & Helwys, 2001.

deSilva, David A. *The Letter to the Galatians*. 2nd ed. NICNT. Eerdmans, 2018.

Dunn, James D. G. *The Epistle to the Galatians*. BNTC. Hendrickson, 1993.

Jervis, L. Ann. *Galatians*. NIBC 9. Hendrickson, 1999.

Gupta, Nijay K. *Galatians*. Story of God Bible Commentary. Zondervan Academic, 2023.

Martyn, J. Louis. *Galatians: A New Translation with Introduction and Commentary*. AYB 33A. Yale University Press, 2008.

Philippians

Belleville, Linda. *Philippians*. New Covenant Commentary. Cascade, 2021.

Bockmuehl, Markus. *The Epistle to the Philippians*. BNTC 11. Hendrickson, 1998.

Cohick, Lynn. *Philippians*. Story of God Bible Commentary. Zondervan, 2013.

Fee, Gordon D. *Philippians*. IVP New Testament Commentary Series. InterVarsity Press, 1999.

Reumann, John. *Philippians: A New Translation with Introduction and Commentary*. AYB 33B. Yale University Press, 2008.

Silva, Moisés. *Philippians*. 2nd ed. BECNT. Baker Academic, 2005.

Thurston, Bonnie B. "Philippians." In *Philippians and Philemon*. SP 10. Liturgical Press, 2009.

8

LETTERS ACROSS ASIA MINOR

Colossians, Philemon, and Ephesians

A General Introduction to These Letters

The letters of Colossians, Philemon, and Ephesians are often studied together because they share many themes. For example, both Colossians and Ephesians use similar body of Christ imagery (Col. 1:18, 1:24, 2:19, 3:15; Eph. 1:22–23, 4:15–16, 5:23). These letters also offer comparable advice about household relationships (Col. 1:18–4:1; Eph. 5:21–6:9), and all three letters reveal early Christian perspectives on slavery (Col. 3:22–4:1; Eph. 6:5–9; Philem. 10–18).

Additionally, the people featured in all three letters bind them together. **Tychicus** was the letter carrier for both Colossians and Ephesians (Col. 4:7–8; Eph. 6:21–22). Colossians and Philemon are connected by Paul's coauthor of Timothy (Col. 1:1; Philem. 1) and the recipients of Onesimus and Archippus (Col. 4:7–9, 4:17; Philem. 2, 12). Both letters also mention Paul's companions of Epaphras, Aristarchus, Demas, Luke, and Mark (Col. 4:12, 4:14; Philem. 23–24). Because of these similarities, we will explore these letters together. We'll begin with the letter to the Colossians.

SUGGESTED READING

Acts 19:1-20:1
Acts 20:17-38
Philemon
Colossians
Ephesians

Colossians

The Story So Far

Colossae was devastated by an earthquake in 60–61 CE (Tacitus, *Ann.* 14.27; or in 64 CE).[1] But in times past, the city was one of the principal cities in the region (Herodotus, *Hist.* 7.30; Xenophon, *Anab.* 1.2.6;

[1]Likely reporting the same event, Tacitus (*Ann.* 14.27) recounts nearby Laodicea being destroyed in 60–61 CE, and Eusebius (*Chron.* 1.21–22) mentions the destruction of Colossae, Laodicea, and Hierapolis in 63–64 CE. If Colossae was destroyed by an earthquake in 60–61 CE, then Paul's captivity must be dated before then. Reicke, "Historical Setting of Colossians," 429–32.

Hierapolis's hot springs include travertine terraces covered with carbonate minerals left by the flowing of thermal spring water.

Diodorus Siculus 14.80.8; Pliny, *Nat.* 5.145). The town was named after its famous wool that was dyed a distinct dark red color called *colossinus* (Strabo, *Geogr.* 12.8.16; Pliny, *Nat.* 21.51). Its fertile valley produced figs, olives, and grapes. Being on the major east–west trade route from the Euphrates River to Ephesus helped to ensure centuries of prosperity.

The city was in the southern portion of the Roman province of Asia (western Turkey) in the Lycus River Valley near the foot of Mount Cadmus. The neighboring city of Laodicea was the administrative and financial center of the region, and Hierapolis was famous for its hot springs (Col. 2:1, 4:13–16).[2] During the Roman period, these cities grew in commercial and social importance, while Colossae declined.

While the population mainly consisted of Phrygians and Greeks, there were several thousand Jewish people in the city.[3] The Greek ruler Antiochus III brought the Jewish people to the region around 200 BCE (Josephus, *Ant.* 12.147–53). The numerous grave inscriptions from Hierapolis indicate that these Jewish people integrated into the region. Philo (*Embassy* 245) also testified to the significant Jewish presence. However, the Jewish people's relationship with the Romans was not always smooth. In 62/61 BCE, the governor, Lucius Valerius Flaccus, attempted to seize the collected the Jewish temple tax of twenty pounds of gold from Laodicea (Cicero, *Flac.* 28.68).

---

[2]Hierapolis's warm water and Colossae's cool water were considered useful, while Laodicea's lukewarm water was not beneficial. Revelation 3:15–16 uses this image of useless lukewarm water to condemn the church of Laodicea for being useless to God.

[3]Dunn, *Colossians and to Philemon*, 21–22. Based on the temple tax from Laodicea (Cicero, *Flac.* 28.68), scholars calculate a Jewish male population of eleven thousand.

Authorship of Colossians

Did Paul really write this letter? Some scholars don't think Paul wrote Colossians based on the unique language and style of the letter.[4] However, language and style are easily accounted for by Paul using a scribe (Col. 4:18). More challenging are arguments claiming that this letter reflects later theological ideas related to Christ, the church, the home, and the end times.

For example, the Christ hymn (Col. 1:15–20) may reflect a higher view of Jesus than Paul's other writings (1 Cor. 8:6; Rom. 8:31–39). However, the Christ hymn of Colossians presents similar high views of Jesus as the Philippians hymn (Phil. 2:6–11) as well as Paul's language about Christ in other early letters (1 Cor. 8:6, 1:24, 2:6–10).

Regarding Christ's relationship to the church, Colossians uses the body of Christ imagery differently from 1 Corinthians and Romans. In Colossians, Christ is the "head" (*kephalē*) of the body of Christ (Col. 1:18, 1:24, 2:19, 3:15), while the other letters focus on believers' relationships within the body of Christ (1 Cor. 12:12–27; Rom. 12:4–5). These differences can be attributed to the different challenges facing the Colossian church (Col. 2:8, 2:20). Likewise, Ephesians uses body imagery similar to Colossians, with Christ as the head of the church (Eph. 4:15–16, 5:23) and over all cosmic powers (Eph. 1:22–23).

Regarding the home, the household codes in Colossians may reflect a more formalized home and church structure (Col. 3:18–4:1; cf. Eph. 5:21–6:9) than what we see in Paul's earlier writings, especially when he wrote, "neither slave nor free, nor is there male and female" (Gal. 3:28 NIV). However, these household concerns complement concerns about household management as found in Philemon. They qualify an overzealous application of Galatians 3:28 (cf. Col. 3:11), much like 1 Corinthians 8–10 qualifies Paul's earlier teaching on freedom in Galatians 5:1–21.

Further, Colossians' views about the end seem to have shifted away from Paul's earlier future hope (1 Thess. 4:13, 5:8; Gal. 5:5) to focus on a present, realized hope (Col. 2:12–13, 3:1). But these differences are overstated. The more present focus in Colossians reflects a similar sentiment as Romans 6:1–14, and Colossians does include future expectations (Col. 3:1–4).

In light of questions like these, it is possible that a disciple or "school" of Paul composed the letter either during his lifetime or shortly after he died, based upon the letter of Philemon and a collection of Paul's teachings.[5] But it seems far-fetched that Colossians would be based on the limited material from the short letter of Philemon. Further, Colossians enjoyed wide acceptance by early church fathers (Irenaeus, *Haer.* 3.14.1; Tertullian, *Praescr.* 7; Clement of Alexandria, *Strom.* 1.1). Thus, it is very likely that Paul wrote this letter.

Because Philemon was written to the same community, it may have accompanied Colossians. These letters are joined by Onesimus being sent by Paul to Colossae (Col. 4:9; Philem. 10–12). If Paul also wrote Ephesians, then it could have accompanied Colossians as a circular letter written to the churches in Asia. Colossians and Ephesians are linked by Tychicus as the letter carrier (Col. 4:7–9; Eph. 6:21–22).[6] More challenging is determining where and when these letters were written—the options include Paul's imprisonments in Ephesus (53 CE), Caesarea (58–59 CE), or Rome (60–62 CE).[7]

---

[4]The modern debate of authorship began in 1838 with Ernst Mayerhoff.

[5]Dunn, *Colossians and to Philemon*, 35–39.

[6]According to 2 Timothy, Paul sent Tychicus to Ephesus while in his Roman prison (2 Tim. 4:12).

[7]See the discussion of Paul's imprisonment in the chapter on Philippians.

Regarding religious practices, Colossae was home to a cult of Cybele, the great mother-goddess of Asia, whose worship may have included fertility rites, asceticism, and ritual mutilation. Various Eastern and Egyptian gods were also worshiped, including Isis, Sarapis, Mithras, Demeter, Helios, and Selene. The cult of Men Ascaenus, the chief god of Pisidian Antioch, was also found in the region. These various gods and goddesses may have contributed to an attitude of religious syncretism in the city. This was fertile ground for false teaching to grow in the church that was influenced by a mixture of the Jewish religion and Greco-Roman philosophy and religion.[8] Due to the similarities between Paul's letter to the Galatians and this letter, it may be that similar Jewish Christian opponents were swaying the Colossian church.[9]

So, when did Paul arrive in Colossae and share his gospel? He didn't. The community was founded by Epaphras, who acted like Paul's personal delegate (Col. 1:7–8). Paul never met the Colossians (Col. 2:1). Instead, he knew them through Epaphras and Onesimus (Col. 4:9). This was not the last time that Paul would write a letter to a church he had not visited. The letter of Romans was also written to a church Paul had not visited (Rom. 1:10).

Marble relief of Cybele in a small temple. Ancient Agora Museum, Athens. (fourth cent. BCE)

Paul identified himself as the author (Col. 1:1) and included a greeting written in his own hand to demonstrate the authenticity of the letter (Col. 4:18). Notably, Paul greeted a woman named **Nympha**. She was one of the patrons of the church and provided her home for some of the believers to gather (Col. 4:15).[10] Paul would have written this letter to the Colossians around the summer of 53 CE while imprisoned in Ephesus. Alternatively, Paul may have sent this letter from his Roman prison around 60–62 CE. Due to his own imprisonment, Paul used Tychicus as his letter carrier (Col. 4:7; cf. Eph. 6:21; 2 Tim. 4:12; Titus 3:12). Another famous letter carrier was Phoebe, who took the letter of Romans to the capital of the empire (Rom. 16:1–2). A significant part of these letter carriers' duties was to convey Paul's personal presence and authority to his audience.

What Colossians Is All About

Christ is at the center of it all. The centrality of Christ is the defining feature of Colossians. All of

[8] Ferguson, *Religions of the Roman Empire*, 217.

[9] Murphy-O'Connor, *Paul*, 247–48.

[10] One may wonder how Nympha, the head of her household, would have felt hearing Paul's household codes that reinforced the leadership positions of the husband, father, and master. See the discussion in Osiek, MacDonald, and Tulloch, *A Woman's Place*, 18.

Christ the King in Almada, Portugal.

Paul's arguments and pleas pointed back to Christ, and he called the Colossians to submit to Christ's lordship. Paul made a case for the supremacy of Christ in the works of creation and redemption. Believers must "perceive the preeminence of Christ in all things, and to recognize that believers already exist in him, having been raised with him and transferred into his kingdom."[11]

Just as Paul encouraged the Colossians to sing hymns, psalms, and spiritual songs (Col. 3:16), he grounded his argument in a traditional hymn about Christ (Col. 1:15–20).[12] This hymn is one of the

[11] Foster, *Colossians*, 35.
[12] Witherington, *Philemon, the Colossians, and the Ephesians*, 130.

premier New Testament passages that shape discussions about Jesus's divinity (Col. 1:15–20; Phil. 2:7–11; John 1:1–18; Heb. 1:1–14). Structurally, the hymn can be divided in half—focusing on Christ and creation (Col. 1:15–18a) and the church (Col. 1:18b–20). However, it can also be divided into thirds, where Christ is the creator (Col. 1:15–16), sustainer (Col. 1:17–18a), and reconciler of all creation (Col. 1:18b–20).[13]

In this hymn, Christ is declared to be the "image" (*eikōn*) of the invisible God (Col. 1:15). As God's image, Christ is in the same form or reflection as God (cf. Col. 4:4; Phil. 2:6; Heb. 1:3). Image language recalls the creation of Adam and Eve, who were made in God's "image" (Heb. *tselem*, Gen. 1:26–27). Now Christ is the new Adam in the renewed creation (cf. 1 Cor. 15:45, 15:47; Rom. 5:12–21). The hymn also frames Christ in light of Jewish traditions about divine Wisdom. Wisdom was the image of God's goodness (Wisd. of Sol. 7:27) and mediated God's presence (Wisd. of Sol. 9:9–12). Wisdom was created first (Prov. 8:22–26), participated in creation (Prov. 8:27–31; Wisd. of Sol. 9:9), and will renew all things (Wisd. of Sol. 7:27).[14] As God's image, Christ tangibly mediates God's presence in creation.

Being the "firstborn" (*prōtotokos*) of all creation (Col. 1:15) denotes Christ's special status and higher rank above creation (cf. Rom. 8:29; 1 Cor. 15:20, 15:23; Heb. 1:6). This is not to be misunderstood as a statement that Christ was a created being. Firstborn imagery is not literal. Instead, it echoes the figurative language used for the special status of the king (Ps. 89:27) and Israel (Exod. 4:22; Jer. 31:9; 4 Ezra 6:58) as God's firstborn. Christ's supremacy over everything in heaven and earth is established by his role in creating (Col. 1:16) and sustaining all things (Col. 1:17). Likewise, Christ is the "firstborn" from the dead (Col. 1:18) because he is the prototype for the new creation.

In addition, this hymn describes the church as the "body of Christ," with Christ as the "head" (*kephalē*, Col. 1:18, 1:24, 2:19, 3:15). With this image, Paul compared Christ to Greco-Roman rulers who were depicted as the "head" of a city and the state as his "body" (Tacitus, *Ann.* 1.12, 1.13; Plutarch, *Galba* 4.3; Philo, *Rewards* 114, 125). As the head of the church, Christ is an authority figure over the church (Col. 2:10; cf. Eph. 1:22). Body imagery reminded the Colossians of the importance of unity within the church and Christ's role in their reconciliation (Col. 3:15). Paul also included a cosmic dimension to Christ's rule by drawing upon the idea that the universe was a "body," with its "head" being the leading principle (Orphic fragment 168; Philo, *QE* 2.117).[15] As Christ's body, the church shares in Christ's rule over everything while also submitting to Christ the head.

Christ's supremacy over all of creation was established by his resurrection (Col. 1:18). Paul proclaimed that the "fullness" (*plērōma*) of God dwells in Christ and that Christ is God's agent in reconciliation. Christ's work of reconciliation is so comprehensive that it includes victory over the hostile, alien, and evil powers that a first-century person would have feared the most (Col. 1:16, 2:15). This cosmic work of Christ is grounded in the historical reality of Jesus's incarnation (Col. 1:22, 2:9, 2:11). Paul also located redemption in Jesus's earthly suffering (Col. 1:24) and the cross where his blood was shed (Col. 1:20). Thus, Christ is Lord over everything. He is the Lord over all of creation—both in the earthly and spiritual

[13]Eduard Norden in 1913 was the first modern scholar to analyze this as a hymn. See a review of the various positions by O'Brien, *Colossians, Philemon*, 32–42.

[14]Bird, *Colossians and Philemon*, 51–52.

[15]Paul modified a hymn that praised Christ as the head of the cosmos by adding "church." Lohse, *Colossians and Philemon*, 54–55; Dunn, *Colossians and to Philemon*, 95.

COLOSSIANS

- Letter's Greetings (1:1–2)
- Thanksgiving and Prayer (1:3–14)
- Christ's Supremacy over All Creation (1:15–23)
- Paul Defends His Ministry of Suffering (1:24–2:5)
- Warning against False Teaching (2:6–23)
- Virtuous Living and the Christian Household (3:1–4:6)
- Letter's Conclusion (4:7–18)

realms. He is also Lord over believers' daily lives.[16] Colossians boldly proclaims that Jesus is in charge of everything.

The grand mystery. Do you like a good mystery? Well, apparently, Paul did. In his letter to the Colossians, he repeatedly talked about a "**mystery**" (*mysterion*, Col. 1:26–27, 2:2–3, 4:3). This mystery had been hidden in the past and was now revealed to the Colossians. What was this mystery? Paul whispers in our ears and tells us the fantastic news that Gentiles have now been included in God's saving plans through Christ (Col. 1:26–27; cf. Rom. 11:25, 16:25–26; Eph. 1:9, 3:3, 3:4, 3:9, 6:19).

Paul's mystery stood in contrast to those who expected Gentile Christians to first become like Jewish Christians by practicing the law in order to be saved. Paul's opponents were promoting the distinctive markers of Judaism, including circumcision (Col. 2:11–14, 3:11), Sabbath observance (Col. 2:16), and food and purity concerns (Col. 2:16, 2:21–22). These concerns pointed to similar antagonists as in Galatia (Gal. 5:2–12, 4:8–10, 2:12–14).[17] Statements about "self-abasement" (Col. 1:18), "do not touch" (Col. 2:21), and the "severe treatment of the body" (Col. 2:23) reflected Jewish purity concerns. These purity concerns were grounded in fear of being defiled through contact with the impure (e.g., Mark 5:1–34; Luke 10:30–32; 1QS 6–7; Philo, *Spec. Laws* 3.205–6; Let. Aris. 142; Lev. 5:2–3, 7:19, 7:21, 13:45–46; Num. 19:11–13; Isa. 52:11).[18] The opponents promised that by following the law believers remain ritually pure and could join angels in the worship of God during their communal gatherings (Col. 2:18; cf. 1 Cor. 11:10).[19]

Paul labeled these opposing views as a "philosophy" (*philosophia*, Col. 2:8) because his opponents were framing their Jewish practices as the best moral philosophy for promoting piety and virtue like

---

[16] Lohse, *Colossians and Philemon*, 178.

[17] There was also an ongoing problem in the early days of the church of believers being attracted to Judaism (e.g., Ign. *Magn.* 8:1, 10:3; Justin Martyr, *Dial.* 47.4; Origen, *Hom. Lev.* 5:8; *Sel. Exod.* 12:46). Dunn, *Colossians and to Philemon*, 29.

[18] Lohse, *Colossians and Philemon*, 123 n. 77; Dunn, *Colossians and to Philemon*, 190–91.

[19] Dunn, *Colossians and to Philemon*, 179–82. While many English translations have "worship of angels" in Colossians 2:18, a better translation is "angelic worship" because we do not have evidence of worshiping angels within first-century Judaism, and, more importantly, this practice was roundly condemned (e.g., Deut. 4:19, 17:3; Jer. 8:2, 19:13; Zeph. 1:5; Rev. 19:10, 22:9; Apoc. Zeph. 6:15; Apoc. Abraham 17:2; Philo, *Flight* 212; *Dreams* 1.232, 238). Further, we have numerous texts that describe the hope to join with the angels in worship (T. Job 48–50, Apoc. Abraham 17; 1QSa 2:8–9). Paul seems to assume an angelic presence in Christian worship (1 Cor. 11:10).

Colossae ruins.

other Jewish writers (e.g., Let. Aris. 256; 4 Macc. 1:1–2, 5:22–24; Philo, *Embassy* 245; *Moses* 2.211–16; Josephus, *Ant.* 18.11). It was the moral clarity of following the law that made his opponents' views attractive to the Colossians. However, Paul dismissed their interpretations of the law as "human tradition" (Col. 2:8; cf. Gal. 1:14; Mark 7:8). Paul also countered that being alive in Christ is all that is necessary for living a virtuous life (Col. 2:5, 3:5–17).

Paul warned that observance of the law would lead to remaining captive to the "elemental spirits of the universe" (*ta stoicheia tou kosmou*, Col. 2:8; cf. Gal. 4:9). These "elemental" forces were broadly understood as cosmic forces influencing and tormenting humanity.[20] While his opponents believed that the law could free people from these forces (Col. 2:8, 2:20), Paul argued that only service to Christ brings true freedom because Christ made all things, including these powers (Col. 1:16), and he has the authority to reconcile all things (Col. 1:21).

Thus, these opponents were Jewish Christians who encouraged the Colossian Gentile Christians to participate in the believing community as Jewish proselytes. These Gentiles were being told to be circumcised (Col. 2:11, 2:13), practice a kosher diet (Col. 2:16), and observe Jewish religious holidays, including the Sabbath (Col. 2:16). While Paul deemed these practices as acceptable for Jewish believers (Col. 4:11), he saw these practices as a threat to the Gentile Christians' freedom in Christ. Because the Colossian church was not under Paul's direct authority (Col. 1:7–8, 2:1, 4:12), he was not as confrontational as he was with churches that he founded like in Philippi or Galatia (Phil. 3:2, 3:18–19, 4:2; Gal. 1:6–9, 3:1–3,

[20] Dunn, 150. See the discussion in the chapter on Galatians.

4:8–10, 5:2–12). Likewise, he took a less forceful approach in Romans, which was another letter written to a church Paul did not establish.

The church as Christ's household. What's your home life like? Does your family look like your neighbors' families? Is there anything unique about it? Like many people in the Greco-Roman world, Paul understood the family as the basic building block of society, and he understood that Christian homes would look very similar to their neighbors' homes, but also very different because they submitted to God's rule.

Specifically, he wanted the Colossians to understand how Christ's supremacy (Col. 1:15–20) reorientated this basic building block of Greco-Roman society (Col. 3:18–4:1). His advice is sometimes called the "**household codes**" (Germ. *Haustafeln*), and we find an expansion of these codes in Ephesians 5:21–6:9 (cf. 1 Pet. 2:18–3:7).[21] These codes contained the fundamental familial relationships in a first-century home of husbands and wives, parents and children, and masters and slaves. This household reflected Paul's patriarchal society and was organized around the male "head of household" (Lat. *paterfamilias*), whom everyone was obligated to obey.

In Colossians, Paul qualified overzealous applications of his equality statement in Galatians—"There is neither Jew nor Gentile, neither slave nor free, nor is there male and female for you are all one in Christ Jesus" (Gal. 3:28 NIV)—by explaining more concretely how the lordship of Christ impacted the social framework for Christian living. Paul made a similar statement of equality in Colossians—"Here there is no Gentile or Jew, circumcised or uncircumcised, barbarian, Scythian, slave or free, but Christ is all, and is in all" (Col. 3:11 NIV). However, he removed Galatians' contrast between male and female and qualified this equality in Christ with a framework for Christian social living in Colossians 3:18–4:1.

For Paul, all social and familial relationships were impacted by Christ's lordship. The lordship of Christ transformed these social interactions as service to Christ rather than to others. Particularly, Christ's lordship in the home displaced the lordship of the male head of the house. Everyone in a Christian home performed their duties in service to Christ, who was the true Lord of the home. With the household codes, Jesus's kingdom of God message entered the home.

While some readers may wish Paul had overturned the social fabric of his day, these codes still reflected Paul's broader patriarchal culture and values. We find similar affirmations of the first-century social order elsewhere in Paul, such as encouraging enslaved people to remain in their station (1 Cor. 7:20–24) and telling wives to learn from their husbands at home (1 Cor. 14:33–38). Yet, Paul also instigated seeds of change and

A. Savin, Wikipedia (Free Art License)

The "tell" (unexcavated mound) of the Colossian acropolis.

[21]This term derives from Martin Luther. Similar thoughts are found in 1 Clem. 21.6–8; Ign. *Poly.* 4.1–6.2; Pol. *Phil.* 4.2–6.1. Hering, *Colossian and Ephesian* Haustafeln.

challenged his culture by introducing the concept of mutual obligation and the motivation for actions based upon duties to Christ as Lord.

When readers recognize the cultural embeddedness of these lists, then interpreters need not reproduce a first-century household. Instead, interpreters may ask how Christ's lordship should transform the modern Christian home. Thus, the lordship of Christ, introduced in the Christ hymn (Col. 1:15–20), impacted every aspect of a Christian's life, including their fundamental domestic relationships because Jesus was in charge.

Philemon

The Story Continues

In addition to writing a general letter to the Colossians, Paul also personally wrote a letter to one of the Colossian Christians, a man named Philemon (Philem. 1–2; cf. Col. 4:9, 4:17). While this was a private letter, it was still read before the church. This communal reading helped ensure that Philemon would feel bound by honor to follow Paul's advice. When Philemon's slave **Onesimus** escaped, he sought refuge with Paul, who was imprisoned in Ephesus or in Rome. According to Athenian law, which

Public Domain

A slave seeks refuge at an altar to escape his master's punishment in a scene from Roman comedy. Louvre Museum, Paris. (ca. first cent. BCE to first cent. CE)

was widespread throughout the empire, an escaped enslaved person could seek asylum in a friend's home.

Onesimus sought Paul's protection because he believed Paul was someone to whom Philemon would have been socially obligated since the church in Colossae was founded by Paul's envoy Epaphras (Col. 1:7, 4:12–13). What is less clear is why Paul wanted to keep Onesimus present with him (Philem. 13) since Roman law required delinquent enslaved people to be sold if they refused to return to their former owners. In fact, Roman law stipulated that whoever gave hospitality to an escaped enslaved person was liable to the master for the value of work lost each day (Philem. 18).

Mosaic floor depicting slaves serving at a banquet. Dougga, Tunisia. (third cent. CE)

Considering this law, Philemon would have felt reassured by Paul's promise to make up the amount of debt incurred by Onesimus's absence (Philem. 19). Further, Paul assured him that he would receive back his delinquent slave (Philem. 12). Although we may wonder if Paul was suggesting that Onesimus return to Philemon so that he would free him and allow him permanently to return to Paul (Philem. 21) because of brotherly love (Philem. 9).

What Philemon Is All About

Slavery in the Greco-Roman world. Slavery was everywhere in the Greco-Roman world and was knitted into the very fabric of society.[22] Slavery was considered part of the natural order of the world (Aristotle, *Politics* 1253–1255b; Philo, *Spec. Laws* 2.123; *Alleg. Interp*. 3.88–89). Out of a population of fifty to sixty million, about twelve million people were enslaved (16 to 25 percent). In addition, many formerly enslaved people became clients of their former masters.

Slavery was not based on ethnicity or race. Rather, people were enslaved through warfare, being the offspring of slaves, voluntary servitude due to poverty and debt, or criminal punishment. Slavery was extensive in rural areas and farms. For example, Caius Caecilus Isidorus claimed he could plow his farm with 3,600 pairs of oxen because he owned 4,116 slaves (Pliny, *Nat.* 33.47).[23] In the first century, a world without slavery was inconceivable.

The social status of slaves was complex. Enslaved people lacked standing because they were the property of their masters. The head of a household could do almost anything he wanted to his slaves, including sexual and physical abuse. Enslaved people were described as "speaking tools" and were just above livestock in status.

---

[22] On slavery, see Bartchy, *First-Century Slavery*; Findley, *Ancient Slavery and Modern Ideology*; Westermann, *Slave System*, 102–3. Slavery was significant as a religious metaphor for early Judaism and could operate independently from any immediate expression in society.

[23] Bartchy, "Slaves and Slavery in the Roman World," 170–71.

Mosaic from Sidi Ghrib in Tunisia portraying two female slaves attending their mistress. National Museum of Carthage. Byrsa, Tunisia. (fourth or fifth cent. CE)

However, earning freedom, called **manumission**, after a period of service, such as around thirty or forty years old, was also possible.[24] One way to free a slave was for the master to deposit money in the temple and for the priests of that particular god to officiate in the purchase of freedom. This freedom was considered a change of ownership from the master to the god.[25] An enslaved person might buy his or her freedom with the savings her or his master allowed him or her to accumulate, but their status as a former slave was part of her or his identity. They were called freedmen and freedwomen (cf. Acts 6:9; 1 Cor. 7:22). In addition, enslaved people did not have the right to purchase the freedom of their children or spouse.

The social standing of their master also determined an enslaved person's status. For example, Christians "of Caesar's household" (Phil. 4:22) were slaves and freedmen in the imperial service. Slaves in these households could enjoy a higher social standing than other poor, free people. Status was also based on an enslaved person's position in the household. Slaves could be better educated than their masters and were entrusted with important business, such as supervising children like a pedagogue who acted as a guardian (not a teacher) and escorted children to and from school (cf. Gal. 3:24).

Philo recorded two rare first-century objections to slavery from Jewish sects. The Egyptian Therapeutae "consider that the ownership of servants is entirely against nature. For nature has borne all men to be free, but the wrongful and covetous acts of some who pursued that source of evil" (*Contempl. Life* 70). The Essenes "denounce the owners of slaves, not merely for their injustice in outraging the law of equality, but also for their impiety in annulling the statute of Nature" (*Good Person* 79).

Among the Greeks and Romans, a more humane attitude toward enslaved persons gained ground under the influence of Stoicism. Seneca (*Ep.* 47.10) wrote, "Kindly remember that he whom you call your slave sprang from the same stock, is smiled upon by the same skies, and on equal terms with yourself breathes, lives, and dies. It is just as possible for you to see in him a free-born man as for him to see in you a slave." Likewise, Epictetus (*Diatr.* 1.13.4) emphasized the equality of slaves and masters, writing, "Will you not recall what you are and over whom you rule; over kinsmen, brothers by nature, offspring of Zeus?"

Paul's appeal for freedom. At times, enslaved people sought to escape their masters. Punishments of escaped slaves could be brutal and included imprisonment, flogging, or crucifixion. Rewards were

[24] Bradley, *Slaves and Masters in the Roman Empire*, 81–112. A negative aspect of manumission allowed masters to free older and less healthy slaves so that they no longer needed to take care of them.

[25] Bartchy, *First-Century Slavery*, 121–25; Martin, *Slavery as Salvation*, 1–63.

offered to anyone who found slaves and brought them back or provided information about their whereabouts. An even higher reward was promised for information about a slave lodging with a private person. This is because the enslaved person would be returned, and the person harboring the slave could be prosecuted and held liable for the loss of the slave's work. For example, one letter says,

> Aurelius Sarapammon, called Didymus . . . to Aurelius. . . . I appoint you by this my instruction as my representative to journey to the most illustrious Alexandria and search for my slave called . . . aged about thirty-five years, with whom you too are acquainted . . . and when you find him you are to deliver him up, having the same powers as I should have myself, if present, to . . . imprison him, chastise him, and to make an accusation before the proper authorities against those who harboured him, and demand satisfaction. (ca. 298 CE)[26]

However, there were occasionally appeals for mercy. For example, Pliny the Younger (*Ep.* 9.21, 9.24) attempted to intercede for a freedman seeking refuge in his home because he feared his former master's wrath. He wrote,

> Your freedman, whom you lately mentioned as having displeased you, has been with me; he threw himself at my feet and clung there with as much submission as he could have done at yours . . . in short, he convinced me by his whole behaviour, that he is thoroughly reformed. I know you are angry with him, and I know too, it is not without reason; but clemency can never exert itself with more applause, than when there is the justness cause for resentment.

Against this background, Paul's request to Philemon had been carefully prepared. He said nothing about Philemon's right to vengeance and did not consider that Onesimus would be punished. Paul promised to accept any liability that Onesimus might have incurred (Philem. 18). He reminded Philemon that he was already in debt to Paul for his salvation (Philem. 19). Paul used gentle language (Philem. 8–9), urging Philemon's cooperation and consent (Philem. 14). Philemon was asked to make his choices "on the basis of

Marble relief depicting the manumission of two slaves. During the ceremony, the slave was touched with a rod and pronounced to be free. The slave's head was shaved, and a pileus hat was placed upon it. Musée de Mariemont. Morlanwelz, Belgium. (first cent. BCE)

[26] Grenfell and Hunt, *Oxyrhynchus Papyri*, 14:70–72.

PHILEMON

- Letter's Greeting (vv. 1-3)
- Thanksgiving (vv. 4-7)
- Paul's Request for Onesimus (vv. 8-20)
- Letter's Conclusion (vv. 21-25)

love" (Philem. 9) and to "refresh [Paul's] heart in Christ" (Philem. 20). Paul asked Philemon to receive Onesimus "as you would welcome me" (Philem. 17). Paul leveraged the idea of his coming to prompt Philemon to do what was asked (Philem. 22). Paul hoped Philemon would go beyond his request, hinting at the possibility of granting Onesimus freedom (Philem. 21). Most likely, Philemon freed Onesimus. Otherwise, we would not have this letter.

Christianity and slavery. Paul's letter to Philemon provides some insight regarding early Christians' attitudes toward the institution of slavery in the ancient world and helps to inform what we find about the relationship between masters and enslaved persons in the household codes (Col. 3:22–4:1; Eph. 6:5–9; cf. 1 Cor. 7:21–23; 1 Tim. 6:1–2; Titus 2:9–10; 1 Pet. 2:18–21).

Because the New Testament never explicitly condemns slavery, it has been considered defective by some at a crucial point. One author writes, "The real problem of the letter is not Onesimus's slavery but Philemon's freedom."[27] However, Paul did challenge social values by calling both Onesimus (Philem. 16) and Philemon (Philem. 7, 20) his brothers, which redefined their social relationships as siblings. Onesimus

Public Domain

Funerary relief of freedpersons Aurelius Hermia and his wife, Aurelia Philmatium, portrayed as Roman citizens. British Museum, London. (ca. 80 BCE)

[27] Lehrmann, *Philémon*, 9.

The remains of the Artemision with one column rebuilt.

was no longer to be treated as Philemon's property but as a family member. Within this common household of Christian faith, Paul highlighted that both Onesimus and Philemon served the same "Master" or "Lord" (*kyrios*), Jesus Christ (Philem. 3, 5, 16, 20, 25). Elsewhere, Paul subverted social expectations with reminders that slaves are serving Christ (Eph. 6:6–8; Col. 3:23–24) and owners have a "Master in heaven" (Eph. 6:9; Col. 4:1). He also negated the differences between slaves and masters, who were united in Christ (Gal. 3:28; Col. 3:11). Thus, under the lordship of Christ, household relationships are redefined.

We can extrapolate from Paul's teaching about slavery to see how he challenged a system that reduced people to property. Paul's letters do not excuse past or present systems of slavery. Unfortunately, it was not until the fourth century that we have a record of a Christian leader, Gregory of Nyssa (In Eccl. 4.1.1–106), clearly condemning slavery.[28] Modern Christians must advocate for social equality, justice, and treating all people with dignity because we are all created in the image of God (Gen. 1:26–27). Although official systems of slavery may not overtly exist in the Western world, we must look beneath the veneer of society and stand against obvious evils, such as human trafficking. We must also ask hard questions of ourselves. Do our personal habits, social positions, and political stances promote systems that reduce people to being less than bearers of God's image? We must follow Paul's exhortation for a heart change and live under Christ's lordship. We should seek to call everyone a brother or a sister and treat one another as part of God's family.

Ephesians

The Story Continues

Ephesus was a coastal city (located in the western part of modern-day Turkey) with an important port on the Aegean Sea. According to legend, Amazonian women established the city (Strabo, *Geogr.* 11.5.1; Apollodorus 2.5.8) and founded the cult of Artemis (Callimachus, *Hymn. Dian.* 3.110). The goddess **Artemis** was the guardian of the city. Yearly games were held in her honor, and one month of the year was named after her. She was the daughter of Zeus and Leto and the twin sister of Apollo (Hesiod, *Theog.* 918–20). Her Roman equivalent was the goddess Diana. Artemis was the virgin goddess of the hunt. She was also associated with midwifery (Euripides, *Hipp.* 160–69; Callimachus, *Hymn. Dian.* 20–25; Plutarch, *Alex.* 3.3).[29]

---

[28] Weisser, "Philo's Terapeutae and Essenes: A Precedent for the Exceptional Condemnation of Slavery in Gregory of Nyssa," 289–310.

[29] Some scholarship sees Artemis as a mother and fertility goddess, but this is not supported by the extant literary evidence. Glahn, *Nobody's Mother.*

Carl N. Toney

Road to the harbor from Ephesus.

The temple dedicated to Artemis of the Ephesians was originally built in 550 BCE (Acts 19:23–41; Pausanias, *Greece* 4.31.8).[30] This enormous sanctuary, called the Artemision, was four times the size of the Parthenon in Athens. It was 450 feet long and 228 feet wide, with 60-foot columns (Pliny, *Nat.* 36.21). It was considered one of the seven wonders of the ancient world (Strabo, *Geogr.* 14.1.20–23; Pausanias, *Greece* 2.2.6, 4.31.8), and people came from all over to visit until it was destroyed in 263 CE.

The Greeks controlled Ephesus from 334 to 133 BCE. Under Emperor Augustus, the city became the capital of the Roman province of Asia in 29 BCE (Dio Cassius, *Hist.* 51.20.6). Previously, Pergamum had been the capital, which created some jealousy between the cities. Ephesus was the third largest city in the empire, behind Rome and Alexandria. With a population between 100,000 and 150,000, it was the largest commercial center in the province of Asia.[31] It was an important center for the Roman imperial cult with temples dedicated to the goddess Roma and the divine Julius Caesar (Dio Cassius,

[30]The temple was rebuilt after it burned down in 356 BCE.

[31]White, "Urban Development and Social Change in Imperial Ephesos," 27–79.

Hist. 51.20.6), but there was also a large Jewish population that enjoyed religious freedoms, including observing the Sabbath (Josephus, *Ant.* 14.262–64). Unfortunately, the city had to be abandoned by the fifteenth century CE because its harbor silted up.

At the end of Paul's second missionary journey, he briefly visited Ephesus, along with fellow church leaders Prisca and Aquila (Acts 18:18–21). He returned to the city on his third missionary journey for an extended stay of about three years (Acts 19:1–41). He used Ephesus as his base of operations for his ministry in Asia and a launching pad for his ministry in Macedonia and Greece. His ministry was so impactful that the temple of Artemis began to lose revenue, and the silversmiths started a riot that ended in the enormous theater in the city, which held twenty-five thousand people.[32] Due to these types of conflicts, Paul was probably imprisoned in Ephesus (1 Cor. 15:32, 16:8–9; 2 Cor. 1:8; Rom. 16:3–4). Eventually, things got so bad that Paul left. When he took his final journey to Jerusalem, he met the Christian leadership outside the city (Acts 20:14–15).

While in Ephesus, Paul wrote several letters to churches facing problems, including Galatians (spring of 53 CE), Philippians (summer of 53 CE), and 1 Corinthians (winter of 54 CE). With all this letter-writing activity, it may come as a surprise that Paul's letter to the Ephesians may not have originally been written to the Ephesians. The earliest and most reliable copies of this letter don't identify the recipients, and the words "in Ephesus" (*en Ephesō*) are missing.[33]

Some have speculated that this letter was the lost letter to the Laodiceans (Col. 4:16).[34] However, the letter lacks any specific greetings, as was customary for Paul. Further, Paul's broad knowledge of his audience indicates that Paul was targeting a general audience (Eph. 1:13, 1:15, 1:16; cf. Eph. 3:2). Matching this general tone, Paul also frequently identified himself with all believers (Eph. 1:3–12, 1:14, 1:19, 2:3–7, 2:10, 2:14–16, 2:18, 3:12, 3:20, 4:7, 4:13–15, 5:2, 6:12). These pieces of evidence indicate that this letter was designed as a general circular letter to be read by all the churches in the region.

Because Ephesus was the capital of the province, the name of the city eventually became attached to the letter.[35] The general nature of this letter, in theory, would allow Paul to write this letter from Ephesus to all the churches in the region around the summer of 53 CE. But it is also possible that Paul wrote it from his Roman prison around 60–62 CE. It may be that Paul wrote this general letter (Ephesians) to churches in the whole region, a more specific letter (Colossians) to the church in Colossae, and a personal letter (Philemon) to one of the members of the Colossian church. It is also possible that this letter was written by one of Paul's disciples shortly after his death using a collection of Pauline materials, such as Colossians and Philemon.

Authorship of Ephesians

Church tradition supports Paul's authorship of this letter (Irenaeus, *Haer.* 1.3–4, 8:4, 5.2.36; Clement of Alexandria, *Paed.* 1.18; *Strom.* 4.65; Tertullian, *Praescr.* 36; *Mon.* 5). This is supported by Paul identifying

[32] Besides theatrical performances, the theater held animal fights and gladiatorial combat.

[33] These words are missing from the original scripts of Codex Sinaiticus (א*) and Codex Vaticanus (B*), as well as the important Greek papyrus P[46] (ca. 200 CE). This is also supported by early writers like Origen and Basil.

[34] Marcion attributed Ephesians to Laodicea (Tertullian, *Marc.* 5.17).

[35] Lincoln, *Ephesians*, 4.

himself as the author in the letter (Eph. 1:1, 3:1, 3:13, 4:1, 6:20). Scholars today either affirm[36] or dispute[37] Paul's authorship. Older objections were based on the unique grammar and syntax in Ephesians, especially its long, pondering sentences (e.g., Eph. 1:3–10, 1:15–23).[38] However, stylistic differences can be explained by the use of a scribe and the genre of the letter.[39] Like other disputed writings, the larger issue of Paul's authorship relates to differences in theology, especially when there are differences between Colossians and Ephesians because these two letters are very similar in content.

Some consider these theological differences to reflect a later post-Pauline period, but others situate Ephesians among Paul's letters. For example, the household codes, which expanded the version found in Colossians, may reflect later, formalized structures (Eph. 5:21–6:9; Col. 3:18–4:1). But if Colossians is accepted as Pauline, then Ephesians could be too. The hope for Christ's imminent return in Paul's earlier writings (e.g., 1 Thess. 4:13–5:11) has faded in Ephesians (Eph. 1:14, 4:30, 5:5, 6:13), and the letter focused upon the church's current benefits (Eph. 1:3, 1:20–23, 2:6). However, other Pauline writings reflect similar attitudes about Christ's return (e.g., 2 Cor. 5:1–10) and present benefits (e.g., Rom. 6:1–14; Col. 3:1–4). The conflict between Jewish and Gentile Christians in most of Paul's letters (e.g., Gal. 5:1–11; Phil. 3:2–11; Rom. 14–15) appeared to be resolved in Ephesians where they are one new humanity (Eph. 2:15–16). This is challenging because Colossians, if written at the same time, revealed this conflict (Col. 2:11–14, 2:16, 2:21–22, 2:3:11). However, if Ephesians is a general letter, Paul may have been expanding upon his ideal of a unified humanity in Christ (Gal. 3:28; Col. 3:11; cf. Rom. 3:22, 10:12, 11:17–24).

Carl N. Toney

Ephesus public bathrooms constructed over a channel of flowing water. Clients used sponges attached to sticks stored in vinegar to clean themselves.

Some Pauline terms gained a new emphasis, so the "church" (*ekklēsia*) referred to all believers (Eph. 1:22, 3:10, 3:21, 5:23–32), when it typically referred to local gatherings (Rom. 16:4, 16:14; 1 Cor. 1:2, 4:17, etc.). However, this broad use of "church" matches the general nature of the letter. Further, Paul referred to the church collectively in his other writings (1 Cor. 10:32, 12:28, 15:9; Gal. 1:13; Phil. 3:6; Col. 1:18, 1:24).[40] The body of Christ imagery differs in this letter from Romans and 1 Corinthians. Ephesians described Christ as the head of the church (Eph. 4:15–16, 5:23) and over all cosmic powers

[36]Bruce, *Colossians, Philemon, Ephesians*, 229–40; Johnson, *Writings of the New Testament*, 360–64; Wright and Bird, *New Testament in Its World*, 458–60.

[37]F. Usteri (1824), W. M. L. de Wette (1826, 1843), and F. C. Bauer (1845) were among the first to dispute Pauline authorship.

[38]In addition, there are numerous prepositions (e.g., Eph. 1:3–23), parallel clauses (e.g., Eph. 4:12–13), and the piling up of synonyms (e.g., Eph. 1:19). For the wider issues, see Patzia, *Colossians, Philemon, Ephesians*, 102–22.

[39]The basic comparative premise that begins with Romans, Galatians, and 1–2 Corinthians is faulty and artificial. A more useful cluster of comparison is (1) Thessalonians, (2) Galatians/Romans, (3) Corinthians, (4) Colossians/Ephesians, (5) Pastorals, (6) Philippians, and (7) Philemon. Johnson, *Canonical Paul*, 1:74–92.

[40]Other words with new twists include "fullness" (*plērōma*, Eph. 1:23) and "mystery" (*mystērion*, Eph. 5:32). See Mitton, *Ephesians*, 11–15.

(Eph. 1:22–23). Yet, this imagery is similar to the portrayal in Colossians of Christ as the head of the church (Col. 1:18, 2:19).[41]

Elsewhere, Ephesians made statements that appear to conflict with previous writings, such as the law being abolished (Eph. 2:15) instead of upheld (Rom. 3:31), or the foundation of the church including prophets and apostles (Eph. 2:20) rather than Christ alone (1 Cor. 3:11; cf. Col. 2:7).[42] Yet, these differences may be accounted for by the different contexts. For example, in the letters of 1 Corinthians and Romans, Paul used weak and strong images differently by describing parties divided by idol food (1 Cor. 8–10) or groups disagreeing about Jewish food laws (Rom. 14–15).

The arguments for and against Pauline authorship are quite close, and nothing in the letter necessitates a time later than the mid-sixties when Paul died.[43] "Whether the epistle is by Paul or not, it is certainly thought to be the crown of Paulinism."[44]

What Ephesians Is All About

Christ rules everything! Christ's rule is a foundational concept for Ephesians, and it is introduced in the opening thanksgiving (Eph. 1:3–14) and prayer (Eph. 1:15–23). Using imagery drawn from Psalm 110:1, Christ is portrayed as resurrected by God and currently exalted in heaven (Eph. 1:20). He sits at God's right hand in a position of victory (Pss. 20:6, 44:3, 48:10; Isa. 41:10), privilege (Ps. 80:18; Jer. 22:24), and power (Exod. 15:6; Ps. 89:13; Isa. 48:13). He presently shares this rule with the church (Eph. 2:6), which he shares every spiritual blessing (Eph. 1:3). The letter of Ephesians proclaims that Christ is in charge.

Carl N. Toney

The theater in Ephesus could hold about twenty-five thousand spectators.

Recalling Psalm 8:6, Christ's authority is portrayed as complete, as God puts everything under his feet (Eph. 1:22). He is over every "ruler" (*archē*), "authority" (*exousia*), "power" (*dynamis*), and "dominion" (*kyriotēs*, Eph. 1:21).[45] These were the hostile cosmic forces in the heavenly realm that stood behind earthly institutions (Col. 1:16; Dan. 10:13, 10:20; 2 En.

[41] Caird, *Paul's Letters from Prison*, 15.

[42] Lincoln, *Ephesians*, lxiii–lxx.

[43] The language of breaking down the dividing wall of hostility in Ephesians 2:14 may point to a post-temple period.

[44] Dodd, "Ephesians," 1224–25.

[45] These spiritual powers may be associated with the "elemental spirits" (Col. 2:8, 2:20). Sometimes these terms can be used for humans. See Colossians 1:16. Wink, *Naming the Powers*, 9.

20–22). People in the Greco-Roman world tried to control these forces through magical practices, such as invoking the names of these powers (Acts 9:10; 1 Kings 18:24). However, Paul told his audience that the name of the Lord Jesus Christ was more powerful (Eph. 1:21; cf. Phil. 2:9–11; Acts 2:21; etc.), and Paul assured them that Christ controlled these hostile spiritual forces (Eph. 2:2, 6:12; cf. Col. 2:10, 2:15; 1 Cor. 15:24; Rom. 8:38).

The devil (Eph. 4:27, 6:11) was the power of evil behind these cosmic forces. He was described as the "ruler of the realm of the air" (Eph. 2:2) and the "evil one" (Eph. 6:16). Unbelievers who sinned followed this ruler (Eph. 2:2). Believers were warned against his influence if they sinned (Eph. 4:27). In other Pauline writings, this figure is called Satan (Rom. 16:20; 1 Cor. 5:5, 7:5; 2 Cor. 2:11, 11:14, 12:7; 1 Thess. 2:18; 2 Thess. 2:9; 1 Tim. 1:20, 5:15), and he was the "god" of this current age (2 Cor. 4:4; cf. 1 John 5:19). The good news, according to Ephesians, was that believers had been freed from the devil's rule (Eph. 2:2), and Christ had already defeated the cosmic forces (Eph. 1:20–22, 4:8–10).

Believers shared in Christ's conquest over evil powers through their common baptism (Eph. 4:5). Because of Christ's victory, they could stand against these evil powers (Eph. 2:2, 6:11–12) and spurn false teaching (Eph. 5:3–20). They could begin new lives of holy and moral living (Eph. 4:1–6, 4:22–24, 4:32, 5:26) in contrast to their former lives of sin and vice (Eph. 4:17–19, 4:25, 4:31, 5:3–5). They "put off" their old nature as they "put on" a new person, created according to God's likeness (Eph. 4:17–24). They were filled and empowered by the Spirit (Eph. 3:16, 5:18). While believers used to be dead through their sins, they were made alive with Christ and saved by his grace through faith, not works (Eph. 2:5, 2:8–9).

Carl N. Toney

Marble relief of gladiator armor in Ephesus.

Believers fought against these forces and the devil (Eph. 6:10–17). They were told that their battle was not against flesh and blood but against these evil cosmic forces (Eph. 6:12). They were called to defend themselves by taking up the armor of God that Christ already used to defeat the devil and forces of evil (Eph. 6:10–17; cf. 1 Thess. 5:8). This image of the armor of God draws upon Isaiah (Isa. 11:5, 49:2, 52:7, 59:17; cf. Wisd. of Sol. 5:17–20a). Believers were called to hold the ground that Christ had already conquered. They would hold this ground through practices like prayer, living righteous lives, loving others, seeking maturity, building up the church, and having a Christ-centered household.

EPHESIANS

- Letter's Greeting (1:1-2)
- Thanksgiving and Prayer: Christ Rules over Everything (1:3-23)
- From Death to Life in Christ (2:1-10)
- Unity of Jews and Gentiles (2:11-22)
- Paul's Ministry and His Prayer for the Church (3:1-21)
- Unity in the Body of Christ (4:1-16)
- Virtuous Living and the Christian Household (4:17-6:20)
- Letter's Conclusion (6:21-24)

The Mystery of Unified Church. Rather than speaking to a localized church, Ephesians envisages the universal church as having been unified in Christ (Eph. 1:21, 2:1–7). This unity was created through Christ's reconciling work on the cross (Eph. 2:16).[46] This unified church has one body, one Spirit, one hope, one Lord, one faith, one baptism, and one God (Eph. 4:4–5).

This letter presents Paul's most idealized vision of unity, countering the divisions between Jews and Gentiles that plagued his ministry. This unified church was a marvel, a "mystery" (*mystērion*) that had only recently been revealed (Eph. 1:9–12, 3:3–6, 3:8–10, 6:19).[47] Ephesians expands Colossians' "mystery" of including Gentiles by uniting Jews and Gentiles. It is only "in Christ" that ethnic divisions could truly be united, and this vision for unity was a natural outgrowth of Paul's earlier wishes:

> There is no longer Jew or Greek, there is no longer slave or free, there is no longer male and female; for all of you are one in Christ Jesus. (Gal. 3:28)
>
> There is no longer Greek and Jew, circumcised and uncircumcised, barbarian, Scythian, slave and free; but Christ is all and in all! (Col. 3:11)

Christ created from the Jews and Gentiles "one new person" (*hena kainon anthropos*) in himself (Eph. 2:15). This new person is the unified body of Christ (Eph. 1:22–23, 3:6, 4:4, 4:12–16, 5:23, 5:29–30), an image drawn from Colossians 1:18, 1:24, 2:19, and 3:15. Christ also leads the church as the head of this body (Eph. 1:22–23, 4:15–16, 5:30). Christ is not only the head of the church, but he is the head over all things (Eph. 1:22). This cosmic dimension of Christ's headship was introduced in Colossians 1:18 and 1:20. As Christ's body, the church no longer has to wait for heavenly blessings because it shares the heavenly life of its exalted Lord (Eph. 1:22, 2:6, 5:27).

The image of Christ's body overlaps with the image of the church as Christ's bride (Eph. 5:25–33). The "mystery" (*mystērion*) of the unity of the husband and wife in marriage is applied to the unity

---

[46] Coggan, "Note on Ephesians 2:14," 242.
[47] Paul also applied this mystery language to marriage (Eph. 5:32).

Carl N. Toney

The eternal flame of Ephesus was kept in the Prytaneion.

of Christ and the church (Eph. 5:31–32). The husband is the "head" (*kephalē*) of his wife as Christ is the head of the church (Eph. 5:23). The church "submits" (*hypotassō*) itself to Christ as the wife to her husband (Eph. 5:24). These marriage roles reflected Paul's patriarchal culture, but Ephesians also subverts these cultural values by exhorting mutual submission (Eph. 5:21). Notably, "submit" (*hypotassō*) is absent in the commands to the wife.[48] In fact, the only distinct command given to the wife is to respect her husband (Eph. 5:33). What is often missed is that most of the commands are directed toward the husband (Eph. 5:25–33a). Rather than establishing his authority, the husband was called to love his wife by following the example of Christ's sacrifice. He is to imitate Christ, who is the savior of the church (Eph. 5:23), and he makes her holy (Eph. 5:26–27). As members of Christ's body, he loves (Eph. 5:25) and cares for the church (Eph. 5:29–30), so the husband should love and care for his wife.

[48] Using verbs from previous clauses is not unusual for Greek and shows verbal dependence. "Submit" (*hypotassō*) is absent in the command to the wife in Ephesians 5:22 and is borrowed from the command for everyone to submit to each other in Ephesians 5:21. Likewise, the verb in Ephesians 5:24b is absent in the command to the wife and must be borrowed from the command to the whole church to "submit" to Christ" in Ephesians 5:24a. This is different from Paul's more direct statement in Colossians 1:18 where the wife is told to submit using the verb.

A Unified Household and Temple. The church is also described as a unified household of God in Ephesians 2:19 (cf. Gal. 6:10; 1 Tim. 5:8). The household codes (Eph. 5:21–6:9) offered guidance within the framework of a patriarchal culture. These codes expanded Colossians 3:18–4:1, which already challenged these patriarchal values by placing mutual obligations on household members. Ephesians further subverts the dominance of the male "head of the household" (Lat. ***paterfamilias***) by expanding his mutual obligations in each pairing of husbands and wives, fathers and children, and masters and slaves.

The household codes begin with a call for all believers to "submit" (*hypotassō*) to each other (Eph. 5:21). In the first pairing (Eph. 5:22–33), the wife is called to submit to her husband, just as all believers submit to Christ (Eph. 5:22–24). In addition to the call to mutually submit (Eph. 5:21), the husband is given extensive instructions beyond the call to mutual submission (Eph. 5:25–33). He must love his wife as Christ loved the church and love her as his own body because marriage partners join together in "one flesh" (cf. Gen. 2:24).

In the second pairing (Eph. 6:1–4), children are encouraged to obey their parents because of the promise found in the command to honor one's parents (Eph. 6:1–4; Exod. 20:12; Deut. 5:16). Fathers are told to not provoke their children to anger. They are also to raise their children in the teachings of the Lord, alluding to Deuteronomy 6:4–9.

In the third pairing (Eph. 6:6–9), Paul significantly reorientated the duties between slaves and masters by subjugating these duties under a common service to the Lord. Slaves obey their earthy masters as they "obey Christ" because they are "slaves of Christ," and they seek to do "the will of God" (Eph. 6:5–6). They are to serve with enthusiasm "as to the Lord," not people (Eph. 6:7). The reciprocity between the master and enslaved persons is highlighted by the command for the master to "do the same" to their slaves (Eph. 6:9). Further, masters are told they must stop mistreating their slaves because they will be held accountable to the same "Master in heaven," who is impartial (Eph. 6:9).

Fresco of Terentius Neo and his wife from Villa di Guilia Felice in Pompeii. (ca. 60 CE)

It may be tempting to reproduce the households described in Ephesians and Colossians. However, we should be cautious of any appeals to the "plain" reading of these texts because a plain reading endorses slavery. Interpreters who describe the master/slave relationship as employer/employee are not reading this passage literally. Instead, we should note how this passage reflects first-century values and a first-century home, and then look for principles espoused by this passage that may be applied to our current contexts. The main principle is that Christ is in charge, and he should be the center of the Christian home.

Paul also used the metaphor of **God's temple** (Eph. 2:20–22) to describe the unity of the Jewish and Gentile believers. The Corinthian correspondence comes closest to Paul's corporate temple image in Ephesians by describing the local congregation (1 Cor. 3:10–17) and individual believers as God's temple (1 Cor. 6:19; cf. 2 Cor. 5:1, 6:16). In Ephesians, the church, as the locus of God's presence, is God's temple. The foundation of this temple are the apostles and prophets, and the exalted Christ crowns the building as its keystone (Eph. 2:20; cf. Ps. 118:22; T. Sol. 22.7–23.3).[49] The apostles, prophets, evangelists, and teachers equip believers for "upbuilding" (*oikodomē*) the body of Christ (Eph. 4:11–12).

With all these images—Christ's body, marriage, the household, and God's temple—Paul created ideal portraits of the unity of believers in Christ. Ephesians represents the culmination of the earlier Pauline teachings about the unity of Jewish and Gentile races and social status being leveled (Gal. 3:28–29; Col. 3:9–11; cf. 1 Cor. 12:13).[50] This letter is grounded in the claim that Christ rules over everything in the heavens and that the church, as his body, should reflect this rule in all their relationships in this world (Eph 1:20–23). Ephesians provides the foundation for Christian claims that the church forms a people united in a new way to reflect God's ultimate design for a broken and sinful world.

Key Terms and People

Artemis: virgin goddess of the hunt, daughter of Zeus, twin of Apollo, and guardian of Ephesus; her temple, the Artemision, was one of seven ancient wonders of the world
God's temple: Paul's metaphor for the church in 1–2 Corinthians and Ephesians
Household codes: guidelines that outline the fundamental family relationships of husbands, wives, parents, children, masters, and slaves, especially in relation to the male head of household
Manumission: after a period of service, when an enslaved person is freed, they became a freedman or freedwoman
Mystery: a theme in both Colossians and Ephesians, where Paul states that God's saving work of the Jews now includes Gentiles
Nympha: a patron of the Colossian believers who gathered in her home
Onesimus: an enslaved person who escaped from his master, Philemon, to whom Paul appealed for forgiveness and potential release
***Paterfamilias*:** the male head of a household whom everyone was required to obey
Slavery: almost a quarter of the population of the Roman Empire was enslaved; slavery was not based on race, but enslaved people were considered the property of their masters
Tychicus: the letter carrier of Colossians and Ephesians

[49] On "keystone" instead of "cornerstone," see Jeremias, "ἀκρογωνιαῖος," *TDNT*, 1:792.
[50] Houlden, "Christ and Church in Ephesians," 271–72.

Conversation Starters

1. Do you think Paul wrote Colossians? Do you think he wrote Ephesians? What is the relationship between Colossians, Ephesians, and Philemon?
2. What does the Christ hymn in Colossians 1:15–20 teach about the divinity of Jesus? What are some specific words and concepts used? How does this relate to Philemon 2:7–11?
3. Why is Christ's lordship so important in Colossians and Ephesians? What does he rule? How does he share this rule with his church?
4. What is the mystery in Colossians? How is this mystery similar and different in Ephesians?
5. How did this mystery impact the relationship between Jewish and Gentile Christians?
6. What was the structure of a typical household in the first century? What was the role of the *paterfamilias*? How were Paul's household codes in Colossians and Ephesians similar and different from the larger Greco-Roman world? What does a Christian household look like today?
7. How would you describe slavery in the ancient world? How was it similar and different from slavery in the United States? Why don't you think the church took a stronger stance against slavery?
8. What is the relationship between the spiritual and earthly realms for Christian moral living?

FOR FURTHER READING

Bruce, F. F. *The Epistles to the Colossians, to Philemon, and to the Ephesians*. NICNT. Eerdmans, 1984.

Cohick, Lynn. *The Letter to the Ephesians*. NICNT. Eerdmans, 2020.

Dunn, James D. G. *The Epistles to the Colossians and to Philemon: A Commentary on the Greek Text*. NIGTC. Eerdmans, 1996.

Fitzmyer, Joseph A. *The Letter to Philemon: A New Translation with Introduction and Commentary*. AYB 34C. Yale University Press, 2008.

Gupta, Nijay K. *Colossians*. Smyth & Helwys Bible Commentary. Smyth & Helwys, 2013.

Keesmaat, Sylvia C., and Brian J. Walsh. *Colossians Remixed: Subverting the Empire*. InterVarsity Press, 2004.

MacDonald, Margaret. *Colossians and Ephesians*. SP 17. Liturgical Press, 2000.

Pao, David. *Colossians & Philemon*. Zondervan Exegetical Commentary on the New Testament 12. Zondervan, 2012.

Thompson, Marianne Meye. *Colossians and Philemon*. Two Horizons New Testament Commentary. Eerdmans, 2005.

9

FINDING RECONCILIATION IN CORINTH

1-2 Corinthians

1 Corinthians

The Story So Far

Corinth had a reputation. The prostitutes at the temple of Aphrodite, who was the goddess of love and life, were legendary. Strabo (*Geogr.* 8.6.20) wrote, "The Temple of Aphrodite was so rich that it owned more than a thousand temple-slaves, courtesans, whom men and women had dedicated to the goddess." "To "Corinthianize" (*korinthiazesthai*) was an expression used to describe fornication. Other colorful words related to the town were used to describe a "pimp" (*korinthiastēs*) and a "prostitute" (*korinthia korē*).[1]

SUGGESTED READING

Acts 18:1-18
Acts 18:24-19:1
1 Corinthians
Acts 20:1-3
2 Corinthians 8-9

The problem with these reputations and rumors is that they simply weren't true. Strabo's reference to temple prostitutes was anachronistic. And the various expressions designed to make Corinth the symbol of commercial sex were probably invented by their Athenian rivals. It's similar to the modern perception of Las Vegas being a den of debauchery while most people living in Las Vegas are quite normal.

So, what was the real reputation of Corinth? What was the city really like?

This ancient city had been occupied since the middle of the seventh millennium BCE. As an ancient Greek city-state, Corinth rivaled the glorious reputations of Athens, Sparta, and Thebes. Some of the most famous wars involving Corinth included fighting alongside Sparta against

[1]On the history of Corinth, see Martin, *2 Corinthians*, 30–36.

Carl N. Toney

Inscription from Delphi identifying Proconsul Gallio (ΓΑΛΛΙΩΝ).

Carl N. Toney

Commemorative inscription in front of the theater in Corinth, saying, "Erastus in return for his aedileship laid [the pavement] at his own expense."

Athens in the Peloponnesian War (431–404 BCE) and joining Athens to fight against Sparta in the Corinthian War (395–387 BCE).

Eventually, the Romans conquered Corinth in 146 BCE. Then the city was rebuilt in 46 BCE by Julius Caesar, who made it a Roman colony. In 27 BCE, the city became the capital of the Roman province of Achaia (modern-day southern Greece). It was governed by a proconsul for one-year terms (July 1 to June 30). During Paul's stay, Lucius Iunius Gallio served as proconsul in 51–52 CE. And Paul's trial before Gallio is one of the few fixed points for reconstructing the chronology of Paul's life since there is an inscription at Delphi dating Gallio's rule.[2]

The population of Corinth included a mixture of Romans, Greeks, Jews, and other foreigners. The Jewish people in the city were given a permanent right of residence and allowed to govern their own internal affairs. The Isthmian Games were held every two years in April or May, and they were second only to the Olympic Games of Athens. Paul's tentmaking business was surely booming, as he helped make tents for those who came for the games.

People came to the city looking for new opportunities. Only those with grit survived in Corinth. As one saying went, "Not for everyone is the voyage to Corinth" (Strabo, *Geogr.* 8.6.20; Horace, *Ep.* 1.17.36). The city was full of inscriptions of people boasting through their own self-promotion. One inscription outside the theater is attributed to an Erastus who paved the street outside the theater. This wealthy man may have been part of the Corinthian congregation, and the church could have gathered in his home for worship (Rom. 16:13; 2 Tim. 4:20).

[2]On Gallio, see Murphy-O'Connor, *Paul*, 15–22.

The city was well-known for its trade and commerce. Corinthian pottery was notable, and Corinthian bronze was a collector's item. Being located on the narrow Isthmus of Corinth allowed the city to control the trade between northern and southern Greece, as well as the east–west trade where sailors would drag cargo across the narrow strip. Corinth oversaw two seaports: Lechaeum on the west and Cenchreae on the east.

When Paul arrived in Corinth for the first time in the winter of 50 CE, he was traveling on his second missionary journey (Acts 18:1–17). The city of Corinth was the final stop of his travels through Macedonia and Greece. He traveled with Silas and Timothy from Philippi to Berea to Thessalonica to Athens.[3] During his initial stay in Corinth, he met fellow tentmakers Prisca and Aquila who were also new to town (Acts 18:2–3). They moved to Corinth after being forced to leave Rome by Emperor Claudius (49 CE; Acts 18:1–2; Suetonius, *Claud.* 25.4; Dio Cassius, *Hist.* 60.6.6; Orosius, *Adv. pag.* 7.6.15).

This couple were leaders in the early church who often worked with Paul (Rom. 16:3; 1 Cor. 16:19; 2 Tim. 4:19). Aquila's name may indicate that they were former slaves of the Acilian family in Pontus (a region on the southern shores of the Black Sea).[4] Because it was unusual to mention a woman's name

Public Domain

Paul Staying in the House of Saints Aquila and Priscilla. Plantin-Moretus Museum, Antwerp, Belgium. (seventeenth cent.)

[3] Martin, *2 Corinthians*, 35–37. For an earlier dating, see Bruce, *New Testament History*, 282, 298; Robinson, *Redating the New Testament*, 31, 35.

[4] Sanday and Headlam, *Romans*, 420. Not everyone is convinced of this reconstruction.

Carl N. Toney

"Synagogue of the Hebrews" inscription in Corinth. (fourth or fifth cent. CE)

first, some think Prisca (also called Priscilla)[5] came from a position of higher social status than her husband, while others speculate that she had a more significant ministry role.

Through Paul's preaching, Stephanas's household was the first to believe (1 Cor. 16:15) and be baptized by Paul (1 Cor. 1:16). Crispus, the official of the synagogue, also became a believer (1 Cor. 1:14; Acts 18:8). After Paul was prevented from meeting in the synagogue, the nascent community of Christ followers began to meet in the house of a Gentile named Titius Justus (Acts 18:7). Upset by Paul's continued teaching, the Jewish community accused Paul of wrongdoing before the proconsul Gallio (Acts 18:12–17). However, Gallio deemed this to be an inner Jewish dispute. His decision secured the safety of this infant group of believers from political pressures by considering them a legal religion as part of Judaism. In frustration over this decision, the crowd beat Sosthenes, the synagogue official. This may be the same Sosthenes who joined Paul in writing 1 Corinthians (1 Cor. 1:1). By the time Paul left Corinth with Prisca and Aquila in the summer of 51 CE, he had stayed there for about eighteen months. He also wrote his first canonical letters of 1–2 Thessalonians during this period (50/51 CE).

After Paul left Corinth, a Jewish Christian named **Apollos**, who was from Alexandria, Egypt, joined the Corinthian community. He was well-versed in the Jewish scriptures and had been discipled by Prisca and Aquila during their stay in Ephesus (Acts 18:24–19:1). While Apollos was in Corinth, Paul settled in Ephesus, where he stayed for about three years (Acts 20:31). During this period, Paul maintained his relationship with the Corinthian church. Paul wrote his "first" letter to the Corinthians (1 Cor. 5:9). Unfortunately, this letter was lost.[6] Then, the Corinthians wrote to Paul asking for advice (1 Cor. 7:1). Members of this church—Stephanas, Fortunatus, and Achaicus—visited and encouraged Paul (1 Cor. 16:15–18). Unfortunately, Chloe's[7] household reported that the church began to split into

[5]Prisca is called Priscilla in Acts 18:2, 18:18, and 18:26.

[6]Kümmel, *Introduction to the New Testament*, 276–77. Alternatively, 2 Corinthians 6:14–7:1 may be a fragment of this letter.

[7]Chloe is another example of an early female leader in the church and a successful businesswoman who seemed to have ties to both Corinth and Ephesus. There is a debate about whether she resided in Corinth or Ephesus.

factions (1 Cor. 1:11). This communication prompted Paul to write his "second" letter in the winter of 54 CE. This letter is 1 Corinthians.[8]

What 1 Corinthians Is All About

Unity and reconciliation. The Corinthians kept fighting. The church divided into various factions identifying with their favorite leader, whether Paul, Apollos, Peter, or Christ (1 Cor. 1:10–17). They could not seem to agree about sexual ethics (1 Cor. 5–7), lawsuits (1 Cor. 6:1–8), idolatry (1 Cor. 8–10), spiritual experiences (1 Cor. 12–14), or beliefs concerning the resurrection (1 Cor. 15). They were even divided by practices surrounding baptism (1 Cor. 1:13) and the Lord's Supper (1 Cor. 11:20–22), which were supposed to bring unity.

Paul's exhortation to reconcile with each other was the primary purpose of this letter (1 Cor. 1:10).[9] Paul believed that the church united under the reign of Christ should be unified (1 Cor. 1:2, 3:23). Even as Paul specifically addressed the issues dividing the Corinthians, he also attempted to cast a grander vision for unity using various images. Two of the most prominent images of unity were a building and a body.

Paul used building language, which included the expression "upbuilding" (*oikodomē*, *oikodomeō*, 1 Cor. 3:9–17, 6:19, 8:1, 8:10, 10:23, 14:3–5, 14:12, 14:17, 14:26; cf. Rom. 14:19, 15:2, 15:20; Gal. 2:18; 1 Thess. 5:11; Eph. 4:12, 4:16, 4:29). "Upbuilding" was a Greco-Roman political metaphor for unifying divided groups (e.g., Aristides, *Or.* 23.31, 24.51). Paul evoked images of "the stable construction, peaceful maintenance and improvement of the Corinthian community" with God as the owner and Christ as the foundation.[10] More specifically, this building was "God's temple" (*ho naos tou theou*, 1 Cor. 3:17), an image that described the unity of Jews and Gentiles in Ephesians 2:19–22.

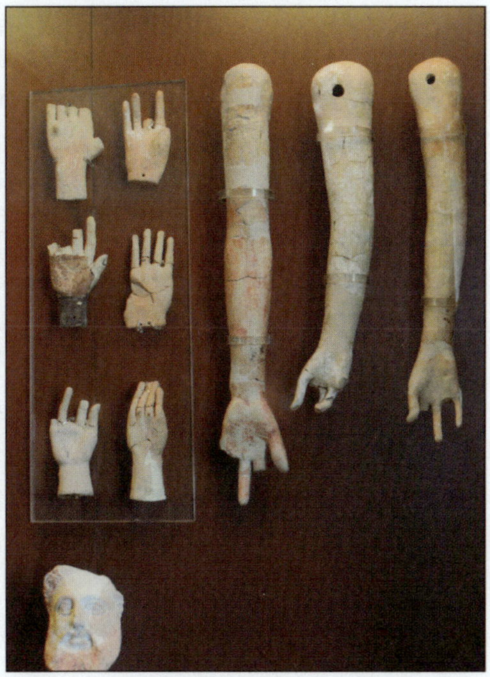

Various votive offerings in the form of body parts found near the Asclepieion in Corinth.

Paul also described the community as the **body of Christ** (1 Cor. 12:12–27; cf. 1 Cor. 1:13, 6:15, 10:16–17). Greco-Roman political writers used body imagery for a functioning society (e.g., Livy, *Hist.* 2.32.12–33; Plutarch, *Cor.* 6.2–4).[11] In Colossians and Ephesians, there was an emphasis on Christ's authority and Christ functioning as the head of this body (Col. 1:18, 1:24, 2:19, 3:15; Eph. 1:23, 2:16, 3:6, 4:4, 4:12–16, 5:23, 5:29–30). For the Corinthians, Paul used this body image as a metaphor for unity among diverse Christian community members (see the similar use in Rom. 12:4–8). In addition, Paul may have been drawing on the personal experiences of the Corinthians, who knew of the clay votive offerings to Asclepius, the god of healing. These clay

[8] Evidence that 1 Corinthians was written from Ephesus includes Paul's reference to Ephesus (1 Cor. 15:32), his greetings from Asia, and his greeting with Prisca and Aquila (1 Cor. 16:19; cf. Acts 18:18–19).

[9] Mitchell, *Reconciliation.*

[10] Mitchell, 99–111, esp. 101.

[11] Mitchell, 157–64; Jewett, *Paul's Anthropological Terms*, 201–87; Sevenster, *Paul and Seneca*, 167–74.

offerings were fashioned into the likeness of diseased, dead, and dismembered body parts. Unlike these offerings, Christ's body was and is living, healthy, and unified.[12]

Sexual ethics. From Paul's Jewish perspective, two significant issues plagued the Gentiles—sexual immorality and idolatry (1 Cor. 5:11, 6:9–10).[13] He challenged the Corinthians' slogan of "all things are lawful" (1 Cor. 6:12) with the qualifications that "not all are beneficial" (1 Cor. 6:12), "I will not be dominated by anything" (1 Cor. 6:12), and "not all things build up" (1 Cor. 10:23). Paul advocated for self-control (1 Cor. 7:5) and dealing with passion (1 Cor. 7:9), which he likened to curbing one's hunger or appetite (1 Cor. 6:13).

Paul's sexual ethics only applied to the believing community (1 Cor. 5:9, 5:11) and were not meant to be projected upon unbelievers (1 Cor. 5:10, 5:12–13). Paul urged judgment against a Christ follower who was living with his father's wife (1 Cor. 5:2). He advocated for the rights of Christian wives, including mutual sexual intimacy (1 Cor. 7:4), providing divorce advice (1 Cor. 7:11, 7:15),[14] and arguing that a wife's faith may save her husband and make their children "holy" (1 Cor. 7:14). According to Paul, anyone who was unmarried should either remain celibate (1 Cor. 7:6–8) or get married if they lacked self-control (1 Cor. 7:9). Notably, Paul elevated singleness as an ideal over marriage, much like Jesus (Mark 12:18–27; Matt. 22:23–33; Luke 20:27–40).[15] Paul's words should encourage single persons in modern churches that often prioritize marriage.

Paul urged married couples not to divorce (1 Cor. 7:1–5, 7:10–16), just as Jesus taught (Mark 10:2–12; Matt. 5:31–32, 19:1–9; Luke 16:8). Both Paul and Jesus conceived of God's ideal for marriage as being between one man and one woman, and they promoted striving for that ideal (1 Cor. 7:2; Mark 10:7–9; Matt. 19:4–6). However, they acknowledged that human sinfulness still breaks relationships. The Jewish rabbinic tradition was divided on the issue of divorce. The school of Shammai permitted divorce only in cases of adultery, while Hillel's school permitted divorce for almost any reason (m. Giṭ. 9.10; b. Giṭ. 90a; cf. Philo, *Spec. Laws* 3.30; Josephus, *Ant.* 4.253; *Life* 72). Jesus allowed divorce due to sexual immorality (Matt. 5:32, 19:9). Paul made his own exception by allowing an unbelieving spouse to divorce (1 Cor. 7:15).

Carl N. Toney

Image from a brothel in Pompeii.

These qualifications of Jesus and Paul are often understood as unique and limited. However, these may be seen as examples of exceptions that allow for various breaks in marriages due to

[12] Murphy-O'Connor, *St. Paul's Corinth*.

[13] Gentiles were stereotyped by Jewish writers as sexually immoral and idolatrous (e.g., Let. Aris. 152; Josephus, *Ag. Ap.* 2.199; Philo, *On Abraham* 135–36).

[14] Only Jewish men could initiate divorce (e.g., Mal. 2:13; Ezra 10:3), but either person could divorce in the Greco-Roman world.

[15] Some argue that Paul's expectation of Jesus's imminent return stood behind his advice. In comparison, advice about marriage and family relationships in other writings like Ephesians, Colossians, and 1 Timothy reflects a church that had experienced a delay in his return.

Carl N. Toney

Corinth was full of temples to various gods and goddesses. This is an agora in Corinth with a reconstructed arch of a shop, and three columns of the Temple of Apollo.

human sinfulness (such as neglect and abuse). However these passages are interpreted, we should avoid interpretations that further victimize the victims. Unfortunately, some interpretations of the teachings of Jesus and Paul make the New Testament more legalistic than the Jewish scriptures, which permitted divorce (Deut. 24:1–4). Ultimately, we should seek interpretations that uphold God's ideal while providing grace to those whose relationships are broken by sin.

Against idolatry. Another problem facing the Corinthians was that some "strong" members were freely eating "idol food" (*eidōlothytos*).[16] In response, Paul provided a nuanced argument against idolatry while also making some allowances for the complexities of living in a Greco-Roman environment (1 Cor. 8:1–11:1). Paul distinguished between eating idol food in temples (1 Cor. 8:1–10:22) and food served in private homes (1 Cor. 10:23–11:1). He reminded the strong to avoid actions that could harm the conscience of the weak (1 Cor. 8:1–13). He provided the principle of considering the needs of others (1 Cor. 9:1–27). But ultimately, Paul drew a firm line in the sand by describing eating food in temples as idolatry (1 Cor. 10:1–22). However, when eating at an unbeliever's home, he permitted eating food that was not explicitly offered as a sacrifice (1 Cor. 10:23–11:1).[17]

Paul was not against eating specific foods. However, as a good Israelite, he was against idolatry (Exod. 20:4–6; Deut. 5:8–10). He was also against cultural compromises for the sake of personal advancement.

[16] The wide range of "idol food" (*eidōlothytos*) sacrificed included grain, fruit, fish, honey, meal, oil, and wine. Also problematic, some of the idol food was sold at the nearby "market" (Lat. *macellum*). Fotopoulos, *Food Offered to Idols*, 208; Gooch, *Dangerous Food*, 53–56.

[17] Toney, *Paul's Inclusive Ethic*, 179–92.

1 CORINTHIANS

- Letter's Greeting (1:1–3)
- Thanksgiving (1:4–9)
- The Corinthian Problems Addressed (1:10–6:20)
    - Divisions in the Church and True Wisdom (1:10–4:21)
    - Addressing Sexual Immorality and Lawsuits (5:1–6:20)
- Paul's Advice and Answers (7:1–16:12)
    - Marriage and Singleness (7:1–40)
    - Food Sacrificed to Idols (8:1–11:1)
    - Orderly Worship, Spiritual Gifts, and Love (11:2–14:40)
    - Resurrection Hope (15:1–58)
    - The Jerusalem Collection and Apollos (16:1–12)
- Letter's Conclusion (16:13–24)

Here, Paul specifically targeted the Corinthians' reputation for doing whatever it took to climb the social ladder, including eating banquets at local temples. However, Paul understood the need to accommodate others to share the gospel (1 Cor 9:19–23). This text should not be used as a proof text for people with "strong" faith acting out their Christian freedom. Instead, it reminds believers to humbly serve the one true God and not claim Christian freedom merely to fit into society or for social advancement.

Orderly worship. Paul turned to the topic of orderly worship in chapters 11–14. Within these chapters are some of the most famous and frequently cited passages, including the words of the Lord's Supper (1 Cor. 11:23–26; cf. Mark 14:22–26; Matt. 26:26–29; Luke 22:14–23), a discussion of spiritual gifts (1 Cor. 12:1–31, 14:1–40), and an extended reflection upon love (1 Cor. 13:1–13).

In contrast to the Greco-Roman practices of eating idol food in temples or private homes, Paul discussed Christian "**love**" (*agapē*) **feasts**, which featured a celebration of the Lord's Supper. The Lord's Supper is also called the "Eucharist," which comes from the Greek word *eucharisteō*, meaning to "give thanks" (1 Cor. 11:24). This expression derives from Jesus "giving thanks" as he broke the unleavened bread and dispersed the wine during his final Passover meal with his disciples (Mark 14:22–23; Matt. 26:27; Luke 22:17, 22:19). The Lord's Supper was meant for believers to reflect on Jesus's sacrificial death (1 Cor. 11:24–25) and his resurrection and return to reign (1 Cor. 11:26). In this letter, Paul confronted the Corinthians who had transformed this meal from celebrating their unity in Christ into a meal that marked divisions based on status and privilege. He challenged them to stop serving those with better food in their private dining room while serving those with lower status in the atrium or other common spaces.

Another key to orderly worship is the work of the Holy Spirit (1 Cor. 12:1–31, 14:1–40). Paul provided a variety of examples of "**spiritual gifts**" (*pneumatikoi*, 1 Cor. 14:1, 14:12; *charismata*, 1 Cor. 7:7, 12:4–7), including celibacy (1 Cor. 7:7–8), wisdom, knowledge, faith, healing, miracles, prophecy, tongues (1 Cor. 12:4–11), service, leadership, and generosity (1 Cor. 12:28–13:3). One of these gifts was speaking in "tongues" (*glōssai*, 1 Cor. 13:1, 14:2, 14:9, 14:23), which was a spiritual language. This is different from speaking in a foreign language such as in Acts 2:6 and 2:11.

We discover a lack of consistency when comparing the various lists of spiritual gifts in the New Testament (1 Cor. 12:4–11, 12:28–13:3; Rom. 12:6–8; Eph. 4:11–12; 1 Pet. 4:9–11). There was not a fixed understanding of these gifts among early Christians. Instead, these lists are examples of manifestations of the Spirit's empowerment. Paul acknowledged that "there are varieties of gifts" but also promoted unity because they were from "the same Spirit" (1 Cor. 12:4). Paul urged the Corinthians to seek prophetic gifts for building up the church (1 Cor. 14:5). He also advised the presence of an interpreter when someone spoke in tongues to build up others (1 Cor. 14:28). Both tongues and prophecy were required to be done in an orderly fashion to contrast the frenetic and ecstatic experiences of cultic priestess and prophets. He reminded the Corinthians that all gifts were manifested for the "common good" (1 Cor. 12:7).

Paul also provided advice concerning women who were praying and prophesying (1 Cor. 11:2–16). We know from the letter to the Romans that there were women leaders in Corinth, including the deacon Phoebe (Rom. 16:1) and Paul's coworker Prisca (Rom. 16:3). Paul's words that "women should be silent in the churches" and that they "should be subordinate, as the law also says" (1 Cor. 14:34) must be interpreted within this broader context. Because churches met in homes, there was a mixture of public and private spaces.

On the one hand, Paul expanded the boundaries for women in his churches by acknowledging the importance of their prophetic voices (1 Cor. 11:5) and by encouraging them to learn during Christian gatherings (1 Cor. 14:34). On the other hand, Paul's advice that wives should wait to ask their questions at home reflected his patriarchal expectations that reinforced husbands as the heads of their homes (1 Cor. 14:35). However, he also noted the interdependence of men and women (1 Cor. 11:11–12) and the ultimate headship of God (1 Cor. 11:3), even while encouraging a cultural practice like head coverings (1 Cor. 11:11–16). We'll look more closely at these passages in our chapter on the Pastorals when we examine a similar passage (1 Tim. 2:8–15). Looking at the big picture, Paul's advice was situational, and his primary concern was to promote order within the Corinthians' worship service, not to create timeless mandates about gender roles. These chapters on orderly

Carl N. Toney

Atrium from Delos. As a public space within the home, the atrium was the center of social and polical life. Patrons received their clients in the atrium.

worship reflect Paul's advice regarding what it meant to center Christian gatherings on the lordship of Christ.

A community of love. In the middle of Paul's discussion on spiritual gifts (1 Cor. 12–14) is his chapter on "love" (*agapē*, 1 Cor. 13). This discussion is at the center of these three chapters because love is the ultimate manifestation of the Spirit's empowering presence and a sign of God's reign in Christ. This chapter focuses on the necessity (vv. 1–3), character (vv. 4–7), and permanence of love (vv. 8–13).

Christianity became distinct in the ancient world for its emphasis on love. However, there is a common misunderstanding about two related terms for love.[18] It is popular to distinguish *agapē* as a sacrificial and superior divine love, versus *philia* as an inferior brotherly love. However, *philia* and *agapē* are nearly synonymous in Greek literature.[19] "The fact that Christian authors typically did prefer *agapē* rather than *philia* as the proper term for 'love' may indicate a wish on their part to distinguish themselves from the surrounding world. . . . But it need not imply that there was a difference of any real substance."[20]

In contrast to the standard philosophical virtues of "prudence" (*phronēsis*), "temperance" (*sōphrosynē*), "fortitude" (*andreios*), and "righteousness" (*dikaiosynē*), Paul highlighted "faith" (*pistis*), "hope" (*elpis*), and "love" (*agapē*) as the three pinnacles of virtue (1 Cor. 13:13). Among these three, love is the greatest Christian virtue.[21] Paul's emphasis on love was rooted in Jesus's command to love one's neighbor (Lev. 19:18; Mark 12:28–34; Matt. 22:34–40; cf. Luke 10:25–28). Paul connected this love command with the activity of the Spirit in Galatians (Gal. 5:13–25) where he called it the "law of Christ" (Gal. 6:2). Paul took up a similar theme of love fulfilling the law in Romans 12:9–11. Paul encouraged the Corinthian community that the ultimate expression of the Spirit's presence was their love, and they distinguished themselves by their acts of love.[22]

Carl N. Toney

In the background, the temple to Aphrodite, the goddess of love, is located on the Acrocorinth. In the foreground is the bema where Gallio may have dismissed the case of Paul.

Resurrection. Paul concluded his letter on a high note with a lengthy treatment of the "**resurrection**" (*anastasis*).[23] Previously, he wrote to the Thessalonians about their resurrection hope because the church was discouraged and believers were dying (1 Thess. 4:13–5:11). However, in this letter, Paul was dealing with the Corinthians'

[18]Lewis, *Four Loves*. Lewis distinguishes between "God's love" (*agapē*), "friendship" (*philia*), "affection" (*storgē*), and "romance" (*eros*).

[19]There has been a shift toward seeing these terms synonymously. Thorsteinsson, *Roman Stoicism*, 159–60; Mitchell, *Reconciliation*, 165; Carson, *Exegetical Fallacies*, 26, 30, 51–54. On love in Paul, see Gupta, *Affections of Christ*.

[20]Thorsteinsson, *Roman Stoicism*, 160–61.

[21]See the discussion of virtue in the chapters on 1–2 Thessalonians and Galatians (Chapters Six and Seven, respectively).

[22]On the importance of love at the heart of Paul's gospel, see Gupta, *Affections of Christ*.

[23]Wright, *Resurrection*; Mettinger, *Riddle of Resurrection*; Elledge, *Life after Death in Early Judaism*; Levenson, *Resurrection and the Restoration of Israel*.

Carl N. Toney

A counter of a "snack shop" (Lat. *thermopolium*) in Pompeii where customers, especially those who did not have kitchens, could purchase food.

overconfident belief that they were experiencing the full effects of their salvation in the present (1 Cor. 4:8). They denied the future resurrection (1 Cor. 15:12). The Corinthians would continue to struggle with their resurrection hope, and Paul would address the issue further in 2 Corinthians 5:1–10.

For Paul, believing in both Christ's historical resurrection and the future resurrection of believers was foundational to the gospel. He wrote, "If there is no resurrection of the dead, then Christ has not been raised; and if Christ has not been raised, then our proclamation has been in vain and your faith has been in vain" (1 Cor. 15:13–14). Further, he stated, "If Christ has not been raised, your faith is futile" (1 Cor. 15:17).

To support these claims, Paul recalled a traditional creed: "Christ died for our sins in accordance with the scriptures, and that he was buried, and that he was raised on the third day in accordance with the scriptures" (1 Cor. 15:3–4). Further, as proof, he highlighted the eyewitness accounts of Christ's appearances to Peter, the twelve disciples, five hundred disciples, James, other apostles, and Paul (1 Cor. 15:5–7, 15:12–19).

Paul claimed that a resurrected person would have a "spiritual body" (*sōma pneumatikon*, 1 Cor.15:44).[24] While the Greco-Roman world created a dualism between the body and the soul/spirit, Jewish thought did not. Paul's language emphasizes the Spirit's empowerment of a believer's new, physical body. Paul's view of the resurrection was holistic. He envisioned God saving the whole person, not just their souls/spirits. "A resurrection mode of existence [is] characterized by the reversal of decay, splendor, power, and being constituted by the direction, control, and character of the Holy Spirit."[25]

For Paul, Jesus's resurrection was the "first fruits" of those who would be made alive in the future. The life Jesus brought contrasts the death brought by Adam (1 Cor. 15:20–23; cf. Rom 5:12–21). Christ's resurrection is also linked to his exalted rule. Jesus is in the process of destroying those who oppose his rule, and the last enemy is death (1 Cor. 15:24–27). Once all his enemies are defeated, Jesus will hand his kingdom to God the Father, securing God's reign (1 Cor. 15:24, 15:28). Thus, Paul fixed the believers' hope on Christ's resurrection and exaltation.

During a chapter that loudly proclaims the resurrection at the center of Christian beliefs, we find that Paul also made a confusing statement about the Corinthians "baptism for [*hyper*] the dead" (1 Cor. 15:29–30 NIV). There are over forty explanations for this expression.[26] Translation options have included "on behalf of the dead (NRSV, ESV)," "for the dead (NIV, KJV)," or "for the sake of the dead." Many interpreters consider this a baptismal ritual done on behalf of recently deceased relatives or friends. Others argue that baptism refers to washing for burial or a metaphor for martyrdom. The best option is to translate this expression as "baptism for the sake of the dead" and to understand this as referring to believers who decided to be baptized because they wished to be identified with believing relatives who had already died.[27] Regardless of one's interpretation, Paul's purpose was to ask the Corinthians to reflect upon their baptismal practices in this life as a means to reinforce their hope for the resurrection in their future life. Thus, the accent of this question and the focus of 1 Corinthians 15 is to place the Christian hope squarely upon a future resurrection when Christ returns and believers "inherit the kingdom of God" (1 Cor. 15:50).

2 Corinthians

The Story Continues

Unfortunately, things went from bad to worse in Corinth with the arrival of new opponents who challenged Paul's authority. This led to Paul making a quick but painful visit in the spring of 55 CE (2 Cor. 2:1). On this trip, Paul was so humiliated before the church that he had to leave. When Paul returned to Ephesus, he wrote a "third" severe letter, which was lost (2 Cor. 2:4).[28]

Finally, in the fall of 55 CE, Paul returned to Corinth after passing through Macedonia (1 Cor. 16:5–12; cf. Acts 20:1–2). Titus met up with Paul during his travels to tell him that the worst of the crisis was finally over (2 Cor. 7:6–16). Paul wrote his "fourth" letter aimed at reconciliation, which is 2 Corinthians 1–9.

---

[24] For more details on this phrase, see Thiselton, *First Corinthians*, 1276–81.
[25] Thiselton, *First Corinthians*, 1279.
[26] Foschini, *Baptized for the Dead*.
[27] Thiselton, *First Corinthians*, 1248.
[28] Some scholars think this letter is 2 Corinthians 10–13.

Unfortunately, opposition soon arose again, resulting in Paul writing a "fifth" letter, which is 2 Corinthians 10–13. These last two letters were eventually combined into 2 Corinthians, following letter-writing conventions of the time. Alternatively, for those who favor the unity of 2 Corinthians, it is also possible that as Paul competed chapters 1–9, he received news that impacted his writing of chapters 10–13.

The Unity of the Corinthian Letters

While we have engaged in several discussions about the authorship of Paul's letters, another compositional issue is the unity of some letters. Scholars debate whether the canonical letters of 1-2 Corinthians are complete compositions or compilations of smaller letters that have been edited together.[29] The practice of joining letters together was known in the first century.

For 1 Corinthians, there are questions about how consistent Paul's thoughts were on various topics, including schisms (as necessary in 1 Cor. 11:18–19 versus not ideal in 1 Cor. 1:10–12), food sacrificed to idols (prohibited in 1 Cor. 10:1–22 versus permitted in 1 Cor. 8:1–13, 10:23–11:1), and Timothy's travel plans (in the future in 1 Cor. 16:5–9 versus in the past in 1 Cor. 4:17–21).[30]

For 2 Corinthians, there appears to be several interruptions to Paul's argument.[31] There was a gap between Paul's travel plans (2 Cor. 2:12–13 and 7:5–16). Traditional material (2 Cor. 6:14–7:1) interrupted Paul's appeal to open their hearts (2 Cor. 6:11–13, 7:2–4). In the middle of the letter, Paul made two requests for the Jerusalem collection, which may be two distinct letters (2 Cor. 8 and 9) added after another letter (2 Cor. 1–7). Finally, the harsh change of tone in the final chapters may indicate a final distinct letter (2 Cor. 10–13).

Rhetorical criticism has been used to defend each letter as a unified composition by showing how the letters maintain a sustained and cohesive argument.[32] While most scholars do not question the unity of 1 Corinthians, many scholars have reservations about the unity of 2 Corinthians. Of the partition theories, it seems most reasonable to distinguish between 2 Corinthians 1–9 and 2 Corinthians 10–13 due to the drastic change of tone between these two parts of the letter. These letters may have been combined, just as Cicero's letters were sometimes compiled.[33] However, since both pieces were written during Paul's journey across Macedonia (Acts 20:1–2), it is also plausible for 2 Corinthians to be one letter.

It was only when Paul reached Corinth by the end of 56 CE that he was able to patch things up (2 Cor. 12:14, 13:1; cf. Acts 20:2). After being reconciled with the community, Paul stayed in Corinth until the winter of 57 CE. During this final stay, he wrote his letter to the Romans (Rom. 16:1–16; Acts 20:3). As the letter carrier, Paul chose Phoebe, who was from Cenchreae, a neighboring city of Corinth (Rom. 16:1–2). She is described as a "patroness" (*prostatis*)—that is, a benefactor to many in the Corinthian church, including Paul (Rom. 16:2). She was also a "deacon" (*diakonos*) like Paul (e.g., 1 Cor. 3:5; 2 Cor. 3:6,

[29] The unity of Philippians is also debated. See Murphy-O'Connor, *Paul*, 215–30.

[30] Thiselton, *First Corinthians*, 36–39, 610–12.

[31] Toney, "Excursus: The Composition of 2 Corinthians (1985–2007)," 50–63.

[32] Mitchell, *Reconciliation*; Long, *Compositional Unity of 2 Corinthians*.

[33] Klauck, "Compilation of Letters," 131–55.

Carl N. Toney

In ancient times, ships and cargo were dragged across the Corinthian isthmus (now a canal) to shorten travel times.

6:4, 11:23), Apollos (1 Cor. 3:5), and Timothy (1 Thess. 3:2), meaning she was also a ministerial leader in the Corinthian church (Rom. 16:1).[34]

What 2 Corinthians Is All About

Paul defends his apostleship of weakness. Issues surrounding Paul's apostleship continued to plague him. In 1 Corinthians, Paul dealt with fractions and opponents within the church. In 2 Corinthians, the opponents came from outside the church with letters of recommendation, possibly from the Jerusalem church (2 Cor. 3:1–3, 10:12). As Paul defended himself from outside opponents in Galatia, he would defend himself in Corinth. Just as Paul's suffering was an issue in Philippi, this continued to plague Paul in Corinth.[35]

Throughout this letter, Paul addressed numerous accusations. He was accused of being a charlatan (2 Cor. 2:17). He was slighted for not having the proper apostolic standing (2 Cor. 11:5, 12:12). He was portrayed as fickle because of his changing travel plans (2 Cor. 1:17–18, 1:23). He seemed to demonstrate weakness rather than strength (2 Cor. 10:10). He was charged with pride (2 Cor. 3:1) and dishonesty (2 Cor. 12:16–19). He was too ordinary (2 Cor. 4:7–10, 10:10, 12:7–10), preached unclearly (2 Cor. 4:3), and had untrained speech (2 Cor. 11:6). He was even described as being out of his mind (2 Cor. 5:13, 11:16–19, 12:6).

---

[34] The translation of "deaconess" incorrectly implies a different Greek word, *diakonissa*, and can unfortunately project a modern, anachronistic understanding of Phoebe's role as being subordinate to men. We should also avoid thinking of this as some form of formal office (see the discussion of "deacon" and "elder" in the Pastorals).

[35] Barnett, "Opposition in Corinth," 3–17.

2 CORINTHIANS

- Letter's Greeting (1:1–2)
- Thanksgiving (1:3–7)
- Paul's Defense of His Ministry (1:8–7:16)
  - Paul Defends His Travel Plans and Severe Letter (1:8–2:13)
  - Paul Defends His Ministry of Reconciliation (2:14–7:4)
  - Titus Reports Their Positive Response (7:5–16)
- The Jerusalem Collection (8:1–9:15)
- Paul Defends His Apostleship of Weakness (10:1–13:10)
- Letter's Conclusion (13:11–13)

His opponents claimed to be true apostles (2 Cor. 11:5, 11:13, 11:23, 12:11), even though they had encroached upon Paul's territory (2 Cor. 10:13–14).[36] They emphasized their strength and qualifications, such as their status as Jews and ministers of the gospel (2 Cor. 11:22–23). They had letters of commendation (2 Cor. 3:1, 10:12, 10:18). They performed miracles by the power of the Spirit (2 Cor. 11:13–15, 12:12) and spoke eloquently (2 Cor. 11:5–6). Paul was concerned that they were exploiting the Corinthians (2 Cor. 11:20). But the real danger was that they preached a rival gospel (2 Cor. 11:3–4).[37]

While his opponents boasted of their strength and accomplishments (2 Cor. 3:1–18, 10:13–16), Paul boasted of his weakness (2 Cor. 11:30, 12:5, 12:10). Paul opposed self-promotion and boasting (2 Cor. 10:12, 10:18; cf. 1 Cor. 13:4; Rom. 1:30). Instead, he believed the only proper boasting was done "in the Lord" (2 Cor. 10:17; cf. 1 Cor. 1:31). This was because Paul took to heart the words of Jeremiah:

> Thus says the LORD: Do not let the wise boast in their wisdom, do not let the mighty boast in their might, do not let the wealthy boast in their wealth; but let those who boast boast in this, that they understand and know me, that I am the LORD; I act with steadfast love, justice, and righteousness in the earth, for in these things I delight, says the LORD. (Jer. 9:23–24)

Carl N. Toney
Corinthian pottery and two mosaics from villa floors.

For Paul, success was found in his suffering, privation, and physical weakness (2 Cor. 11:23–33, 12:1–10). He understood that his weakness kept him humble (2 Cor. 12:8). Unlike his opponents,

[36] Barnett, *Second Corinthians*, 28–30.
[37] Martin, "The Setting of 2 Corinthians," 3–19.

who relied upon human authority (2 Cor. 10:12), Paul understood that true authority came only from God (2 Cor. 1:1; cf. Gal. 1:1, 1:15–16). Paul's concern was that by rejecting him as God's messenger, the Corinthians risked rejecting the gospel message and God. Paul's apostolic aim was to upbuild the church (2 Cor. 13:10) rather than dominate (2 Cor. 1:24) or divide it (2 Cor. 11:2–4, 12:20).

Ultimately, Paul patterned his own life of suffering and weakness on the death of Jesus as the means for him to minister to others (2 Cor. 4:7–15; cf. 1 Cor. 1:23–24; Phil. 2:6–11). Further, he understood that human weakness makes room for divine empowerment (2 Cor. 4:7–10, 12:8–10). He took to heart Jesus's promise, "My grace is sufficient for you, for my power is made perfect in weakness" (2 Cor. 12:9). And he concluded his letter with a Trinitarian blessing that begins with the "grace" (*charis*) of Jesus, the "love" (*agapē*) of God, and the "fellowship" (*koinōnia*) of the Holy Spirit (2 Cor. 13:14).[38]

How about some money? One of the Corinthians' chief concerns was how Paul handled money. Like a televangelist, Paul was accused of preaching for self-gain (2 Cor. 2:17) and being a financial scammer (2 Cor. 8:16–24, 11:8–11, 11:12, 12:13, 12:18–19). They were suspicious of Paul's refusal to allow them to support him (2 Cor. 11:8, 11:12, 12:13), especially since they knew that Paul was receiving support from Macedonian churches such as the church in Philippi (2 Cor. 8:1–5, 11:8–11). Paul asked the Corinthians to contribute to his collection for the Jerusalem church to assure them of his good intentions and integrity in handling the money (2 Cor. 8–9).

Carl N. Toney

The Lechaion Road was how people entered the city of Corinth.

[38]See discussion on Matthew 28:18-20. The New Testament is full of Trinitarian references (Eph. 4:4-6; 1 Pet. 1:2; cf. 1 Cor. 6:11, 12:4-6; 2 Cor. 1:21-22; Gal. 3:11-14, 4:4-5; 2 Thess. 2:13-14; 1 Pet. 1:3-5; Jude 20-21).

The Order of Paul's Letters and the Jerusalem Collection

Four of Paul's letters potentially discuss a collection for the Jerusalem church (Rom. 15:14–32; 1 Cor. 16:1–4; 2 Cor. 8:1–9:15; Gal. 2:10). These passages are used to determine the scope and chronology of the Pauline collection.[39] It is often assumed that letters that do not speak about the collection were written either before the collection became a priority for Paul (e.g., 1–2 Thessalonians) or sometime after the collection was delivered (e.g., the Pastorals). Typically, Galatians, 1–2 Corinthians, and Romans are all considered to have been written during the period of Paul's collection.

However, the general statement about being concerned for the poor in Galatians 2:10 does not need to refer to the Jerusalem collection mentioned in 1–2 Corinthians and Romans. Rather, it refers to Paul's earlier collection efforts on behalf of the poor, including a relief fund for the Jerusalem church from the Antioch church (Acts 11:27–30).[40] If Galatians is not referencing the Jerusalem collection, then it is possible that Philippians, Colossians, Ephesians, and Philemon could have been written around the same time from Ephesus. If Galatians mentions the collection, then the absence of the collection in these letters would be surprising during this time period.

This reading allows us to place Philippians in a time before 1–2 Corinthians. In this reconstruction, the Philippians' generosity (Phil. 4:10–20) inspired Paul to take up a collection for the Jerusalem church. The collection is first mentioned in the Corinthian letters (1 Cor. 16:1–4; 2 Cor. 8:1–9:15). Romans 15:14–32 (written from Corinth) also speaks about this collection from Paul's Gentile churches. Acts 24:17 may record Paul's delivery of the collection; however, Acts may be silent about the collection, and these "alms" for Israel may demonstrate Paul's Jewish piety.

Often today, giving is framed within appeals of generosity. However, gift giving was bound to the patronage system in the first century. Wealthy patrons would give their clients gifts. In return, clients were obligated to show loyalty to their patron. This worldview helps us to understand Paul's efforts to collect resources for the Jerusalem church. Paul avoided becoming obligated to the Corinthian church by refusing to take their money for his ministry. But the Corinthian church would understand their obligation to the Jerusalem church because the gospel spread from Israel (Rom. 15:25). However, the gospel presented an even more radical challenge to this system of obligations because it claimed that God was the ultimate benefactor, so allegiance was now expected to be shown to God (2 Cor. 9:8, 13). Generosity toward other believers was a response to God's patronage through the work of Christ (2 Cor. 8:9).[41]

Paul's collection for the Jerusalem church was inspired by the generosity of the Macedonian churches (2 Cor. 8:1–5, 8:8). This collection occupied a central place in Paul's missionary strategy during his Corinthian ministry. On the most basic level, Paul sought to relieve poverty, particularly in the Jerusalem church (2 Cor. 8:13–14, 9:12; cf. Rom. 15:26).[42] The cause of poverty among Jerusalem Christians was due

---

39 Wedderburn, "Paul's Collection: Chronology and History," 95–110; Downs, "Paul's Collection and the Book of Acts Revisited," 50–70; Longenecker, "Good News to the Poor," 58–63.

40 Martyn, *Galatians*, 19–20, 222–28.

41 deSilva, *Honor, Patronage, Kinship, & Purity*; Bates, *Gospel Allegiance*; McKnight, *King Jesus Gospel.*

42 For present-day ethical issues related to Paul's concern for the poor and equality, see Wheeler, *Wealth as Peril and Obligation: The New Testament on Possessions*, 73–89.

Carl N. Toney

The Pierene Fountain was a major water source for Corinth.

to a combination of factors, including their radical sharing of wealth (Acts 2:42–47, 4:32–37), persecution by non-Christians, and a food shortage and famine (Acts 11:28–30).[43]

The **Jerusalem collection** was also part of Paul's strategy of ethnic reconciliation. The sharing of resources created solidarity between Jewish and Gentile believers, as well as between the separate Gentile churches of the Pauline mission. Paul also saw this collection as fulfilling the expectation that Gentiles would bring gifts to Israel in the last days (Isa. 2:1–5, 60:5–14, 66:18–20; cf. Mic. 4:1–4; Zech. 14:16).[44] For the Corinthians, Paul hoped the common cause of the collection would unite those fighting. Paul asked for their generosity based upon their own past kindness (2 Cor. 8:6, 8:10–11, 9:2), the model of the Macedonian churches (2 Cor. 8:1–5, 8:8), and the model of Christ (2 Cor. 8:9).[45] When Paul wrote to the Roman church from Corinth, he considered his collection a success (Rom. 15:26). Unfortunately, how this collection was received in Jerusalem remains a mystery.

Speaking about the resurrection (again). Paul's views about the resurrection and Christ's return continued to develop between 1 Corinthians 15 and 2 Corinthians 5. Most notably, in 1 Corinthians 15, Paul thought he would be alive when Christ returned and that he would have a resurrected body (1 Cor. 15:51; cf. 1 Thess. 4:15). However, in 2 Corinthians 5, Paul considered the possibility that he may be dead before

[43] Winter, "Acts and Food Shortages," 59–78.

[44] Donaldson, "Proselytes or 'Righteous Gentiles'? The Status of Gentiles in Eschatological Pilgrimage Patterns of Thought," 3–27.

[45] Harrison, *Paul's Language of Grace*, 294–332; Downs, *Offering of the Gentiles*; Barclay, *Paul and the Gift*.

this occurred (2 Cor. 5:1–10, 5:15; cf. 2 Cor. 1:9–11, 4:7–18). This change was due to Paul's confrontation with his own death (2 Cor. 1:9–11, 4:7–18), and he explained how his resurrection hope empowered him to face trials on behalf of others.

Like 1 Corinthians, there is a question regarding what kind of resurrection Paul was talking about, particularly if it was physical or spiritual.[46] In 2 Corinthians 5:1, the new body is "eternal" (*aiōnios*), "not made with hands" (*acheiropoiētos*), and "heavenly" (*ouranois*). Fitting within the Jewish hope of an embodied existence, Paul longed for his new resurrected body when he wrote, "we do not wish to be unclothed but to be clothed" (2 Cor. 5:4 NIV). Further, Paul likened his earthly body to a "tent" (*skēnos*), subject to wear and tear. Still, it would be replaced by a new, permanent "house" (*oikia*). Paul's imagery echoes the tabernacle/temple motifs in the Jewish scriptures. Paul wanted to encourage the Corinthians that God remained present with his people via the Spirit during their pilgrimage until they reached the promised land upon Christ's return.[47]

It is unclear whether Paul was expressing his hope that he would have this new body immediately when he died or if he assumed that the dead would exist in a temporary bodiless period in heaven with Christ (2 Cor. 5:8; cf. 1 Cor. 15:35–38, 15:42–44; Phil. 1:23). Paul's hope (like all believers) was that Christ would return to reign and that he would skip the interim state of death. Paul viewed Christ's return as the climax of Christian transformation. In 2 Corinthians, Paul offered the hope of being in the presence of Christ for anyone who died before Christ's return. Paul's main purpose was not to explain this future existence but to remind his audience of the impact of the future upon the present (2 Cor. 5:9, 5:10, 5:15). Because of this future resurrection hope, believers should live ethical lives of love, build up one another, and allow themselves to be guided by the Spirit in the present. These kinds of lives demonstrate to others that God is in charge.

Key Terms and People

Apollos: a Jewish Christian leader in the Corinthian church who had been discipled by Prisca and Aquila

Body of Christ: image used by Paul in 1 Corinthians and Romans to describe the unity and diversity of the church that draws upon political images for society; in Colossians and Ephesians, Christ is described as the head of this body

Jerusalem collection: Paul's efforts to gather funds to support the Jerusalem church were based on his understanding that Gentiles would share their wealth with Israel in the last days

Love feasts: Christians gathered for communal meals that included sharing in the Lord's Supper

Resurrection: Christians believe that God physically raised Jesus from the dead and that Christians will be bodily raised from the dead in the future

Spiritual gifts: manifestations of the Spirit's empowerment in believers' lives, such as faith, generosity, healing, prophecy, and tongues

---

[46] For a survey of views, see Toney, "Excursus: Resurrection in 2 Corinthians," 250–56.

[47] Harris, *Second Corinthians*, 370–71.

Conversation Starters

1. What are some things you learned about the city of Corinth? How would you describe Paul's relationship with the Corinthians?
2. What sort of issues were dividing the Corinthian church? What advice did Paul give to help unify the church?
3. What was Paul's understanding of sexual ethics? How does this relate to the teachings of Jesus? Why do you think Paul and Jesus promoted singleness?
4. How did Paul encourage orderly worship? Why were his teachings about love in the middle of teaching about spiritual gifts?
5. What was Paul's understanding of his weakness? How was this an asset for his gospel and ministry?
6. Why was Paul collecting money for the Jerusalem church? How was this collection related to the generosity of the Philippian church?
7. Why did Paul spend so much time discussing the resurrection in these letters? How is this similar and different from the Thessalonian letters?

FOR FURTHER READING

Baker, William, Ralph P. Martin, and Carl N. Toney. *1 Corinthians, 2 Corinthians*. Cornerstone Biblical Commentary 15. Tyndale House, 2009.

Barrett, C. K. *The Second Epistle to the Corinthians*. BNTC 8. Hendrickson, 1993.

Belleville, Linda L. *2 Corinthians*. IVP New Testament Commentary 8. InterVarsity Press, 1996.

Fee, Gordon D. *The First Epistle to the Corinthians*. NICNT. Eerdmans, 1987.

Harris, Murray J. *The Second Epistle to the Corinthians: A Commentary on the Greek Text*. NIGTC. Eerdmans, 2005.

Martin, Ralph P. *2 Corinthians*. 2nd ed. WBC 40. Zondervan, 2014.

Murphy-O'Connor, Jerome. *St. Paul's Corinth*. Rev. ed. Michael Glazier, 1990.

Oropeza, B. J. *1 Corinthians*. New Covenant Commentary. Cascade, 2017.

Thiselton, Anthony C. *The First Epistle to the Corinthians: A Commentary on the Greek Text*. NIGTC. Eerdmans, 2000.

Witherington, Ben, III. *Conflict and Community in Corinth: A Socio-Rhetorical Commentary on 1 and 2 Corinthians*. Eerdmans, 1995.

10

A LETTER OF INTRODUCTION

Romans

The Story So Far

According to one legend, the twin founders of Rome, Romulus and Remus, were descendants of Aeneas, the great hero who survived the fall of Troy (Virgil, *Aen.*; cf. Livy, *Hist.* 1.1–3). According to others, the boys were conceived by the god Mars with their virgin mother Rhea Silvia, but then they were left to die on the banks of the Tiber River by their great-uncle Armulius (Livy, *Hist.* 1; Plutarch, *Quaest rom.*; Dionysius, *Ant. rom.* 1.72–2.29). Fortunately, a she-wolf and a woodpecker saved them by nursing and feeding them until a shepherd found and raised them. When the boys grew up, they discovered the truth about their birth. Seeking revenge, they killed their great-uncle. Then, they set out to establish their own city. Tragedy struck when Romulus accidently killed Remus during a quarrel while choosing the location of the city. Finally, Romulus founded the city of Rome, naming it after himself.

While these are interesting stories, we can trace the historical origins of Rome to the tradition reported by Marcus Terentius Varro that Rome began as a small agricultural village on the Palatine Hill near the Tiber River around 753 BCE. Around 600 BCE, a people called the Etruscans conquered the city, drained the marshy land, and built a city wall. Rome grew into a city-state that expanded control over the entire Italian peninsula. This Archaic period (753–509 BCE) ended with the expulsion of the king of Rome.

SUGGESTED READING

Acts 28:14-31
Romans

In the new era of the Roman Republic (509–31 BCE), the people were governed by a senate and two annually elected magistrates (initially called praetors, then consuls). This Republic consisted of four classes of people—land-owning patricians (nobles), equestrians (knights) who fought for Rome, free citizens called plebeians, and slaves. As Rome expanded east, it conquered the former territories of Alexander the Great. While Latin was spoken in Rome and

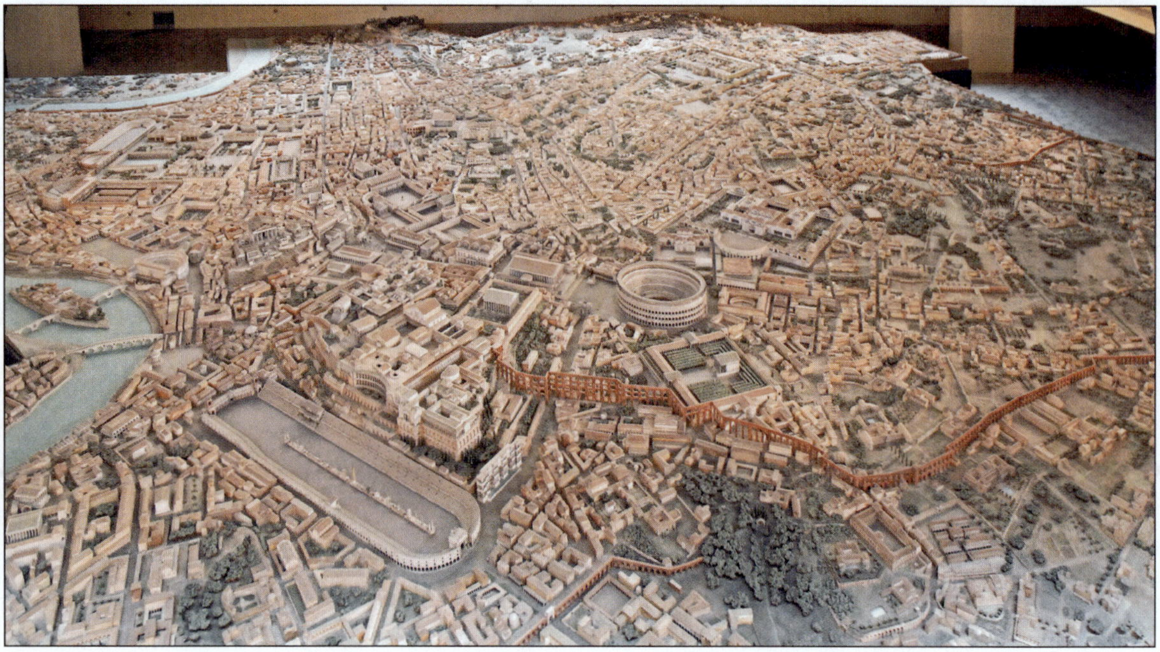

Scale model of Rome from the age of Constantine by Italo Gismondi. Museo della Civiltà Romana, Rome.

the western provinces, Greek was the dominant language of the eastern provinces that were formerly under the control of the Greeks.

Notably, during this period, Pompey conquered Jerusalem in 63 BCE. He let the Jewish people know that Rome was now in charge. He brought a sizable number of Jewish slaves to Rome, who were later emancipated and given citizenship (Josephus, *Ant.* 14.4.1–5). When Paul wrote Romans, it was estimated that the Jewish population was between fifteen thousand and sixty thousand people (out of a population between seven hundred thousand to one million). These Jews and many Christians lived in the less desirable, poorer districts occupied by immigrants, including the Trastevere district across the Tiber River (Philo, *Embassy* 155–56) and an area near the old Porta Capena (Juvenal, *Sat.* 3.10–18).[1]

Rome was a crowded urban environment with an estimated population density nearly three times higher than Manhattan.[2] About 90 percent of people lived in rooms that measured about 100 square feet to 1,200 square feet, found in the upper levels of the four- to five-story apartment buildings (Lat. *insulae*) or in the rear of shops. It has been estimated that the Jewish district had 4,405 apartment buildings and 24 bakeries.[3] In contrast, the wealthy lived in multiroom apartments (Lat. *cenacula*) that were about 1,600 square feet to 3,200 square feet, or in mansions located in better parts of the city.[4]

The final days of the Roman Republic were marked by three civil wars (91–89, 80s, 40s BCE) and Julius Caesar's rise to power. The Roman Republic died with the assassination of Julius Caesar in 44 BCE. However, it was reborn as the Roman Empire in 31 BCE with the ascendance of Augustus Caesar, who

[1] Lampe, *From Paul to Valentinus*, 19–65; Jewett, *Romans*, 55–58.

[2] Jewett, *Romans*, 54.

[3] Lampe, *From Paul to Valentinus*, 53–54.

[4] Jeffers, *The Greco-Roman World of the New Testament Era*, 59.

restored the "Roman peace" (Lat. *Pax Romana*). This empire would last into the fifth century CE.

Early Christian tradition attributes the founding of the Roman church to Peter and Paul (e.g., Irenaeus, *Haer*. 3.3.1–2; cf. Eusebius, *Hist. eccl.* 6.1). However, the biblical evidence provides the most plausible explanation for the origins of the church (Acts 2:10, 18:2; Heb. 13:24; 1 Pet. 5:13). According to Acts 2:10, Jewish pilgrims from Rome heard the gospel from Peter during the festival of Pentecost. When they returned to Rome, they shared their beliefs with other Jews in the local synagogues. Among these early Christians were Prisca and Aquila (Rom. 16:3; Acts 18:1–2). **House churches** in Rome consisted of fifteen to twenty-five people who met in some of the smaller apartments (Acts 20:7–12), larger apartments of wealthier members (16:3–5; cf. Acts 18:7), lecture halls (Acts 19:9–10), or other public spaces.[5]

Insulae were multiple-story apartment buildings that included a common staircase, shops, small upper floor housing, and a central courtyard. Ostia Antica, Italy. (second cent. CE)

A rift occurred between the Jewish Christians and other Jews during the reign of Emperor Claudius (41–54 CE). As a result, the emperor expelled the Jewish Christian leadership around 49 CE. Prisca and Aquila were among those expelled, and they met Paul in Corinth (Acts 18:1–2). Suetonius (ca. 120 CE) recounted this **Edict of Claudius**: "Since the Jews constantly made disturbances at the instigation of Chrestus, he expelled them from Rome" (*Claud*., 25.4; cf. Acts 18:1–2; Dio Cassius, *Hist*. 60.6.6; Orosius, *Adv. pag*. 7.6.15).[6] With the Jewish Christian leadership gone, the Roman church separated from the Jewish synagogues and became predominantly Gentile (Rom. 1:13, 11:13, 11:19–22, 11:25, 11:28).

When Emperor Nero first rose to power (54–62 CE), he permitted the Jewish Christian leadership to resettle in Rome. During this time, Prisca and Aquila returned to the city (Rom. 16:3). Unfortunately, the return of the Jewish Christian leadership created tension between the Jewish and Gentile Christians. In the winter of 57 CE, Paul wrote his letter to the Romans from Corinth, and he addressed these tensions (Rom. 14:1–15:13). He also expressed his desire to visit the church for the first time (Rom. 1:11–15, 15:22–29; cf. Acts 20:2–6). Later, Paul got his wish, but he arrived in Rome as a prisoner (Acts 28). We do

Claudius Caesar. Napels National Archaeological Museum.

[5]Some churches may have also met outside cities (Acts 16:13, 16:16). Adams, *The Earliest Christian Meeting Places: Almost Exclusively Houses?*; Kloppenborg, *Christ's Associations*, 97–130, esp. 110.

[6]Suetonius probably confused the common name for slaves and freedmen, *Chrēstus*, which means "good/useful," with "Christ" (*Christos*). The edict is probably dated to 49 or 50 CE (Orosius). Lampe, *From Paul to Valentinus*, 12–13.

Public Domain

Nero Caesar. Glyptothek Museum, Munich.

not know when Peter arrived, but according to Dionysius, bishop of Corinth, Peter and Paul eventually "together taught in Italy" (Eusebius, *Hist. eccl.* 2.25.8, 4.23).

Rome found itself ablaze during the second half of Nero's reign (62–68 CE). At midnight on July 19, 64 CE, a fire consumed ten out of the fourteen districts in Rome. While people suspected that Nero started the fire (Pliny, *Nat.* 17.5), the emperor blamed the Christians.[7] They probably made excellent scapegoats because the Roman elite perceived Christians as having a "hatred of the human race," being atheists for not believing in the Roman gods, and not participating in the civic cults (Tacitus, *Ann.* 15.38). While Claudius's edict indicated that the Romans had not yet distinguished between Jews and Christians in 49 CE, by the time of Nero's edict in 64 CE, these groups were seen as distinct. Although the Jews were protected by Roman law as adherents of a "legal religion" (Lat. *religio licita*), Christians were not.

The aftermath of Nero's fire was a period of persecuting Christians in Rome. They were executed for entertainment in Nero's garden (Tacitus, *Ann.* 15.44).[8] It was also during Nero's reign that Peter and Paul were both martyred. According to tradition, Peter was crucified upside down (Acts of Peter 37–38; Eusebius, *Hist. eccl.* 2.25.5; cf. John 21:18–19), and his bones were eventually buried in the crypt beneath St. Peter's Basilica in Rome. According to other traditions, Paul as a Roman citizen was beheaded in a private setting at the traditional site at the Church of the Three Fountains (Mart. Paul 3–5; Tertullian, *Scorp.* 15.4; cf. Tertullian, *Praescr.* 36; Eusebius, *Hist. eccl.* 2.25.7–8, 3.1.3).

What This Letter Is All About

Romans is a letter of introduction since Paul had never been to Rome (Rom. 1:10).[9] Romans 16 contains Paul's longest list of greetings because Paul wanted the church to know that he knew people in the city who could act as his character references. For example, he greeted his longtime ministry partners Prisca and Aquila (Rom. 16:3–4). He also greeted the apostles Andronicus and Junia (Rom. 16:7), who were probably part of a group of Jewish Christians appointed as apostles by Jesus after his resurrection (1 Cor. 15:7). Junia was also notable for being the only named female apostle in the New Testament.[10] Not only were this couple apostles, but Paul highlighted their outstanding reputation as "esteemed among the apostles" (Rom. 16:7).[11] The word "esteemed" (*episēmos*) can be understood like a flag or figurehead that

---

[7] Dio Cassius (*Hist.* 62.16) suggested that unknown enemies of the emperor did the job.

[8] However, the Romans were shocked by the manner of the executions. Merrill, *Essays in Early Christian History*, 129.

[9] Romans has a general tone, like Ephesians, and it is written to an audience he has not met, like Colossians. Some manuscripts omit "in Rome" (Rom. 1:7), and the greetings from chapter 16 may be from another letter to the Ephesians.

[10] Due to mistranslations, some have thought Junia was a male. Martin Luther translated the name as the male "Junias." However, Junia is only used as a woman's name in over 250 ancient texts. Early Christians like John Chrysostom knew she was a woman. He wrote, "Oh, how great is the devotion of this woman, that she should be counted worthy of the appellation of apostle" (Chrysostom, *Hom. Rom.* 31.2)!

[11] My translation. A less plausible translation is "esteemed by the apostles." Paul's comments about being "in Christ before him" indicate they were witnesses of Jesus's resurrection. See Jewett, *Romans*, 963. But "apostle" could also mean someone "sent" (2 Cor. 8:23; Phil. 2:25) or a "commissioned missionary" (e.g., 1 Cor. 9:5–6). See Moo, *Romans*, 939–40.

identifies one ship from another (Herodotus, *Hist.* 8.88). In other words, they stood out. Paul greeted them because of their stellar reputation in the early church. He hoped they would give a favorable word about him to their fellow Roman believers since they were previously imprisoned with Paul for the sake of the gospel (cf. Col. 4:10; Philem. 23).

Paul wrote Romans to explain his apostleship and gospel (Rom. 1:1–7) and to gain the support of the church for his mission to Spain (Rom. 15:22–29). He also wanted them to contribute to his collection for the Jerusalem church (Rom. 15:25, 15:31). Romans is often divided into three major movements: (1) Paul's gospel message (chapters 1–8), (2) God's faithfulness to Israel (chapters 9–11), and (3) ethical advice for the community (chapters 12–16). Paul wrote using the engaging style of **diatribe**, which involved asking his audience questions, giving answers, and addressing imaginary dialogue partners (called imaginary interlocutors) in Romans 2:1–5, 2:17–24, 9:19–21, 11:17–24, and 14:4–12. This style of writing was designed to teach and shape the moral character of the audience.

Romans was written to a people living at the heart of the Roman Empire. Anyone living in the city knew that Rome was in charge, and Paul directly addressed Roman rule in chapter 13. Paul wrote his letter to encourage believers that a righteous God was in charge. As such, God had judged the whole world—both Gentiles and Jews—as sinners who were accountable to God (Rom. 1:18–3:20). God's authority over everyone also meant that God desired to save everyone (Rom. 3:21–8:39). God's plans to save everyone included his plans to save Israel (Rom. 9:1–11:36). In response to salvation, Paul gave practical advice for submitting to God's rule within the community, as well as its posture toward their Roman rulers (Rom. 12:1–15:13).

Righteousness of God

Paul set out to prove that God put people in right relationships as they trusted in him. Paul's main idea of Romans is found in Romans 1:16–17, which states, "For I am not ashamed of the gospel; it is the power of God for salvation to everyone who has faith, to the Jew first and also to the Greek. For in it

The Roman Forum was the center of civic, commercial, and religious life. It included the temples of Julius Caesar, Vespasian and Titus, Vesta, Saturn, and Castor and Pollux; the Basilica Julia; and the senate meeting house.

the righteousness of God is revealed through faith for faith; as it is written, 'The one who is righteous will live by faith.'"

To help us understand this thesis better, let's unpack some of its key terms. First, "**righteousness of God**" (*dikaiosynē theou*) is an expression that is almost entirely unique to Romans (Rom. 1:17, 3:5, 3:21, 3:22, 3:25, 3:26, 10:3).[12] This expression reminds us of the God-centered focus of the letter. Paul expounded upon God's righteousness, not human righteousness. This phrase can be understood in one of several ways. God's righteousness is treated as an object or possession where God gives his righteousness as a gift to believers. Alternatively, God's righteousness is a quality or characteristic so that a righteous God makes righteous people. Others emphasize that righteousness is imputed, meaning believers are deemed righteous because of Christ's righteousness, despite continuing to sin. While others consider this effective righteousness, meaning believers are actually changed into righteous people who can now please God.[13]

Rather than getting bogged down in the quagmire of theological debates, it may be more useful to think of righteousness as "right relationships."[14] Righteousness is not something that individuals can

ROMANS

- Letter's Greeting (1:1–7)
- Thanksgiving (1:8–15)
- God's Righteousness Makes Righteous People by Faith (1:16–8:39)
    - The Gospel of God's Righteousness (1:16–17)
    - Condemnation of All Sinners (1:18–3:20)
    - Saving People by Faith and Abraham's Example (3:21–4:25)
    - Results of Being Justified by Faith (5:1–8:39)
- God's Faithfulness to Israel (9:1–11:36)
    - Salvation of Israel's Remnant (9:1–11:10)
    - Salvation of All Israel (11:11–36)
- Christian Living in Response to God's Righteousness (12:1–15:13)
    - Community Conduct (12:1–13:14)
    - The Weak and Strong (14:1–15:13)
- Paul's Travel Plans (15:14–33)
- Letter's Final Greetings and Conclusion (16:1–27)

[12] It is also found once in 2 Corinthians 5:2. Bultmann, "ΔΙΚΑΙΟΣΥΝΗ ΘΕΟΥ," 12–16.

[13] Protestants have traditionally argued that righteousness is "imputed" by God, meaning a sinner is granted a new *status*. However, Catholics have favored righteousness as "imparted," so that a sinner gains a new *nature*.

[14] See the chapter on Galatians.

have on their own, independent of others. Righteousness is something a person has in one's relationships as a social being. People are righteous when they meet the expectations others have placed on them in their relationships.[15]

For the Jewish people, the law represented these expectations (Rom. 2:17–20, 9:4–5, 10:5; cf. Exod. 20–24). Their relationship centered on God's covenantal faithfulness to his people (Rom. 3:2–3, 11:1–2, 11:28–32). To be in a right relationship with God, a person must obey the law (Rom. 2:13, 2:25). Right relationships brought rewards (Rom. 2:7, 2:10). Breaking these laws created wrong relationships that brought punishments (Rom. 2:8–9). The law was holy and good (Rom. 7:12, 7:16, 8:4) and helped people identify sin (Rom. 3:19–20, 7:7). Unfortunately, the law was too weak to overcome sin (Rom. 5:20, 8:3) and could not keep people in right relationship with God (Rom. 3:20, 4:15). Christ came to put all people in right relationship with God, apart from the law (Rom. 3:21–31).

The Circus Maximus in Rome was the largest stadium in the empire and could accommodate 150,000 spectators.

The relational and social concept of righteousness helps eliminate a false dichotomy between God's love (and mercy) and God's righteousness (and judgment). Paul argued that God is the only righteous and proper judge, and his good character judges the world so that he is in right relationship with evil and sin (Rom. 1:18–3:20). Because of the reconciling work of Christ, God can forgive sins and is put in right relationship with humanity as an expression of his love for humanity (Rom. 3:21–31, 5:1–11, 5:18–21, 6:5–11, 7:4–6, 8:1–4).

After a person is put in right relationship with God, he or she can have right relationships with others (Rom. 12:9–21, 13:8–10, 14:1–15:13). Loving God is an expression of being put in right relationship with God and letting God be in charge (Rom. 8:28; Deut. 6:5). Loving one's neighbors is an expression of being in right relationship with others (Rom. 13:8–10; Lev. 19:18). If the order is reversed (loving others, then loving God), we discover a skewed standard of righteousness that can lead to false boasting (Rom. 2:17, 2:23, 3:27, 4:2).[16]

God's Faithfulness

What did Paul mean that God's righteousness is revealed "from faith to faith" (*ek pisteōs eis pistin*) in his opening statement (Rom. 1:17)? This "from-to" expression can be understood as "from faith's beginning to end" to communicate the all-encompassing nature of the faith (cf. Ps. 83:8; Jer. 9:2; 2 Cor. 2:16, 3:18). More likely, Paul was referencing two distinct but linked kinds of faith—from God's faithfulness *to* humanity's faith.

---

[15] Dunn, *Romans*, 1:40–41.

[16] The idea of ordered love is explored in Augustine, *On Christian Teaching*, esp. book 1.

Temple of Mars in the Forum of Augustus. Rome.

To reinforce this idea of God's faithfulness inspiring faith, Paul quoted his own version of Habakkuk 2:4.[17] This quotation is among the four different ancient forms of Habakkuk 2:4 that we possess:

> The righteous one will live by his faith[fulness]. (MT)
> My [God's] righteous one will live by faith[fulness]. (LXX A and C; cf. Heb. 10:38)
> The righteous one will live by my [God's] faith[fulness]. (LXX S and W)
> The righteous one will live by [his? or God's?] faithfulness. (Rom. 1:17; Gal. 3:11)

In the first and second quotations, the emphasis is upon the faith(fulness) of the righteous person. The third quotation highlights God's faith(fulness) to the righteous one. The last quotation comes from Paul, who omitted any pronouns and made the phrase ambiguous.

Paul intentionally made the phrase vague by dropping the personal adjectives *my* and *his* so that Habakkuk 2:4 includes both meanings of "God's faithfulness" and the "righteous person's faith." "In the tradition of Jewish interpretation, Paul would not necessarily want to narrow the meaning to *exclude* other meanings self-evident in the text forms used elsewhere, so much as to *extend* and broaden the meaning to include the sense he was most concerned to bring out."[18]

This quotation from Habakkuk 2:4 summarizes God's expectations for his people. Paul was not unusual as a Jewish thinker in the first century. We find a later rabbinic tradition attributed to Rabbi

[17] On Habakkuk 2:7, see the debate among Campbell, *Deliverance of God*, 377–81; Watson, "By Faith (of Christ)," 147–63; Dunn, *Romans*, 1:44–46.

[18] Dunn, *Romans*, 1:45.

Simelai that also reduces all 613 laws of the Jewish scriptures down to Habakkuk 2:4 (b. Mak. 23b–24a). This Jewish tradition that summarizes the law as living by faith may surprise those with Christian stereotypes that Judaism is a legalistic religion focused on the works of the law.

Paul wrote Romans to remind his audience that God is faithful to keep his covenantal promises through the work of Christ. In the Jewish scriptures, these promises included saving Israel and punishing her enemies (e.g., Exod. 9:27; 1 Sam. 12:7; Dan. 9:16; Mic. 6:5; Ps. 31:1; Isa. 45:8, 46:13, 63:1; cf. Bar. 5:2, 5:4; 1QS 11.2–5, 12–15; 1QH 4.37, 11.17–18, 11.30–31). Paul's assurance of God's faithfulness was meant to inspire the faith of the Roman Christians. Paul's logic was that the natural response to a trustworthy God is to trust. Another way to understand this concept is that God's loyalty to his people should generate loyalty or allegiance from his people.[19]

Paul's concern to prove **God's faithfulness** to save *all* people is expressed throughout the letter. He hoped that by presenting God's faithfulness, the Roman church would respond by deepening its trust in God. In Romans 3:21–31, Paul explained how everyone, both Jews and Gentiles, could be saved through the work of Christ apart from the law. He grounded his argument with the example of God's faithfulness to Abraham (Rom. 4:1–25), who "believed God, and it was reckoned to him as righteousness" (Rom. 4:3, citing Gen. 15:6).[20] He contrasted the sin of Adam with the life-giving grace of Christ (Rom. 5:12–21). He continually linked both the problem and the solution to the wider story of creation (Rom. 1:18–32, 5:12–21, 8:18–30).

However, Paul's claim that salvation comes apart from the law generated questions regarding God's past promises made to Israel through the law (Rom. 3:1–2, 9:6–18). While the law effectively points out sin, it is insufficient for helping people overcome sin. Paul also spoke against Jewish particularism that grounded salvation in the works of the law. The works of the law, such as circumcision (Rom. 3:25–29), Sabbath observance (Rom. 14:5), and kosher diet (Rom. 14:2–3, 14:17), were identity markers distinguishing Jews from Gentiles. Paul spoke against relying upon these for securing salvation (Rom. 3:17–24). Rather, salvation is available for all people apart from the law through the work of Chris in (Rom. 3:21).

If the law as God's covenant no longer ensured salvation for Israel, then had God broken his promises to Israel? How did people know he would not break his new promises in Christ? This prompted Paul to explain how God remained faithful to past promises to Israel while making room for new promises in chapters 9–11. Paul argued that God had saved a faithful remnant of Israel, including Jewish people like Paul (Rom. 9:6–11:10), and that God had plans to save the rest of Israel when they came to recognize their Messiah (Rom. 11:11–27). Because God remained faithful to Israel, he could be trusted with his new promises to save all people in Christ (Rom. 11:28–36). By explaining God's faithfulness, Paul hoped that people would respond with faith by living according to God's will (Rom. 12:1–8).

Loyalty for Gifts

Paul had a lot to say about role of faith in salvation. Paul made it clear that people are saved by faith, not the works of the law. Greek has a whole family of words to describe faith, including the verb "to believe"

---

[19] Campbell, "Romans 1:17—A Crux Interpretum," 227; Dunn, *Romans*, 1:43–44.

[20] Abraham functioned as an example to both Jews and Gentiles. As the founder of Israel, he was the ideal Jew, and because this story occurred prior to his circumcision, he was also an ideal Gentile.

Carl N. Toney

Clients would pay respects and ask favors from their patrons early in the morning. Some patrons had extra seating outside their homes for those seeking an audience. Pompeii.

(*pisteuō*), the noun "faith" (*pistis*), and the adjective "faithful" (*pistos*). In our English translations, it is important to note the relationship among this word family, which can be translated in a variety of ways, such as "faith," "faithfulness," "belief," "trust," "entrust," and "loyalty."

Unfortunately, the English words for "faith" or "belief" often get reduced to a mental acceptance of ideas. People say that to be saved, someone must understand that they are a sinner, and Jesus saves them through his death and resurrection. While it is true that Christians must believe correct ideas, Paul's concept of "**faith**" (*pistis*) was far more robust and complex. In some contexts, Paul talked about belief (Rom. 10:9–11). At other times, he talked about a response of trust or confidence (Rom. 4:5, 4:13). Still at other times, faith aligned more closely with the ideas of faithfulness and loyalty (Rom. 1:17). Paul's language of faith corresponded with his ideas of grace, and both terms were connected to the broader Greco-Roman cultural system of patronage and honor.[21]

We were introduced to this patronage system in our discussion of Acts, but let's do a quick refresher. In the patronage system, "**grace**" (*charis*) was a term that referred to the gift or benefit given to a client by their benefactor. This gift was not earned and was not expected to be repaid (Rom. 3:24, 5:2, 6:23). In response to the patron's gift, the client was expected to show "faith" or "loyalty" (*pistis*) to their benefactor (Rom. 3:22, 4:24). In a system of honor, the greater the "gift" (*charis*) the greater response of "loyalty" (*pistis*) was required.

Paul understood salvation to be a "grace" or "gift" (*charis*) from God, who is the ultimate benefactor of humanity. Jesus's sacrifice is not a *free* gift, but it is instead a *priceless* gift (Rom. 5:17). Because of the invaluable nature of this "gift" (*charis*), believers are expected to respond with "loyalty" (*pistis*) to God, which Paul called the "obedience of faith" (Rom. 1:5, 16:26). Further, by accepting this gift, all other loyalties are realigned and subjugated to the lordship of Christ. When we read the words "faith" or "believe" in the English Bible, it is often helpful to understand these as faithfulness or loyalty. Faith is a means of expressing allegiance to the reign of God embodied in the lordship of Christ.

Sin and Jesus's Death

Paul talked a lot about sin in Romans. He uses a variety of terms to describe sin. The most common is "sin" (*hamartia*, Rom. 3:20, 4:7–8, 5:13, 5:20, 6:1, etc.). Others include "evil" (*kakos*, Rom. 1:30, 2:9, 3:8, 7:19, 7:21, etc.) in contrast to "good" (*agathos*, Rom. 12:21, 16:19). People can be "disobedient" (*parakoē*, Rom. 5:20). They can "stumble" (*proskoptō*, Rom. 9:32, 14:21). A "transgression" (*parabasis*, Rom. 2:23,

[21] deSilva, *Honor, Patronage, Kinship, & Purity*; Bates, *Gospel Allegiance*; McKnight, *King Jesus Gospel*; Gupta, *Language of Faith*.

5:14) describes breaching particular commands, while a "trespass" (*paraptōma*, Rom. 5:15–18, 5:20) is more general and does not necessitate violation of law. "Injustice" (*adikia*, Rom. 1:18, 1:29, 2:8, 3:5, 6:13, 9:14) describes horizontal wrongs between people, while "impiety" (*asebeia*, Rom. 1:18, 11:26) describes vertical wrongs between people and God.

The first part of Romans establishes that all of humanity sinned by not meeting the expectations that God had placed on them (Rom. 1:18–3:20). Both creation (Rom. 1:19–20) and the law articulate God's character and expectations (Rom. 2:18). Gentiles, who did not have the law, were controlled by sinful vices (Rom. 1:18–31). Likewise, the Jewish people also failed because the law could not control sin (Rom. 2:1–3:9). The bad news was that everyone had sinned (Rom. 3:10–20). Further, because of their sin, people were God's enemies (Rom. 5:6–10).

"Sin" (*hamartia*) describes a person's moral failure (Rom. 3:20, 4:7–8, 5:13, 5:20, 6:1, etc.)[22] and is connected to people's humanity through "flesh" (*sarx*) language (Rom. 7:5, 7:14–25). A person who does wrong is a "sinner" (*hamartōlos*, Rom. 3:7, 5:8, 5:19). However, Sin is also a power or force (Rom. 3:9, 5:21, 6:12–14, etc.) that enslaves people and causes them to sin (Rom. 6:6, 6:17, 6:20, etc.). Although the law helps to identify sin (Rom. 3:19–20, 7:7), the law is powerless to help people overcome the power of Sin (Rom. 7:5, 7:14–25). In fact, the power of Sin uses the law to multiply people's sins (Rom. 5:20, 7:8).

Paul voiced the struggle of humanity with the power of Sin in Roman. 7:14–25. At face value, many readers assume the "I" in this chapter is Paul. However, Paul was using a rhetorical device called "speech in character." With this "I," he took on the persona of a Gentile proselyte since this person did not have

Trajan's Market included shops and may have been the administrative offices for the emperor. Rome. (ca. 100-110 CE)

[22] It is popular to connect this to the image of "missing the mark" (e.g., Judg. 20:16 LXX; Homer, *Il.* 5.287), but this etymology is disputed because more evidence favors the moral sense of doing wrong (e.g., Luke 15:18; Plato, *Phaedr.* 242e).

the law in their life (Rom. 7:9), and Paul as a Jewish person always had the law. Another interesting suggestion is this may have been the persona of Adam and Eve. Regardless of the identity of this person, Paul described the utter despair of a person who was captive to the power of Sin (Rom. 7:14, 7:23, 7:25).

The power of Sin entered the world and corrupted creation through the sin of Adam, and it brought the power of Death (Rom. 5:12–21).[23] This passage has been understood as describing Adam's "original sin," or the Fall (cf. Gen. 3). It raises the question about the relationship between Adam's sin and the sin of humanity. Some think Adam represents everyone, resulting in the guilt of his sin being imputed to all people. Alternatively, people inherit his sinful nature, predisposing them to sin. Or they follow his example when they sin. Finally, some read this passage as describing the entry of the power of Sin into the world and exerting its influence upon people to sin.

While "all have sinned" (Rom. 3:23), all have the opportunity to be made righteous by God's grace as a gift (Rom. 3:24). The grace of God brings justification and eternal life because Christ as the new Adam breaks the power of Sin and Death over humanity (Rom. 5:12–21) and ultimately frees creation from its bondage to decay (Rom. 8:18–25). With Christ's death, people are "redeemed" (*apolytrōsis*) from the power of Sin (Rom. 3:24; cf. Rom. 3:9). Language of redemption evokes images of the exodus and exile where Israel was redeemed from their Egyptian enslavement (e.g., Exod. 6:6, 15:13; Deut. 7:8, 9:26 LXX), and the exiles were redeemed from their Babylonian captivity (Isa. 45:13, 52:3 LXX).[24] Those baptized into Christ's death and resurrection align with his defeat of the powers of Sin and Death (Rom. 6:9, 6:12, 6:14) and become slaves to God's righteousness, submitting to his rule (Rom. 6:18).

Further, Jesus's death is portrayed as an **atoning sacrifice** (Rom. 3:25) with God placing Jesus's blood on the "mercy seat" (*hilastērion*) of the Ark of the Covenant like the high priest sprinkled blood from a goat and bull on the Day of Atonement (cf. Lev. 16:14–16; Exod. 25:17–22).[25] This image of atonement has been understood as Jesus's sacrifice placating God's wrath (called propitiation) or canceling the debt of sin (called expiation), or a combination of both ideas. Like a sin offering, Jesus took on the sin of humanity by coming in the "likeness of sinful flesh" to deal with sin (Rom. 8:3; cf. Rom. 6:5; 2 Cor. 5:21; Lev. 5:6–7, 5:11, 16:3) and allowing believers to fulfill the law via the power of the Holy Spirit (Rom. 8:4). The Spirit, who gave life to Christ, now indwells and gives life to believers (Rom. 8:11). In addition, Christ reconciles sinners to God through his death and life, proving God's love and providing the Holy Spirit (Rom. 5:1–11).

Public Domain

Ark of the Covenant. Auch Cathedral, France.

[23] Pauline writings blame both Adam and Eve for the Fall, reflecting other Jewish literature. In Romans 5:12, Adam is blamed (cf. 4 Ezra 7:118), while 1 Timothy 2:13–15 blames Eve (cf. Sir. 25:24; Life of Adam and Eve, 3).

[24] See the discussions of the "ransom" sayings in Mark 10:45 and 1 Peter 1:18 in Chapters Two and Fourteen.

[25] Romans, Hebrews, and 1 John use a cluster of words to link Jesus's death with the Day of Atonement. Romans references the "mercy seat" (*hilastērion*, Rom. 3:25; cf. Heb. 9:5), where the sacrifice's blood is placed. Hebrews uses "makes atonement" (*hilaskomai* Heb. 2:17), and 1 John speaks of the "atoning sacrifice" (*hilasmos*, 1 John 2:2, 4:10).

Sexual Ethics of the Early Christians

One of the most significant passages in the New Testament addressing sexual ethics is Romans 1:18–24. When it comes to approaching the sexual ethics of the New Testament, there are three broad camps: (1) those who deem these ethics as having some kind of timeless quality and remain applicable today, (2) those who reinterpret these ethics to make them applicable today, and (3) those who reject these ethics because they reflect the values of the first century. "Biblical" sexual ethics is a problematic concept because the Jewish scriptures include a variety of sexual ethics not deemed appropriate by most Christians today, such as allowing polygamy (Exod. 21:10) or stoning someone caught performing same-sex intercourse (Lev. 20:13). Instead, Christians turn to the New Testament as their source of ethics.

One dimension of the debate is the translation of terms. The Greek word *porneia* broadly means "sexual misconduct" that is condemned (e.g., Matt. 15:19; Mark 7:21; Acts 15:20; 1 Cor. 6:18; Eph. 5:3; Col. 3:5; 1 Thess. 4:3; Rev. 2:21, 14:8), but Greek translators sometimes used this term for "adultery" (Exod. 20:14 LXX). Because the concept of sexual misconduct is so broad, this term is not terribly helpful on its own. Rather, we'll have to look at specific passages in the New Testament that describe sexual misconduct.

Arsenokoitai and *malakos* are two terms associated with modern debates about homosexuality. Modern discussions about human sexuality often distinguish between gender identity, sexual attraction, and biological sex. We need to remember that our descriptions of human sexuality and identity are relatively new. For example, *arsenokoitai* (1 Cor. 6:9; 1 Tim. 1:10) was first translated as "homosexual" in 1946, whereas the King James Version translated this as "abusers of themselves with mankind." Some argue that Paul coined this term that means "man-bedder" to refer to male same-sex activity based on Leviticus 18:22 and 20:13. Others see this term narrowly reflecting pedophiles. Another controversial term is *malakos* (1 Cor. 6:10), which can refer to an effeminate man (Dio Chrysostom, *Or.* 49; Diogenes Laertius, 7.173). Paul may have been describing a male prostitute.[26] Alternatively, the pairing of *malakos* and *arsenokoitai* in 1 Corinthians 6:10 may refer to male same-sex partners.[27]

In Romans, Paul described same-sexual activity between men and men as well as women and women as a sign of human sinfulness and rebellion against God (Rom. 1:18–24). Some interpreters note that Paul's polemic could reflect his own Jewish prejudice that considered Gentiles to be sexually immoral idolaters (Let. Aris. 152; Josephus, *Ag. Ap.* 2.199; Philo, *On Abraham* 135–36; Ps.-Phoc. 3–5; cf. Acts 15:20, 15:29, 21:25; Rev. 9:21). More importantly, the thrust of Paul's example and argument was that people should not judge others (Rom. 2:1).

Others turn to Jesus's definition of sexual activity, marriage, and singleness. In the Sermon on the Mount, Jesus reiterated the prohibition of "adultery" (*moicheuō*) in the Ten Commandments (Matt. 5:27). He heightened the command for husbands by including looking at another woman with "desire" (*epithymeō*) as also sinful (Matt. 5:28). Some will note that Jesus did not speak about the sexual activity of

[26] See, for example, Scroggs, *New Testament and Homosexuality*, 106.
[27] See, for example, Witherington, *Conflict and Community in Corinth*, 166.

non-married people in this passage. However, Jesus identified both "adultery" (*mocheia*) and "sexual immorality" (*porneia*) as human vices of everyone (Mark 7:21–22; Matt. 15:19).

Jesus defined marriage as between one man and one woman (Mark 10:1–12; Matt. 19:1–9) and grounded this in the creation of humanity (Gen. 1:27, 2:24). In these passages, he also prohibited most cases of divorce, except for "sexual immorality" (*porneia*). Elsewhere, Jesus noted that marriage is an earthly, temporary institution, and he exalted singleness as the heavenly ideal and final state of humanity (Mark 12:18–27; Matt. 22:23–33; Luke 20:27–40).

Paul also offered guidelines about marriage and singleness, and he limited the marriage relationship to be between one man and one woman (1 Cor. 7:2) and rooted his understanding in creation (Eph. 5:31; cf. Gen. 2:24). Paul presented the relationship between a husband and wife as an earthly reflection of Christ and the church (Eph. 5:25–33). He cited Jesus's prohibition of divorce (1 Cor. 7:10–14) but allowed for an unbeliever to divorce their spouse (1 Cor. 7:15). Like Jesus, Paul elevated singleness as the ideal (1 Cor. 7:1, 7:8), but he conceded that some people may not be able to control their desires and should get married (1 Cor. 7:2, 7:9).

Both Jesus and Paul described marriage as between one man and one woman. Jesus's definition of marriage between two different sexes has been used either to exclude all other forms of sexual practice or to exemplify the importance of monogamist, committed relationships. Those critical of using these passages as timeless ethics emphasize the contextual nature of these passages and point to inconsistent stances in some churches on divorce and remarriage. They also highlight the values of love and inclusion. Those who affirm traditional marriage note the consistent teachings of Jesus and Paul. Jesus and Paul both elevated singleness as an ideal, and they urged submitting one's passions and desires to God, including sexual desires, as part of the Christian life.

Church and State

What do you imagine Paul was attempting to achieve when he wrote, "Let every person be subject to the governing authorities, and those authorities that exist have been instituted by God" (Rom. 13:1)? Did Paul write Romans 13:1–8 to flatly support the state? Was he telling believers that Rome was in charge? Was he writing from a position of power since he was a Roman citizen who, thanks to the empire, enjoyed the protection of his rights through the judicial process? Did he recognize that the general progress of the gospel had been aided by Rome and ongoing Roman peace? Were these the reasons that he saw the powers of Rome needed to be respected and preserved?[28]

It is more likely that Paul was writing from the perspective of an ethnic minority living on the margins. His advice was essentially, "Keep your head down low, and don't make trouble" (cf. Rom. 12:18). To put Paul's advice in context, we need to recall that the founder of Christianity, Jesus, was executed by the Roman government for alleged crimes of insurrection. Further, the leadership of the Roman church had been expelled by Claudius in 49 CE for causing social disturbances. Finally, this advice (Rom. 13:1–7) occurred right before Paul addressed the new social tensions between the weak and the strong

[28] Hengel, *Christ and Power*, 34–35.

(Rom. 14:1–15:13). Paul sought to resolve their differences because additional social unrest could lead to another edict by Nero. Paul's advice was meant to protect the church, not to protect the Roman government. Further, Paul's advice was not simply "pay your taxes because you owe the government." Rather, his discussion of taxes was subversive, just like Jesus's response to the question of paying taxes to Caesar (Mark 12:13–17; Matt. 22:15–22; Luke 20:20–26).[29]

Carl N. Toney

The Roman Colosseum was built by the emperors Vespasian and Titus (ca. 72-80 CE) and could hold fifty thousand to eighty thousand spectators.

Like Jesus, Paul prioritized the obligations of his audiences to God. In other words, he wrote from the perspective that God is ultimately in charge. He began by placing the authority of the empire under his Jewish God when he wrote, "There is no authority except from God" (Rom. 13:1). He then limited Roman authority by declaring, "Pay to all what is due them—taxes to whom taxes are due, revenue to whom revenue is due, respect to whom respect is due, honor to whom honor is due" (Rom. 13:7). His next line, "Owe no one anything, except to love one another; for the one who loves another has fulfilled the law" (Rom. 13:8), further relativized the demands of the Roman government. Paying taxes and participating in the Roman systems of honor became lesser obligations to the higher obligation to obey God's law as summarized by the command to "love one another" (Rom. 13:8; cf. Lev. 19:18).

Paul's exhortation of obedience to the state was practical advice in light of the Roman Christians' situation. Paul's aim was not to reinforce the corrupt power of the Roman Empire. Rather, he encouraged Christians to act as model citizens to avoid scrutiny and potential persecution. Unfortunately, the relationship between the Roman Christians and the government broke down by 64 CE when Nero identified Christians as a distinct group and began to arrest and execute them. We also should not project the more radical polarization between Christianity and culture that occurred later. For example, Tertullian (*Praescr.* 7) famously wrote, "What is there in common between Athens and Jerusalem? Between the Academy and the Church" (ca. 155–220 CE)?[30]

---

[29] See the discussion on paying taxes to Caesar in the chapter on Mark.

[30] For Christian attitudes to social institutions, see Hengel, *Christ and Power*, 38–39; Meeks, *First Urban Christians*; Theissen, *Social Setting of Pauline Christianity*.

Who Are the Weak and Strong in Romans?

The identity of the **weak and strong** is debated. Traditionally, the "weak" were understood to be Jewish Christians who continued to cling to the law while the "strong" were Gentile Christians who had become free from the law.[31] The restricted diet of the "weak" may have reflected Jewish kosher dietary restrictions (Lev. 11:1–23; Deut. 14:3–21), abstaining from wine may have reflected the Nazarite vow (Num. 6:2–4; Judg. 13:4–5, 16:7; Amos 2:11–12), and refraining from meat and wine may have been a sign of repentance (T. Reu. 1.10; T. Jud. 15.4).

However, none of these backgrounds precisely fit the Roman situation. As early as Origen (*Comm. Rom.* 9.36.1–2, 9.38.1), commentators have noted that the core difficulty for Jewish backgrounds was that the Mosaic law did not actually demand vegetarianism (Rom. 14:2, 14:6). Looking for parallels in the Greco-Roman world, the weak have been identified as Gentile Christians practicing asceticism (e.g., Plato, *Leg.* 6.782c; Philostratus, *Vit. Apoll.* 1.8, 8.7.4). More broadly, the "weak" may simply be a label for the less mature (Philodemus, *On Frank Criticism*). The categories of weak and strong may have also reflected inferior and superior social status (e.g., Pliny the Younger, *Ep.* 1.18.3; Cicero, *Off.* 2.51; Seneca, *Ep.* 14.4.1; Tacitus, *Dial.* 8.3.7).[32]

Due to the ambiguity of Paul's language, some favor a mixed view of Jewish and Gentile backgrounds behind the issue.[33] Others argue that we cannot pinpoint the background because these groups did not exist; rather, Paul was adapting his weak-strong language from 1 Corinthians 8–10. From a rhetorical standpoint, Paul may have been intentionally oblique because he assumed that every Roman believer would consider himself or herself the "strong" person who was charged to accept others "weaker" in faith (Demetrius, *Eloc.* 287, 292; Quintilian, *Inst.* 9.2.71).[34]

Judea Capta coins were struck for twenty-five years and commemorated Emperor Vespasian's victory over the First Jewish Revolt. On this coin, Emperor Vespasian is on the front, and a captive Jewish male and female are on the back.

Daniel provides the most useful background for understanding the issues dividing these two groups. Daniel and his friends ate only vegetables and avoided wine due to purity concerns while living in a Gentile environment (Dan. 1:12–16). Also, Daniel 10:2–3 connects abstaining from meat and wine broadly with fast days. We have additional stories of Jewish heroes maintaining their Jewish identity by refusing Gentile food (Tob. 1:10–12; Jth. 12:2, 19; Add. Esth. 14:17; Jos. Asen. 7.1, 8.5).

[31]Marxsen, *Introduction to the New Testament*, 98–100; Toney, *Paul's Inclusive Ethic*, 49–124. An alternative is that Paul was only addressing Gentiles. See Stowers, *Diatribe and Paul's Letter to the Romans*; Rodríguez, *If You Call Yourself a Jew*.

[32]Stowers, "Paul on the Use and Abuse of Reason," 253–86; Reasoner, *Strong and Weak*, 46–55.

[33]Käsemann, *Romans*, 365–69.

[34]Sanday and Headlam, *Romans*, 384–87, 400–403; Karris, "Romans 14:1–15:13," 65–84; Sampley, "Weak and Strong," 40–52.

Further, the Maccabean crisis highlighted dietary concerns as indicative of the conflict between Jews and Gentiles (1 Macc. 1:62–63; 2 Macc. 5:27; 4 Macc. 4–18; Josephus, *Ant.* 11.346).

Returning to the evidence from Romans 14–15, Paul's contrast between "unclean" (*koinos*, Rom. 14:14) and "clean" (*katharos*, Rom. 14:20) matches these Jewish purity concerns related to the issues of food and days (e.g., 1 Macc. 1:47, 1:62; Josephus, *Ant.* 3.181, 11.346, 12.3.20, 13.4).[35] While the Mosaic law did not demand vegetarianism or abstaining from wine, the eating habits of the "weak" reflected the Jewish practice of avoiding potentially unclean meat and wine when among Gentiles. Observance of Jewish holy days, including the Sabbath, also served as an important boundary marker between Jews and Gentiles (Exod. 31:16–17; Deut. 5:15; Neh. 9:13–14; Ezek. 20:16; 1 Macc. 1:43; Josephus, *Ant.* 11.346). During the Jewish Diaspora, both Jewish dietary concerns and Sabbath observance became central identification markers (e.g., Let. Aris. 139, 142; Philo, *Moses* 1.278), and these practices seemed to be causing division between the weak and strong.

Inclusive Ethic

Romans 14–15 may be the most important chapters for understanding Romans. Paul sought to broker peace and unity between "strong" and "weak" groups that disagreed about dietary issues connected to eating meat and drinking wine (Rom. 14:2–3, 14:6, 14:14–17, 14:20–21) and the observance of holy days (Rom. 14:5–6). "Weak" language tied into Paul's broader convictions that human weakness created either an opportunity for sin (Rom. 5:6, 6:19, 8:3) or an opportunity to be empowered by God (Rom. 4:19–21). Rather than relying upon human strength, the "strong" (Rom. 15:1) were those who relied upon God's strength (e.g., Rom. 1:16, 1:20, 9:17, 9:22, 11:23).[36]

The "weak" were Jewish Christians (but also included Gentile God-fearers and proselytes) who sought to maintain their ethnic identity and place within the wider Jewish community. They only ate vegetables at community gatherings due to purity concerns about the food served by Gentiles, and they only worshiped on Sabbaths and Jewish holy days. The strong were Gentile Christians (but also included Jewish Christians like Paul, Prisca, and Aquila) who considered themselves free from the law. They did not practice a kosher diet or observe the Sabbath because of their freedom found in Christ.

Unfortunately, the disagreements between the "weak" and the "strong" over diet and days threatened worship practices and the unity of the Roman believers. These issues were not marginal or "indifferent matters" (*adiaphora*). Instead, they were at the heart of Christian practice. Issues of food consumption would have impacted the food served at love feasts. Further, avoidance of wine by the "weak" would have been problematic because it could prevent full participation in the Lord's Supper (1 Cor. 11:20–26). The desire of the "weak" to worship on Sabbath and Jewish holy days would conflict with desire of the "strong" to worship on Sundays in honor of the resurrection (1 Cor. 16:2; Acts 20:7; Rev. 1:10).

---

[35] In the Jewish scriptures, there are two categories of purity. Ritual purity is avoidable, from natural substances, communicable, bathed away, not an abomination, and not sinful. Moral purity is avoidable, from an action, noncommunicable, dealt with by atonement/punishment, an abomination, and sinful. Theissen, *Jesus and the Forces of Death*, 13, 15.

[36] Toney, *Paul's Inclusive Ethic*, 75–80.

Carl N. Toney

The Arch of Titus in Rome displaying the Roman armies looting the Jerusalem temple in response to the First Jewish Revolt.

As a solution, Paul drew upon insights from previous conflicts in Galatia and Corinth. In Galatians, Paul insisted that nothing be added to the gospel, so he argued against Jewish Christians who demanded that Gentiles become Jewish proselytes and observe the law in addition to faith in Christ (Gal. 5:1–12). Ironically, in Romans, it was the Gentile Christians who were making the additional demands of Jewish Christians to abandon practicing the law along with faith in Christ. In 1 Corinthians, Paul explained his fundamental principle to "become all things to all people so that I might by all means save some. I do it all for the sake of the gospel" (1 Cor. 9:22–23). In Romans, Paul wanted the strong to accommodate the weak for the sake of the gospel. Paul was not concerned about "earning" salvation. Rather, Paul argued against linking the freedom of the gospel with particular ethnic and cultural practices.

Paul challenged both groups to find their common identity through the presence of the Holy Spirit (Rom. 15:13). Paul understood "**holy**" (*hagios*) to mean consecrated, set apart, or marked off to God in light of the boundary markers between sacred and profane.[37] "Holiness" identified believers with God and recalled the Levitical refrain, "Be holy, for I am holy" (Lev. 11:44). Paul wanted the Roman believers to know that the presence of God's Holy Spirit was what marked them apart to God. It was not religious,

[37] Priests were instructed "to distinguish between the holy and the common, and between the unclean and the clean" (Lev. 10:10). For the relationship between holy/common and clean/unclean, see, Thiessen, *Jesus and the Forces of Death*, 9–10.

cultural, or ethnic markers that set believers apart from others. In other words, the goal was not to push others away through distinct practices and beliefs. Rather, the aim was to draw closer to a holy God while pulling others toward God by calling all people into right relationship with him. Paul's words still challenge us today to create groups that are inclusive of others based on our relationship with God rather than putting up artificial boundary markers that exclude others.

Paul taught that the Holy Spirit dwells in every believer and gives them life (Rom. 8:9–11). Unlike the law, the Spirit empowers believers to obey God's will (Rom. 8:1–4) and to put to death the deeds of the flesh (Rom. 8:12–13; cf. Gal. 5:16–21). The Spirit helps with human weakness and intercedes with God on their behalf (Rom. 8:26–27). Through the Spirit, believers are adopted as children of God, calling him "Abba, Father" (Rom. 8:15; cf. Gal. 4:6).[38] As siblings, Paul encouraged believers not to judge each other (Rom. 14:10) or do things to harm each other (Rom. 14:15). The Spirit enables believers to serve one another as it bestows a variety of "gifts" (*charisma*) related to prophecy, serving, teaching, exhorting, giving, leading, and compassion (Rom. 12:6–8). The virtues of the Holy Spirit like righteousness, peace, and joy are manifestations of the kingdom of God (Rom. 14:17; cf. Gal. 5:22–26). Thus, the Spirit's presence among believers unifies them and demonstrates that God is in charge.

Key Terms and People

Atoning sacrifice: one image for Jesus's death is the blood of a sacrificial goat sprinkled on the mercy seat of the Ark of the Covenant on the Day of Atonement to either placate God's wrath (propitiation) and/or cancel the debt of sin (expiation)

Diatribe: dialogue style of writing involving asking rhetorical questions to an imaginary person and giving answers

Edict of Claudius: Claudius expelled Jewish Christian leaders such as Prisca and Aquila from Rome in 49 CE; under Nero, Christians were allowed to return

Faith: for Paul, faith was the only requirement for salvation; faith has been understood as belief, trust, or loyalty

Faithfulness of God: because God was trustworthy to keep his promises to Israel, Jews and Gentiles can trust God's promises to save the world through the work of Christ; God's faithfulness produces faith

Grace: means "gift" and is the gift of salvation from God, which people accept through faith

Holy: means "set apart to God"; holiness is a characteristic of God that believers share because of the presence of the Holy Spirit

House church: the small Christian gatherings of around fifteen to twenty-five people who met in homes, apartments, shops, lecture halls, and other public spaces

Righteousness of God: because God is a good God, he puts the world in right relationship with him.

[38] *Abba* does not mean "Daddy." Paul translates this Aramaic word for his audience using the Greek word *patēr*, which means, "Father."

- **Weak and strong:** the labels for divisions based on Jewish identity markers in the Roman community, members of which were called to find unity and their identity under the lordship of Christ
- **Women leaders in the church:** Phoebe, Junia, and Prisca

Conversation Starters

1. What did you find interesting about the history of Rome? What was the Edict of Claudius, and how did it impact the Roman church?
2. How would you describe the Roman church? What was their social standing and ethnic makeup? Where did they gather?
3. Explore Paul's understanding of faith. What is the difference between understanding faith as belief, trust, and/or loyalty? What is the relationship between grace and faith?
4. What did Paul mean by the "righteousness of God"?
5. How did Paul understand Jesus's sacrificial death as it relates to redemption, atonement, and reconciliation?
6. Why was God's faithfulness so important to Paul in Romans?
7. What did Paul mean by his advice to obey the governing authorities?
8. What does Paul's advice to the weak and strong teach us about including others, especially if we disagree with them? How does Paul's concept of holiness help?
9. What kinds of things does the Holy Spirit provide believers?

FOR FURTHER READING

Bates, Matthew. *Gospel Allegiance: What Faith in Jesus Misses for Salvation*. Brazos, 2019.

Bird, Michael. *Romans*. Story of God Bible Commentary. Zondervan, 2016.

Dunn, James D. G. *Romans*. 2 vols. WBC 38A–38B. Word Books, 1988.

Fitzmyer, Joseph. *Romans: A New Translation with Introduction and Commentary*. AYB 33. Yale University Press, 2008.

Gaventa, Beverly Roberts. *When in Romans: An Invitation to Linger with the Gospel According to Paul*. Baker Academic, 2016.

Grieb, A. Katherine. *The Story of Romans: A Narrative Defense of God's Righteousness*. Westminster John Knox, 2002.

Jewett, Robert. *Romans: A Short Commentary*. Fortress, 2013.

Johnson, Luke Timothy. *Reading Romans: A Literary and Theological Commentary*. RNT. Smyth & Helwys, 2001.

McKnight, Scot. *Reading Romans Backwards: A Gospel of Peace in the Midst of Empire*. Baylor University Press, 2019.

Moo, Douglas J. *The Epistle to the Romans*. 2nd ed. NICNT. Eerdmans, 2018.

Rutledge, Fleming. *Not Ashamed of the Gospel: Sermons from Paul's Letter to the Romans*. Eerdmans, 2007.

Westerholm, Stephen. *Understanding Paul: The Early Christian Worldview of the Letter to the Romans*. Baker, 2004.

11

THE LEGACY OF PAUL

The Pastoral (1-2 Timothy and Titus)

The Story So Far

The Last Days of Paul

Acts 28:30–31 concludes with Paul being under house arrest in Rome for two years. Readers of the New Testament are left with a mystery regarding the close of Paul's life. Combining church tradition and information gleaned from 1–2 Timothy and Titus results in two different speculations regarding Paul's final days.

Early Christian writers reconstructed a full picture of Paul's life after the ending of Acts (Acts of Paul; 1 Clem. 5.6–7; Eusebius, *Hist. eccl.* 2.22.2–3). Paul was released after two years in prison, and then he continued various missionary activities, including at a Spanish mission. During this time (ca. 62–64 CE), Paul wrote to Timothy in Ephesus (1 Tim. 1:3), and he wrote to Titus in Crete (Titus 1:5).[1] After his final missionary journey to Spain, Paul was arrested again, wrote his second letter to Timothy (2 Tim. 4:16–18), and was executed by Nero around 67/68 CE (Jerome, *Vir. ill.* 11.5).[2]

SUGGESTED READING

1 Timothy
Titus
2 Timothy

Alternatively, we can take the silence of Acts to mean that Paul was never released from prison. Rather, Paul and Peter were executed during the outbreak of Nero's persecution of the church in 64/65 CE (1 Clem. 5–6). Paul, a Roman citizen, was beheaded. In contrast, Peter, who was not a citizen, was crucified upside down.[3] If this second model is correct, and we believe that Paul was the author of these letters, then we can attempt to fit

---

[1] Barrett, "Titus," 1–14.

[2] For a plausible reconstruction of Paul's release and subsequent imprisonment and martyrdom, see Murphy-O'Connor, *Paul*, 341–71.

[3] Cadbury, "Roman Law," 338; Cullmann, *Peter: Disciple, Apostle, Martyr: A Historical and Theological Study*, 87–98.

A reconstruction of Paul's fourth missionary journey.

these letters in the chronology of Acts, possibly close to his time in Ephesus (Acts 19:21–40, 20:1–4; ca. 51–54 CE).[4] If we believe that Paul was not the author, then we need to explain how and why these letters were written after his death by one of his disciples. Most scholars argue that one of Paul's disciples wrote Titus, 1 Timothy, and 2 Timothy.[5] Titus and 1 Timothy were based on a collection of Pauline teachings that his disciples assembled and composed shortly after his death (e.g., 1 Tim. 1:11, 1:12–16).[6] Some scholars think that 2 Timothy was written by Paul just before his death as Paul's last will and **testament**. However, most scholars see 2 Timothy fitting the testament genre (like 2 Peter), which could be pseudonymous.[7]

Icon of Timothy.

Who Were Timothy and Titus?

Two of these letters are addressed to Paul's coworker **Timothy,** whose name means "one who honors God." He was from Lystra (in modern-day Turkey). During Paul's first missionary journey, he visited the city with Barnabas and healed a man who could not walk (Acts 14:8–20). The people misunderstood and thought that the "gods have come down to us in human form" (Acts 14:11). However, Paul and Barnabas quickly corrected the townspeople, and they tried to share the gospel. This didn't go well. Some of Paul's Jewish enemies showed up and convinced the town to stone Paul and leave him for dead. But after the believers gathered around Paul, he got up and left the city.

[4] Johnson, *Letters to Timothy*, 144–45. There are several notable parallels between 1 Timothy and the Corinthian correspondence lending support that these letters could have been written during a similar time in Paul's ministry.

[5] Friedrich Schleiermacher was the first scholar to question these letters' authorship in 1807. For the history, see Johnson, 42–54.

[6] One of the most creative proposals is by Jerome Quinn. He proposed that the Pastorals, which recount the story of the end of Paul's ministry, are the third volume completing Luke's project of the early church. Quinn, *Titus*, 62–75.

[7] Testaments include Jacob (Gen. 48–49), Moses (Deut. 22–23), Joshua (Josh. 22–24), David (1 Chron. 28–29), Jesus (Mark 13; John 13–17), Paul (Acts 20), and Peter (2 Peter). Pseudepigraphic testaments include Rebecca and Isaac (Jub. 35–36) and the twelve sons of Jacob (T. 12 Patr.).

Authorship of the Pastorals

Some scholars affirm the claim that the letters were written by the apostle Paul (1 Tim. 1:1; 2 Tim. 1:1; Titus 1:1). Others argue that these letters were written by an unknown disciple of Paul based on a collection of his teachings. Neither view of authorship should challenge the canonical authority of these letters, but it will impact the dating of the composition of the letters. The following are reasons for doubting Pauline authorship, as well as responses that defend Pauline authorship.

First, the language and style of the Pastorals differ from the undisputed letters of Paul.[8] However, this could be due to scribal practices.

Second, certain Pauline themes are different. For example, the Pastorals use "faith" as "trust" in God and "trustworthy sayings" (1 Tim. 1:15, 3:1, 4:9; 2 Tim. 2:11; Titus 3:8; cf. Titus 1:9). They have unique emphases, such as piety and good works. However, the differences are negligible when comparing individual letters to the Pauline corpus.[9]

Third, it is unclear where these letters, especially 1 Timothy and Titus, fit into a chronology of Paul's life as presented in Acts. However, it is plausible to fit 1 Timothy and Titus's composition during Paul's Ephesian ministry (Acts 19:21–41) or shortly after (Acts 20:1–4). Second Timothy fits at the end of Paul's two-year Roman imprisonment (Acts 28).[10] Church tradition places all these letters after Paul's release from his first Roman imprisonment, as recorded in Acts.

Fourth, the opponents may reflect second-century Gnostic heresies (e.g., 1 Tim. 6:20).[11] **Gnosticism** was an early Christian heresy that saw the material world as evil, while the spiritual world was good. Gnostics believed people were trapped in this material world but could be saved through secret knowledge. However, nothing is distinctly Gnostic in these texts, and proper "knowledge" is found much more prominently in Paul's letters to the Corinthian in Rome. (e.g., 1 Cor. 1:5, 8:1, 8:7, 8:10; 2 Cor. 4:6, 6:6).

Fifth, it isn't easy to understand circumstances in which Paul would write Timothy and Titus these kinds of letters. The letters of 1 Timothy and Titus outlined the basics of church ministry, but these men were veteran co-leaders who helped Paul establish churches. The Jewish disciple Timothy had represented Paul in the past

One of three altars with a relief of Paul's head at the Church of the Three Fountains in Rome.

[8] Easton, *Pastoral Epistles*, 171–237; Ellis, "The Authorship of the Pastorals," 49–57; Grayston and Herden, "Authorship of the Pastorals," 1–15.

[9] One of the most vocal supporters of this view is Johnson, *Letters to Timothy*, 55–99.

[10] Towner, *Timothy and Titus*, 13–15; Johnson, *Letters to Timothy*, 135–37.

[11] Kelly, *Pastoral Epistles*, 10–12.

(1 Cor. 4:17, 16:10–11; Phil. 2:19–24; 1 Thess. 3:2-3, 3:6) and was a co-sender or coauthor of six epistles (2 Cor. 1:1; Phil. 1:1; Col. 1:1; 1 Thess. 1:1; 2 Thess. 1:1; Philem. 1). The Gentile disciple Titus had previously helped Paul with significant church conflicts (e.g., Gal. 2:1–3; 2 Cor. 2:13, 7:5–16, 8:6, 8:16–24, 12:18).

It is plausible that an unknown author presented Paul as the ideal teacher instructing his ideal Jewish and Gentile disciples regarding church leadership. Alternatively, these letters may have been written by Paul, and they are the sort of letters we would expect Paul to send with his delegates when they were struggling, and the ultimate target audience was all the community members (1 Tim. 6:21; 2 Tim. 4:22; Titus 3:15).

1 TIMOTHY

- Letter's Greeting (1:1–2)
- Contrast between False Teachers and Paul (1:3–20)
- Proper Conduct of Men and Women in Worship (2:1–15)
- Virtuous Characteristics of Overseers and Deacons (3:1–16)
- Contrast between False Teachers and Timothy (4:1–16)
- Church Order as the Household of God (5:1–6:2)
- Contrast between False Teachers' Vices and True Teachers' Virtues (6:3–21a)
- Letter's Closing (6:21b)

Paul made such a deep impression that both Timothy's grandmother, Eunice, and mother, Lois, became followers of Jesus (1 Tim. 1:5). While Timothy's mother was Jewish, his father was Greek, and he wasn't circumcised as a baby. After his mother became a Christ follower, she led him to his own faith and taught him about the Jewish scriptures (2 Tim. 3:15), which are "inspired by God and useful for teaching, for reproof, for correction, and for training in righteousness" (2 Tim. 3:16).

When Paul revisited the town with Silas on his second missionary journey, he invited Timothy to join his team (Acts 16:1–5). Paul also asked Timothy to be circumcised so that he would not be a stumbling block to fellow Jews who knew the importance of circumcision and observing the law as part of their ethnic identity (Rom. 3:1–2; 1 Cor. 9:20). Paul quickly brought Timothy alongside him as a church leader, and he regularly called him a coworker (Rom. 16:21; 1 Thess. 3:2). He was the coauthor of six of Paul's letters (1 Thess. 1:1; 2 Thess. 1:1; Phil. 1:1; Col. 1:1; Philem. 1; 2 Cor. 1:1). Paul and Timothy were close, and he sometimes called Timothy his son (Phil. 2:22; cf. 1 Cor. 4:17; 2 Tim. 1:2).

Timothy also was one of Paul's trusted emissaries. He remained with Silas in Beroea, helping strengthen the church after Paul left (Acts 17:15). Paul also sent him to the Thessalonians to encourage the persecuted church (1 Thess. 3:1–2). While imprisoned, Paul planned to send Timothy to encourage the Philippians (Phil. 2:19–24). However, not every church responded favorably. While Timothy worked closely with Paul to help establish the church in Corinth (2 Cor. 1:19), Paul had to remind them not to despise him

(1 Cor. 16:10–11) when Paul sent Timothy as his emissary (1 Cor. 4:17, 16:10; cf. Acts 19:21–23). Timothy also worked with Paul in Ephesus (Acts 19:22), and according to Eusebius (*Hist. eccl.* 3.4), he became the first bishop of Ephesus. Being an emissary of Paul, his leadership in Ephesus, and the difficulties he had with churches accepting his leadership all provide the background for the implied social setting of 1–2 Timothy.

Paul's other emissary was **Titus,** who was also called a coworker (2 Cor. 8:23) and a "loyal child" (Titus 1:4). While Titus does not grace the pages of Acts, we discover from Paul's letters that he had a prominent role in Paul's ministry. According to Galatians, Titus was a Greek Christian, who accompanied Paul and Barnabas to the Jerusalem Council (Gal. 2:1, 2:3). Titus was presented as a test case for Paul's Gentile mission. Titus helped the early church determine that Gentiles did not need to be circumcised to be part of God's people (Gal. 2:1–10).

From the material found in 2 Corinthians, we learn that Titus was involved in another crisis in Corinth (2 Cor. 8:23). When this new conflict arose between Paul and the Corinthian church, he sent Titus to determine the cause of the trouble (2 Cor. 7:15, 12:18). Before Paul arrived in Corinth, he reunited with Titus (2 Cor. 7:5–6). He reported that he was welcomed by the Corinthians, who had repented and eagerly awaited Paul's arrival (2 Cor. 7:7, 7:10). This resulted in Paul dispatching Titus ahead of him to assist the Corinthians with the Jerusalem collection (2 Cor. 8:6, 8:10–11, 8:17; cf. 1 Cor. 16:1–4). Unfortunately, this triggered another misunderstanding between Paul and the Corinthians, and Paul concluded his letter by defending himself and Titus (2 Cor. 12:17–18).

Turning to the Pastoral letters, we learn that Paul entrusted Titus to establish churches across the island of Crete (Titus 1:3–5). This reflected Paul's great confidence in Titus's leadership abilities, and this island is the implied setting of the letter to Titus. When Titus completed this task, Paul wished for him to join him in Nicopolis, located in the province of Macedonia (modern-day northeast Greece).

Carl N. Toney

The commercial agora in Ephesus, located near the theater and harbor.

An odeon (small theater) in Crete.

According to 2 Timothy, Titus spent some time comforting Paul in prison before he went to Dalmatia (2 Tim. 4:10). Finally, tradition identifies the Church of Saint Titus in Gortyn, Crete, as his burial place.

Both Timothy and Titus, to whom these letters are addressed, represented the next generation of Christianity after Paul and the apostles. Their biographies reveal that they were both capable leaders in the church, so it would be a mistake to think that Paul was addressing novices in these letters. Just as Paul struggled at times with people respecting his authority, so Paul came alongside them in their struggles.

What the Pastorals Are All About

The Opponents in the Pastorals

Once again, people were leading Pauline churches astray (1 Tim. 1:19–20; 2 Tim. 2:17, 3:13; Titus 1:10–11) and dividing the church (1 Tim. 5:4; 2 Tim. 3:8–9; Titus 3:10–11). In all three letters, these opponents spread their teachings in the church through vulnerable women (1 Tim. 2:12–13, 5:13; 2 Tim. 3:1–6; Titus 1:3). In contrast to these women, Paul commended female deacons (1 Tim. 3:11), women caring for widows (1 Tim. 5:16), and godly teachers like Timothy's mother and grandmother (2 Tim. 1:5).

To undergird his authority, Paul recalled his commission as an apostle to the Gentiles (1 Tim. 2:7; 2 Tim. 1:11; cf. Rom. 11:13). He presented his divine commission as the premier example of divine mercy because he was saved, despite being "the foremost" (1 Tim 1:12–15) of sinners and a blasphemer, persecutor, and man of violence (1 Tim. 1:12–17). Unfortunately, Paul's statement is sometimes exaggerated to describe Paul as someone who killed Christians. This more negative portrayal contrasts Philippians 3:4–6, in which Paul called himself blameless according to the law.

Paul accused his opponents of promoting myths (1 Tim. 1:4, 4:7; 2 Tim. 4:4; Titus 1:14), which conveyed the broad sense of falsehood as opposed to truth (2 Pet. 1:16).[12] Their teaching led to vicious living

[12]See also Herodotus, *Hist.* 2:45; Plato, *Resp.* 330D, 377A; *Leg.* 636C; *Tim.* 26E; *Phaed.* 61B; Epictetus, *Diatr.* 3.24.18; Josephus, *Ag. Ap.* 2:256. Johnson, *Letters to Timothy*, 163. For more specific speculation about these myths as either related to proto-Gnosticism or Jewish teaching, see Dibelius and Conzelmann, *Pastoral Epistles*, 16–17.

(1 Tim. 5:24; 2 Tim. 3:1–6, 3:13; Titus 1:12) and the promotion of greed (1 Tim. 3:3, 5:9–10, 6:9–10; 2 Tim. 3:2; Titus 1:11). In response, Timothy was exhorted to model virtuous living (1 Tim. 6:11–16), and the wealthy were called to place their trust in God (1 Tim. 6:17–19).

These opponents were likely Jewish Christians. In Titus, they were identified as the "circumcision" (*peritomē*, Titus 1:10; cf. Gal. 2:7–9; Col. 4:11; Rom. 15:8; Acts 10:45, 11:2) who promoted Jewish myths (Titus 1:14). They may have been part of the large Jewish population in Crete (Josephus, *J.W.* 2.7.1; *Ant.* 17.12.1; *Life* 48; Philo, *Alleg. Interp.* 282). The genealogical concerns raised in Titus and 1 Timothy (Titus 3:9; cf. 1 Tim. 1:4) may be likened to the retelling of biblical stories as in Jubilees.[13] All three letters disputed the opponents' interpretation and application of the Jewish scriptures (1 Tim. 1:7–11; 2 Tim. 3:14–17; Titus 3:9). Rather, the law was good when properly used (1 Tim. 1:8–9), and each letter argued for an inclusive salvation of Gentiles (1 Tim. 2:7; 2 Tim. 4:17; cf. Titus 2:11).

The opponents of each letter also had some distinctive views. In 1 Timothy, the opponents promoted asceticism and disparaged marriage (1 Tim. 4:3; cf. 1 Tim. 5:11).[14] Similarly, in Titus, their teaching disrupted whole households (Titus 1:11). In response to the promotion of asceticism, Timothy was encouraged to deem everything God created as good (1 Tim. 4:4–5), to be content with food and clothing (1 Tim. 6:8), and to drink a little wine (1 Tim. 5:23). As a rebuttal of their views on marriage, traditional Greco-Roman family values were promoted, including the subordination of women (1 Tim. 9–15; cf. Titus 1:5), respect for older men and women (1 Tim. 5:1–2; cf. Titus 1:3–8), submission of slaves (1 Tim. 6:1–2; cf. Titus 1:9–10), and encouraging widows to marry and have children (1 Tim. 5:14; Titus 1:4).

In 2 Timothy, the opponents argued that the resurrection had already occurred (2 Tim. 2:17–18), but Paul looked forward to Jesus's future appearance (2 Tim. 4:9). In fact, Paul considered their presence to be a sign of being in the last days (2 Tim. 3:1–6). In Titus, the opponents were discredited with a local, stereotypical saying: "Cretans are always liars, vicious brutes, lazy gluttons" (Titus 1:12).

To shore up against false teaching, all three letters place a unique emphasis upon the expression "a trustworthy saying" (*logos ho pistos*, 1 Tim. 1:15, 3:1, 4:9; 2 Tim. 2:11; Titus 3:8; cf. Titus 1:9). This may either be understood as endorsing a shared faith tradition or a rhetorical device used to affirm the arguments of the letters.[15] All three letters were written to encourage "believers" (*pistoi*, 1 Tim. 4:3, 4:10, 4:12, 5:16, 6:2; Titus 1:6) in the "faith" (*pistis*, 1 Tim. 1:2, 1:14, 3:9, 3:13, 4:1, 4:6, 5:8, 5:12, 6:10, 6:12, 6:21; 2 Tim. 1:13, 2:18, 3:8, 4:7; Titus 1:4, 1:13, 2:2, 3:15).[16] The audience was called to lives of "faithfulness" (*pistos*, 1 Tim. 1:12, 3:11; 2 Tim. 2:2, 2:13), and "good works" (*erga agatha*) were evidence of the Christian life (1 Tim. 2:10, 5:10, 5:25; 2 Tim. 2:21, 3:17; Titus 1:16, 2:7, 2:14, 3:1, 3:8, 3:14; cf. 2 Cor. 9:8; Col. 1:10; 2 Thess. 2:17). Yet, these works did not save people because people were justified by grace (2 Tim. 1:9; Titus 3:5–7).

---

[13] Karris, "Background and Significance of the Polemic," 549–64.

[14] Some see proto-Gnostic elements in these beliefs. However, these views may also be tied to Jesus's teaching about the end of marriage after the resurrection (Mark 12:18–27; Matt. 22:23–33; Luke 20:27–40).

[15] Knight, *Faithful Sayings*; Campbell, "Identifying the Faithful Sayings in the Pastoral Epistles," 73–86.

[16] Faith is a major theme in these letters, with various cognates of the term appearing sixty-one times: "faith" (*pistis*, 33x, e.g., 1 Tim. 1:2, 1:4, 1:5, 1:14; 2 Tim. 1:5, 1:13, 1:22, 2:18; Titus 1:1, 1:4, 1:13), "faithful" (*pistos*, 17x, e.g., 1 Tim. 1:12, 1:15; 2 Tim. 2:11; Titus 1:9, 3:8), "to believe" (*pisteuō*, 6x, 1 Tim. 1:11, 1:16, 3:16; 2 Tim. 1:12; Titus 1:3, 3:8).

The Inspiration of Scripture

One of the most important passages speaking about the nature of Scripture is 2 Timothy 3:15–16, which says, "All scripture is inspired by God."[17] The word "inspired" (*theopneustos*) combines "God" (*theos*) and "breathe" (*pneō*), literally translated as "God-breathed," and evokes the concept of the creative and prophetic Word of God. Second Peter 1:20–21 makes a similar claim that "no prophecy of scripture is a matter of one's own interpretation, because no prophecy ever came by human will, but men and women moved by the Holy Spirit spoke from God." These New Testament statements about the inspiration of Jewish scriptures align with other first-century Jewish thinkers.[18]

The collection of inspired writings was expanded by the early church to include other New Testament works, such as when 2 Peter 3:15–16 equated Paul's letters with other scriptures. The stories of Jesus's life and teachings in the Gospels were also considered authoritative because of Jesus's identity as the Son of God. Eventually through the canonization process, the church recognized all sixty-six books of the Bible as inspired.

Discussions have arisen concerning the meaning of "inspiration" since the Bible was written by human authors during specific historical circumstances.[19] Some models emphasize the divine aspect of inspiration. So, inspiration was a kind of divine dictation where the author was a scribe writing down God's revealed message word-for-word (e.g., Deut. 31:19–22; Jer. 30:2). Other models attempt to account for some element of human agency in the composition of divine revelation (e.g., 1 Cor. 13:3; 1 Thess. 2:13; Rev. 1:11). Some evangelical groups use the technical term "plenary verbal inspiration," meaning God guided the minds and personalities of the authors while they used their own words to convey the intended meaning God revealed. Others describe the Bible as somehow being fully God's word and fully human word and use models like Jesus's incarnation. In this sense, the authors wrote within their specific cultural contexts, but the principles revealed are divine. Other models emphasize human authorship. Some conceptualize the author like an artist whom God inspired, like a muse inspires the verbalization of their divine experiences. Others deem inspiration more like a divine endorsement, after the fact, of the author's own words. Last, some would describe the Bible as books written by people

William Tyndale was the first person to translate the New Testament in 1526. He was martyred in 1536 before he could complete his translation of the Old Testament. Oxford's Bodleian Library.

[17]Good discussions on the nature of the Bible are by Marshall, *Biblical Inspiration*; Wright, *Scripture and the Authority of God*; Wright, *Surprised by Scripture*; Bird, *7 Things I Wish Every Christian Knew*.

[18]The concept of biblical inspiration is described by other Jewish writers, including Josephus, *Ag. Ap.* 1.37 and Philo, *Decalogue* 35; *Confusion* 44; *Dreams* 2.172; *On Moses* 2.188, 2.263; *Spec. Laws* 1.65, 4.49).

[19]Postulating a variety of models of inspiration is not new. Philo (*On Moses* 2.188) describes a variety of ways: "Of the divine utterances, some are spoken by God in His own Person with His prophet for interpreter, in some the revelation comes through question and answer, and others are spoken by Moses in his own person, when possessed by God and carried away out of himself."

about God—as such, there are parts that get God "right," but there are also portions where the author misunderstood God.

Intersecting with this discussion of inspiration is the extent that the Bible is true. Numbers 23:19 says, "God is not a human being, that he should lie." Insofar as the Bible is the revelation of God, then it is true. A broad term used to describe this concept of the Bible as trustworthy to reveal God's truth is "infallibility." Some make stronger claims about the trustworthiness of the Bible using the word "inerrancy" to claim that the original autographs of the Bible are without any kind of error. The logic is that if God is perfect, then Scripture must be perfect.[20]

In examining the truthfulness of the Bible, we may ask how the Bible relates to other fields of knowledge. How do we understand the scientific descriptions in the Bible, like the sun standing still (Josh. 10)? How do we understand historical details, such as the chronology of events? For example, did Jesus's temple actions occur at the end (Mark 11:15–19) or at the beginning of his ministry (John 2:13–23)? How do we understand tensions created by theological claims in the Bible, like who bears the guilt for sin—individuals only (Ezek. 18:20) or multiple generations (Exod. 20:5)? How do we deal with factual inconsistencies like different census numbers for the same group of people (2 Sam. 24:9; 1 Chron. 21:5)? How do we deal with archaeological questions raised by evaluating evidence related to the exodus or Joshua's conquest? What do we do with those who object to the morals of the Bible, such as the treatment of women (Deut. 21:10–14; Num. 31:17–18, 31:35) or the portrayal of genocide (e.g., Josh. 6:21, 10:37; 1 Sam. 15:2–3, 15:17–18)?[21]

Readers asking these kinds of questions are engaging with the complexity of Scripture. One side musters explanations that bolster views of inerrancy. For example, Michael Bird writes,

> God's revelation in Scripture is accommodated to the worldview and expectations of its original audience in matters of the way the physical world works, the understanding of history, notions of literary genres, and standards of truth-telling. That said, the accommodation is never a giving in to sheer error. God does not speak erroneously, nor does he feed us nuts of truth lodged inside shells of falsehood.[22]

The other side deems mistakes as evidence that the Bible is a limited, human document that functions like signposts recording the search for truth placed by previous seekers. These signposts are not for us, but the Bible does provide guidance for us to ask our own theological questions. Sometimes these signposts accurately point toward God, but sometimes they misdirect. Peter Enns writes,

> The Bible—from back to front—is the story of God told from the limited point of view of real people living at a certain place and time. . . . What makes the Bible God's Word isn't its uncanny historical accuracy, as some insist, but the sacred experiences these stories point to, beyond the words themselves. Watching these ancient pilgrims work through their faith, even wrestling

[20] Inerrancy is not a claim about modern Bibles, which include errors introduced by copyists and translators.
[21] We will look at the issue of violence in our chapter on Revelation.
[22] Bird, *7 Things I Wish Every Christian Knew*, 61.

> with how they did that, models for us our own journeys of seeking to know God better and commune with him more deeply.[23]

Those taking middle positions acknowledge that the Bible contains mistakes that reflect the human authors, but it should still be trusted as divine revelation, especially in matters of faith and morals. For example, I. Howard Marshal writes,

> We started from the view that the Bible is entirely trustworthy for the purpose for which God has inspired it. We have seen, however, that the Bible has not been handed down in the form of a perfectly accurate text which can be interpreted throughout without the possibility of error. . . . It certainly does contain statements which can be regarded as erroneous by some standards but which are consistent with its intended purpose; one does not fault a carpenter for measuring a table leg accurately to only one decimal place when the standard of accuracy in a laboratory runs to several places of decimals.[24]

When considering our own understanding of the Bible's inspiration, we are challenged to contemplate the kind of testimony the Bible provides about God and his relationship with the world. Readers must evaluate the complex relationship between God and the human authors. We must decide to what extent we believe that Bible conveys the message of a trustworthy God. More importantly, we must ask ourselves if and how we will live our lives in light of the Bible's teachings about God's reign.

Church Order: Bishops, Elders, and Deacons

The letters of 1 Timothy and Titus reveal churches growing concerned with the qualifications of church leadership. Leadership was carefully selected. Prominent roles were given to "elders" or "presbyters" (*presbyteroi*, 1 Tim. 4:14, 5:17–22; Titus 1:5–6; cf. Acts 14:23, 20:17; 1 Pet. 5:1–5; James 5:14; 2 John 1; 3 John 1); the "bishop" or "supervisor" (*episkopos*, 1 Tim. 3:1–7; Titus 1:7–9; cf. Acts 20:28; Phil. 1:1); "deacons" or "helpers" (*diakonoi*, 1 Tim. 3:8–13; cf. Rom. 16:1; Phil. 1:1); and "widows" (*chērai*, 1 Tim. 5:3–16).

However, the Pastorals do not reflect the formal system with singular bishops developed by the second century (Ign. *Magn.* 2.1, 3.1). These roles were still largely undefined as seen by "elders" being equated with the "bishop" in Titus 1:5 and 1:7 (cf. Acts 20:17, 20:28). These letters reflect a period when the clarification of leadership roles was still developing. According to Acts 14:23, Paul established elders in every church. We see similar roles in the Philippian church, when Paul greeted the "bishops" (*episkopoi*) and "deacons" (*diakonoi*, Phil. 1:1). In light of the more informal nature of these positions, it may be helpful to translate "presbyter" (*presbyteros*) as "elder," "bishop" (*episkopos*) as "supervisor," and "deacon" (*diakonos*) as "helper."

"**Elders**" (*presbyteroi*) were appointed male leaders. Broadly speaking, an elder was any older person who deserved respect (e.g., 1 Tim. 5:1–2; Acts 2:7; John 8:9) and would have authority, such as in a

[23] Enns, *The Bible Tells Me So*, 62–63, 77; Hooker, "The Bible and the Believer: A. S. Peake Memorial Lecture 1978," 77–89.
[24] Marshall, *Biblical Inspiration*, 69–70.

Carl N. Toney

Marble road leading to the city's large theater in Ephesus.

household (Gen. 50:7; Ps. 105:22) or local councils (Deut. 21:19, 22:15; Prov. 31:23). Appointing elders was based upon the Jewish pattern of having elders as leaders in local synagogues (Luke 7:3).[25] Elders were sometimes called "**supervisors**" (*episkopoi*). They were tasked with teaching duties and guarding against heresy. The supervisor may have had a similar function as the "superintendent" (Heb. *mebaqqer*) in the Qumran community (1QS 6.10–11; CD 13.7–16, 14.8–12).[26]

"**Helpers**" (*diakonoi*) supported the supervisor and could be either males or females (1 Tim. 3:8, 3:11). They cared for those in need. Phoebe is an example of a helper or deacon recognized by Paul (Rom. 16:1). Although the term "helper" is not used in Acts 6:1–6, these seven men who were appointed to take care of the needs of the widows may be the foundation for the roles of service, as seen in 1 Timothy (cf. Rom. 16:1; Phil. 1:1; Did. 15:1–2). A final group identified were "**widows**" (*chērai*), who were women

[25] However, *prebyteros* was not a formal title of elders in the first-century synagogue, and there were a variety of terms used to describe leaders including "elder" (*gerousia*), "ruler" (*harchontes*), "administrator" (*phrontistēs*), "scribe" (*grammateus*), etc. (Bornkamm, "πρέσβυς κτλ," *TDNT*, 6:655–61, 664–68).

[26] Kelly, *Pastoral Epistles*, 73–74; Thiering, "*Mebaqqer* and *Episkopos*," 59–74.

TITUS

- Letter's Greeting (1:1-4)
- Virtuous Characteristics of Elders and Overseers (1:5-16)
- Virtuous Households, Individuals, and Civic Duties (2:1-3:2)
- Salvation Produces Virtuous Living (3:3-11)
- Travel Plans (3:12-14)
- Letter's Closing (3:15)

over sixty that spent their lives serving the church in prayer, hospitality, helping the afflicted, washing the feet of saints, and doing good works (1 Tim. 5:3–16).

Despite the nickname "Pastorals," the word "pastor" (*poimēn*) is absent in these letters. In fact, "pastor" is only mentioned alongside apostles, prophets, evangelists, and teachers in Ephesians 4:11, which should caution modern readers from projecting current church leadership roles onto these texts. The closest mixture of the pastor and elder role in the New Testament comes from 1 Peter 5:1–11, which encouraged elders to care for God's "flock" (*poimnion*) on behalf of Jesus, the "chief shepherd" (*archipoimēn*).

The appointment of church leadership included the laying on of hands by the elders (1 Tim. 4:14, 5:22; cf. 2 Tim. 1:6). Leaders were responsible for teaching sound doctrine (1 Tim. 5:17; Titus 1:9). However, there was not an extensive list of specific duties for these leaders. Rather, these letters focused on the *character* of leadership. Both 1 Timothy 3:1–13 and Titus 1:5–9 provide virtue lists of the qualifications for leadership. These virtuous qualities promoted "piety" (*eusebeia*, 1 Tim. 2:2, 3:4, 3:8, 3:11, 3:16, 4:7, 6:3, 6:5, 6:6, 6:11; 2 Tim. 3:5; Titus 1:1) and a "good conscience" (1 Tim. 1:5, 1:19, 3:9; cf. 2 Tim. 1:3)—two distinct emphases in these letters.[27] These characteristics provided concrete moral criteria to undermine the qualifications of the opponents whose consciences were seared (1 Tim. 4:2; Titus 1:15).

One qualification for a male "supervisor" (*episkopos*) and male "helper" (*diakonos*) deserves special attention. These men were required to be "married only once" (*mias gynaikos anēr*, 1 Tim. 3:1, 3:16; Titus 1:6), and there was a parallel qualification for older widows to be "married only once" (*henos andros gynē*, 1 Tim. 5:9). These expressions are literally "a husband of one wife" and "a wife of one husband," leaving them open to a variety of interpretations. This could refer to a widowed person who does not remarry, a monogamous versus polygamous marriage, or being faithful to one's spouse. Regardless of the interpretive decision, the overall purpose of these qualifications was to highlight the importance of character and having a stable home as qualifications for leading the household of God, reflecting God being in charge.

Female Leaders in the Early Church

First Timothy 2:8–15 instructed both men and women concerning orderly worship. Men were told to pray with their hands raised and to avoid anger and arguments (1 Tim. 2:8). During gatherings, wives

[27] A good conscience is also a notable theme in the Corinthian letters (1 Cor. 8:7, 8:10, 8:12, 10:25, 10:27–29; 2 Cor. 1:12, 4:2, 5:11).

should adorn themselves with good works and not dress immodestly (1 Tim. 2:9–10). They should learn in "quietness" (*hēsychia*) and "submission" (*hypotagē*) and not teach or have authority over their husbands (1 Tim. 2:11–12).

These instructions were grounded in an interpretation of the creation story that highlights Adam being made first, along with the claim that Eve was deceived (1 Tim. 2:13–14; Gen. 2–3). The passage concludes with a promise that a woman, Eve, will be saved by "childbearing" (*teknogonia*), which is perhaps an allusion to the birth of Jesus (Gen. 3:15) and is tied to an exhortation for women to practice virtues (1 Tim. 2:15).[28]

This passage exposes the question of proper behavior raised by Christian worship services in private spaces such as homes, which mixed the public and private settings.[29] We find Paul addressing similar problems in 1 Corinthians 12–14. In 1 Timothy 2:13–14, the appeal to Adam and Eve gives the impression that the command for a woman to quietly learn and fully submit is a timeless truth. The exhortation for women to live virtuously was modeled on the hope of Jesus's salvific birth (1 Tim. 2:15). But the commands for men to raise their hands in worship and for women not to wear braided hair, gold, pearls, or expensive clothes remind us that these instructions were also culturally conditioned (1 Tim. 2:8–9). We cannot pick and choose the parts we literally follow versus the parts that are principles.

Gender roles in Pauline churches were complex. The call for women to quietly learn and not to teach men so as not to disrupt public worship parallels 1 Corinthians 14:34–36. A similar remark about Eve's deception is found in 2 Corinthians 11:3, but, and this is important, it was applied to men who were false teachers. In other words, it was not Eve's gender that Paul was emphasizing; instead, she served as a model of deception.[30] The submissive role of wives aligned with the household codes in Colossians 3:18–19 and Ephesians 5:21–33 (cf. 1 Cor. 11:3–16; Titus 2:3–5). The comment about being saved by "childbearing" (*teknogonia*) is echoed by the later command for younger widows to marry, "bear children" (*teknogoneō*), and manage their household (1 Tim. 5:14).

In the Pastorals, women are included with church leadership as helpers/deacons (1 Tim. 3:11) and charged with taking care of elderly widows (1 Tim. 5:16). Timothy's mother and grandmother were praised for teaching him from Scripture (2 Tim. 1:5, 3:14–16). Elsewhere, women spoke in church settings when prophesying, but they also had to wear head coverings that signified gender roles and the supremacy of Christ and God (1 Cor. 11:2–16). Paul included women in leadership roles, such as helpers/deacons and apostles (Rom. 16:1–3, 16:6–7). In addition, several churches gathered in women's homes, indicating female patronage and leadership (1 Cor. 1:11; Col. 4:15). Finally, Paul made statements about gender equality (Gal. 3:28–29; cf. 1 Cor. 12:13; Col. 3:11).

Some interpreters see a consistent Pauline teaching reinforcing gender roles and a universal prohibition of women teaching and holding church leadership roles. Others see the earliest Pauline churches

---

[28] The singular "she" refers to Eve, who was deceived and fell into sin (1 Tim. 2:13–14). The salvation brought through the birth of a child alludes to the promised offspring of Genesis 3:15, which is fulfilled via the birth of Jesus (Ign. *Eph.* 19; Irenaeus, *Haer.* 3.22, 5.19; Justin Martyr, *Dial.* 100; Tertullian, *Carne Chr.* 17). The plural pronoun "they" in the second half of the verse refers to the Ephesian women who are to emulate Eve through the godly living of "faith, love, holiness, and self-control."

[29] Towner, *1–2 Timothy & Titus*, 197.

[30] There is a similar logic to 1 Timothy 2:13–15 in Romans 5:12–21, where sin enters the world through Adam (Rom. 5:12), and redemption comes through Jesus (Rom. 5:17-19). For various views, see Marshall and Towner, *Pastoral Epistles*, 469–70.

Carl N. Toney

Artemis of the Ephesians statue. Vatican Museums.

championing the leadership of women (Gal. 3:28–29; Rom. 16:1–3, 16:7). But the Pastorals, Colossians, and Ephesians represent a more conservative social reaction developed by later Pauline churches, with 1 Corinthians 14:34–36 being added later to the letter.[31]

More productively, we should read these passages considering their first-century cultural values and specific church contexts before drawing out broader principles.[32] The command in 1 Timothy 2:11–15 for women to quietly learn arises from a particular situation in Ephesus. Paul warned about younger widows "gadding about from house to house . . . saying what they should not say" (1 Tim. 5:13; cf. Acts 2:46, 5:42; 2 Tim. 3:6), which could be describing the spread of false teaching.[33]

But what was this false teaching? There are several plausible reconstructions of this situation. Many think the Artemis cult was influencing these women.[34] Alternatively, they were promoting an unhelpful form of asceticism. Or, they were part of the "new women movements" in this region that rejected traditional female duties.[35] Finally, this command may reflect that women were typically not as educated as men, so their teaching was uninformed and disruptive.[36]

The prohibition against wives talking in churches in 1 Corinthians 14:34–36 was because questions from these women were disturbing services. They were told to ask their husbands for explanations at home. Likewise, the command to quietly learn in 1 Timothy 2:11 was intended to prevent disruption. In fact, both 1 Timothy 2:11–15 and 1 Corinthians 14:34–36 challenged cultural norms by encouraging women to participate in worship and calling for women's education. This contextual interpretation allows us to ask what an orderly church service looks like in our cultural context and to promote the education of both men and women. It also gives permission to not replicate these same social values today.[37]

[31] Fee, *First Corinthians*, 699–702. As a counter, see Wire, *The Corinthian Women Prophets*, 149–52; Johnson, *Letters to Timothy*, 205–6.

[32] First-century values included the following: the modesty of women's dress (1 Tim. 2:9–10; cf. Philo, *Spec. Laws* 1.102, 3.51, 169–71; Phyntis, *On the Temperance of a Woman* 153.15–28; 1 Pet. 3:1–7) and wives' submitting to their husbands (1 Tim. 2:11–12; cf. Xenophon, *Oec.*; Aristotle, *Politics*; Josephus, *Ag. Ap.* 2.200; Philo, *Hypothetica* 7.3, 7.5). Johnson, *Letters to Timothy*, 207.

[33] Glahn, *Nobody's Mother*, 122–23.

[34] Glahn argues that Paul was quoting a local proverb, "She will be saved through childbearing," to describe Artemis's role as a midwife helping during childbirth in order to offer the counterclaim that Christ now offers such protection to those women who remain faithful. See Glahn, 146–56.

[35] The "new woman" movement attracted the wealthy women in Corinth and Ephesus. They flaunted traditional dress and social norms, redefined women's roles, and were so disruptive that Augustus issued legislation. Winter, *Roman Wives, Roman Widows*, 153–57. When women were educated, it was for their domestic roles (1 Tim. 2:11; cf. Musonius Rufus, *Or.* 3.10.2–4, 11–14).

[36] When women were educated, it was for their domestic roles (1 Tim. 2:11; cf. Musonius Rufus, *Or.* 3.10.2–4, 11–14).

[37] For a helpful interpretive model navigating these cultural issues, see Webb, *Slaves, Women & Homosexuals*.

We find in Pauline literature a reflection of traditional first-century values that subordinated wives to their husbands. However, we also see moments where Paul pressed beyond these boundaries by making statements and treating women as equals. In sum, we recognize that these texts reflect their first-century culture. Still, we should also look for how they challenged this culture and allow us to trace trajectories from the New Testament that ask interpreters to contextualize such passages for today.[38]

The Model Household of God

The "household" (*oikos*) was the basic building block of society and was considered a microcosm of the state. Colossians and Ephesians encouraged the ideal Christian household through the household codes. First Timothy and Titus guided believers' behavior in the "household of God" (*oikō theou*, 1 Tim. 3:15). Using the image of "God's household management" (*oikonomian theou*, 1 Tim 1:4), 1 Timothy encouraged "faithful attention to God's way of ordering things."[39] The result of living according to God's household management was an ethic of love (1 Tim. 1:5).

Leaders in the church were exhorted to be good managers of their homes (1 Tim. 3:4–5, 3:12, 5:4, 5:8; Titus 1:7; cf. 2 Tim. 4:19), while the opponents were disrupting homes (Titus 1:11; cf. 2 Tim. 1:16, 3:6). Likewise, younger widows and women were charged to manage their homes (1 Tim. 5:14; Titus 2:5), in contrast to certain widows disrupting homes (1 Tim. 5:13).

Believers' homes reflected first-century values, and these ideal households served as a form of gospel witness because they reflected families who lived under God's rule. Wives were called to submit to their husbands (1 Tim. 2:11–12; Titus 2:5). Women were to dress modestly (1 Tim. 2:9). Both older men and women were to be treated with honor (1 Tim. 5:1–2). The purity of younger women was to be protected (1 Tim. 5:2). Widows were to be cared for by their children and grandchildren (1 Tim. 5:4). Marriage was to be encouraged (1 Tim. 5:11, 5:14; Titus 2:4–5). Women should raise children and manage their households (1 Tim. 5:14; Titus 2:4–5). Enslaved people must obey their masters, especially if the master was a believer (1 Tim. 6:1–2; Titus 2:9–10).

Carl N. Toney

Interior room in the House of Castor and Pollux in Pompeii.

Each letter urged the church to model the best social behavior according to the values of the first century. Believers were called to submit to rulers (Titus 3:1–2) and to supplicate, pray, intercede, and offer thanksgiving for everyone, especially those governing figures (1 Tim. 2:1–2). The aim was to lead a quiet and peaceable life, exhibiting piety and dignity (1 Tim. 2:2; cf. 1 Tim. 3:8, 3:11 3:16, 4:7–8, 5:4, 7:3, 7:5–6, 7:11), and most importantly, for the sake of saving everyone (1 Tim. 2:4; cf. 1 Tim. 1:5). This advice made sense for a marginalized group to survive in a hostile first-century

[38] Johnson, *Letters to Timothy*, 198–211.
[39] Translation and quotation by Johnson, 148–49.

2 TIMOTHY

- Letter's Greeting (1:1–2)
- Thanksgiving for Timothy's Faith (1:3–5)
- Contrasting Examples of Suffering (1:6–18)
- Be Strong in Christ during Suffering (2:1–26)
- Avoid Wicked People and Equip the Church in the Last Days (3:1–4:5)
- The Example of Paul Finishing Well (4:6–18)
- Letter's Closing (4:19–22)

environment. However, modern readers are not called to reproduce these first-century homes. Rather, Christians should follow the principles in these texts and ask how our Christ-centered homes can be lifted up as ideals that would attract people in our culture.

Fortitude in Suffering: 2 Timothy

Second Timothy is presented as Paul's last will and testament. Paul wrote to Timothy as he faced his impending death. As such, the letter called for Timothy to remain faithful to the gospel, even when

Remains of a victory monument at Nicopolis, which was founded in 29 BCE by Augustus to commemorate his victory over Mark Antony and Cleopatra at the Battle of Actium.

facing suffering, because of the faithfulness of God (2 Tim. 1:8; cf. 2 Tim. 3:10–12). Paul presented himself as an example of fortitude during his apostolic ministry and current imprisonment for the sake of the gospel (2 Tim. 1:8–14, 2:9–10). Paul reminded Timothy of when he brought the gospel to Timothy's home region in Antioch, Iconium, and Lystra (2 Tim. 3:10–11).

Other people worthy of emulation included Timothy's mother, Eunice, and grandmother, Lois, who provided him with the foundation of his sincere faith (2 Tim. 1:5, 3:14–15). Timothy was called to follow the example of the household of Onesiphorus, who supported Paul during his imprisonment. He should not be like Phygelus and Hermogenes, who turned away from Paul (2 Tim. 1:15–18). Nor should he be like Hymenaeus and Philetus, who claimed the resurrection had already happened (2 Tim. 2:17–18).

Timothy was encouraged to share in Christ's sufferings and to follow Christ's model of faithfulness (2 Tim. 2:1–3, 2:9–13). He was to endure like a good soldier, a winning athlete, and a successful farmer (2 Tim. 2:3–7, 4:6–7). He was to avoid "wrangling over words" (2 Tim. 2:14), "profane chatter" (2 Tim. 2:16), "senseless controversies," and quarrels with his opponents (2 Tim. 2:23–24). Rather, he must be patient and kind, hoping they may repent (2 Tim. 2:24–26). He must shun youthful passions (2 Tim. 2:22) and avoid outward forms of godliness that allow a person to be full of vices (2 Tim. 3:2–5). Instead, he should pursue virtues like faith, love, peace, and righteousness (2 Tim. 2:22). As such, readers of 2 Timothy are called to emulate Timothy's example, and this letter teaches us how to let God reign in our personal lives.

Key Terms and People

Elder/presbyter: early church male leader, based on the synagogue practice of having elder males
Gnosticism: an early Christian heresy that saw the material world as evil, while the spiritual world was good; people were trapped in this material world but could be saved through secret knowledge
Helper/deacon: men and women leaders in the early church who helped supervisors; their duties included taking care of the poor
Pastoral epistles: Paul's three letters written to his coworkers (1 Timothy, 2 Timothy, Titus)
Supervisor/bishop: a lead elder, similar to the Jewish office of superintendent, with responsibilities including teaching and guarding against heresy
Testament: a genre where an author gives their final exhortations before they die
Timothy: Paul's Jewish disciple from Lystra, whom Paul used to develop churches; he was the co-sender/coauthor of six of Paul's letters (2 Corinthians, Philippians, Colossians, 1–2 Thessalonians, Philemon)
Titus: Paul's Gentile disciple, whom Paul took to Jerusalem to argue that Gentiles were free from the law; he worked with Paul to develop churches
Widow: a woman over sixty in the church who could not marry but spent her life in prayer, hospitality, helping the afflicted, washing saints' feet, and doing good works

Conversation Starters

1. Who were Timothy and Titus? Why did Paul write them letters?
2. How do you think Paul's life ended? What did his final years look like?
3. Where would you situate these letters? Were they written during Paul's ministry in Acts? After being released from Rome? Or were they written by one of his disciples?
4. What kind of opposition did the author of these letters face? Why were Jewish Christian opponents often looming behind Paul's letters? How can the church avoid adding sociocultural practices or ethnic identity markers to the gospel?
5. What is your understanding of the inspiration of Scripture? To what extent do you consider it trustworthy and true?
6. How do these Pastorals envision church leadership? Who were named as leaders? How formal were these leadership roles? What were the characteristics of leaders? Could women lead, and if so, in what capacity?
7. What is your understanding of the relationship between men and women in the early church? What should the relationship between men and women look like in the modern church?
8. What models did Paul give for those who suffer? How should a Christian face suffering?

FOR FURTHER READING

Belleville, Linda, Jon C. Laansma, and J. Ramsey Michaels. *1 Timothy, 2 Timothy, Titus, Hebrews.* Cornerstone Biblical Commentary 17. Tyndale House, 2009.

Johnson, Luke Timothy. *The First and Second Letters to Timothy: A New Translation with Introduction and Commentary.* AYB 35A. Yale University Press, 2008.

Kelly, J. N. D. *The Pastoral Epistles.* BNTC 14. Hendrickson, 1993.

Mounce, William D. *Pastoral Epistles.* WBC 46. Thomas Nelson, 2000.

Quinn, Jerome D. *The Letter to Titus: A New Translation with Notes and Commentary.* AYB 35. Yale University Press, 2008.

Spencer, Aída Besançon. *1 Timothy.* New Covenant Commentary. Cascade, 2013.

———. *2 Timothy and Titus.* New Covenant Commentary. Cascade, 2014.

Towner, Philip H. *1–2 Timothy & Titus.* The IVP New Testament Commentary Series 14. InterVarsity Press, 1994.

PART THREE

THE HOPE OF GOD

The Wider Church

12

A NEW COVENANT

Hebrews

What Do We Know about the Author?

The historical backgrounds of Hebrews are murky. We may wish to know the identity of the author, but the work does not provide a name. However, speculations abound. Tertullian (*Pud.* 20) proposed Barnabas (Acts 13:2, 15:39). Origen dismissed views that Clement of Rome or Luke were the composers (Eusebius, *Hist. eccl.* 6.25.14). Martin Luther argued for Apollos's authorship due to his background as an eloquent and educated Alexandrian Hellenistic Jew (Acts 18:24) and coworker of Paul (1 Cor. 3:5–6, 3:16:12).

Silas (also known as Silvanus) has also been considered because he was a coauthor in several Pauline epistles (1 Thess. 1:1; 2 Thess. 1:1) and was a known associate of Timothy (Acts 17:14–15, 18:5; 2 Cor. 1:19; cf. Heb. 13:23), and Hebrews bears stylistic affinities to 1 Peter, which may have also been written by Silas (1 Pet. 5:12).[1] Another intriguing proposal is that Prisca and Aquila were coauthors because they taught Apollos (Acts 18:26), were closely associated with Timothy (Acts 18:5, 19:21–23; 1 Cor. 16:10, 16:19; cf. Heb. 13:23), hosted a church in Rome (Rom. 16:5), and fit with the authors' transitions between "we" and "I."[2]

SUGGESTED READING

Genesis 14:17-24
Leviticus 16
Psalm 2
Psalm 110
Hebrews

While each alternative theory is creative, none has yet to capture the level of consensus as the long-standing tradition of Pauline authorship (e.g., Clement of Alexandria, Jerome, Augustine). Broadly speaking, both Hebrews and Paul highlight the importance of faith, contrast the law, and present Abraham as a model of faith. However, the specific development of these topics is very dissimilar. Particularly, Hebrews lacks Paul's notion of justification by faith. Structurally, Hebrews looks nothing like a Pauline letter. It lacks Paul's usual epistolary introduction and thanksgiving. It also is one sustained argument

[1] Hewitt, *Hebrews*, 26–32.
[2] Harnack, "Probabilia über die Addresse und den Verfasser des Hebräerbriefes," 16–41.

Public Domain

Icon of Jesus as High Priest by Michael Damaskinos. Dionysios Loverdos Collection, Greece. (sixteenth cent. CE)

based on Psalms 2 and 110, while Paul's arguments contain various movements on a variety of topics.

Hebrews also uses **tabernacle** imagery (e.g., Heb. 8:2, 8:5, 9:1–10), while Paul more regularly used temple images (1 Cor. 3:16–17, 6:19; 2 Cor. 6:16; Eph. 2:21). Hebrews is the only New Testament writing to present Jesus as high priest.[3] Hebrews focuses on Jesus's heavenly exaltation (e.g., Heb. 1), while Paul focused on his resurrection (e.g., 1 Cor. 15; 2 Cor. 5). Hebrews claims to receive secondhand tradition (Heb. 2:3, 13:7), while Paul affirmed his apostolic authority and being an eyewitness to the resurrected Christ (Gal. 1:11–16; 1 Cor. 15:8; Rom. 1:1). In the end, Pauline authorship is unlikely, and we are left with a mystery. We may quip with Origen, "But who wrote the epistle, in truth God knows" (Eusebius, *Hist. eccl.* 6.25.14).

The Story So Far

We may also wish to know more about the first readers of Hebrews. However, the audience and date are also shrouded in mystery. Early manuscripts attempted to identify the audience with the title "To the Hebrews." But the document itself provides little evidence concerning the ethnic makeup of the community. The use of Jewish scriptures and Jewish interpretive techniques indicates an audience familiar with Jewish concepts. However, both Jewish and Gentile believers who came from synagogue backgrounds would have similar knowledge.

The opaque conclusion of Hebrews, "Those from Italy send you greetings" (Heb. 13:24), doesn't help. It has been understood as either identifying the letter being written from Rome to an audience in Israel[4] or Italian Christians living abroad writing back to Rome.[5] At best, we can say that this letter fits with other Christian writings associated with the Roman church (e.g., 1 Peter, 1 Clement, Shepherd of Hermes).

Unfortunately, we can only provide an approximate compositional date range. The earliest date for Hebrews is determined by the reference to Timothy (Heb. 13:23), who joined Paul's missionary team around 49 CE. The latest date is determined by the allusion to Hebrews 1–3 in 1 Clement 36, which was written by 96 CE. Descriptions of past persecutions, including imprisonment and property confiscation (Heb. 10:32–39; cf. Heb. 12:2–4), give us various choices. These may refer to Claudius expelling Jewish Christians from Rome (ca. 49 CE), Nero's persecutions (64/65 CE), Vespasian and Titus's campaign during the Jewish revolt (66–73 CE), or Domitian's persecutions (90s CE).

[3] Although Scot Hafemann argues that 1 Peter 1:2 may also convey high priestly imagery of the exalted Jesus sprinkling his blood (cf. Heb. 12:24).

[4] E.g., Hughes, *Hebrews*, 2.

[5] E.g., Bruce, *Hebrews*, xxiv–xxv.

In favor of an earlier date, before the destruction of the temple in 70 CE, are passages describing ongoing sacrifices (Heb. 7:27–28, 8:3–5, 9:6–7, 9:25, 10:1–3, 10:8, 13:10–11). However, other writings dated after the destruction of the temple in 70 CE use similar language (1 Clem. 41.2; Josephus, *Ant.* 3.224–57; *Ag. Ap.* 2.77).[6] Also favoring an earlier date is the absence of language about the destruction of the temple since the destruction would have fit well within arguments in Hebrews about the temporal nature of the old covenant. However, the author may have specifically chosen the tabernacle to situate the argument within the exodus narrative that included Moses, Joshua, and the promised rest of God. The tabernacle highlights the temporary and transitory nature of the earthly sanctuary and its rituals.

In favor of a date in the eighties or nineties, several passages describe the author and audience as either second- or third-generation Christians (Heb. 2:3, 13:7). Time had passed for this community, so Hebrews addressed concerns about the delay of Christ's return (Heb. 10:25, 10:35–39). There were also long-standing believers who had been baptized (Heb. 6:4–5, 10:22) but were in danger of growing weary in their Christian walk (Heb. 3:12–13, 5:11–6:8, 10:35–36, 12:12–13).

We are left with myriad vague details about Hebrews. Reading Hebrews can feel like being given a book today with the comment, "Here, you may enjoy this. It was written in America or Russia or France, I'm not sure, by a Jew—or was it a Gentile?—anyway, it was written sometime between 1920 and 1970. Enjoy."[7]

What Hebrews Is All About

Good to Great

Hebrews presents a dualist picture of the world, sometimes described as a modified Platonic worldview where earthly things reflected heavenly ideals. But this dualism also fits within the larger Greco-Roman worldview that favored the spiritual over the material world. However, unlike Greco-Roman thought, Hebrews does not deem the earthly realm as bad. Rather, it is simply inferior to the heavenly world.

More helpful, the dualism of Hebrews was grounded in Jewish apocalyptic thought. Hebrews situates the audience in the "last days" (Heb. 1:2; cf. Isa. 2:2; Ezek. 38:16; Hos. 3:5; Mic. 4:1; cf. Deut.

Carl N. Toney

Ruins of the Jerusalem temple and Robinson's Arch, which was part of the staircase connecting Jerusalem's lower market to the temple.

[6] Manson, *Hebrews*, 43–44; Robinson, *Redating the New Testament*, 200–204.

[7] Long, *Hebrews*, 2.

Tabernacle replica. Timna Park, Israel.

4:30, 4:32, 8:16) and reminds them of the hope for a future city where God will rule (Heb. 13:14). The author peeled back the physical world to reveal the heavenly reality that was controlling and transforming the world. Heaven is God's eternal realm, while the earth is the temporal realm of humanity. The author pointed beyond the material world to superior, permanent heavenly realities. The audience was told that the earthly tabernacle, priesthood, and sacrifices reflected the true heavenly sanctuary (Heb. 9:1–10), Jesus's eternal priesthood (Heb. 4:14–7:28), and his ultimate sacrifice (Heb. 9:11–10:31).

The arguments use a good-to-great framework rather than bad-to-good. Angels gave the good, old covenant, but the Son of God gave the new, better covenant (Heb. 2:1–4, 8:1–13). Moses led people to rest in the promised land, but Jesus offered a new, greater heavenly rest (Heb. 3:1–4:13). The old Levitical priesthood was effective on earth, but it had been replaced by the sinless Jesus, who serves as a priest in heaven, offering eternal salvation (Heb. 4:14–5:10, 7:1–28). As a tent, the earthly tabernacle is temporary; however, there is a permanent, heavenly sanctuary (Heb. 9:1–10). The old, ongoing sacrifices offered the forgiveness of sins, but the new, one-time sacrifice of Jesus perfects people (Heb. 9:11–10:18). For Hebrews, these good things all pointed to great things.

Ways to Read the Bible

How do we approach reading the Bible? Statements like "the Bible says it, so I believe it" hide the complex process of reading and interpretation. The study of methods of interpretation is called **hermeneutics**. **Exegesis** describes interpretations that draw meaning out of the text. **Eisegesis** describes readers projecting meaning upon the text.[8]

The New Testament authors' primary lens for interpreting Scripture was the life and work of Jesus, and their interpretations were guided by the Holy Spirit (e.g., Peter spoke about Jesus fulfilling Psalms 16:8–11 and 110:1 in Acts 2:25–36). These writers also sometimes employed typological readings that compared people, events, or things from one period to another (e.g., Jesus was like Melchizedek in Hebrews 7:1–28). We also find at least one occasion of allegorical reading, which understood the text symbolically (e.g., Paul read the stories of Sarah and Hagar symbolically in Galatians 4:21–31).

By the medieval period, a method called the *quadriga* articulated a four-pronged strategy (named after a chariot drawn by four horses) that connected interpretation with the Christian virtues of faith, hope, and love.[9] First, the literal approach looked for the historical meaning of the text. Second, the

[8] For a brief history of interpretation, see Stanglin, *Letter and Spirit of Biblical Interpretation*.

[9] Augustine of Dacia (*Rotulus pugillaris*) created a limerick to summarize this approach: "The letter teaches what happened, the allegory what you should believe, the moral sense what you should do, the anagogy what you should hope."

allegorical approach looked for symbolic meanings in the text to unlock spiritual meanings enhancing faith. Third, the moral (also called tropological) approach looked for ethical teachings that promoted love. Fourth, the futurist (also known as anagogical) approach looked for prophetic meanings to inspire hope. However, after the Protestant Reformation, the literal approach rose to prominence over the other three.[10]

With the Enlightenment, scholars began to emphasize more scientific approaches, and many of these are still used by scholars today. For example, the historical-critical method seeks to understand the original meaning of the text for its original audience (e.g., learning about the Corinthian church helps to understand 1–2 Corinthians). Source criticism looks for the sources used by authors for writing their works (e.g., Matthew and Luke using Mark). Redaction criticism focuses on how authors edited materials together (e.g., how the Gospels put pericopes together). Rhetorical criticism examines the elements that made works persuasive (e.g., comparing Paul's letters to ancient speeches). Literary criticism reads the Bible as literature, and narrative criticism analyzes elements like character and plot (e.g., how the relationship between Jesus and his disciples furthers Mark's plot).

With the recognition that every interpreter brings their own life experiences to the text, many newer approaches examine the text by asking specific questions. For example, reader-response criticism studies how readers understand texts, including their assumptions. Feminist criticism examines and evaluates the text from female perspectives, asking questions about gender, sexuality, and power. Womanist interpretations look at the text from the perspectives of women of color, including questions of racism and sexism. Liberation theology, developed in Latin America, emphasizes God's preferential

Marie-Lan Nguyen / Wikimedia Commons (Public Domain)

Illustrating the *Quadriga* (four-horsed chariot) is François-Joseph Bosio's *Peace Riding in a Triumphal Chariot* on the Arc de Triomphe du Carrousel in Paris.

[10] Both Luther and Calvin stressed the importance of the literal. Calvin, in his commentaries, specifically rejected allegorical interpretations and stressed authorial intent.

concern for the poor and marginalized. Postcolonialism reads the Bible in light of the impacts of colonization and notes that much of the Bible was written under the imperial powers of Assyria, Babylon, and Rome.

Others prefer devotional readings that focus on spiritual application. For example, *lectio divina* (divine reading) involves "reading" (Lat. *lectio*) a passage, then "reflecting" (Lat. *meditatio*) by listing for God's voice, then "responding" (Lat. *oratio*) in prayer, and finally "resting" (Lat. *contemplatio*) in silent contemplation. Alternatively, Ignatian meditation invites readers to use their imagination and five senses while reading. Readers immerse themselves in the stories of Scripture by imagining what they see, hear, smell, touch, and taste.

One approach for personal Bible study is the inductive method, which provides a step-by-step reading strategy.[11] The acronym *OIDA* (from the Greek word meaning "I understand") can help us remember the steps. Readers make *Observations* about the text, such as its genre, key characters, repeated themes, major arguments, quotes or allusions to other passages, and so forth. Then, readers *Interpret* the text in its ancient historical and literary contexts by asking about the significance and meaning of these observations. Clear passages are used to help interpret unclear passages. Next, readers *Dialogue* with others by consulting trusted authorities and literature (like study Bible notes and commentaries). Finally, readers *Apply* the text to the contemporary world and their lives.

When interpreting a biblical passage, one mantra is "context is king (or queen)." We ought to do our best to understand a passage considering its ancient historical and literary contexts. Also, we should be aware of how a passage has been understood historically and by people with different perspectives. Finally, we must be attentive to our own personal contexts and how they might influence or contribute to our own interpretations.

When using the Bible to formulate Christian beliefs, the Wesleyan Quadrilateral advocates that interpreters should draw upon four areas in the following order: Scripture, reason, experience, and tradition (these can be rearranged to form the acronym REST).[12] To this, we would add that many practicing Christians also include prayer and illumination by the Holy Spirit. In navigating the variety of approaches, keeping in mind the purpose for reading Scripture is important. In one of the earliest works about interpreting the Bible, Augustine (*On Christian Teaching* 1.36) offered the insight that proper interpretation of the Bible always leads to a greater love of God and love of neighbor.

Jesus as God's Son

Hebrews 1:1–4, Philippians 2:6–11, Colossians 1:15–18, and John 1:1–18 are foundational texts for how the early church understood Jesus's incarnation. These opening verses introduce one of the Hebrews' favorite descriptions of Jesus as God's "Son" (*hyios*, Heb. 1:2, 1:5, 1:8, 3:6, 4:14, 5:5, 5:8, 6:6, 7:3, 7:28, 10:29). The title "son of God" was associated with the Roman Emperor and Greco-Roman heroes. For Jewish audiences, Israel was called God's son (e.g., Exod. 4:22–23; Jer. 31:20). More importantly, the son of God

[11] A good starting point for personal Bible study is Fee and Stuart, *How to Read the Bible for All Its Worth*.

[12] John Wesley never used this expression; rather, Albert Outler is credited with coining the concept.

King David. St. George's Collegiate Church. Tübingen, Germany. (1491)

was the Davidic king (2 Sam. 7:14; 1 Chron. 17:13; Ps. 2:7). Hebrews claims that Jesus is the messianic Son of God (Heb. 1:5), who is the agent of God's reign, and supports this with a daisy chain of citations from Jewish scriptures (Heb. 1:5–13), including Psalm 2:7, 2 Samuel 7:14, and Psalm 110:1.[13]

As the Son of God, Jesus was not merely the Davidic Messiah. Hebrews also uses "Son of God" language to argue for Jesus's superiority to angels (Heb. 1:4). "**Angels**" (*angeloi*), literally meaning "messengers," were also called sons of God (Gen. 6:1–8; Job 1:6; Dan. 3:25).[14] Jesus as the Son of God embodied the final prophetic message of God (Heb. 1:1–2). His superior salvific message was confirmed by the testimony of the apostles, signs, wonders, and gifts of the Holy Spirit (Heb. 2:1–4). As the "apostle" (*apostolos*; lit. "sent one"), the Son was the unique and ultimate "one sent" by God (Heb. 3:1). While angels were agents of salvation and intermediaries between God and people (Heb. 1:14), the Son was the new agent of eternal salvation and a superior intermediary. Although angels mediated the law as the old covenant (Heb. 2:2; cf. Acts 7:38, 7:53; Gal. 3:19; Jub. 1.27, 1.29), the Son mediated a new covenant (Heb. 7:22), which

[13] The daisy chain includes Psalm 2:7; 2 Samuel 7:14 (cf. 1 Chron. 17:13); Deuteronomy 32:43; Psalms 104:4, 45:6–7, 102:25–27, 110:1. Harris and Burch, *Testimonies*.

[14] The topic of angels is mainly in the opening chapters and only two references in the end (Heb. 12:22, 13:2). Some argue that Hebrews combats angel worship. Jewett, *Letters to Pilgrims*.

HEBREWS

- Opening about God's Son (1:1–4)
- New Ruler and New People (1:5–2:18)
- New Rest (3:1–4:13)
- New Covenant (4:14–10:31)
    - New High Priest (4:14–7:28)
    - New Covenant (8:1–13)
    - New Tabernacle (9:1–10)
    - New Sacrifice (9:11–10:31)
- New Faith (10:32–13:19)
- Letter's Closing (13:20–25)

overcame the inability of the law to perfect people (Heb. 7:11, 7:18–19).

Jesus is also superior to angels because of his divine preexistence (e.g., Heb. 1:2–3, 7:3, 10:5). Like the Father, Jesus is eternal and unchanging (Heb. 1:12), being the same "yesterday and today and forever" (Heb. 13:8). The Son is also the same "essence" (*hypostasis*)[15] as God (Heb. 1:3). Drawing upon the traditions that God created the world through his Word (Ps. 33:6; Gen. 1) and heavenly wisdom (Prov. 8:30; Wisd. of Sol. 7:22, 9:9), the Son is described as creating and sustaining the world (Heb. 1:2–3). Like wisdom, the Son reflects God's glory and mediates God's benefits to creation (Heb. 1:3; Wisd. of Sol. 7:26).

Citing Psalm 2:7, which says, "You are my son; today I have begotten you," Jesus is described as the "begotten" (*gennaō*) Son of God (Heb. 1:5; cf. Heb. 5:5). Early Christians understood Jesus's "begetting" as the incarnation (Chrysostom) and his eternal generation (Augustine, Aquinas). Hebrews links Psalm 2:7 with Jesus's resurrection and exaltation (Heb. 1:5; cf. Acts 13:33; Rom. 1:4), while the four Gospels link this psalm to Jesus's baptism (Mark 1:11; Matt. 3:17; Luke 3:22; John 1:34) and transfiguration (Mark 9:7; Matt. 17:5; Luke 9:35; cf. 2 Pet. 1:17).

According to Hebrews, Jesus was temporarily made lower than angels when he became a human. He was exalted as ruler of all as a reward for his suffering and death (Heb. 2:9). After completing his priestly work of purifying people from sin, the Son sat at the right hand of God, where he continues to mediate salvation and the new covenant (Heb. 1:3–4). Like Jesus, believers can be glorified and perfected through their suffering (Heb. 2:10), and they have the hope of one day sharing in Jesus's kingdom (Heb. 12:28). Salvation will be fully consummated in the future when Christ returns (Heb. 9:28, 10:37) and subjugates his enemies (Heb. 10:13).

Jesus as High Priest

Hebrews is also well-known for its unique presentation of Jesus as the ultimate and heavenly "**high priest**" (*archiereus*, Heb. 2:17, 3:1, 4:14, 4:15, 5:1, 5:5, 5:10, 6:20, 7:26–28, 8:1, 9:11).[16] Elsewhere in the New Testament, believers are described as priests (1 Pet. 2:5, 2:9; Rev. 1:6, 5:10, 20:6). However, Hebrews is the only work to describe Jesus as a high priest (Heb. 4:14–7:28).

---

[15] This term is difficult to define and had a variety of meanings in the first century (e.g., "essence, plan, situation, title deed"). Hebrews uses it differently ("substance," Heb. 1:3; "confidence," Heb. 3:14; "assurance," Heb. 11:1). In the Nicene Creed (325 CE), this word is used to insist that the Father and Son are the same "essence" (*hypostasis*). However, the Second Council of Chalcedon (553 CE) describes the Trinity as one "essence" (*ousia*) consisting of three "persons" (*hypostaseis*).

[16] Cullmann, *The Christology of the New Testament*, 89–107; Fitzmyer, "Further Light on Melchizedek from Qumran Cave 11," 25–41; Aune, "A Note on Jesus' Messianic Consciousness and 11Q Melchizedek," 161–65; Vanhoye, *Our Priest Is Christ*.

Hebrews links Jesus's priesthood with his sonship by connecting Psalm 2:7 with both Psalm 110:1 (Heb. 1:5, 1:13) and Psalm 110:4 (Heb 5:5–6). Like many other Christian writers, Hebrews cites Psalm 110:1—"Sit at my right hand until I make your enemies your footstool"—to establish Jesus's kingship, along with his resurrection and exalted rule (e.g., Mark 12:35–37, 14:62; Acts 2:34; 1 Cor. 15:25). Then, Hebrews cites three times (Heb. 5:6, 7:17, 7:21) an additional verse from this same psalm: "You are a priest forever, according to the order of Melchizedek" (Ps. 110:4). By connecting Psalm 2:7 with Psalm 110:4, Hebrews argues that Jesus was not only a king, but he was also a high priest in the order of Melchizedek.

According to the Mosaic law, priests could only come from the tribe of Levi. However, Jesus was a descendant of David, not Levi, which was a problem. Hebrews uses the story of **Melchizedek** (Gen. 14:17–24) to create a new priestly office linked to the Davidic line via Psalm 110 (Heb. 7:13–14). As a descendant of David, Jesus was recognized as a priest in the order of Melchizedek through this psalm. Hebrews makes an etymological argument that Jesus reflects Melchizedek's name, which means "king of righteousness," and as "king of Salem," he is the "king of peace" (Heb. 7:2; cf. Philo, *Alleg. Interp*. 3.79; Josephus, Ant. 1.180).[17] Finally, because Melchizedek is presented in Genesis without parents or lineage, he is like Jesus, the eternal Son of God, who remains a priest forever (Heb. 7:3).

Public Domain

Mosaic of Abraham meeting Melchizedek. Basilica di San Marco. Venice, Italy. (thirteenth cent. CE)

[17] "Melch" = "king," "zedek" = "righteousness," "Salem" = "peace."

Hebrews argues that Melchizedek and Jesus were superior to the Levitical priesthood (Heb. 7:11–22). It contends that Abraham recognized Melchizedek's higher status when he paid tribute to Melchizedek after rescuing Lot (Heb. 7:7; cf. Gen. 14:17–24). As heirs of Abraham, the Levites shared the same status as him. Being in the order of Melchizedek meant that Jesus shared the same status. Since Melchizedek was superior to Abraham, Jesus was superior to the Levitical priests. Further, while all Levitical priests eventually died, Jesus holds his office permanently as a new priest and lives forever (Heb. 7:23–25). Although Levitical priests were weak and sinful, Jesus is holy and blameless (Heb. 7:26, 7:28). While the Levitical priests needed to sacrifice animals daily for their sins and people's sins, the sinless Jesus offers himself as a superior, one-time, and heavenly sacrifice (Heb. 7:27). Although the

On the Day of Atonement, Aaron cast lots to pick a scapegoat. Lincoln Cathedral, England. (1855)

Levites were the proper earthly priests in the tabernacle (Heb. 8:4–5), Jesus is the ultimate high priest who sits at the right hand of God in heaven (Heb. 8:1, 8:6; cf. Ps. 110:5).

The New Covenant and New Sacrifice

The change in priesthood also necessitated a change in the covenant (Heb. 7:12). According to Hebrews, the law was good but was insufficient and incapable of perfecting people (Heb. 7:11, 7:18–19, 9:9, 10:1). While Moses mediated the **old covenant** of the law at Mount Sinai, Jesus mediates a new and better covenant, which makes the old covenant obsolete (Heb. 7:22, 8:7, 8:13, 9:15–17, 10:16, 10:29, 12:24). This **new covenant** is described in Jeremiah 31:31–34 as God's law being written on people's hearts (Heb. 8:8–12, 10:16–17). God establishes this new covenant, including a new high priest (Heb. 4:14–7:28), a new sanctuary (Heb. 9:1–10), a new sacrifice (Heb. 9:11–10:31), and a new promise of Sabbath rest (Heb. 4:1–11).

The earthly tabernacle of Moses was created to reflect the true, heavenly sanctuary revealed at Sinai (Heb 8:5–6).[18] The tabernacle and its furnishings are described (Heb 9:2–5; cf. Exod. 25–31, 35–50), along with the high priest's duty to offer the atoning sacrifice (Heb. 9:6–10). The atoning sacrifice was performed yearly on the Day of Atonement (Lev. 16:1–34). After offering bulls as sin sacrifices, the high priest would kill one goat for all the sins of Israel and spread its blood on the mercy seat of the Ark of the Covenant. He also released a "scapegoat," which had the people's sins symbolically placed on its forehead. In contrast to this ongoing ritualistic sacrifice of a goat and bulls, Jesus entered the heavenly sanctuary as the new high priest, "making an atoning sacrifice" (*hilaskomai*) for the sins of the people (Heb. 2:17; cf. Rom. 3:25; 1 John 2:2, 4:10).[19] He offered his own life as this new and final act of atonement (Heb. 9:11–10:18).

Hebrews uses the analogy of wills ratified at death to explain the necessity of Jesus's death (Heb. 9:16–17). The first covenant was ratified by the blood of "calves and goats," and it required the yearly sacrifice on the Day of Atonement (Heb. 9:18–22; cf. Heb 10:19–22). However, the new covenant is established once and for all by the superior blood of Jesus (Heb. 9:12, 9:14, 10:19, 12:24). As high priest, Jesus ratifies the new covenant with his blood and makes an atoning sacrifice for people's sins (Heb. 2:17, 13:11–15; cf. Rom. 3:25). His death also frees people from the power of the devil (Heb. 2:14–15).

Because people's sins had been forgiven, there was no longer a need for further sacrifices (Heb. 10:18). The sacrifices of the law could not "purify" (*katharizō*) or "perfect" (*teleioō*) God's people. Instead, these sacrifices only reminded people of their sins (Heb. 10:1–4). Jesus continues to minister on behalf of believers in the heavenly sanctuary as high priest (Heb. 7:26–27, 8:1, 9:24–28, 10:12–14; cf. Ps. 110:1). God's people are "purified" (*katharizō*, Heb. 9:14), "perfected" (*teleioō*, Heb. 10:14), and "made holy" (*hagiazō*, Heb. 2:11, 10:10, 10:14, 10:29; 13:12) by Jesus's sacrifice. They can now approach God in his heavenly sanctuary because of their clean hearts (Heb. 10:19–22; cf. Heb. 9:18–22).

---

[18] There were also some anomalies with the furnishings. Specifically, the altar of incense's placement was inside with the ark (cf. Exod. 40:5) versus outside the sanctuary (cf. Philo, *Moses* 2.101–4; possibly Exod. 30:6).

[19] The verb *hilaskomai* describes performing the atoning sacrifice. For a brief discussion of the atonement, see the footnote on "mercy seat" (*hilastērion*) in Romans 3:25 in Chapter Ten.

Judea wilderness near the Dead Sea.

Faithfulness versus Unbelief

Habakkuk 2:3–4 is quoted in Hebrews 10:37–38, including the verse, "My righteous one will live by faith" (Heb. 10:38).[20] This important text also is quoted by Paul in Romans 1:17 and Galatians 3:11, and later Jewish traditions identify this as the ultimate summary of the law (b. Mak. 23b–24a). With this quote from Habakkuk, Hebrews stresses faith in the sense of faithfulness or loyalty directed toward God (Heb. 6:1, 11:6; cf. Heb. 10:36, 11:1–40, 12:1–2). And Jesus is the ultimate example of this lived-out faith (Heb. 4:2–9, 10:36–39, 12:1–4).[21]

The so-called "**hall of faith**" in Hebrews 11 presents an idealized list of Jewish heroes who exemplify this faith that is "confidence in what we hope for and assurance about what we do not see" (Heb. 11:1 NIV). Abel's faith enabled him to offer a better sacrifice than his brother (Gen. 4:1–16). Enoch did not die because of his faith (Gen. 5:24). Noah's faith led to building the ark (Gen. 7–9). Abraham and Sarah trusted God's promises for land and heirs (Gen. 15:1–6, 21:1–7, 22:1–14). Isaac, Jacob, and Joseph also trusted these promises (Gen. 48:8–16, 50:22–25).

Moses's faithful leadership is remembered (Exod. 2:1–10, 12:31–51). Israel's faith is rehearsed from crossing the Red Sea to conquering the land. The faith of Rahab, Gideon, Barak, Sampson, Jephthah, David, Samuel, and the prophets is also recounted. Finally, a whole litany of tests of faith are rehearsed,

[20] There are four versions of Habakkuk 2:4. Paul's citation is different. See the discussion in our chapter on Romans.

[21] Michel ("πίστις," *TDNT*, 1:604) writes, "Heb. represents an independent tradition of teaching in regard to the meaning of 'faith' (*pistis*)."

from jeers to flogging to being put to death. These examples of faith focus on these characters' strengths rather than highlighting their failures to encourage the audience as they endured hardships.[22] Finally, the audience is called to emulate Jesus's ultimate model of faith, as he endured the cross so that he could be exalted to his heavenly rule by God (Heb. 12:1–4).

Conversely, Hebrews warns against unbelief (Heb. 3:12, 3:19), rebelliousness (Heb. 3:16), disobedience (Heb. 4:6, 4:11), hard-heartedness (Heb. 3:13, 3:15, 4:7) caused by neglect (Heb. 2:1–3, 10:24–25), and disillusionment over the non-arrival of Jesus's return (Heb. 10:35–39). The audience was warned not to follow "strange teachings" that appear rooted in Jewish particularism, including food laws (Heb. 13:9; cf. Heb. 9:10). They should avoid "dead works" (Heb. 6:1, 9:14). They were called to uphold marriages and avoid adultery (Heb. 13:4) and to be content rather than greedy (Heb. 13:5). The audience was chastised for their lack of maturity because they needed "milk, not solid food" (Heb. 5:11–17; cf. 1 Cor. 3:1–4).[23]

These warnings are significant because Hebrews includes several passages indicating believers could lose their salvation (Heb. 6:4–8, 10:26–31). The audience was cautioned against sharing the fate of the wilderness generation of Israel, whose disbelief kept them from entering the promised land (Heb. 3:16–19), and Esau, who gave up his birthright for a single meal (Heb. 12:16–17). Yet, these warnings ended with confidence that the audience would not share these fates (Heb. 6:9–12, 10:32–39). They were reminded that Jesus empathized with their weaknesses and provided a model of obedience because he was tested and was without sin (Heb. 4:15–16).

Positively, believers are called to maturity (Heb. 5:11–14) and to "persevere" (*hypomonē*) in their struggle against sin (Heb. 10:36, 12:1, 12:4). They are reminded that Jesus is the perfector of their faith (Heb. 10:14, 12:2, 12:23). They should obey and imitate the faith of their leaders (Heb. 13:7). They are charged to hold fast to the confession of faith of the community, which centers upon Jesus as the Son of God and high priest (Heb. 3:1, 4:14, 10:23; cf. Heb. 13:15). They demonstrate their faith by showing hospitality to strangers and caring for those in prison (Heb. 13:2–3). The community of faith is called to endure trials, understood to be God disciplining his children, to produce the "peaceful fruit of righteousness" (Heb. 12:11). They are exhorted to pursue love and good works through faith (Heb 6:10–12, 10:24, 13:1) as they await in hope for Christ's return (Heb. 10:23–25). These acts of faith will help members of this community as they journey on the road of salvation, hoping to reach the rest of their heavenly homeland where Christ rules (Heb. 13:14).

Key Terms and People

Angels: "messengers" from God, also called "sons of God," and according to tradition, mediated the Mosaic covenant

Eisegesis: interpretations where readers project meaning upon the text

Exegesis: interpretations that draw meaning out of the text

Hall of faith: Hebrews 11 presents a list of Jewish heroes as examples of faith

[22] For example, there is no mention of Abraham's encounters with Abimelech, Jephthah sacrificing his daughter, or David committing adultery and murdering his friend.

[23] This is a common Greco-Roman metaphor for instruction (Philo, *Husbandry* 9; *Good Person* 160; *Migration* 29; *Preliminary Studies* 19; *Dreams* 2.9; Epictetus, *Diatr.* 2.16.39).

Hermeneutics: the study of methods of interpretation
High priest: the head priest of Israel who was a descendant of Aaron and part of the tribe of Levi; once a year, the high priest entered God's presence in the Holy of Holies on the Day of Atonement
Melchizedek: a mysterious priest to whom Abraham paid tribute after rescuing Lot; his priesthood was connected to the enthronement of the Davidic king in Psalm 110
New covenant: according to Jeremiah 31, the law would be written on people's hearts, and this covenant was for both Jews and Gentiles
Old covenant: the law, including the Ten Commandments, was given to Moses on Mount Sinai exclusively for the Jewish people
Tabernacle: the tent that God commanded Moses and the Israelites to construct during the exodus; it was considered the house of God and the center of Israelite sacrifice and worship

Conversation Starters

1. Who do you think wrote Hebrews, and why? Does the anonymous authorship of Hebrews impact its authority as part of the canon?
2. What do you think are the best ways to approach interpreting and applying Scripture?
3. What does the use of the title "Son of God" in Hebrews teach us about Jesus?
4. Why does Hebrews compare Jesus to angels?
5. How is Jesus understood as a high priest in Hebrews? How did the author use Melchizedek to explore this theme?
6. Trace the exodus themes in Hebrews in light of the good-to-great schema of the work.
7. How did Jesus's death help establish a new covenant? How was his death an atoning sacrifice?
8. What was faith in Hebrews? Knowing that many people in the hall of faith led imperfect lives, how does this list help exemplify faith?
9. What is the consequence of unbelief? How does a person avoid unbelief?

FOR FURTHER READING

Bruce, F. F. *The Epistle to the Hebrews*. Rev. ed. NICNT. Eerdmans, 1990.

Cockerill, Gareth Lee. *The Epistle to the Hebrews*. 2nd ed. NICNT. 2012.

deSilva, David A. *Perseverance in Gratitude: A Socio-Rhetorical Commentary on the Epistle "to the Hebrews."* Eerdmans, 2000.

Guthrie, Donald. *Hebrews: An Introduction and Commentary*. InterVarsity Press, 1983.

Isaacs, Marie E. *Reading Hebrews and James: A Literary and Theological Commentary*. RNT. Smyth & Helwys, 2002.

Koester, Craig. *Hebrews: A New Translation with Introduction and Commentary*. AYB 36. Yale University Press, 2008.

Lane, William L. *Hebrews*. 2 vols. WBC 47A–47B. Word Books, 1991.

Martin, Ralph P., and Peter H. Davids, eds. *Dictionary of the Later New Testament and Its Developments*. InterVarsity Press, 1997.

13

JESUS'S BROTHERS SPEAK UP

James and Jude

An Introduction to the Catholic Epistles

Before we turn to James and Jude, let's take a minute to talk about the other letters in the New Testament that are associated with these two books. The letters of James, Jude, 1–2 Peter, and 1–3 John are collectively called the **Catholic epistles.**[1] "Catholic" (*katholikos*) means "universal," and these letters addressed a general Christian audience.[2] The division between the seven Catholic epistles and fourteen Pauline epistles (if Hebrews is included) may be due to the symbolism of the number seven as the divine number of completion (Pauline epistles = 2 x 7; Catholic epistles = 7).

While the Pauline collection of letters is arranged from longest to shortest, the order of these seven letters may be influenced by the order of names of Peter, James, and John found in Galatians 2:9.[3] These letters are currently found after Hebrews in modern Bibles, but they were located between Acts and Paul's writings in several early collections, including the Codex Vaticanus (fourth century CE) and Athanasius's Easter Letter (367 CE). This alternate arrangement might reflect a value judgment of the superior apostolic status of these "pillar" apostles or because they were apostles prior to Paul.

SUGGESTED READING

Acts 15:1-21
Acts 21:17-26
James
Genesis 6:1-8
Jude

[1]Eusebius (*Hist. eccl.* 2.23.25) writes, "James, who is said to be the first of the Epistles called Catholic . . . the case with the Epistle called Jude's, which is itself one of the seven called Catholic." Elsewhere he writes, "John the apostle, whose are the Gospel according to John and the Catholic Epistle" (*Hist. eccl.* 7.25.7).

[2]Painter, *1, 2, and 3 John*, 33–34. Most of these letters have a broad audience. However, 2 John is written to a specific church, and 3 John is written to Gaius.

[3]Brown, *Epistles of John*, 3; Painter, *1, 2, and 3 John*, 35–36. The length of each letter: James (1,749 words), 1 Peter (1,678 words), 2 Peter (1,099 words), 1 John (2,137 words), 2 John (245 words), 3 John (219 words), and Jude (461 words).

Carl N. Toney

Tapestry of Jacob dreaming of angels ascending to and descending from heaven at Bethel (Gen. 28).

Another intriguing aspect of their arrangement is that James and Jude seem to be paired together in a fashion that matches the pairing of 1 Peter and 2 Peter. Both James and 1 Peter are Christian "dispersion" (*diaspora*) letters (James 1:1; 1 Pet. 1:1) addressed to believers spread across the Roman Empire.[4] The Jewish "dispersion" (*diaspora*) was the scattering of the Jewish people among the Gentile nations (e.g., John 7:35; Deut. 28:25, 30:3–4; Jer. 13:13–14). This Diaspora image is found among a variety of Jewish letters written to those living in exile (Jer. 29:4–23; 2 Bar. 78–87; 2 Macc.1:1–10a, 1:10b–2:18). Thematically, James and 1 Peter encouraged believers to joyfully face trials that refined their faith. For James, these internal trials were personal and communal temptations fueled by desires (James 1:2–4). For 1 Peter, these were external trials from a hostile world (1 Pet. 1:6–9).

Both James and Jude are paired with a second letter that makes a literary connection with the previous letter. Jude claimed to be the brother of James (Jude 1), and 2 Peter claimed to be the second letter written (2 Pet. 3:1). Thematically, both Jude and 2 Peter deal with false teachers and share similar content. Thus, from a canonical perspective, reading James and Judc as parallel letters to 1 Peter and 2 Peter can be useful.[5]

James

Who Was James?

English Bibles translate the author of this letter as "**James**" (*Iakōbos*). However, a more accurate translation of this name is "Jacob" (cf. Matt. 1:2; Luke 3:34), recalling the Jewish patriarch Jacob (Gen. 25–50; Isa. 41:8, 43:22; Jer. 30:10; Ezek. 28:25).[6] The greeting of the letter uses language that echoes Jacob's farewell address to his twelve sons (Gen. 48–49). Like the patriarch, this author was writing his letter to the twelve tribes of the "dispersion" (*diaspora*). His audience was Jewish Christians dispersed among the Gentile nations in the Roman Empire (e.g., John 7:35; Deut. 28:25, 30:3–4; Jer. 13:13–14).[7]

While we know the author's name, we have several choices about his identity. Casting our gaze over the New Testament, we find several men named James. Most prominent was the disciple James (Mark 1:19; Matt. 4:21; Luke 5:10; Acts 1:13). However, his early execution by Herod Agrippa I by 44 CE

[4] Michaels, *1 Peter*, xlv–xlvii.

[5] See Lockett, *Letters from the Pillar Apostles.*

[6] Although "Jacob" is a better translation, this chapter will identify the author as James in accordance with most English translations.

[7] *Diaspora* could also refer to the remnant of Israel (cf. Jer. 31:8; Ezek. 37:19, 37:25; 1QS 8.1; 2 Bar. 78.2–7).

JAMES

- Letter's Greeting (1:1)
- The Testing of Faith (1:2–27)
- The Deeds of Faith (2:1–26)
    - No Partiality between Rich and Poor (2:1–13)
    - Consistency between Faith and Deeds (2:14–26)
- Pure Speech (3:1–4:12)
    - Taming the Tongue (3:1–12)
    - Two Ways: God versus the World (3:13–4:12)
- Warnings to the Wealthy (4:13–5:6)
- Conclusion (5:7–20)
    - Enduring Testing (5:7–12)
    - The Prayer of Faith (5:13–20)

makes him an unlikely contender (Acts 12:2). Other men named James included the son of Alphaeus (Mark 2:14, 3:18; Matt. 10:3; Luke 6:15; Acts 1:13), the son of Mary (Mark 15:40; cf. Mark 16:1; Matt. 27:56; Luke 24:10), and the father of Judas (Luke 6:16; Acts 1:13).

Traditionally, most identify the author of this letter with James the brother of Jude (Jude 1) and the brother of Jesus (Mark 6:3; Acts 12:17, 15:13, 21:18; Gal. 1:19, 2:9, 2:12; 1 Cor. 15:7; cf. Josephus, *Ant.* 20.200).[8] After Jesus's resurrection, James became a believer (Acts 1:14) and rose to prominence as the head of the Jerusalem church (Acts 12:17, 15:13–21, 21:18; cf. Gal. 2:9). The historian Eusebius (*Hist. eccl.* 2.23) identified James as the first bishop in Jerusalem. According to church tradition, he died as a martyr, being stoned by Jewish leadership around 62 CE (Josephus, *Ant.* 20.200; Eusebius, *Hist. eccl.* 2.23).

There are several reasons to favor this traditional view. This letter shows familiarity with Jesus's teaching from the Sermon on the Mount without having verbal dependence upon Matthew's Gospel (Matt. 5–7).[9] The letter also includes accurate knowledge of the Palestinian environment, which you would expect from a brother of Jesus.[10]

---

[8] The Protevangelium of James presents James, Jude, and the other brothers of Jesus as sons of Joseph by a former marriage (Prot. Jas. 19:27). Jerome argued that James and the other brothers were children of Clopas and Mary, sister to the mother of Jesus. Another popular reading is to consider "brother" to mean "foster brother" and may denote a first cousin. McHugh, *The Mother of Jesus in the New Testament*, 246.

[9] Johnson, *James*, 55–57. Allusions to the Sermon on the Mount include rejoicing in trials (James 1:2; Matt. 5:12); asking and receiving from God (James 1:5; Matt. 7:7); being perfect (James 1:4; Matt. 5:48); being against oaths (James 5:12; Matt. 5:33–37); hoarding (James 5:2–3; Matt. 6:19); anger (James 1:20; Matt. 5:22); lip service (James 2:14–16; Matt. 7:21–23); condemning murder and adultery (James 4:2, 4; Matt. 5:21–30); challenging a divided loyalty (James 4:4; Matt. 6:24); blessing the poor (James 2:5; Matt. 5:3); and opposing the wealthy (James 2:6–7; Matt. 6:19–24).

[10] Palestinian references include agriculture (James 1:11, 5:7), the cultivation of figs and olives (James 3:12), seasonal rains (James 5:7), day laborers (James 5:4), the sea (James 1:6), a morning mist (James 4:13), salt and bitter springs (James 3:11), and Gehenna (James 3:6). Ropes, *St. James*, 295–97; Hadidian, "Palestinian Pictures in the Epistle of James," 227–28.

It is also plausible that the letter was written during James's lifetime. This letter has several characteristics of early Christian writings. First, the letter emphasizes the imminent return of Jesus (James 1:12, 5:7–11). In addition, the letter does not show any concerns about formal church structure. Instead, there is a focus on community practices, such as not judging others (James 2:1–4), helping the needy (James 2:14–17), teaching (James 3:1–2), praying and singing (James 5:13), anointing the sick (James 5:14), and mutual confession (James 5:16, 5:19). Finally, the lack of attention on the nature of Jesus (James 1:1; 2:1) and salvation (James 1:21, 2:14, 4:12, 5:15, 19–20) while emphasizing the role of God and moral living (James 1:19–27, 2:1–13, 2:14–26, etc.) could reflect an earlier period of the church.[11]

Those who disfavor this traditional view observe that the letter was composed in Greek, mimicking the Septuagint. An uneducated Palestinian Jew would not be able to pen this kind of Greek, but it could be written by a scribe conveying James's thoughts.[12] One early tradition proposed by Jerome (*Vir. ill.* 2) was that the letter had two authors, James and a later editor. James the brother of Jesus was responsible for writing the core content of the letter during his time in Jerusalem in the fifties. After James's martyrdom in 62 CE, his disciples fled and took his teachings to Antioch, where an editor composed the final form of the letter in the sixties based on his original content.[13] In support of this, several places in the New Testament note James's connections with Antioch (Gal. 2:12; Acts 15:13–21). Further, the bilingual setting of the city would be perfect for completing this letter. Finally, this letter is connected to other writings associated with Antioch—the Gospel of Matthew and the Didache.[14]

However, not everyone was impressed with this letter. According to Eusebius (*Hist. eccl.* 3.25; cf. *Hist. eccl.* 2.23), James was not accepted as Scripture by all the early Christians. Origen (*Comm. John* 19.6) provided the first known endorsement (200 CE). The letter was also included in Athanasius's Easter Letter that listed all twenty-seven works of the New Testament (367 CE). It was also accepted by heavy hitters like Jerome (ca. 340–420 CE) and Augustine (ca. 354–430 CE). During the Protestant Reformation, Martin Luther (1483–1546) disliked the "epistle of straw" because he thought it contradicted Paul's view of justification by faith. However, he still included it in his Bible.

In terms of genre, James was written as a piece of **wisdom literature** meant as a moral exhortation. As such, it includes numerous imperatives (e.g., James 1:3, 3:1, 4:4, 5:20). Also, it makes appeals to follow models like Abraham (James 2:21–23), Rahab (James 2:25), Job (James 5:11), and Elijah (James 5:17). It also challenged the audience not to emulate the false beliefs of demons (James 2:19). Characteristic of this kind of literature, this letter converses with an imaginary dialogue partner (James 2:18–19, 4:13, 5:1) and poses a series of rhetorical questions (James 2:14, 2:21, 3:13, 4:1, 4:5). While the letter may appear to lack a formal structure,[15] the opening chapter presents six themes that are developed throughout the letter: (1) enduring testing (James 1:2–4, 1:12; cf. James 5:7–11), (2) the prayer of faith (James 1:5–8; cf.

---

[11] Johnson, *James*, 119.

[12] Johnson, 116–18; Sevenster, *How Much Greek Could the First Jewish Christians Have Known?*, 3–21; Argyle, "Greek Among the Jews of Palestine in New Testament Times," 87–89.

[13] For a more developed treatment of this argument, see Martin, *James*, lxix–lxxvii.

[14] All three works are notable with their calls to perfection (James 1:4; Did. 6:1–2; Matt. 5:48; 19:21). James and the Didache have similar topics, like warning against being double-minded/tongued (James 4:4; Did. 2:4), condemning indifference to those fellow Christians in need (James 19:21; Did. 5:2), confession and the forgiveness of sin (James 5:9, 5:16; Did. 11:7, 14:2), and an imminent eschatology (James 5:9; Did. 10:6, 10:16).

[15] Dibelius and Greeven, *James*, 2, 11.

James 5:13–18), (3) the poor and rich (James 1:9–11, 1:27; cf. James 2:1–7, 4:13–5:6), (4) true wisdom (James 1:13–18; cf. James 3:13–4:10), (5) proper speech (James 1:19–20; cf. James 3:1–12), and (6) the consistent action between faith and deeds (James 1:22–27; cf. James 2:14–26).[16]

What Was James All About?

This is just a test. What do you do when you are faced with a test? Do you get nervous and think the person giving the test hopes you'll fail? Or do you think the test is an opportunity to show what you can do well? Our lives are filled with tests. When you get in an elevator, you see the maximum weight. That is based on a test to keep you safe. When you take a driver's license test, the aim is to guarantee you'll be a good driver. When you get an A on a school test, it shows that you've mastered the material.

James talks a lot about facing "**tests**" or "**trials**" (*peirasmos*). This is the central theme of the letter (James 1:2–4). James says facing tests should produce "joy" (*chara*) rather than anxiety or alarm. This may come as a surprise since these tests included difficult things like being socially and economically disadvantaged (James 1:9–11; cf. James 2:7, 4:7–10, 5:1–6) and being tempted to have evil thoughts or do evil actions (James 1:12–15). In his approach to trials, James drew upon wider Jewish traditions that called God's people to rejoice when facing trouble because of their trust in God (cf. Jth. 8:25; Wisd. of Sol. 3:4–9; 4 Macc.7:22; Josephus, *J.W.* 1.653; 2 Bar. 52.5–6).

Carl N. Toney

Sunset on the Sea of Galilee.

[16] Johnson, *James*, 174–75.

Carl N. Toney

Basalt millstones for grinding wheat into flour in Capernaum. (See Mark 10:42.)

For James, tests or trials did not indicate that God was mad with a person, nor was God the source of temptations (James 1:13; cf. Sir. 15:11–13). Instead, people were tempted by their own "desires" (*epithymia*, James 1:14), such as "pleasure" (*hēdonē*, James 4:1–3), "jealousy" (*zēlos, zēloō*, James 3:14, 4:2), and "selfish ambition" (*eritheia*, James 3:14, 3:16). Temptations also come from the world (James 4:4–5) and the devil (James 4:7). These sources of temptation attempt to rule a person. People must be careful not to misstep when facing tests or trials because everyone will be held accountable for their actions (James 1:14). Temptation is not a sin nor a sign of sinfulness. But giving in to temptations leads to sin and can ultimately bring death (James 1:15).

Resisting temptation begins by personally submitting to God's rule. God can purify a person's heart and cause the devil to flee (James 4:7–8). Like other New Testament writers (Rom. 5:2–4; 1 Pet. 1:6–7), James engaged with the Greco-Roman idea of testing a person's virtue in order to strengthen a person's character (Seneca, *Prov.* 2.1–6; cf. 4 Macc. 7:22, 9:29–30, 11:22). For James, it was a "testing [*dokimion*] of faith" (James 1:3). This process creates "endurance" (*hypomonē*) that results in maturity. James saw a virtuous person as humble (James 1:9, 4:10), meek (James 1:21), merciful (James 2:13), gentle (James 3:13), peaceful (James 3:18), and patient (James 5:7–8, 5:10). He challenged his audience to avoid vices like selfish ambition and boasting (James 3:14–16). James not only challenged the faith of individuals, but he also connected this to the faith of the community as indicating their "fidelity to God as its source of being and worth."[17]

A mature faith. Another critical idea from James is the maturity of faith (James 1:2–4). He used the language of "**perfection**" or "completion" (*teleios*, *teleō*, *teleioō*), to convey this idea (James 1:4, 1:17, 1:25, 2:8, 2:22, 3:2). James understood perfection to be when something lives up to its full potential. It is like a seed that is complete when it grows into a tree.

For James, perfection was a statement about a person's maturity through achieving the highest moral character. This perfection was revealed through a person's "deeds" (*erga*, James 1:4, 2:22), "wisdom" (*sophia*, James 1:5, 1:17), "faith" (*pistis*, James 2:22; cf. James 1:6), and obedience to the "law" (*nomos*, James 1:25, 2:8, 2:10). People who submit to God's reign and live according to God's will by acting according to their beliefs are complete or mature. They are people living up to their full potential. A perfect person does not get distracted. They are "singlehearted," not "double-minded" (James 1:8, 4:8).[18] They are not "unstable" (*akatastatos*, James 1:8), or "disordered" (*akatastasia*, James 3:16).

For James, "**deeds**" or "works" (*erga*) were how faith was concretely lived out. People act according to their beliefs. Failing to perform deeds according to God's will reveals a lack of true faith. For James, deeds were not done to earn salvation. Rather, they proved that God had saved a person. James provided several examples from Jewish scriptures of models to follow. Believers should practice deeds of faith like Abraham and Rahab (James 2:20–25). Their faith should include obedience like Job (James 5:10–11). They should offer prayers of faith like Elijah (James 5:17–18). This maturity of faith is not achieved by human effort. Instead, maturity comes as a divine gift (James 1:17–18; cf. James 1:5). James also saw this as a maturity that looked to the future when God's purposes were achieved (James 1:18).[19]

Marie-Lan Nguyen (CC BY 2.5)

Athena was the goddess of wisdom. Pictured is the Owl of Athena on a tetradrachm coin. Museum of Fine Arts of Lyon.

Be wise. Proverbs 1:7 famously states, "The fear [or awe] of the Lord is the beginning of knowledge; fools despise wisdom and instruction." Likewise, James encouraged his audience to seek after divine wisdom (James 3:17) instead of earthly wisdom (James 3:15) when facing trials (James 1:2). He assured his readers of God's generous desire to impart his wisdom upon any righteous person in their time of need (James 1:5; cf. Prov. 27:21; Sir. 2:1; Wisd. of Sol. 3:4). This wisdom leads to appropriate attitudes and actions.

James was indebted to Jewish wisdom traditions (e.g., Prov. 1:7, 2:6, 22:4; Sir. 1:1, 1:14, 1:26,

[17] Johnson, "Letter of James," 188.
[18] Schweizer, "ἀνάψυξις," *TDNT*, 9:665.
[19] Dibelius and Greeven, *James*, 17.

James uses agrarian imagery of olive trees, fig trees, and grapevines.

19:20; Wisd. of Sol. 1:6; 7:15).[20] James 4:6 quotes Proverbs 3:34 to remind the audience that "God opposes the proud." Also, the language describing the restoration a sinner as covering a multitude of sins in James 5:20 echoes "love covers all offenses" from Proverbs 10:12. In addition, James provides Job's suffering as the ultimate example of wise living (James 5:11; cf. Job 1:21–2:10).

James drew attention to how community members should wisely relate to others. A wise person submits to God's rule by following the "royal law" of loving one's neighbor (James 2:8; cf. Lev. 19:18; Prov. 10:12, 17:17). For James, this love was expressed by caring for widows and orphans (James 1:27; cf. Prov. 15:25, 23:10). A loving person takes care of the poor by clothing and feeding them (James 2:14–15; cf. Prov. 19:17, 21:3, 31:9, 20; Sir. 4:9, 28:8–9, 35:2). Wisdom also includes controlling how one speaks to others (James 1:26, 3:5–10; cf. Sir. 5:13, 19:6–12, 23:7–8, 28:12). A wise person should avoid harmful speech (Prov. 16:27; Sir. 28:14–18), such as not cursing those made in God's image (James 3:9–10), not speaking evil (James 4:11), or grumbling against others (James 5:9). Further, a wise person should be quick to listen but slow to anger (James 1:19; cf. Prov. 15:1; Eccl. 7:9). A wise and loving community is dependent upon God and uses their speech to pray for each other (James 4:13–17, 5:13–17; cf. Prov. 15:8, 15:29). Finally, a wise person can also restore a sinner in his or her community with love (James 5:20; cf. Prov. 10:12).

[20] However, James lacks the Jewish personification of Wisdom (Prov. 8:1-36; Wisd. of Sol. 7:15-30; Sir. 24:1-24).

Wealth and the piety of the poor. James addressed a stratified community divided by wealth and status. In his community, the poor lacked daily food (James 2:15) and adequate clothing (James 2:2, 2:15). They were represented by orphans and widows (James 1:27) and day laborers (James 5:4). Sadly, they were being marginalized and dishonored during community gatherings (James 2:3–4, 2:6, 2:9). In contrast, the wealthy possessed fine clothes and rings (James 2:2) and lived in luxury (James 5:5). They oppressed the poor by dragging them to court (James 2:6) and did not pay fair wages (James 5:4). Unfortunately, the wealthy were being given honor and preferential treatment by other believers (James 2:3).

James condemned the greed of the wealthy, such as landowners whose love of possessions came at the expense of the poor (James 5:1–6; cf. Matt. 6:19–34; Luke 12:13–34). Likewise, he confronted the pride of merchants (James 4:13–17; cf. Prov. 27:1) calling for humility when making plans by asking "if the Lord wishes" as a means of submitting to God's rule (James 4:15). James compared wealth to a flower withering in a field to remind his audience that wealth is uncertain, and its ruin is swift (James 1:9–11; cf. 1 Tim. 6:9–10, 6:17–19). Rather than accumulating these transitory goods, true religion (James 1:27) involves taking care of those who are exploited (e.g., Exod. 22:21; Deut. 14:28; Isa. 1:17; Jer. 5:28; Zech. 7:10).

James called for believers to stand on the side of the poor, who were being oppressed by the wealthy (James 2:2–4, 2:15–16). His concern for the poor was grounded in Jewish scriptures (Deut. 10:18; Ps. 68:5; Sir. 4:10), which also denounced their wealthy oppressors (Isa. 3:11–15, 5:8–10, 9:18–10:4; Amos 2:6–7, 5:11–12, 6:4–6, 8:5–6; Mic. 2:1–5). In James, God prefers the poor; their cries reach God, who will judge their oppressors (James 5:4). While some people may be poor now, they will be elevated by God in the future (James 1:9) and become heirs in God's kingdom (James 2:5). However, the poor were not intrinsically godlier because of their lack of possessions. Instead, their poverty made them more dependent upon God (James 4:5; cf. James 1:12). Their poverty resulted in their sole allegiance to God's rule because they could not be double-minded (James 1:8, 4:8) or distracted by wealth (James 4:2–4, 4:13–15).

The believing community was called to reflect God's great kingdom reversal, where he raises the lowly and brings down the wealthy (James 1:9–10). Jesus's command to love one's neighbor is redefined with the poor person as their neighbor (James 2:8; cf. James 1:25, 2:12; Lev. 19:18). This love for the poor is concretely demonstrated by the status given to poor members in community gatherings (James 2:2–4) and by providing food and clothing to those in need (James 2:15–16). The wealthy should give away their possessions to care for the poor rather than buy fine clothes (James 2:2) or hoard wealth for an uncertain future (James 4:13–15). Believers are reminded that the poor are God's exemplars chosen "to be rich in faith and to be heirs of the kingdom" (James 2:5).

Jordan River headwaters. James includes the metaphors concerning freshwater and saltwater springs to illustrate consistent speech.

> **JUDE**
>
> - Letter's Greeting (vv. 1-2)
> - Contend for Faith (vv. 3-4)
> - Warning and Judgment of False Teachers (vv. 5-19)
> - Call to Remain Faithful (vv. 20-23)
> - Doxology (vv. 24-25)

Do what you believe. James is well-known for emphasizing faith and works in James 2:14–26. James is often compared with Paul (Gal. 2:15–16, 3:6; Rom. 3:21–28, 4:3) because both authors spoke of faith and works. Some think James wrote independently before Paul, or he was responding to a conflict with Paul. If this was an antagonistic relationship, then James emphasized works, while Paul emphasized faith. If this was a complementary relationship, then Paul talked about faith alone as the key to getting saved, while James spoke of the necessity of works as demonstrating saving faith.

Placing these two authors in conversation with one other can be a helpful for comparison, but it is not a reflection of their historical circumstances. Paul's discussion of faith and works centered upon his concern about the salvation of Gentiles independent from the works of the law, such as circumcision, Sabbath observance, and food laws. James argued that works result from true faith because people act according to their beliefs.[21] As an illustration, both writers cited Genesis 15:6 to the opposite effect. Paul emphasized Abraham's faith apart from the law and used God's promises in Genesis 17 to make his "faith alone" point. James argued that Abraham's faith was demonstrated by his deeds, as seen in the story of Abraham's willingness to sacrifice Isaac in Genesis 22.

Most likely, James and Paul addressed specific concerns and were independent of each other. One way to avoid conflating James and Paul is to use the language of "deeds" rather than "works" for the Greek word *erga* in James. For James, the "perfect person" (*teleios anēr*, James 3:2) shows consistency between his or her words and actions. Deeds that demonstrate a living faith include tangibly taking care of the poor (James 2:15–16) and practicing hospitality (James 2:25). Faith is perfected by such deeds (James 2:22). James is an excellent reminder to Christians that since we act according to our beliefs, we need to center our beliefs on the grace and mercy of Christ.

Jude

Hey Jude, Who Are You?

What's in a name? The Greek name *Ioudas* is translated three different ways in our English Bibles as **Jude**, Judas, and Judah. Thus, we have a few choices for how we translate the name of this letter's author. "Judas" is a less helpful translation because of the association with the disciple who betrayed Jesus. A more useful translation is "Judah" because it reveals that he was named after the patriarch Judah (e.g., Gen. 35:5; Exod. 1–5; cf. Matt. 1:2–3; Luke 3:33), who was the figurehead of the tribe of David (Judg. 1:2; cf. Heb. 7:14; Rev. 5:5, 7:5).[22]

---

[21] This motif is also found among Greco-Roman moral philosophers (Epictetus, *Diatr.* 2.1.31, 2.9.21; Dio Chrysostom, *Or.* 35.2).

[22] Although "Judah" is a more helpful translation in light of the parallels with Jewish scriptures, this section will use the English translations of the names, like "Jude" and "Judas."

Some argue that the author can be identified as the disciple Judas, the son of James (Luke 6:16; Acts 1:13; John 14:22). However, most early Christians favored him to be the brother of Jesus (Matt. 13:55; Mark 6:3). This identification was reinforced by calling himself the "brother of James" (Jude 1). James and Jude were among the four named brothers of Jesus. Like James, he probably didn't follow Jesus during his ministry (Mark 3:21, 3:31; John 7:5). But Jesus's resurrection changed his perspective, and he became a believer (Acts 1:14). According to church tradition, Jude shared the gospel throughout the land of Israel (Eusebius, *Hist. eccl.* 1.7.14). It's possible that Jude lived into his eighties, having several grandsons (Eusebius, *Hist. eccl.* 3.19.19–3.20.8).

Modern commentators agree upon this identification as Jesus's brother but disagree on whether he wrote this letter.[23] Evidence for a pseudonymous person writing at a later date includes the shift in understanding faith from the concept of belief to describing the content of a fixed tradition (Jude 3, 20). Some argue that this letter opposed later Gnostic heresies. Language of "remember[ing]" the apostles (Jude 17) may show distance from the apostolic age. However, this letter lacks any hint of Gnostic cosmology, and the dualism and apocalyptic outlook of the letter stress living in the final days, which reflects an early period of Christianity. In addition, Jude's use of apocryphal works like 1 Enoch and the Testaments of the Twelve Patriarchs indicates an earlier period when the church had fewer clear definitions of canonical authority. The biggest challenge to the authorship of this letter comes from the careful Greek composition, but the use of a scribe explains this.

If the letter was written by the brother of Jesus, then it was probably written in the fifties or sixties to a Jewish Christian audience in the land of Israel. The identity of the Jewish Christian community was rooted in images used for Israel. They were "called" by God (Jude 1; cf. Isa. 42:1, 42:6, 48:12, 48:15, 49:1, 49:7) and were God's "beloved" (Jude 3, 17, 20; cf. Deut. 32:15, 33:5, 33:26; 2 Chron. 20:7; Ps. 28:6; Isa. 5:1, 44:2; Bar. 3:36). If the letter was written by someone else using Jude's name, then it had to be written sometime before the middle of the second century.

This letter was considered authoritative by many in the early church, as reflected by its inclusion in the Muratorian Canon (ca. 170–190 CE). Clement of Alexandria (ca. 150–215 CE) also wrote a short commentary on Jude.[24] However, some people were unsure about this letter. Eusebius (*Hist. eccl.* 2.23.25, 3.25; ca. 264–339 CE) considered Jude, James, 2 Peter, and 2–3 John among the disputed books. But Jude was included in the full list of New Testament books in Athanasius's Easter Letter (367 CE). With these backgrounds in mind, let's now turn to this short, strange work.

Public Domain

Lithograph of Enoch by William Blake. (1807)

[23] Pseudonymous: e.g., Reicke, *James, Peter, and Jude*; Sidebottom, *James, Jude, 2 Peter*.

[24] Clement, *Comments on the Catholic Epistles*.

What Is Jude All About?

False teachers. Jude really did not like false teachers. A significant portion of the body of his letter warned against them (Jude 5–19). He othered them by describing them as "those" people (Jude 8, 10, 12, 16, 19) in contrast to his "beloved" (Jude 3, 17, 20). They were "intruders" (Jude 4) in the love feasts in the community (Jude 12; cf. Acts 2:46; 1 Cor. 11:17–34; Did. 9–10; Ign. *Smyrn.* 8:2; Acts of Paul 25). Jude worried that their presence and false teaching were endangering the community (Jude 4).[25]

Itinerant preachers were a common problem for the early church (Matt. 7:15; 2 Cor. 10–11; 1 John 4:1; 2 John 10; Did. 11–12). They took advantage of financial support from the churches (Rom. 16:18; 1 Tim. 6:5; Titus 1:11; Did. 11:5–6, 12). Jude portrayed his opponents as malcontents (Jude 16), scoffers (Jude 18), grumblers (Jude 16), flatterers (Jude 16), and lustful (Jude 16, 18). He described them as being outsiders of the community, who were impious sinners (Jude 15), worldly (Jude 19), and devoid of the Spirit (Jude 19). They brought harm to the community. They were described as "irrational animals" (Jude 10), "waterless clouds" (Jude 12), "wandering stars" (Jude 13), and "wild waves" (Jude 13). Jude compared these false teachers with six examples of past notorious sinners from Israel's history to illustrate the severe danger they posed to the community (Jude 5–19).

Fountain of the Fallen Angel by Ricardo Bellver. Retiro Park. Madrid, Spain. (1877)

The first three sets of sinners were the rebellious Israelites in the desert (Jude 5; cf. Num. 14; 1 Cor. 10:1–11; Heb. 3:7–19), the immoral people of Sodom and Gomorrah (Jude 7; cf. Gen. 19; Matt. 10:15, 11:23–24; Luke 10:12, 17:29; Rom. 9:29), and the fallen angels chained in deepest darkness awaiting judgment (Jude 6; cf. Gen. 6:1–8; 1 En. 6–19). These fallen angels reflect something called the **Watchers' tradition**, which is based on the preflood story of the "sons of God" who were thought to be fallen angels that slept with the "daughters of men" (Gen. 6:1–8). This episode illustrated the great wickedness of humankind, which led to God judging the world with the flood (Gen. 6:5–7). The story was expanded by writings attributed to Enoch (1 En. 10.13, 13.2, 14.5, 15.8–12). It was a tradition found in Jude 6, 1 Peter 3:19, and 2 Peter 2:4–5.

In the second group of three sinners, the false teachers are compared to the first murderer, Cain (Jude 11; cf. Gen. 4:1–16; Heb. 11:4; Josephus, *Ant.* 1.52–66; Philo, *Posterity* 38–39); the false prophet Balaam, who encouraged idolatry and sexual

[25] Martin, "Theology of Jude, 1 Peter, and 2 Peter," 68–86.

immorality (Jude 11; cf. Num. 25:1–3, 31:16; Rev. 2:14); and Korah, who led a rebellion against Moses (Jude 11; cf. Num. 16). According to Jude, these false teachers were the latest examples of rebellious and impious sinners whose fate had long been known. Their presence meant that the community was living in the last days. As such, the community needed to be wary of them and contend for their faith.

Public Domain

Triumph of Faith over Idolatry by Jean-Baptiste Théodon. Church of the Gesù in Rome. (1646-1713)

God is in charge. Despite living in the last days, Jude wanted his audience to know that God was in control. He used the language of "keeping" (*tēreō*, *phylassō*) to reinforce this point. The audience was "kept" (*tēreō*) safe by God (Jude 1). However, rebellious angels did not "keep" (*tēreō*) their heavenly position (Jude 6), so they were "kept" (*tēreō*) in eternal chains (Jude 6). Likewise, the deepest darkness was "kept" (*tēreō*) for false believers (Jude 13). The audience was charged to "keep" (*tēreō*) themselves in God's love (Jude 21), and God would "keep" (*phylassō*) believers from stumbling (Jude 24).

Because God was in control (Jude 4), the fate of the opponents was already sealed (Jude 13–15). Because of this, Jude did not call them to repent. Instead, he pronounced prophetic judgment against them. Jude looked to the past to reiterate God's consistent judgment of sinners. History revealed a pattern for his opponents' future judgment of eternal fire (Jude 7) and deepest darkness (Jude 13). The fate of his opponents served as a warning to those tempted to follow their path of rebellion against God's rule (Jude 22–23).

Apostolic faith. Since most of the letter focuses upon the condemnation of his opponents (Jude 4–19), it can be tempting to see this as the primary purpose of the letter. However, Jude framed this condemnation with positive appeals for believers to "contend for the faith" (Jude 3). This "faith" (*pistis*) was the body of apostolic teaching that Jude urged his audience to adhere to (Jude 3, 17, 20).

Unfortunately, Jude did not describe the content of this faith. Yet, some of its content may be discerned from his reactions to his opponents. True faith did not deny the sovereignty of Jesus as "Lord" (*kyrios*, Jude 4, 21, 25) or "Master" (*despotēs*, Jude 4). Further, Jesus acted as God's agent, judging the wicked and saving the faithful. God was also understood as both "Father" (Jude 1) and "Savior" (Jude 25). The stakes were high because people's faith was tied to their choice between eternal life (Jude 21) versus eternal punishment (Jude 7, 13–15).

Believers must live out this faith that keeps them in God's love (Jude 21). They were filled with the Holy Spirit (Jude 20; cf. Jude 19) so that they lived ethically, free of "impious desires" (*epithymias tōn asebeiōn*, Jude 18). This faith was communal, and believers were called to abide in Christ, who kept them from stumbling (Jude 24). They should contend for the faith together and "snatch" (*harpazō*) others out of the fire of judgment through acts of mercy (Jude 23). Thus, Jude reflects a period where the faith of his community was getting shaped and crystalized in response to false teaching. This positive focus on faith is reflected in Jude's closing doxology that praises the reign of Christ:

> To him who is able to keep you from stumbling and to present you before his glorious presence without fault and with great joy—to the only God our Savior be glory, majesty, power and authority, through Jesus Christ our Lord, before all ages, now and forevermore! Amen. (Jude 24–25 NIV)

Key Terms and People

Catholic epistles: letters written to the general church (James, Jude, 1–2 Peter, 1–3 John)
Deeds/works: for James, deeds resulted from a person's faith lived out; they did not earn salvation, but they were proof of salvation
James: the brother of Jesus, leader of the Jerusalem church, and author of the letter bearing his name
Jude: the brother of Jesus and author of the shortest letter in the New Testament
Perfection: understood as completion, meaning something acts according to its full potential
Trials/tests: in James, trials were opportunities to test a believer's faith
Watchers' tradition: fallen angels called the "sons of God" who slept with the "daughters of men"; a shared tradition in Jude and 1–2 Peter
Wisdom literature: writings that present moral guidelines by offering general principles for living

Conversation Starters

1. What are some parallels between James and Jude with 1–2 Peter?
2. What do we know about James, and who do you think wrote this letter?
3. What was the role of tests/trials in James? How were these meant to be positive and faith-building?
4. What does mature faith look like?
5. What does wise living look like for James?
6. How is faith lived out through deeds? How was James's discussion of deeds different from Paul's discussion of works?
7. What was James's attitude toward wealth? How should we treat the poor? How does treating the poor tie into Jesus's love command?
8. Who was Jude?

9. Why did Jude spend so much space writing against false teachers? Who are they compared to, and why?
10. How does God being in control help believers as they hold fast to their faith?

FOR FURTHER READING

James

Jobes, Karen H. *Letters to the Church: A Survey of Hebrews and the General Epistles*. Zondervan, 2011.

Johnson, Luke Timothy. *The Letter of James: A New Translation with Introduction and Commentary*. AYB 37A. Yale University Press, 2008.

Kamell, Mariam, and Craig Blomberg. *James*. Zondervan Exegetical Commentary Series: New Testament 16. Zondervan, 2008.

Lockett, Darian. *Letters from the Pillar Apostles*. Pickwick, 2017.

Mason, Eric Farrel, and Darian Lockett, eds. *Reading the Epistle of James: A Resource for Students*. Resources for Biblical Study 94. SBL Press, 2019.

Perkins, Pheme. *First and Second Peter, James, and Jude*. Interpretation. Westminster John Knox, 1995.

Jude

Watson, Duane F. "The Letter of Jude." In *The New Interpreters Bible: General Articles & Introduction, Commentary, & Reflections for Each Book of the Bible*, 12:473–500. Abingdon, 1994.

Most of the Jude resources are found in the next chapter.

14

THE FIRST AND LAST TESTAMENTS OF PETER

1-2 Peter

1 Peter

What Do We Know about Peter?

He was called the "Rock," but you probably know him as **Peter**. Jesus gave him this nickname (Matt. 16:17–18; John 1:42). "Peter" (*Petros*) is the Greek translation of the Aramaic "Cephas" (*kefa*), which means "Rock." Elsewhere in the New Testament, the Greek transliteration "Cephas" (*Kēphas*) is used instead of "Peter" (1 Cor. 1:12, 3:22, 9:5, 15:4; Gal. 1:18, 2:9, 2:11, 2:14; John 1:42). His original name was "Simon" (*Symeōn*, *Simōn*), from the Hebrew *shimeʿon* (Acts 15:14; 2 Pet. 1:1; cf. Matt. 4:18), which means "[the Lord] has heard." He was named after Simeon, the second son born to Leah and Jacob (Gen. 29:33).

> **SUGGESTED READING**
>
> Matthew 4:18-22
> Matthew 8:14-17
> Matthew 14:22-33
> Matthew 16:13-20
> Matthew 26:69-75
> 1 Peter
> 2 Peter

Peter was the most prominent member of the twelve disciples and often acted as their spokesperson in the Gospel stories. According to John's Gospel, Peter was from Bethsaida (John 1:44). According to the Synoptic Gospels, he was married and lived in Capernaum, the city that became the center of Jesus's Galilean ministry (Mark 1:29; Matt. 8:14; Luke 4:38; cf. 1 Cor. 9:5). Peter and his brother Andrew were fishermen on the Sea of Galilee, along with the brothers James and John. According to the Synoptic Gospels, they left their fishing profession after Jesus called them to become his disciples (Mark 1:16–20; Matt. 4:18–22; Luke 5:1–11). According to John's Gospel, Andrew introduced Peter to Jesus (John 1:40–42). Peter, James, and John were the core group of Jesus's disciples. They witnessed the raising of Jairus's daughter (Mark 5:37), Jesus's transfiguration (Mark 9:2–8; Matt. 17:1–8; Luke 9:28–36), and his final prayers in the Garden of Gethsemane (Mark 14:32–41; Matt. 26:36–46).

Miraculous Draught of Fishes by Raphael. Sistine Chapel. (1515)

One of Jesus's first miracles involved the healing of Peter's mother-in-law (Mark 1:29–34; Matt. 8:14–17; Luke 4:38–41). When Jesus walked on the Sea of Galilee, Peter asked to join him (Matt. 14:22–33). He is probably best known for confessing that Jesus was the Messiah (Mark 8:27–30; Matt. 16:13–16; Luke 9:18–20). When Jesus washed the disciples' feet at the Last Supper, Peter initially protested. But then he accepted this gesture of foot washing (John 13:6–9). During Jesus's arrest, Peter tried to protect Jesus by cutting off the ear of the slave of the high priest (John 10:10). However, after following Jesus to the high priest's house, he became afraid and denied Jesus three times (Mark 14:66–72; Matt. 26:69–72; Luke 22:54–62; John 18:15–18, 18:25–27). Following Jesus's resurrection, Peter was one of the first witnesses of the empty tomb (Luke 24:12; John 20:1–10). In the final scene of John's Gospel, Jesus restored and commissioned Peter by telling him three times to tend his sheep (John 21:15–19).

At Pentecost, Peter was filled by the Holy Spirit and gave the first recorded sermon in Acts (Acts 2:14–42). Among Peter's miracles, he healed a crippled man (Acts 3:1–10) and raised Tabitha from the dead (Acts 9:36–42), but he also killed Ananias and Sapphira (Acts 5:1–11). Twice Peter was imprisoned but also was freed by God (Acts 5:17–42, 12:6–19). At pivotal points in Acts, he imparted the Holy

Spirit—first to the first Jewish believers at Pentecost (Acts 2:14–42), then to the first Samaritan followers of Jesus (Acts 8:14–25), and finally to the first household of Gentile converts (Acts 10:1–48).

During the Jerusalem Council, Peter argued in favor of the Gentiles being freed from obeying the Jewish law (Acts 15:6–11). According to Paul, Peter and Paul came to an agreement that Peter and James would share the gospel with the Jews, while Paul would reach the Gentiles (Gal. 2:8). However, Peter and Paul also had several disputes during their ministries (Gal. 2:11–21; 1 Cor. 1:12, 3:22). Ultimately, according to church tradition, Peter and his wife died as martyrs in Rome under Nero. He watched her executed before he was crucified upside down (John 21:18–19; 1 Clem. 5.4; Acts of Peter 37–38; Eusebius, *Hist. eccl.* 2.25.5; Clement of Alexandria, *Strom.* 7.11). Many Christians believe that Peter's remains are buried in the crypt beneath St. Peter's Basilica in Rome.[1]

What Do We Know about 1 Peter?

The author of 1 Peter identified himself as the apostle Peter (1 Pet. 1:1). He claimed to be a firsthand witness of Jesus's sufferings (1 Pet. 5:1; cf. 1 Pet. 1:11, 4:13).[2] The letter of 1 Peter was accepted as authoritative by the early church. Early writings, such as 1 Clement and Polycarp's *Letter to the Philippians*, regularly cite it. Irenaeus (*Haer.* 4.9.2, 4.16.5, 5.7.2) affirmed Peter's authorship. Likewise, Eusebius (*Hist. eccl.* 3.25.1–3) confirmed the canonical status of 1 Peter.

However, in modern times, some scholars understand 1 Peter to be a pseudonymous letter.[3] They question how a Galilean fisherman, an "uneducated and ordinary" man (Acts 4:13), could have written good Greek and relied upon the Greek translation of the Hebrew Bible. As a solution, it may be possible that Silvanus was Peter's scribe (1 Pet. 5:12). Silvanus may have been Silas (2 Cor. 1:19; 1 Thess. 1:1; 2 Thess. 1:1), who was described as a church leader (Acts 15:22), a prophet (Acts 15:32), and a companion of Paul (Acts 15:40, 16:19, 16:25, etc.).[4]

Others object to Petrine authorship, citing the persecutions mentioned in 1 Peter 4:12–16 as referring to events after Peter's death when the Roman Empire showed hostility to the church under Nero (64–68 CE), Vespasian (69–79 CE), Domitian (81–96 CE), or Trajan (111–112 CE).[5] However, these formal times of hostility do not match the positive description in the letter of the government "punish[ing] those who do wrong and . . . prais[ing] those who do right" (1 Pet. 2:14). Instead, the sufferings in 1 Peter feasibly align with the sort of localized challenges Christians faced, as described regularly in Acts. These smaller skirmishes fit in a setting in the early sixties, just before Nero persecuted the Christians in Rome and the execution of Peter and Paul (ca. 64/65 CE). The letter was likely written from Rome, which the letter identifies as "Babylon" (1 Pet. 5:13; cf. Rev. 14:8, 16:19, 17:5, 18:2; 2 Esd. 3:1–36; Sib. Or. 5.143). Babylon was an apt name for Rome since it symbolized a city opposed to God's rule and where God's people were exiled.

---

[1]Peter's body was buried at or near his place of execution. It was taken to the Christian catacombs under San Sebastiano around 258 CE. His body was transferred to the basilica built by Constantine (fifth cent. CE). Chadwick, "St. Peter and St. Paul in Rome," 31–52; Marco, *Tomb of Saint Peter*.

[2]Selwyn, *First Peter*, 28.

[3]E.g., Achtemeier, *1 Peter*, 43; Kelly, *Peter and Jude*, 32; Beare, *First Peter*, 48; Best, *1 Peter*, 49.

[4]Silvanus authored letter: Selwyn, *First Peter*, 9–17, 369–84. However, he may be the letter carrier (cf. Acts 15:23), but this would still allow an unnamed scribe to pen the letter. Elliott, *1 Peter*, 123–24, 872–74.

[5]For a survey, see Best, *1 Peter*, 39–42.

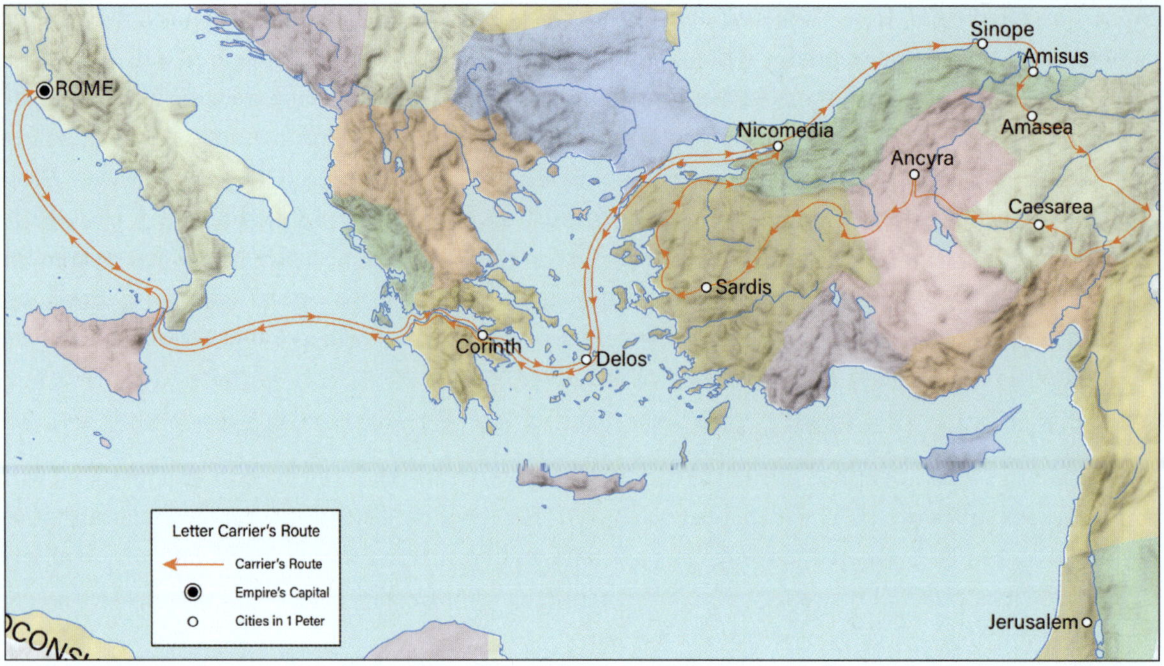

Route of the letter carrier for 1 Peter reconstructed using 1 Peter 1:1.

The audience was from the provinces in northern Asia Minor of Pontus, Galatia, Cappadocia, Asia, and Bithynia (1 Pet. 1:1). The order of provinces listed in 1 Peter is curious because the single province of Pontus-Bithynia is split in two. This may reflect the letter carrier's route. He would sail from Rome to Pontus and then journey clockwise through the regions to arrive in Bithynia and depart by ship.[6] This vast area covered about 129,000 square miles. While Paul evangelized northern Galatia in the fifties (Acts 16:6, 18:23), we do not know how the gospel reached others in this area, and we do not have any record of Peter's presence in the region.

Like James 1:1, Peter described his audience as "exiles of the Dispersion" (1 Pet. 1:1), and those outside the community were called Gentiles (1 Pet. 2:12, 4:3). It is easy to assume that Peter was also addressing Jewish Christians dispersed among the Gentile nations (John 7:35; Deut. 28:25, 30:3–4; Jer. 13:13–14; cf. Eusebius, *Hist. eccl.* 3.4.2–3). However, certain passages in the letter reveal that Peter was actually writing to Gentile Christians but applying Jewish labels to them. As Gentiles, their past lives were under "desires that you formerly had in ignorance" (1 Pet. 1:14). They lived an "empty way of life" (1 Pet. 1:18 NIV). Their previous lifestyle is described using Jewish polemical language about Gentiles, such as performing acts of immorality; being lustful; participating in drunken orgies, feasts, and revelries; committing idolatry; and blaspheming (1 Pet. 4:3–5).

First Peter applies Israelite language to these Gentile Christians to indicate that they were now part of God's chosen people (possibly seeing them as the new Israel). He called them a "chosen race, a royal priesthood, a holy nation" (1 Pet. 2:9; cf. Exod. 19:6) and included the qualifier, "once you were not a people" (1 Pet. 2:10; cf. Hos. 2:23). As the new people of God, Jesus was their "cornerstone" (1 Pet. 2:6)

[6] Elliott, *1 Peter*, 316–17.

laid in Zion and "the very head of the corner" (1 Pet. 2:7) of the temple (quoting Isa. 28:16 and Ps. 118:22). Peter wrote this letter to encourage this community of Gentile Christians to remain true to their faith even while suffering and facing social pressures.

What Is 1 Peter All About?

How to endure the suffering caused by others. Human suffering is not a new phenomenon. Job, which tells the story of a wealthy man losing his family and facing financial ruin, is probably the most famous work in the Jewish scriptures dealing with suffering. Job pushes back against the idea that rewards are given for righteous behavior and that troubles are the consequences of sinful behavior (Deut. 27–28; cf. 2 Chron. 7:12–22). James appealed to the example of Job as he addressed suffering caused within the Christian community. First Peter agrees that suffering is not linked to God's displeasure, and the work guides Christians' responses to suffering caused by the outside world antagonistic to God's rule (1 Pet. 1:6–8, 2:12, 2:19–23, 3:9, 3:13–17, 4:12–16, 5:10).

Peter encouraged his audience to emulate Christ's faithfulness and perseverance during suffering, of which he claimed to have been an eyewitness (1 Pet. 5:1). This reference to Jesus's sufferings probably does not include his crucifixion since Peter was not present at the cross. Instead, Peter was broadly describing his witness to Jesus's suffering during his earthly ministry at the hands of his opponents. Like Jesus, believers should expect to endure suffering and pushback from their broader culture, but they can also expect a similar vindication by God as Jesus experienced through his resurrection and exaltation (e.g., Mark 8:34–38; Matt. 16:24–28; Luke 9:23–27).

How had these Christians suffered? Their suffering was the product of local opposition rather than an official Roman policy of persecution (e.g., Acts 16:16–40, 17:5–9).[7] As a minority group, these Christians had been marginalized and misunderstood by society. They were called "evildoers" (1 Pet. 2:12), and they were insulted (1 Pet. 3:9) and slandered (1 Pet. 3:14). More significantly, slaves were abused by their

Carl N. Toney

Shoreline of Sea of Galilee at Capernaum.

[7] Selwyn, "Persecutions in 1 Peter," 39–50; Kelly, *Peter and Jude*, 28–32.

1 PETER

- Letter's Greeting (1:1–2)
- Rejoice in Trials (1:3–12)
- Call to Holy Living (1:13–2:10)
- Submitting to Authorities as Christian Witness (2:11–4:11)
- Call to Endure Suffering (4:12–5:11)
- Letter's Closing (5:12–14)

masters (1 Pet. 2:20–23). The believers' divergent practices, which were considered antisocial, as well as religiously and politically suspect, had caused the consternation of their Greco-Roman neighbors (1 Pet. 2:12).[8]

In response, Peter encouraged his audience to keep a good conscience by remaining steadfast under provocation as part of the Christian life. They should act as ideal citizens, submitting to every human authority, whether the emperor, governors, or local officials (1 Pet. 2:13–14). Like Romans 13:1–8, Peter's words were directed to a marginalized community, offering advice about how to avoid unnecessary trouble. Just as Paul placed governing authorities under the authority of God, Peter did the same. Both authors understood that God is truly in charge. Sprinkled throughout Peter's advice were constant reminders that believers submit because their obligation was to God, not human rulers. Their actions were "for the Lord's sake" (1 Pet. 2:13) and because "it is God's will" (1 Pet. 2:15). They were "servants of God" (1 Pet. 2:16), and they must "fear God" (1 Pet. 2:17).[9]

Language of exile conveyed these believers' social situation of displacement while they awaited their heavenly hope (1 Pet. 1:1, 1:17, 2:11). Exodus motifs are also found throughout the letter (e.g., 1 Pet. 1:18–19), including Passover allusions (1 Pet. 1:3–12). Christ was described as the perfect sacrificial lamb who "**ransomed**" (*lytroō*, 1 Pet. 1:17–19; cf. Luke 24:21; Titus 2:14; Mark 10:45; Matt. 20:28) them by his blood (cf. Acts 20:28; Rom. 3:24–25; Eph. 1:7; Heb. 9:12).[10] The Jewish scriptures are full of images of God ransoming—that is, setting Israel free from slavery in Egypt (e.g., Exod. 6:6, 15:13; Deut. 7:8, 9:26 LXX) and Babylonian exile (Isa. 45:13, 52:3 LXX). In 1 Peter, the audience has been ransomed (i.e., set free) from the values, norms, and commitments of their former Greco-Roman lives. In 1 Peter 2:9–10, the language of being "a chosen people, a royal priesthood, a holy nation" comes from Exodus 19:4–5, which describes the exodus deliverance that culminated with gaining a new identity as God's people and the giving of the law on Mount Sinai.

The admonition to endure during this time of testing (1 Pet. 4:7, 4:19, 5:8–11) echoes other New Testament writers (e.g., Mark 13; Matt. 24–25; Luke 21). Peter reminded his audience of the honor they

[8] Kelly, *Peter and Jude*, 25; Moule, "Nature and Purpose of 1 Peter," 10–11.

[9] Paul's advice to the enslaved in Ephesians 6:5–8 employs a similar strategy and uses similar expressions.

[10] See the discussions on the "ransom" sayings in Mark 10:45 and Romans 3:24 in Chapters Two and Ten.

would receive from their suffering: "If any of you suffers as a Christian, do not consider it a disgrace, but glorify God because you bear this name" (1 Pet. 4:16). Of note, this is one of only three New Testament passages to use the label "Christian" (*Christianos*) to identify believers (cf. Acts 11:26, 26:28), and it appears to have been used as a derogatory label by outsiders.

These Christians were encouraged to be patient, persistent, and prayerfully vigilant during these difficult times. Ironically, when Christians were later formally accused of sedition, their refusal to succumb during trials was regarded by the Roman magistrates as "stubbornness and inflexible obstinacy" (Pliny, *Ep.* 10.96.3). In response to troubles and persecution, believers were encouraged to:

> Always be ready to make your defense to anyone who demands from you an accounting for the hope that is in you; yet do it with gentleness and reverence. Keep your conscience clear. (1 Pet. 3:15–16)

Thus, 1 Peter transformed suffering into a positive opportunity for gospel witness. However, we must be careful not to read 1 Peter or other New Testament writers as celebrating suffering (1 Pet. 1:3–5; cf. James 1:2–4; Matt. 5:4–5, 5:10, 5:12; Rom. 5:3–5, 8:18; 2 Cor. 4:17–18). Suffering is hard. Instead, 1 Peter looks beyond suffering to the joy of trusting in the sovereign God's future vindication (1 Pet. 4:13–14). "Neither Peter nor Paul nor James knows of a 'paradox' of joy in suffering. Suffering produces sorrow, while joy is the result of vindication. In the present passage, suffering and sorrow belong to the present, while vindication and joy, although very near, belong to the future."[11]

Baptism traditions. This letter is sometimes thought to include instructions for early Christian baptism, especially considering 1 Peter 3:18–22, which connects baptism to the flood story (Gen. 7–9).[12] Because of the baptismal language, 1 Peter may address a group of recently baptized believers. As new believers, Peter's audience had an exuberant and undaunted joy (1 Pet. 1:8). They are called "newborn infants" who should desire "spiritual milk," a metaphor for the word of God (1 Thess. 2:7; Heb. 5:12–13, 6:5; Barn. 6:17).[13] By feeding upon the good word of God, these newly baptized believers were encouraged to mature in their salvation, giving them the strength to endure suffering (1 Pet. 2:2, citing Ps. 34:8; cf. 1 Pet. 3:10–12, citing Ps. 33:13–17).

Christian baptism, using water in the name of the Father, Son, and Holy Spirit and accompanied by a believer's confession of faith, was part of the conversion process in accordance with the command of Jesus (Matt. 28:18–20; cf. Acts 2:38). It was rooted in the Jewish practices of baptizing Gentile proselytes, as well as regular baptisms for ritual purity. Jesus's baptism by John the Baptist recalled the crossing of the Jordan at the end of the exodus (Mark 1:9–11; Matt. 3:13–17; Luke 3:31–22; John 1:29–34). According to Acts, being filled with the Holy Spirit accompanied baptism (Acts 1:5, 8:16–17, 9:44–48). Both individuals and whole households were baptized (Acts 8:36–38, 9:18, 10:44–48, 11:14). Didache 7:1–4 describes baptism by immersion but also makes allowances for sprinkling. In 1 Peter, the model of Christ's suffering, death, resurrection, and exaltation is connected to a believer's baptism (1 Pet. 3:18–22). Paul has a

---

[11] Michaels, *1 Peter*, 37.
[12] Kelly, *Early Christian Creeds*, 18.
[13] Elliott, *1 Peter*, 399–401.

comparable extended meditation on baptism in Romans 6:1–14, where he linked baptism to the death and resurrection of Jesus.

Christ's model of suffering (1 Pet. 3:18, 3:22) sandwiches a confusing passage, stating that Christ witnessed to the "imprisoned spirits" (1 Pet. 3:19; cf. Gen. 6:1–8) from the days of Noah. Does this mean Christ somehow preached through Noah to those "imprisoned" by sin? Or were they the spirits of those who died during the flood? Considering Ephesians 4:8–10, which describes Christ descending "into the lower parts of the earth," could this be understood as Christ's descent into hell?[14] Or is it possible that these were Christians who died before the return of Christ?[15]

Most likely, Peter was engaging with the Watchers' tradition of the fallen angels who were imprisoned for sleeping with the "daughters of men" (1 Pet. 3:19–21; cf. Gen. 6:1–8; 2 Pet. 2:4; Jude 6).[16] Christ is portrayed as visiting the underworld and announcing the fate of these wicked spirits. Christ's message of doom was meant to assure the church that these evil angels' dominion was broken. The wicked spirits also contrast Noah and his family, whom God saved. The story of the Watchers was meant to encourage believers that God was really in charge and that God would judge the wicked as he judged the Watchers. It also gave them hope because God would save and vindicate the baptized community, like Noah's family.[17]

Living as a Christian. The Christian life is centered on the hope of "new birth" (1 Pet. 1:3; cf. John 3:3–8; Titus 3:5)—that is, new origins as God's children (1 Pet. 2:2). It is sustained by faith in God who proved himself by resurrecting and glorifying Christ (1 Pet. 1:21). Because Peter saw Christians as a "royal priesthood" and a "holy nation" (1 Pet. 2:9), he urged them to pursue the standard priestly holiness conduct, citing the central theme of Leviticus: "You shall be holy, for I am holy" (1 Pet. 1:16; cf. Lev. 11:44, 11:45, 19:2). In Leviticus, holiness is the quality of being set apart to God manifested by the conduct of God's people by obeying the law.[18] In 1 Peter, believers are also called to holy living by following the summary of the law found in Leviticus 19:18, the command to love one another (1 Pet. 1:22, 2:17, 3:8, 4:8, 5:14).

Carl N. Toney

Mikveh were ritual purity pools found throughout Israel. Magdala.

The Christians' self-control (1 Pet. 1:13) would be attractive to nonbelievers (1 Pet. 1:18, 2:11, 2:16), especially when they were unjustly provoked and harassed.[19] Believers were urged to cast their anxieties caused by social unrest upon God because

[14] Some interpret the descent as Christ going to hell, but it probably refers to his descent as his incarnation (cf. John 3:13). Barth, *Ephesians*, 2:433–34.

[15] Dalton, *Christ's Proclamation to the Spirits*, 51–66.

[16] See the discussion about the Watchers' tradition in our chapter on Jude.

[17] On the Noahic tradition, see Elliott, *1 Peter*, 693–705.

[18] On holiness, see the discussion in Chapter Ten. Theissen, *Jesus and the Forces of Death*.

[19] Stauffer, "Critique of Paganism in I Peter 1:18," 129–42.

he cared for them (1 Pet. 5:7). They were told to be courteous and patient when facing trouble (1 Pet. 3:8–17). They were to uphold the Greco-Roman social order as a form of gospel witness.

First Peter provides its own version of household codes, which focus on the relationship between believers and the unbelieving world (1 Pet. 2:13–3:7).[20] By obeying political authorities, believers silenced ignorant detractors (1 Pet. 2:13–17). Mistreated slaves were called to endure out of submission to God (1 Pet. 2:18–25). Wives were to submit to their unbelieving husbands (1 Pet. 3:1–6). Believing husbands should treat their wives with respect (1 Pet. 3:7). And Christians were warned to avoid antisocial acts like theft and murder (1 Pet. 4:15–19).

Good Shepherd statue. Catacombs of Domitila. Rome. (fourth cent. CE)

Following Christ's example, Christians were called to humility. They were told not to repay evil with evil so that God may bless them (1 Pet. 3:8). They were reminded that God opposes the proud but exalts the humble (1 Pet. 5:5–6). As the church faced these difficult times, they needed "elders" (*presbyteroi*) to serve and "to shepherd" (*poimainō*) their community (1 Pet. 5:1–4; cf. Acts 20:28). The English word "**pastor**" is a translation of the Greek word that means "shepherd" (*poimēn*; cf. Eph. 4:11).[21]

An elder is to be like a shepherd who cares for the church as God's "flock" (*poimnion*). First Peter draws upon this pastoral image from the Jewish scriptures, where the Jewish leadership was called to shepherd Israel as God's flock (Jer. 23:1–4; Ezek. 34:1–34). Psalm 23 famously describes God as a shepherd (cf. Matt. 18:10–14). Jesus also called himself the Good Shepherd (John 10:1–18; 1 Pet. 2:25; Heb. 13:20; cf. Mark 14:27; Matt. 2:6, 26:31), whom church leaders are called to emulate (John 21:16; Acts 20:28). As shepherds, these elders need to protect their flock from the true enemy, the devil, who prowls like a lion (1 Pet. 5:8). These elders are to steward God's flock while waiting for Christ the "chief shepherd" (*archipoimenos*) to return (1 Pet. 5:1–5).[22]

---

[20] This is different from the codes in Pauline literature, which focus on Christian households.

[21] Only in Ephesians 4:11 are leaders of the church called "pastors" (*poimenes*), but the image is applied to elders in 1 Peter 5:2 who are called "to shepherd/pastor" (*poimainō*) God's flock. Likewise, Peter is called to the role of a shepherd by Jesus in John 21:15–19. Because of the limited use of these terms, we should be cautious of directly importing the modern profession of pastor on these texts.

[22] Elliott, "Ministry and Church Order in the New Testament," 367–91.

Faith and Politics

How should Christians relate to their government? During New Testament times, Roman citizenship was limited, and people did not elect their rulers. The relationship between the church and the Roman government was mixed, and New Testament authors provided a variety of views on the relationship between the church and state. Some texts called believers to submit to (1 Pet. 2:11–17; Rom. 13:1–8; Titus 3:1) and pray for (1 Tim. 2:1–2) ruling authorities, while other texts challenged Christians to submit to God's rule (Mark 1:15; Matt. 4:17) and to resist the Roman Empire (Rev. 13:7–10, 20:4).

Some interpret Jesus's words, "Give to the emperor the things that are the emperor's, and to God the things that are God's" (Mark 12:17), as distinguishing between obligations to the church and state. Others argue that God extends his rule through governments, quoting verses like, "for there is no authority except from God, and those authorities that exist have been instituted by God" (Rom. 13:1). Others envision a good government promoting justice and punishing sin, following verses like, "It [the governing authority] is the servant of God to execute wrath on the wrongdoer" (Rom. 13:4) and "to punish those who do wrong and to praise those who do right" (1 Pet. 2:14). Other traditions highlight the positive responsibility of the government for cultivating a common good, citing verses like "it is God's servant for your good" (Rom. 13:4).

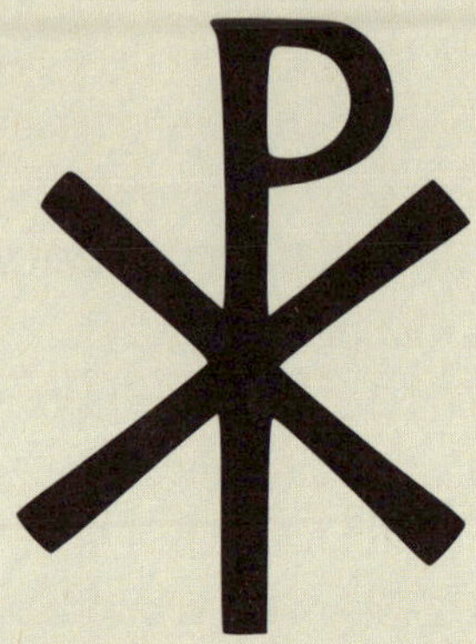

The combined letters of chi and rho, the first two letters in the name of Christ, was the symbol of the first Christian emperor, Constantine, as part of his military standard.

Others note the hostile relationship between the church and state in the New Testament and question Christians' participation in politics. Jesus's gospel message was perceived by some as a political message that challenged the authorities of his day. He announced God was in charge, calling people to "Repent, for the kingdom of heaven has come near" (Matt. 4:17). His ministry challenged the authority of the religious leaders (Matt. 23). And he was executed as a political insurrectionist with the charge, "This is Jesus, the King of the Jews" (Matt. 27:37). However, others point to the spiritual dimension of Jesus's kingdom message, noting Jesus's words to Pilate, "My kingdom is not from this world" (John 18:36).

Jesus predicted his followers' future persecutions by the government (Mark 13:9; Matt. 24:9; Luke 21:12). Acts reports several points of persecution. Herod Agrippa executed James (Acts 12:2). Paul, Silas, and Jason were arrested by city officials (Acts 16:19–24, 17:9). Jews like Prisca and Aquila were exiled from Rome because of disturbances related to Christianity (Acts 18:1–2). Other New Testament writings describe Christians suffering for their so-called antisocial behavior (1 Pet. 1:6–8, 2:12, 2:19–23, 3:9, 3:13–17, 4:12–16, 5:10; Phil. 1:29, 2:15, 3:10). Hebrews describes Christians being imprisoned and having their property confiscated (Heb. 10:32–39; cf. Heb. 12:2–4). Revelation speaks about Christians being killed for their faith (e.g., Rev. 2:10, 2:23, 7:14). It warns about participating in an anti-God society (Rev. 13:11–18, 14:9–10), and it promises God's judgment of evil nations (Rev. 18, 19:11–21, 20:7–15).

In assessing this material, it is important to recall that the New Testament was written from the perspective of a minority, disenfranchised population group. Texts like 1 Peter 2:11–17, Romans 13:1–8,

1 Timothy 2:1–2, and Titus 3:1 that urge the submission to and prayer for governing authorities can be understood as sage advice for a group struggling for survival and should not be understood as blind allegiance. Jesus's teaching about paying taxes to Caesar may have actually been subverting the authority of Rome (Mark 12:13–17; Matt. 22:15–22; Luke 20:20–26). Revelation portrays the Roman Empire as the agent of Satan and the enemy of the church (Rev. 13:1–2). Those who chose loyalty to the empire over loyalty to God would be judged along with the empire (Rev. 14:9–11).

Overall, the New Testament calls believers to place their allegiance with God, challenges them to be wary of other demands for loyalty, and reminds them that God is ultimately in control. As we consider applying these texts to our contexts, we must examine both the first-century context and our own socioeconomic and political contexts.

Thoughts on God. First Peter is notable for its emphasis on the character and actions of God. The triple construction in 1 Peter 1:2 of Father, Spirit, and Jesus is among the many New Testament passages standing behind the Trinitarian formulation in the Nicene Creed (325 CE; 1 Pet. 1:2; Matt. 28:18–20; 2 Cor. 13:13; Jude 20–21; cf. 1 Pet. 1:3–5; 1 Cor. 6:11, 12:4–6; 2 Cor. 1:21–22; Gal. 3:11–14, 4:4–5; Eph. 4:4–6; 2 Thess. 2:13–14).

Faith is directed to God (1 Pet. 1:21, 3:18) and mediated by the Son. Jesus is portrayed in light of the imagery in Jewish scriptures as the true Passover lamb (1 Pet. 1:19; cf. Exod. 12:1–20; Num. 9:1–14; Deut. 16:1–8; Ezek. 45:21–25) and servant of Yahweh (1 Pet. 2:22–23; cf. Isa. 52:13–53:12). Jesus was an exemplar for this suffering community because he also suffered (1 Pet. 2:23–25). Because God ultimately vindicated and exalted Jesus, the community could also expect vindication and a final reward (1 Pet. 1:3, 1:21, 3:18–22). Because Jesus was expected to return soon (1 Pet. 1:7, 1:13, 4:13, 5:1), the audience should continue to live ethical lives, anticipating his return (1 Pet. 4:7).[23]

The letter praises the merciful acts of God the Father (1 Pet. 1:3–5). God's present and future work is the foundation of the appeal of the letter for the audience to rejoice while suffering trials because this produces genuine faith (1 Pet. 1:6–9). Using the image of refinement, their faith, which was being tested, would prove to be purer and more precious than gold. Thus, Peter saw this period of testing and trial as something positive.

Carl N. Toney

Ancient anchor. Israel Museum.

[23]Best, *1 Peter*, 46; Russell, "Eschatology and Ethics in 1 Peter," 78–84.

Public Domain

Saint Peter by Marc Zoppo. National Gallery of Art. Washington, DC. (1468)

The author described God as the Holy One (1 Pet. 1:15), Father (1 Pet. 1:17), Creator (1 Pet. 4:19), and Judge (1 Pet. 4:5). Reflecting his ultimate authority, God's will determines everything that occurs—both the bad and good. It shapes the destiny of the church. "God determines the actions of those whom He has chosen for His own, who sustains them through the sufferings which He sends to test them, and who at last will vindicate them and reward them eternally."[24] The audience of 1 Peter would find comfort in knowing God is in charge.

2 Peter

What Else Do We Know about Peter?

Second Peter is often considered Peter's last will and testament, publishing his thoughts as he faced death. It follows the pattern of Deuteronomy, which is presented as Moses's last will and testament recorded before his death. Like other testaments, 2 Peter notes Peter's imminent death (2 Pet. 1:13–14), reassures his audience (2 Pet. 1:15), contains biographical materials (2 Pet. 1:16–18; 3:1), warns against deception (2 Pet. 1:4, 1:16, 2:1–2, 3:3–4, 3:16–17), and provides ethical admonitions (2 Pet. 1:5–7, 2:21, 3:2).[25] As we turn to these last words of Peter, let's imagine what he would say to us as he faced his martyrdom under Nero in 64/65 CE.

Authorship of 2 Peter

Figuring out who wrote this second letter is complicated. If we take the letter at face value, it claims to be the second letter (2 Pet. 3:1) written by Simon Peter (2 Pet. 1:1), who was an eyewitness of Jesus's transfiguration (2 Pet. 1:16-18).[26] It may be puzzling to hear that the letter was only slowly accepted into the New Testament canon.[27]

Even more surprising, many scholars today do not think the apostle wrote the letter. Second Peter was written in the style of a testament, which was a genre associated with pseudonymous authors. Some doubt that Peter would have deemed Paul's writings as authoritative (2 Pet. 3:15-16) because there was little evidence that Paul's letters received authoritative status before his death.[28] More challenging

[24] Beare, *First Peter*, 52.

[25] Testaments are farewell speeches modeled on heroes from Jewish scriptures like Jacob (Gen. 48-49), Moses (Deut. 22-23), Joshua (Josh. 22-24), and David (1 Chron. 28-29). We also find them in other New Testament writings, such as Jesus (Mark 13; John 13-17) and Paul (Acts 20; 2 Timothy). Testaments are also used in pseudepigraphic literature (e.g., Jub. 35-36; T. 12 Patr.).

[26] Robinson, *Redating the New Testament*, 175-85.

[27] For example, Eusebius (*Hist. eccl.* 3.25.3) placed the book among those in dispute. He (*Hist. eccl.* 3.3.1-4) considered it noncanonical, as did Didymus of Alexandria (ca. 313-398 CE), who considered it a forgery.

[28] Green, *2 Peter Reconsidered*, 30.

are the extensive parallels between 2 Peter and Jude. For example, the false teachers were condemned in both letters (2 Pet. 2:1–3; Jude 4). Angels were chained in the deepest darkness (2 Pet. 2:4–5; Jude 6). God judged Sodom and Gomorrah (2 Pet. 3:6–8; Jude 7). The false teachers were like irrational animals (2 Pet. 3:12; Jude 10), Balaam (2 Pet. 3:15–16; Jude 11) and waterless clouds (2 Pet. 2:17–18; cf. Jude 12). References were made about polluting the flesh (2 Pet. 2:10; Jude 8), boastful people (2 Pet. 2:18; Jude 16), and the presence of scoffers in the last days (2 Pet. 3:2–3; Jude 17–18).

These parallels could mean that 2 Peter is dependent upon Jude, that Jude is dependent upon 2 Peter, or that both letters are dependent upon a common, lost source. Of these choices, most scholars believe that 2 Peter is using Jude because 2 Peter appears to improve and expand upon material found in Jude. This use of Jude would indicate that the letter of 2 Peter was probably not directly written by the apostle.[29]

Carl N. Toney

An ancient church, memorializing the house of Peter's mother-in-law in Capernaum, is shelterd by a modern building.

This raises the issue of pseudonymity. Would the church really accept a document misleading readers by claiming to be written by Peter? At first glance, early evidence seems to say no. For example, Paul seemed to combat forged letters in his early ministry (2 Thess. 2:2, 3:17). But what if the author intentionally wrote this letter to embody Peter's teaching but was not trying to deceive readers? What if this letter was produced as part of the school of Peter (like the school of the prophets in Jewish scriptures or the Gospel of John)? In other words, Peter's disciples may have compiled and published Petrine traditions and teachings in their master's name.[30]

This letter could have been written by Peter or could have been based on the gathered traditions of Peter presented as his last will and testament as he faced his death by Nero.[31] Whatever informed decision a reader makes about the authorship of the letter, this should not undermine its authority as God's Word and its place as an accepted part of the New Testament canon.

What Is 2 Peter All About?

Virtuous living. Second Peter begins with a virtue list (2 Pet. 1:5–7; cf. Gal. 5:19–23; Mark 7:21–22; etc.). This list connects with several important terms found in Greco-Roman moral philosophy, including

[29] Second Peter arranges his examples in chronological order—the fallen angels (2 Pet. 2:4; Jude 6), flood (2 Pet. 2:5), Sodom and Gomorrah (2 Pet. 2:6; Jude 7), and Lot (2:7–8). Second Peter omits references to apocryphal works (e.g., 2 Pet. 2:10–11; Jude 8).

[30] Barker, Lane, and Michaels, *New Testament Speaks*, 352.

[31] Kümmel, *Introduction to the New Testament*, 430.

2 PETER

- Letter's Greeting (1:1–2)
- Reminder to Live a Life of Godliness (1:3–15)
- Eyewitness of Christ's Glory (1:16–21)
- Warning and Judgement of False Teachers (2:1–22)
- The Delay of Day of the Lord (3:1–13)
- Call to Persevere and Letter's Closing (3:14–18)

Carl N. Toney

A millstone (left) and olive grinder (left) along with an olive press (right) in Capernaum.

the concepts of "virtue" (*aretē*), "self-control" (*egkrateia*), and "piety" (*eusebeia*).[32] The author gave his list a distinctive Christian flavor by bookending it with the Christian virtues of "faith" (*pistis*) and "love" (*agapē*). This allowed the author to demonstrate how Christian virtues share some values with the wider world when they are subordinated to the Christian virtues of faith and love.

Like other virtue lists found among Greco-Roman and Jewish authors, Peter presented these virtues in a daisy chain of causality to provide a summary of the good life (e.g., Seneca, *Ep.* 85.2; Wisd. of Sol. 6:17–20; m. Soṭa 9:15). This daisy-chain construction created the impression that "Christian faith is the root from which all these virtues must grow, and Christian love is the crowning virtue to which all the others must contribute."[33] As the last virtue, love is presented as the most significant, and it serves as the overriding principle that encompasses all others (cf. 1 Cor. 13:13).

By opening with these virtues, Peter summarized the character of true believers who were "pious" (*eusebēs*, 2 Pet. 2:9), in contrast to his opponents, who were driven by "desire" (*epithymia*, 2 Pet. 1:4, 2:10, 2:18, 3:30), which is the enemy of virtue. According to Peter, anyone who did not possess these virtues acted like they were not saved in the present (2 Pet. 1:9). Similarly, Paul described the manifestation of Christian virtue as the "fruit of the Spirit" (Gal. 5:22–23) in contrast to the "desires" (*epithymiai*, Gal. 5:16) and vices of the flesh (Gal. 5:19–21). Without these virtues, Peter argued that believers lacked any assurance of their ultimate salvation and entry into Christ's kingdom (2 Pet. 1:10–11). James had a similar litmus test when he wrote, "faith without works is also dead" (James 2:26).

---

[32] Bauckham, *2 Peter, Jude*, 174–76; Neyrey, *2 Peter, Jude*, 154–62.
[33] Bauckham, *2 Peter, Jude*, 193.

Jesus's return and final judgment. Unfortunately, false teachers, who were greedy and exploitative, infiltrated the community (2 Pet. 2:1, 3). By appealing to Christian freedom (2 Pet. 2:19; cf. Gal. 5:1, 5:13), they encouraged believers to sin (2 Pet. 2:2, 2:7, 2:18). This may reflect similar problems found in the Corinthian church (e.g., 1 Cor. 6:12, 10:23). This unnamed Christian community also may have been founded as part of Paul's mission, which would explain the author's appeals to Paul's writings as authoritative (2 Pet. 3:15–16).

Problems arose because believers were concerned about the failure of Christ to return during the first generation of Christianity (2 Pet. 3:4, 3:9).[34] Peter urged patience because God's timing is not the same as humans' (2 Pet. 3:8–9). However, the opponents insisted that Jesus's future return was an invention (2 Pet. 1:16) and a misinterpretation of prophecy (2 Pet. 1:20–21). The lack of Christ's return (2 Pet. 3:4) raised doubts concerning Christ's rule and final judgment (2 Pet. 2:3). It allowed the opponents to indulge in their desires (2 Pet. 3:3). They understood Christ as freeing them from the law (2 Pet. 2:7–8, 2:19), leading them to promote greed and sexual immortality (2 Pet. 2:2, 2:10, 2:13–14, 2:18).

Because Peter's opponents denied Jesus's future return and the final judgment, they did not feel compelled to live moral lives in the present. However, Peter argued that this posture did not actually free people from desires; rather, they became controlled by them. Instead, Peter encouraged his audience to live "pious" (*eusebeia*) lives in the present, with an expectant hope of Christ's return to reward and judge (2 Pet. 1:3–11). Peter's concept of final judgment draws upon the **day of the Lord** (2 Pet. 3:10–13), presented in Amos 5:18–20 as a time of ultimate reckoning, demonstrating that God is in charge.

Peter claimed that the presence of these opponents was a sign of the last days (2 Pet. 2:1, 3:3–4). The future judgment of the wicked (2 Pet. 2:4–7, 2:10–22) and the salvation of the "pious" (*eusebēs*, 2 Pet. 2:8–9) repeated patterns from Israel's past. Peter drew upon similar images found in Jude and 1 Peter. He recalled the Watchers, who are described as sinful angels that had been imprisoned in "hell" (*tartarus*) for judgment (2 Pet. 2:4; cf. Jude 6; 1 Pet. 3:19–20; Gen. 6:1–8; Jub. 5, 6, 10; 1 En. 10.4–6, 20.2). Their actions and the sinfulness of the world resulted in God destroying the world by the flood (2 Pet. 2:5; cf. Gen. 6:11–9:17). Because Peter thought the world was a corrupting influence that believers needed to resist (2 Pet. 1:4, 2:20, 3:14), it needed to be destroyed again (2 Pet. 3:7, 3:12–13). Fortunately, believers would be saved like Noah and his family (2 Pet. 2:5; cf. 1 Pet. 3:20).

Public Domain

Last Judgment by Michelangelo. Sistine Chapel. (1536-41)

[34]Smalley, "Delay of the Parousia," 41–56; Talbert, "II Peter and the Delay of the Parousia," 137–45.

Peter then recounted the destruction of Sodom and Gomorrah by fire, as well as Lot's deliverance (2 Pet. 2:6–8; cf. Jude 7; Gen. 18–19), to foreshadow the future fiery judgment of the unrighteous and the salvation of the pious (2 Pet. 2:9–10, 3:10, 3:12).

Peter shared further imagery with Jude as he portrayed his opponents as stupid, "irrational" (*alogos*) animals who acted on instinct and would be caught and killed (2 Pet. 2:12; cf. Jude 10). Like Balaam, their false teaching endangered the community (2 Pet. 2:15–16; cf. Jude 11; Num. 25:1–3, 31:16). They were also compared to waterless springs speaking "bombastic nonsense" (2 Pet. 2:18) enticing people who had just escaped from error (cf. Jude 12). Although they promised freedom, they were actually enslaved by corruption (2 Pet. 3:19–21), and they were like unclean dogs and pigs (2 Pet. 2:22).

The certainty of God's judgment was tied into the creation story (Gen. 1). Just as the Word of the Lord created the world, God's same Word will destroy the world and judge the "impious" (*asebēs*, 2 Pet. 3:5–7, 3:12). God was being patient with humanity because he wished for people to repent rather than perish (2. Pet. 3:9). Further, the timing of God's judgment was not the same as the timing for humanity since "with the Lord a day is like a thousand years, and a thousand years are like a day" (2 Pet. 3:8), but it will arrive suddenly "like a thief" (2 Pet. 3:10; cf. Matt. 24:43; Luke 12:39; 1 Thess. 5:2, 5:4; Rev. 3:3, 16:15; 1 Clem. 23.5). However, after the day of the Lord, when God judges the heavens and earth, God will form from the ashes a new heaven and earth, according to his promises (2 Pet. 3:11–13; cf. Amos 5:18–20). God's ultimate purpose after judgment is to restore creation to its pristine beauty. Considering this final fate, believers were urged to live virtuous lives of "holiness" (*hagios*) and "piety" (*eusebeia*, 2 Pet. 3:11).

Knowing Jesus. Themes of knowing and remembering are prominent in 2 Peter.[35] They were keys to salvation and pious living. With this emphasis on knowledge, Peter was not confronting the sort of knowledge found in later Gnosticism where salvation was attained through secret knowledge. Instead, Peter engaged with the Jewish idea that "knowledge" (Heb. *yadaʿ*) is relational. Correct knowledge of God leads to obeying God (Jer. 24:7, 31:33–34; cf. Isa. 1:2–4; Jer. 9:2–3).[36]

In Jewish scriptures, knowledge is a gift from God (Prov. 1:7) and is connected to divine Wisdom (Prov. 1–9). Knowledge is gained through familiarity and personal experience (Exod. 3:7; Num. 24:15–16). Likewise, Peter stressed the personal quality of knowledge when he wrote, "For we did not follow cleverly devised myths . . . but we had been eyewitnesses of his majesty" (2 Pet. 1:16). Peter wished to convey his personal knowledge of Jesus to his audience, and he reaffirmed their relationship with their exalted Lord. This knowledge would enable them to live pious lives and ensure their ultimate salvation (2 Pet. 1:3).

Knowledge of Jesus helped believers escape the current corrupting influence of the world, and it allowed them to participate in Jesus's divine nature, giving them a foretaste of their ultimate glory (2 Pet. 1:3–4). Conversely, a person leading a sinful life forgets being cleansed from past sins (2 Pet. 1:9). Knowledge of Jesus also results in the fruits of Christian virtues and love (2 Pet. 1:5–8). This knowledge helped believers escape any present entanglements with the defilement of the world (2 Pet. 2:20).

[35] Key terms include "to know" (*oida*, 2 Pet. 1:12, 1:14 2:9), "knowledge" (*gnosis*, 2 Pet. 1:5, 1:6, 3:18; *epignōsis*, 2 Pet. 1:2, 1:3, 1:8, 2:20), "to remember" (*hypomimnēskō*, 2 Pet. 1:12), and "memory" (*hypomnēsis*, 2 Pet. 1:13, 3:1).

[36] Fretheim, "יָדַע," *NIDOTTE*, 2:409–14.

St. Peter's Square. Vatican City.

Knowledge also provides hope. Believers were reminded of the prophetic promises of Jesus's future coming and the judgment of the wicked (2 Pet. 3:1–7). In sum, Peter argued that knowledge of Jesus (2 Pet. 1:3–4) impacted the present through believers' virtuous living (2 Pet. 1:5–9), and it impacted the future through the promise of their admittance into Christ's kingdom (2 Pet. 1:10–11).

Key Terms and People

Baptism: the Christian practice of immersing or sprinkling a convert with water and asking for their confession of faith symbolizes participation in Jesus's death and resurrection
Day of the Lord: an image from the Jewish scriptures to describe the time of final judgment
Pastor: means "shepherd"; a metaphor describing the role of church leaders caring for and protecting God's people as emulating Jesus the Good Shepherd
Ransom: an image of salvation where Jesus's sacrificial death sets people free and redeems them from slavery
Simon Peter: the most prominent of the twelve disciples; after Peter confessed that Jesus was the Messiah, Jesus called Simon the nickname Peter/Cephas, which means "Rock"

Conversation Starters

1. What did you learn about Peter's life? What were some of the most significant events? Do you think he wrote both 1 Peter and 2 Peter?

2. What does 1 Peter teach us about the suffering caused by others? How does 1 Peter give hope to people who are suffering?
3. What did you learn about baptism from 1 Peter? How was baptism linked to the exodus in Jesus's life? How does 1 Peter link this to the flood?
4. What does living a holy life look like in 1 Peter? How does this holy living connect Leviticus's love command with the holiness code?
5. How is the image of a pastor or shepherd helpful for understanding church leadership?
6. What did you learn about the early Christians' relationship to the Roman government? How do you conceive the relationship between faith and politics?
7. Why do you think 1–2 Peter and Jude used the Watchers' tradition?
8. How does 2 Peter present Christian virtues?
9. How does 2 Peter talk about Jesus's second coming and the day of the Lord?
10. What does 2 Peter teach about knowledge in relation to the Christian life?

FOR FURTHER READING

First Peter

Achtemeier, Paul J. *1 Peter: A Commentary on First Peter*. Herm. Fortress, 1996.

Davids, Peter H. *The First Epistle of Peter*. NICNT. Eerdmans, 1990.

Elliott, John H. *1 Peter: A New Translation with Introduction and Commentary*. AYB 37B. Yale University Press, 2008.

Green, Joel B. *1 Peter*. Two Horizons New Testament Commentary. Eerdmans, 2007.

McKnight, Scot. *1 Peter*. The NIV Application Commentary. Zondervan, 1996.

Peter and Jude

Bauckham, Richard J. *2 Peter, Jude*. WBC 50. Word Books, 1983.

Green, Michael. *2 Peter and Jude: An Introduction and Commentary*. Tyndale New Testament Commentaries 18. InterVarsity Press, 1987.

Kelly, J. N. D. *Epistles of Peter and Jude*. BNTC. Continuum International, 1990.

Mason, Eric F., and Troy W. Martin, eds. *Reading 1–2 Peter and Jude: A Resource for Students*. Resources for Biblical Study 77. SBL Press, 2014.

Mbuvi, Andrew Mũtũa. *Jude and 2 Peter*. New Covenant Commentary. Cascade, 2015.

Neyrey, Jerome H. *2 Peter, Jude: A New Translation with Introduction and Commentary*. AYB 37C. Yale University Press, 2008.

Perkins, Pheme. *First and Second Peter, James, and Jude*. Interpretation. Westminster John Knox, 1995.

Watson, Duane F. "The Second Letter of Peter." In *The New Interpreters Bible: General Articles & Introduction, Commentary, & Reflections for Each Book of the Bible*, 12:323–62. Abingdon Press, 1994–2004.

15

JESUS ABIDES

The Gospel of John

Who Was John?

Together, the Fourth Gospel, 1–3 John, and Revelation are called **Johannine literature** because certain church traditions identify John of Zebedee as either the author or the person associated with these works. These works account for about one-third of the New Testament. In these closing chapters, we will turn to this Johannine collection of five works. But first, let's sketch a brief biography of John the disciple.

John was one of Jesus's twelve disciples (Mark 3:13–19; Matt. 10:1–4; Luke 6:12–16). He was known as the son of Zebedee, whose brother was James (Mark 1:19–20, 3:17, 10:35, etc.). John's mother, whose name may have been Salome, was also a disciple of Jesus, and she witnessed Jesus's crucifixion (Matt. 27:56; cf. Mark 15:40). His family lived in Capernaum. The brothers partnered with Peter and Andrew as fishermen before Jesus called the four of them to be his first disciples (Mark 1:16–20; Matt. 4:18–22; Luke 5:2–11). Less flatteringly, James and John were called the "sons of thunder" (Mark 3:17). This nickname reflected their impassioned disposition that sometimes caused them to exclude people (Mark 9:38; Luke 9:49), while at other times zealously wishing to bring judgment upon those who rejected Jesus (Luke 9:54).

SUGGESTED READING

John 1:1-12:19
John 13:1-15:17
John 18:1-21:25

John was part of the inner core of disciples, along with his brother James and Peter. They experienced several privileged moments with Jesus, including witnessing the reviving of Jairus's daughter (Mark 5:35–43; Luke 8:49–56), seeing Jesus's transfiguration (Mark 9:2–8; Matt. 17:1–8; Luke 9:28–36), receiving private instructions (Mark 13:3), and being called to pray with him during his last hours (Mark 14:32–42; Matt. 26:36–46). His mother also famously asked Jesus to appoint her two sons to positions of rule in his future kingdom (Mark 10:35–45; Matt. 20:20–28). However, Jesus replied that he did not have the authority to grant that request. Instead, he promised that they would suffer like him. Then, at the end of Jesus's ministry, John

Public Domain (Getty Images 2C03.35.2)

Saint John, from a Crucifixion. J. Paul Getty Museum. Los Angeles. (c. 1420)

and Peter were entrusted by Jesus to prepare his final Passover meal (Luke 22:8).

After Jesus's resurrection, John continued to lead the church. Paul recognized John, along with Peter and Jesus's brother James, as leaders of the Jewish church (Gal. 2:9; cf. Acts 15). Acts reports several episodes of John's leadership. He was with the disciples as they witnessed Jesus's ascension (Acts 1:6–11). John was with the twelve when they received the Holy Spirit at Pentecost (Acts 2:1–12). He was with Peter when he healed a lame man at the temple (Acts 3:1–10), which led to their arrest and appearance before the Sanhedrin (Acts 4:1–22). As the church grew, John and Peter were sent to Samaria to verify those who were converted by Philip (Acts 8:4–25). When John and Peter laid their hands on these new believers, they received the Holy Spirit.

While the Bible is silent about the end of John's life, later traditions fill out his portrait. Irenaeus (*Haer*. 3.1.1) recorded John moving to Ephesus, where he authored the Fourth Gospel in the eighties or nineties (cf. Justin Martyr, *Dial.* 81). Eusebius (*Hist. eccl.* 3.1.1) wrote that John was allotted the province of Asia when the church was scattered from the land of Israel at the outbreak of the Jewish revolt in 66 CE. According to 1–3 John, the Johannine churches struggled during a period of internal threats from heretics.

Tertullian (*Praescr.* 24) reported that John's time in Ephesus ended after he was submersed in boiling oil. However, he miraculously survived. He was banished by Emperor Domitian to Patmos, where he wrote Revelation in the nineties in order to encourage the churches in Asia Minor that were being persecuted by the emperor (Eusebius, *Hist. eccl.* 3.18.1–3; Irenaeus, *Haer*. 5.30. 3). After Domitian's death, John was permitted to return to Ephesus, where he lived until at least 98 CE (Eusebius, *Hist. eccl.* 3.23.1–6; Irenaeus, *Haer*. 2:22.5). Additional legends about John are recorded in the apocryphal Acts of John.

Who Wrote the Johannine Literature?

While several church traditions identify John of Zebedee as the author of the Fourth Gospel, 1–3 John, and Revelation, the evidence for John's authorship found in these works is more ambiguous. One challenge in determining the authorship of Johannine literature is that the author identified himself differently in the various works. Revelation is the only work to name its author as "John" (Rev. 1:1, 1:4, 1:7, 22:8). The "beloved disciple" is identified as the author of the Fourth Gospel (John 21:20, 21:24). First John does not name its author. Finally, the "elder" is the identity of the author in 2–3 John (2 John 1; 3 John 3).

While the same person may have written all these works, it is unusual that the same author would identify himself so differently. In light of these different identities, it is possible that several people helped write the Johannine literature and were part of a school of disciples entrusted with the traditions of the disciple. Using this model, John the "beloved disciple" wrote the Fourth Gospel, John the "elder" wrote the letters, and John the "seer" wrote Revelation. However, even if a reader accepts the church traditions that identify John of Zebedee as the common author of all these works, it can be helpful to describe the authors of these works by using their self-identifications.

The Fourth Gospel

The Fourth Gospel introduces the "**beloved disciple**" into the narrative during the Last Supper (John 13:23), and he was present at key events during Jesus's last days.[1] He was the only male disciple to witness Jesus's crucifixion, and Jesus entrusted his mother to him while dying (John 19:26–27). After Jesus's resurrection, the beloved disciple witnessed Jesus's empty tomb (John 20:1–10). When Jesus appeared by the Sea of Galilee, the beloved disciple recognized Jesus as he miraculously provided a catch of fish (John 21:1–14). During Jesus's last encounter with Peter and the beloved disciple, a rumor started that he would not die until Jesus returned (John 21:22–23).

According to John 21:24, the author responsible for the traditions used in the Fourth Gospel is the beloved disciple. It says, "*This is the disciple* who is testifying to these things and has written them, and *we know* that his testimony is true" (emphasis added) The first half of the verse claims apostolic authority behind the Gospel because this "disciple" provided his eyewitness testimony. The second half of the verse reveals an editor of these traditions with the expression "we know" his testimony is true. The "we"

Traditional tomb of John the Baptist in Ephesus.

[1] Bultmann (*John*, 484) argues that he is a fictional creation.

represents the community of disciples surrounding the beloved disciple, which verified "his testimony." This "school" of John was responsible for compiling the beloved disciple's traditions and editing in the late eighties or early nineties the final version of the Fourth Gospel that appears in our Bible.

While the disciple is described as "beloved," he is never named. This anonymity allows for several options regarding the disciple's identity. Because he is called "beloved," one option is Lazarus, who was the only male disciple that the Gospel says that Jesus "loved" (John 11:5, 11:36). However, according to tradition, this beloved disciple was John of Zebedee (Irenaeus, *Haer*. 3.1.1; ca. 185 CE).

Johannine Letters

While it is very likely that John of Zebedee was the "beloved disciple" who wrote the Fourth Gospel, the Johannine Letters may have been written by one of his disciples. The letters do not identify the author as John or the "beloved disciple." Instead, the author of 1 John is anonymous, and the author of 2–3 John identified himself as the "elder." A distinction between John the disciple and John the elder was an early church tradition since the days of Papias (ca. 130 CE), who wrote:

> I inquired . . . what Andrew or Peter or Philip or Thomas or James or ***John*** or Matthew, or any other of the Lord's disciples, had said, and what Aristion and the ***elder John***, the Lord's disciple, were saying. (Eusebius, *Hist. eccl.* 3.39.3–4—emphasis added)

The Johannine letters were written in response to heresies growing in the church (1 John 2:18–19, 2:26, 3:7). First John was written by the elder as a commentary illuminating the proper understanding of the Fourth Gospel. Second and Third John were written by the elder as guidance for the community as they navigated these heresies.

Carl N. Toney

Collection of pottery. Israel Museum.

Revelation

Revelation does identify its author as "John" (Rev. 1:1, 1:4, 1:9, 22:8), and some early Christian traditions affirm this was the apostle (Justin Martyr, *Dial.* 81.4).[2] However, this was not a unanimous position (Eusebius, *Hist. eccl.* 3.28.2; Tertullian, *Marc.* 4.5). As early as the third century, Dionysius of Alexandria (Eusebius, *Hist. eccl.* 7.25.6–8, 12–16, 22) distinguished between the author of Revelation and the author of the Fourth Gospel and Johannine epistles. Eusebius thought that John the elder wrote Revelation (*Hist. eccl.* 3.39.3–7).[3]

[2]See also Eusebius, *Hist. eccl.* 3.18.1, 4.18.8; Irenaeus, *Haer.* 4.20.11; Tertullian, *Marc.* 3.14.3, 3.24.4; Clement of Alexandria, *Quis div.* 42; *Strom.* 6.106; *Paed.* 2.108, 2:119; Hippolytus, *Antichr.* 36–42. Some commentators favor the same author for the Gospel and Revelation. For example, Smalley, *Thunder and Love*, 37–40; Mounce, *Revelation*, 31.

[3]Hengel, *The Johannine Question*, 126–27. Some scholars propose that the apostle John wrote Revelation, but not the Gospel. For example, Beasley-Murray, *Revelation*, 33; Barrett, *St. John*, 62, 133–34.

The poor Greek of Revelation is distinct from the Fourth Gospel and the letters, which may indicate someone whose native language was Aramaic or Hebrew.[4] It seems plausible that the author was an unknown Palestinian Jew who immigrated to Asia Minor, possibly due to the Jewish revolt around 66–70 CE, in order to join John's community. To distinguish this author from John the disciple and John the elder, we may call him John the seer.[5] John the seer wrote Revelation to churches in Asia Minor as they faced persecution from the Roman Empire and offered encouragement regarding the return of Christ.

Distinguishing between these three authors is meant to account for the literary differences among these works. But they are all bound together by common themes, and they were likely all written to the same communities in Asia Minor. For some, this distinction will prove useful, and this follows church traditions that identify different authors. Others may wish to stick with the traditions that identify John of Zebedee as the author of all these works.

Carl N. Toney

Stone jars like this one found in Cana may have been what Jesus used to turn water into wine.

What Was John's Version of the Story?

With the Fourth Gospel, we now return to telling stories about Jesus. As we already noted, the Gospel of Mark invented the Gospel genre. Then, Matthew and Luke used his work to create their versions of Jesus's story. While these three Synoptic Gospels tell a similar story, the Fourth Gospel, which was probably the last Gospel written, offers a completely fresh perspective.

Jesus's ministry looks different in the Gospel of John. The Fourth Gospel portrays Jesus as having a three-year ministry with three recorded Passover visits (John 2:13, 6:4, 11:55). In contrast, Jesus's ministry appears to last under one year in the Synoptics with Jesus visiting Jerusalem once at the end of his ministry (Mark 11; Matt. 21; Luke 19). John also rearranges the timeline of Jesus's ministry. For example, in the Fourth Gospel, Jesus began his ministry alongside John the Baptist (John 3:24), while the Synoptics indicate that Jesus's ministry began after John's imprisonment (Mark 1:14–15; Matt. 4:12–17; Luke 4:14–15). In addition, the Gospel of John places Jesus's temple act at the start of his ministry (John 2:13–25), while the Synoptics record it at the end (Mark 11:15–19; Matt. 21:12–17; Luke 19:45–48).

The episodes of Jesus's ministry also look different. In John, Jesus only performed eight miracles, while the Synoptics present a multitude of miracles. Further, Jesus's first miracle was at the **wedding of Cana** (John 2:1–11), while the first recorded miracle in the Synoptics is Jesus exorcising a demon

---

[4] Aune, *Revelation*, 1:clxii–ccxi.

[5] Brown, *An Introduction to the New Testament*, 804.

(Mark 1:21–28; Luke 4:31–37).[6] On the rare occasions when John recounts the same stories, they are given a new twist. According to John, Jesus healed an official's son (John 4:46–54), but the Synoptics record Jesus healing a centurion's servant (Matt. 8:5–13; Luke 7:1–10). John replaced the Eucharistic words of the Last Supper (Mark 14:22–25; Matt. 26:26–29; Luke 22:14–23) with Jesus washing his disciple's feet (John 13:1–20). The day of crucifixion is also different. It occurs on the Day of Preparation in John to coincide with the sacrifice of lambs (Nisan 14; John 19:31). In the Synoptic Gospels, it is portrayed as being on the Passover (Nisan 15; e.g., Mark 14:12, 14:16).[7]

Thus, John offers a unique perspective on Jesus. These differences indicate that the Fourth Gospel tells stories based on traditions independent from the Synoptics, and John provides a distinct historical witness to the life and ministry of Jesus.

Carl N. Toney

The Western Wall of the temple in Jerusalem. The "wall" is the retaining wall of the foundation of Herod's temple. The large stones at the bottom are from Herodian times.

Jesus as the Word of God

Like the other Gospels, the beginning of John offers insight into the purpose of the work. The most distinctive feature of the Gospel of John is its opening chapter or prologue (John 1:1–18). The prologue provides the lens to understand Jesus and read the entire Gospel.[8] It opens with, "In the beginning was the Word [*logos*], and the Word was with God, and the Word was God" (John 1:1). This Word "became flesh and lived among us" (John 1:14). The prologue ends by connecting the Word with Jesus as the Son of God: "No one has ever seen God. It is God the only Son, who is close to the Father's heart, who has made him known" (John 1:18).

"In the beginning was the Word" echoes the first words of the Bible: "In the beginning" (Gen. 1:1 LXX). John connected his story about Jesus as the Word made flesh with the story of creation. In Jewish literature, divine Wisdom acted as God's agent of creation (Prov. 8:22–31; Sir. 24; Wisd. of Sol. 7). Likewise, Jesus as the Word of God is portrayed as the agent of creation (John 1:3–5). The figure of divine Wisdom serves as a vehicle for John to portray the divinity of Jesus in a way that

[6] Matthew's general summary of healings (Matt. 4:23–25) could have included Jesus exorcising the demon from Mark. His first described miracle is the cleansing a leper (Matt. 8:1–4).

[7] On the various views for reconciling these dates, see France, "Chronological Aspects of 'Gospel Harmonization,'" 43–54; Meier, *A Marginal Jew*, 5:1:372–409.

[8] Hoskyns, *Fourth Gospel*, 137.

his audience would understand. As the agent of creation, Jesus's authority and divine rule was established. Jesus's authority is conveyed throughout the Gospel, such as his authority to drive sellers out of the temple (John 2:13–25); perform miracles (e.g., John 5:17); and being in control of his arrest (John 18:4–9), trial (John 18:36–37), and death (John 10:15–18, 19:30).

John's choice of the "**Word**" (*logos*) of God rather than the "Wisdom" of God helped him to engage with larger conversations within Greco-Roman philosophy. "Word" (*logos*) also means "reason." The Greek writer Heraclitus (sixth cent. BCE) described the "Word" (*logos*) as the eternal principle of order in the universe. Stoic philosophers thought divine "Reason" (*logos*) was the foundational principle of the world. Among Jewish thinkers, Philo integrated these ideas and spoke of "reason" (*logos*) as the mediator between God and his creation. By describing Jesus as the Word of God, John connected Jesus to God's creative, life-giving Word that spoke creation into existence (John 1:3; e.g., Gen. 1:3; Pss. 33:6, 33:9; cf. 4 Ezra 6:38; 2 Bar. 14:17). In his ministry, Jesus, as the Word of God, brought life through his healing miracles and eternal life to those who believed in him (John 3:16).

Further, John alluded to the prophetic word of the Lord (Isa 38:4; Hos. 1:1; Joel 1:1; etc.). This prophetic word was associated with God's covenantal promises (Deut. 32:46–47; Pss. 119:105, 119:130) and was effective in accomplishing God's purposes (Isa. 55:11). While prophets and sages came with a fragmentary and incomplete revelation from God, Jesus embodied the full and final disclosure of God (John 14:9; cf. Heb. 1:1–2). For John, the incarnation of Jesus was the revelation of God's ultimate creative activity and his final revelatory Word (John 1:3, 1:10, 1:14, 1:18).[9]

Because of the prologue, the audience perceives Jesus's actions in the rest of the Gospel through a divine lens. Readers know Jesus is divine, and he exerts God's authority. However, the characters in John's story did not have this insight, and they were attempting to figure this out. One way that Jesus revealed his divine identity to characters was through his seven "I am" (*egō eimi*) statements. These statements echoed God's revelation of his divine name to Moses: "I Am Who I Am" (Exod. 3:14). The "I am" statements also emphasized Jesus's life-giving activity. Jesus stated, "I am the . . ."

> "bread of life" (John 6:35)
> "light of the world" showing the life-giving way (John 8:12, 9:5)
> "gate" to the life-giving pasture for the sheep (John 10:9)
> "good shepherd" who lays down his life for the sheep (John 10:11)
> "resurrection and the life" (John 11:25)
> "the way and the truth and the life" (John 14:6)
> "vine" giving life to the branches (John 15:1, 15:5)

In John's narrative, Jesus's opponents were confused because they thought they were talking with Jesus of Nazareth, but according to the Fourth Gospel, they were listening to the incarnate Word of God. By the end of the Gospel, both the audience and characters are meant to agree with the disciple Thomas, who submitted to Jesus's authority and rule when he confirmed Jesus's divine identity by declaring, "My Lord and my God" (John 20:28).

[9] Manson, "Johannine Logos Doctrine," 136–59, esp. 144–45.

Carl N. Toney

John tells the story of Jesus healing a lame man at the Pool of Bethesda in Jerusalem. (John 5:2-9)

However, John did not simply portray Jesus as a divine being. John also emphasized Jesus's humanity. He wrote, "The Word became flesh [*sarx*]" in John 1:14 (cf. 1 John 4:2; 2 John 7). Using the language of "flesh" (*sarx*), the narrative reinforces this idea of the Jesus being a human. For example, Jesus had human emotions like grief (John 11:33–35), feeling anguish (John 12:27, 13:21), being suspicious (John 2:24–25), and getting irritable (John 2:4, 6:26, 7:6–8, 8:25). He had a real body that got tired (John 4:6) and thirsty (John 19:28). When Jesus died, the Fourth Gospel gave details to underscore a real death (John 19:34–35). Likewise, the resurrection stories highlight a real, bodily resurrection (John 20:20, 20:24–27, 21:12–25).[10] By stressing both Jesus's divinity and humanity, John gives a full-orbed presentation of the incarnation of Jesus.

God as Father

The prologue ends by introducing the close relationship between Jesus as the Son with God as his Father. It says, "No one has ever seen God. It is God the only Son, who is close to the Father's heart, who has made him known" (John 1:18).

The fatherhood of God was an essential concept for the Jewish people. Israel understood God as their Father who loved his children (Ps. 103:13).[11] As Father, God founded the nation and called Israel into existence (Jer. 31:9; Deut. 32:4–6). Israel, as God's firstborn son, was saved during the exodus (Exod. 4:23) and given the land of Israel as an inheritance (Jer. 3:19, 31:9; Isa. 61:7–10, 63:16). The king, who was also God's son, represented Israel and was God's agent for dealing with the nation (2 Sam. 7:12–14; Ps. 2:6–8). As Father, God continued to bring salvation to his children (Isa. 63:15–16; Jer. 31:9; Exod. 4:22–23; Hos. 11:1, 11:3). He expected honor and obedience from them (Mal. 1:6, echoing Exod. 20:12) and demanded his children to be faithful to each other (Mal. 2:10). He was also the Father of the most vulnerable Israelites—the orphans and widows (Pss. 27:10; 68:5).

John took this Father-son relationship between God and Israel and applied it to the unique relationship between the Father and Jesus. Jesus repeatedly referred to God as *his* "Father" (*patēr*, eight-three times) and only once called God the Father of the disciples (John 20:17). Just as the Israelite king

---

[10] Thompson, *Incarnate Word.*

[11] Thompson, *God of the Gospel of John*, 64. Interestingly, Philo and Josephus made God's fatherhood more universal (e.g., Josephus, *Ant.* 7.380, 1.230, 2.152; Philo, *Heir* 20; *Dreams* 1.67, 1.76; *Decalogue* 61, 64–65).

represented the nation, so Jesus, as God's Son, was his agent in the world, functioning as God's true and final representative (John 6:57). He was a king, but his kingdom was not of this world (John 18:36–37). As the Son, Jesus shared with his Father intimate knowledge—the same will, mutual love, and common works (John 3:35, 5:20, 10:17). Jesus affirmed his unity with his Father (John 10:30, 14:10–11). But he was also subordinate as the Son (John 5:19, 5:30), and he did only what the Father commanded (John 5:19, 10:18, 14:31).

Jesus's unique relationship with the Father is expressed by describing Jesus as the "only begotten" (*monogenēs*) Son (John 1:14, 1:18, 3:16; cf. Heb. 1:4, 5:5; Ps. 2:7). Only Jesus was the "Son" (*hyios*) of God (mentioned fifty-five times), while his disciples could become "children" (*tekna*) of God (John 1:12). Jesus excluded his opponents by disputing their Israelite claim of God as their Father (John 8:41–42).[12] In fact, only the righteous could be true children of God, and they must believe in Jesus as the Son (John 8:31–59). These believers are described as children "born of God" (John 1:13), and they receive eternal life, which began in this life (John 3:16). The Father is the source of life, and Jesus as God's Son receives this life to give it to others, who were adopted as fellow children of God (John 5:24–29).[13]

The Spirit of God

After the prologue (John 1:1–18), the Fourth Gospel describes the ministry of John the Baptist and introduces the Spirit. The religious leaders approached John asking about the purpose of his baptism (John 1:19–28). John informed them that he was the herald of the messianic "coming one" (*erchomenos*, John 1:15, 1:27; 11:27, 12:13).[14] Upon seeing Jesus, he identified him as "the Lamb of God, who takes away the sin of the world" (John 1:29; cf. John 1:36) to foreshadow Jesus's death like a Passover lamb (John 19:31; cf. Exod. 12:1–20; Num. 9:1–14; Deut. 16:1–8; Ezek. 45:21–25). John also testified that he saw the "Spirit" (*pneuma*) descend upon Jesus like a dove during his baptism as a means of anointing Jesus as Messiah (John 1:32–33). From this point forward, the Spirit is frequently mentioned in the story (John 3:5–6, 3:8, 3:34, 4:23–24, 6:63, 7:39, 11:33, 13:21, 14:17, 14:26, 15:26, 16:13, 19:30, etc.).

Only the Fourth Gospel describes the Spirit as the "**Paraclete**" (*paraklētos*, John 14:15–17, 14:26, 15:26, 15:27, 16:7–11, 16:13–14). The Paraclete is presented in a fashion that emphasizes a personal nature. The term for Paraclete has been translated as "Mediator," "Intercessor," "Counselor," or "Helper." Of

The baptism location of John the Baptist, as depicted by the Madaba mosaic (the oldest surviving map of the Holy Land). (sixth cent. CE)

[12] Thompson, 57–100; Thompson, *Promise of the Father*.

[13] Thompson, "John," 189.

[14] Fitzmyer, *One Who Is to Come*.

GOSPEL OF JOHN

- Prologue: Concerning the Word of God (1:1–18)
- Book of Signs (1:19–12:50)
    - Jesus's Baptism and Andrew's Confession (1:19–51)
    - Ministry from Cana to Cana (2:1–4:54)
        - Sign 1: Changing Water into Wine (2:1–12)
        - The Temple Act, Nicodemus, and the Samaritan Woman (2:13–4:45)
        - Sign 2: Raising the Official's Son (4:46–54)
    - Four Feasts of the Jewish People (5:1–10:39)
        - Sign 3: Sabbath and Healing the Paralytic (5:1–47)
        - Signs 4–5: Passover and Feeding Five Thousand and Walking on Water (6:1–71)
        - Sign 6: Feast of Tabernacles and Healing the Blind Man (7:1–9:41)
        - Feast of Rededication (Hanukkah) and Jesus as the Good Shepherd (10:1–42)
        - Sign 7: Foreshadowing Jesus's Glorification including Raising Lazarus (11:1–12:50)
- Book of Glory (13:1–20:31)
    - Last Supper and Last Discourses (13:1–17:26)
    - Arrest, Trial, and Crucifixion (18:1–19:42)
    - Resurrection (20:1–31)
- Epilogue: Stories of the Resurrection including the Miraculous Catch of Fish (21:1–25)

these, it is best understood in the legal sense as "Advocate," and the Spirit could provide a legal defense (e.g., T. Jud. 20.1, 20.5). Some rabbis understood the Spirit interceding for Israel as its defender (Lev. Rab. 6).[15] Conversely, the Spirit could also prosecute wrongdoing (e.g., Wisd. of Sol. 1:7–9). Likewise, John emphasized the Spirit as a legal advocate in passages such as John 14:15–17 and John 15:26 in which the Spirit prosecuted sin and defended persecuted believers (John 16:7–11).[16]

However, John's usage was not limited to a legal sense. The Advocate was known as the Spirit of Jesus (John 7:38–39, 19:30, 20:22), representing the risen, unseen Lord.[17] The Advocate was portrayed as Jesus's alter ego, which would convey his presence after he was gone (John 16:7). According to John, Jesus is still with his followers because the Spirit is present with believers and mediates his presence. The Spirit made a final dramatic appearance when Jesus imparted the Spirit upon the disciples (John 20:22). And by receiving the Spirit, the disciples possessed the source of eternal life (John 3:3–10, 6:63–65).[18]

[15] Str-B, 2:644–47; Montefiore and Loewe, *Rabbinic Anthology*, 677.

[16] Barrett, *St. John*, 386; Johnston, *Spirit-Paraclete*, 123.

[17] Brown, "Paraclete in the Fourth Gospel," 128; Johnston, *Spirit-Paraclete*, 92–94, 123–25.

[18] Jesus imparted the Spirit while present with his disciples in this upper room, which is a different perspective than Luke's account of the Spirit's coming at Pentecost (Acts 2:1–13).

After Jesus was gone, the Spirit would have the same relationship with the disciples as Jesus did (John 16:28). As the "Spirit of truth" (John 14:17, 15:26), it would teach what Jesus taught (John 16:13). It would remind the disciples of Jesus's actions and words (John 14:26, 16:14). It would lead them to the truth, as embodied in Jesus (John 14:6, 16:13). It would announce the future (John 16:13) as Jesus did (John 4:25–26). It would convict the world of sin (John 16:8) as Jesus did (John 7:7).

The Spirit's presence fulfilled the Jewish hope of the Spirit's coming in the last days (Isa. 32:14–15, 44:3; Ezek. 11:17–19, 36:26–27, 39:29; Joel 2:28–29). Because the Spirit conveyed Jesus's presence, the Fourth Gospel offered hope to a community experiencing persecution and despair because of the delay of Jesus's promised return (John 21:20–25). The Spirit renewed a link, broken by the death of eyewitnesses, for John's community that connected them to the apostolic age. The Spirit's abiding presence with the church fulfilled Jesus's promise to remain with them (John 14:18, 14:19, 14:23, 14:28, 16:16, 16:22). The Advocate provided hope that Jesus remains with his church (John 14:16), guiding (John 16:13) and enabling it to face new problems.[19] The Spirit also anticipated Jesus's future return to raise the dead and grant eternal life, as well as to judge those who had done evil (John 5:26–29, 11:24–26).

Jesus's Friends

The Fourth Gospel includes its version of the calling of the disciples (John 1:29–51) after the prologue (John 1:1–18) and the ministry of John the Baptist (John 1:19–28). The twelve disciples are never identified as a formal group in John. Instead, John introduces several new characters, such as Philip and Nathaniel (John 1:43–51). Rather than Jesus walking along the Sea of Galilee calling Peter, Andrew, James, and John as in the Synoptics, the Fourth Gospel highlights how John the Baptist was responsible for providing Jesus with his first two disciples, including Andrew (John 1:35–42). After encountering Jesus, Andrew encouraged his brother Peter to also follow Jesus. When Jesus returned to Galilee, he called his next two disciples, Philip and Nathanael (John 1:43–51).

After these encounters, Jesus took his disciples to a wedding in Cana, where he performed his first miracle of turning water into wine (John 2:1–12). This miracle, where Jesus created a vast supply of wine, conveyed the abundant power and provision of Jesus. When paired with the feeding of the five thousand (John 6:1–15), these miracles illuminated the wine and loaves of the Lord's Supper.[20] This miracle was the first of seven miracles that formed the distinct structure of the

Carl N. Toney

In Jerusalem, Jesus healed a blind man after he washed in the Pool of Siloam. The pool was fed by waters from the Gihon Spring via Hezekiah's tunnel.

[19] Brown, "Paraclete in the Fourth Gospel," 113–32.

[20] While John did not include the wine and bread of the Eucharist, he told stories of Jesus providing wine and bread that echo the Lord's Supper. After the feeding of the five thousand, Jesus described himself as the "bread of life" and his "flesh" that must be eaten (John 6:22–59).

ministry of Jesus in the Fourth Gospel, and five of these miracles are unique to John. These seven miracles may reflect an early version of the Gospel called the **Signs Source**.[21]

For his second miracle, Jesus healed an official's son at Cana (John 4:46–54). Third, he healed a paralytic on the Sabbath at the pool of Bethesda (John 5:1–47). Fourth, Jesus fed five thousand people (John 6:1–15; Mark 6:30–44; Matt. 14:13–21; Luke 9:10–17). Fifth, Jesus walked across the Sea of Galilee (John 6:16–21; Mark 6:45–52; Matt. 14:22–33). With his sixth miracle, Jesus healed a blind man who washed in the Pool of Siloam (John 9:1–41). The seventh miracle involved Jesus reviving Lazarus from the dead in Bethany (John 11:1–44). These seven miracles were meant to be "signs" (*semeia*) that instilled faith in the disciples (e.g., John 2:11). This is different from the Synoptics where "miracles" (*dynamies*, Mark 6:2; Matt. 11:20–21; etc.) often required faith (e.g., Mark 9:23–24). As the Fourth Gospel concludes, we see the link between Jesus's miracles, faith, and discipleship in the purpose statement, which says,

> Now Jesus did many other signs [*semeia*] in the presence of his disciples, which are not written in this book. But these are written so that you may continue to believe that Jesus is the Messiah, the Son of God, and that through believing you may have life in his name.[22] (John 20:30–31)

Carl N. Toney

Landscape near the Jordan River between Galilee and Judea. John's Gospel is unique in portraying Jesus traveling with his disciples at least three times between Galilee and Judea.

[21] Bultmann, *John*, 6–7.

[22] On this translation, see Brown, *John*, 2:1056.

Jesus was arrested in the Garden of Gethsemane.

Jesus Abides with His Disciples

The Fourth Gospel defines discipleship as simply "**abiding**" (*menō*) with Jesus.[23] Discipleship as abiding is introduced when Jesus called his first disciples, who were invited to abide with him (John 1:38–39). Abiding is linked to following Jesus (John 12:26), which shows the dedication of discipleship (John 8:12, 10:4, 10: 27, 12:26, 13:36, 21:19, 21:22; cf. Mark 1:18, 2:14).[24] For example, Jesus's mother, Mary, is presented as an ideal disciple who followed Jesus from Cana to the cross (John 15:26–27).[25]

Jesus also abided with his disciples (John 2:12, 4:40, 7:9, 10:40, 11:6, 11:54). The concept of Jesus mutually abiding with his disciples is conveyed by Jesus's vine and branch metaphor (John 15:1–17). Abiding in Jesus's love is extended to abiding in God's love and is linked to keeping Jesus's commandments (John 15:9–10). Those who abide with Jesus are set free from sin (John 8:31–38) and will receive eternal life (John 6:55–58).

This emphasis upon abiding helps to explain a tension in the Fourth Gospel created by Jesus continually promising to depart (e.g., John 13:1, 13:33–36, 14:1–5, 14:7–12, 16:4–6, 16:10, 16:28, 17:11, 17:12, 17:13). Yet, the Gospel concludes with Jesus never leaving. In fact, the Fourth Gospel includes the most

[23] Over half of the total uses (118x) of "abide" (*menō*) in the New Testament are found in Johannine literature (68x). The Fourth Gospel (40x), 1 John (24x), 2 John (3x), and Revelation (1x).

[24] Brown, *John*, 1:78.

[25] Latz, "Theology of Abiding in John's Gospel," 161–68.

post-resurrection scenes of all four Gospels. John crafted this conclusion to emphasize the continued abiding presence of Christ among his followers. This is because the mark of discipleship is to abide with Christ, and Jesus had promised to abide with them. John's community was promised that it would continue to experience the abiding presence of Christ through the Spirit.

Correct knowledge is also important for discipleship, and John frequently used terms like "to know" (*ginōskō*) and "to understand" (*oida*), and John's use of these terms reflected the relational aspect of "knowledge" (Heb. *yada*ʿ) from Jewish scriptures.[26] The Father and Son mutually knew each other (John 7:29, 8:55, 10:15, 17:25). Likewise, Jesus and his disciples had a reciprocal relationship. Jesus said, "I am the good shepherd. I know my own and my own know me" (John 10:14). The disciples' knowledge of Jesus and the Father (John 14:7) continued to grow after his glorification (John 12:16, 13:7, 14:9, 16:18, 16:30). In contrast, Jesus's opponents never knew Jesus or the Father (John 7:28, 8:19, 8:27, 8:55, 16:3, 17:25). For John, right knowledge led to right relationships, and proper knowledge led to covenantal obedience (Jer. 24:7, 31:33–34; cf. Isa. 1:2–4; Jer. 9:2–3).

The Call to Love

The Fourth Gospel is also noteworthy for its emphasis upon "**love**" (*agapē*) as the ultimate expression of discipleship and covenantal obedience. The most famous verse in the Bible is John 3:16, which declares that God "loved the world," so he sent his Son to save it. Jesus commanded his disciples to love each other because Jesus loved them (John 13:34–35, 15:12–13, 15:17–19). Love in the Fourth Gospel is community-focused, omitting the Synoptics' inclusion of loving outsiders (Mark 12:28–34; Matt. 22:34–40; Luke 10:25–28). The disciples were also told what not to love—they should not love their own life (John 12:25) or the praise of people (John 12:43). They should hate the darkness but love the light (John 3:19).

Surprisingly, the Fourth Gospel never defines love. Instead, love is shown through the relationships in the story. The Father and Son showed a mutual and reciprocal love for each other (John 3:35, 5:20, 10:17, 14:21, 14:31, 15:9, 17:23–26). Together, the Father and Son loved the disciples (John 13:1, 14:21, 14:23, 15:9–10, 16:27). Jesus's love for Martha and Lazarus led to Lazarus's being revived (John 11:3, 11:5, 11:36). The ideal disciple was beloved by Jesus (John 13:23, 19:26, 20:2, 21:7, 21:20). Jesus's **foot washing** replaced the words of the Lord's Supper found in the Synoptics with a concrete example of loving service (John 13:1–20).

These loving relationships were models for John's community to love each other after Jesus's departure. This love for each other was a sign that John's community lived under the reign of God. When John's community loved each other, they fulfilled Jesus's commands and demonstrated their love for Jesus (John 14:15, 14:21, 14:23, 15:9–10). Disciples were empowered to love each other because the Father and Son loved them. The Gospel concludes with a call to love Jesus and care for fellow believers with the story of Peter being asked to shepherd Jesus's flock as an expression of his love for Jesus (John 21:15–19).[27]

---

[26] Fretheim, "ידָע," *NIDOTTE*, 2:409–14.

[27] Peter's triple response of "I love you" (*phileō*, John 21:15–17) uses the same verb. Jesus changes verbs from "Do you love me?" (*agapaō*, John 21:15–16) to "Do you love me?" (*phileō*, John 21:17) as a stylistic choice using synonyms just as Jesus changes from "lambs" (*arnion*, John 21:15) to "sheep" (*probaton*, John 21:16–17). There is shift toward seeing *agapaō* and *phileō* as synonymous words for love. Thorsteinsson, *Roman Stoicism*, 159–60; Mitchell, *Reconciliation*, 165; Carson, *Exegetical Fallacies*, 26, 30, 51–54.

Jesus's Foes

Carl N. Toney

Ossuary of the high priest Caiaphas. Ossuaries were used to collect the bones of the dead. Israel Museum.

In contrast to Jesus's disciples, "the Jews" (*hoi Ioudaioi*) were Jesus's opponents. The Fourth Gospel was known for its particularly negative portrayal of the religious leaders.[28] Their conflicts with Jesus (John 1:19, 2:13–22) resulted in plotting to kill him (John 5:18, 11:45–53). After pressing Pilate to crucify Jesus (John 18:28–19:16), they witnessed his death (John 19:17–22). Sadly, John's portrayal of the Jews has sometimes been understood as condemning all ethnic Jewish people. This has led to justifying horrific acts, such as the Holocaust.

To avoid antisemitic readings, looking at John's language within its historical context is important. First, Jesus and all the early believers were Jewish. Second, the author, editor, and much of John's audience were Jewish. As such, John's harsh tone reflected insider language of one Jewish group in conflict with another. For the Fourth Gospel, "the Jews" is not a racial designator. Instead, it applies to those who rejected Jesus's messiahship (John 9:24–29).[29]

John's community believed Jesus was the Messiah, while their opponents rejected this claim. This conflict led to the Johannine community being separated from the local synagogue. Modern readers must not confuse John's language as our own. We should be careful how we use language to describe the Jewish people and avoid slipping into intentional or unintentional antisemitic rhetoric.

The Messiah Brings Salvation

John is the only Gospel to transliterate the Hebrew "Messiah" (Heb. *mashiah*) into the Greek (*Messias*, John 1:41, 4:25). It also uses the more common "Christ" (*Christos*). In Johannine literature, Jesus's messianic identity is so entwined that "Jesus Christ" is often used (John 1:17, 17:3; cf. 1 John 1:3, 2:1, 3:23, 4:2, 5:6, 5:20).

While the Synoptics delay and conceal Jesus's messiahship until Peter's confession (Mark 8:27–30; Matt. 16:13–20; Luke 9:18–20), John opens with Peter's brother, Andrew, confessing Jesus to be the Messiah (John 1:41). Later, Peter would confess Jesus to be the "Holy One of God" (John 6:69). Throughout the Gospel, characters wrestled with the nature of Jesus's messiahship, including John the Baptist (John 1:20, 3:28), the Samaritans (John 4:29–30), the Jewish authorities (John 7:52), and the common people (John 7:25–31, 7:40–43, 12:34).[30]

---

[28] This expression is found in John (71x), Matthew (6x), and Luke (5x).
[29] Moloney, *John*, 11.
[30] Barrett, *St. John*, 59–60.

Carl N. Toney

Pilgrims to Jerusalem follow the Via Dolorosa ("Way of Suffering") with fourteen stations of the cross that represent Jesus's journey to his crucifixion.

The Gospel ends by resolving these questions and linking Jesus's messiahship with salvation. John 20:30–31 states that salvation is based on belief in Jesus as the Messiah, the Son of God. As Messiah, Jesus's death on the cross is portrayed as a vicarious martyrdom (John 10:11–18, 11:50–52, 15:13; cf. 4 Macc. 17:22). He died during the slaying of the Passover lambs (John 19:14, 19:31–37; cf. Exod. 12:10, 12:46; Num. 9:12) because he was the "Lamb of God, who takes away the sin of the world" (John 1:29). He remained in control of his life and death, and Jesus only died after he declared, "It is finished" (John 19:30; cf. John 10:17–18).

Throughout the Gospel, Jesus spoke of his death and resurrection as his "hour" (*hora*) of "glorification" (*doxa, doxazō*) (John 17:1–5; cf. John 7:39, 12:16, 12:23–24, 13:1).[31] Jesus described his death as being "lifted up" (*hypsoō*), which has the double meaning of being raised on the cross and being exalted to heaven as he returns to his Father for his glorification and heavenly rule (John 3:14, 8:28). Positively, the cross was the concrete demonstration of Father's love for the world (John 3:14–16) and Jesus's love of his disciples (John 15:13).

God used Jesus's death to bring life to the world (John 17:1–5) and judgment upon the "ruler of the world" (i.e., Satan), who was driven out (John 12:31; cf. John 14:29). The Spirit brought eternal life and cleansed people from sin (John 20:22–23; cf. Jer. 31:31–34; Ezek. 36:25–28; Jub. 1:23; 1QS 4.18–23; 1QH 8.19–20). After Jesus was "lifted up," the life-giving Spirit (John 6:63, 7:38–39) was given to his disciples (John 7:39, 16:7, 19:30, 20:22). Throughout the story, "life" (*zōē, zaō, zōopoieō*) is shorthand for "eternal life" (*zōē aiōnios*). Because life comes when God imparts his "Spirit" (*pneuma*; Heb. *ruah*), eternal life is not simply the extension of limited human life. Life is the impartment of the very life of God that is unending by its nature.

In the closing chapters, Jesus breathed the Spirit upon his disciples, echoing God breathing life into Adam (John 20:19–23; Gen. 2:7). Eternal life was not just for the future (John 14:2–4; cf. Mark 10:17–31; Matt. 18:8–9), nor was it merely symbolic (John 4:13–14).[32] Instead, it begins in the present through faith (John 5:24–26). Both baptism (John 3:3–16) and the Lord's Supper (John 6:54) help connect the present benefits of this life to the future eternal life experienced by knowing God through Christ (John 17:3). These present benefits help assure believers of their future hope of everlasting life.[33] For John, salvation was not some sort of eternal life insurance. Rather, because God is in charge, God's eternal life invades the present and actively transforms the believer and the world.

---

[31] Barrett, 159; Beasley-Murray, *John*, 34–35; Brown, *John*, 1:99–100.

[32] Bultmann, *John*, 302–5; Ashton, *Understanding the Fourth Gospel*, 217; Kysar, *Fourth Evangelist*, 172.

[33] Brown, *John*, 1:cxx–cxxi.

Key Terms and People

Abiding: Jesus abides with his disciples through the Holy Spirit, and discipleship is understood as abiding in Jesus

Beloved disciple: this character is introduced during the Last Supper; the Fourth Gospel presents this disciple as standing behind its account of Jesus's life; the Johannine community affirmed his authority

Disciple John: son of Zebedee, brother of James, and core disciple of Jesus, who, according to tradition, authored the Fourth Gospel, moved to Ephesus, and cared for Mary the mother of Jesus

Foot washing: Jesus washed his disciples' feet as an act of service to demonstrate his love concretely; this scene replaces the words of the Lord's Supper from the Synoptics

Johannine literature: the Gospel of John, 1–3 John, and Revelation are the collection of writings associated with John of Zebedee

Love: the premier Christian virtue; believers are commanded to love each other because of Jesus's love for them

Paraclete: meaning "Advocate," the name uniquely used by John to describe the Holy Spirit

Signs source: the seven miracles recorded in the Gospel of John and possibly the basis of the Fourth Gospel

Wedding of Cana: the first recorded miracle in the Gospel of John where Jesus turns water into wine to illustrate the abundant love of God

Word/Logos: Jesus is described as the divine Word of God who is the ultimate revelation of God; this image draws upon the Jewish tradition of divine Wisdom and the Greek tradition of divine Reason

Conversation Starters

1. What were some highlights from John's life and ministry? What do you think about what some of the later traditions say about John's life?
2. Who was the beloved disciple? How does John 21:24 help us identify the author of the Fourth Gospel?
3. How does the Fourth Gospel tell a unique story about Jesus?
4. What are some significant themes that John's prologue introduces? How does this help connect Jesus's story to the Jewish scriptures?
5. Why was Jesus's abiding presence important in John? How did Jesus convey the Father's presence, and how did the Spirit convey Jesus's presence? How does abiding help explain why Jesus never departed at the end of the Gospel?
6. What do we learn about the Spirit in John? Why did John describe the Spirit as the Paraclete?
7. How does the Fourth Gospel describe love?
8. What are some of the benefits of salvation, according to the Fourth Gospel?

FOR FURTHER READING

Brown, Raymond E. *The Gospel According to John*. 2 vols. AYB 29–29A. Doubleday, 1966.

Burge, Gary M. *The Letters of John: From Biblical Text . . . to Contemporary Life*. The NIV Application Commentary. Zondervan, 1996.

Coloe, Mary L., Mary Ann Beavis, and Barbara E. Reid. *John*. 2 vols. Wisdom Commentary 44A–44B. Liturgical Press, 2021.

Culpepper, R. Alan. *The Gospel and Letters of John*. Interpreting Biblical Texts. Abingdon, 1998.

———. *The Johannine School: An Evaluation of the Johannine School Hypothesis Based on an Investigation of the Nature of Ancient School*. SBLDS 26. Scholars Press, 1975.

Keener, Craig. *The Gospel of John: A Commentary*. Hendrickson, 2003.

O'Day, Gail. "The Gospel of John." In *The New Interpreters Bible: General Articles & Introduction, Commentary, & Reflections for Each Book of the Bible*, 9:493–865. Abingdon, 1994–2004.

Thompson, Marianne Meye. *John: A Commentary*. The New Testament Library. Westminster John Knox, 2015.

16

JOHN'S COMMUNITY IN CRISIS

1-3 John and Revelation

Internal and External Problems

It's a good thing that Jesus promised to abide with John's churches. They needed him as they faced conflicts within their communities. They quickly became divided over how to understand the message of the Fourth Gospel, and these conflicts from the early to mid-nineties were recorded by **John the elder** in his letters of 1–3 John. However, by the end of the century (95–96 CE), these same churches faced external oppression from the Roman Empire, and this conflict was recorded by **John the seer** in Revelation.[1]

The letters of John recorded the struggle of the Johannine community with false teaching. First John provided the standards for correct teaching based on the principles explained in the letter (1 John 2:21, 2:26, 5:13). This letter created a dualist framework of "us versus them" where believers were called to be the children of God, not the children of the devil (1 John 2:18–25, 3:8–9).[2]

SUGGESTED READING

1 John
Revelation 1:1-13:18
Revelation 15:1-16:21
Revelation 18:1-10
Revelation 19:1-2
Revelation 19:11-22:21

Second John recorded the next stage in the struggle. The elder urged the entire church to be on guard against deceivers (2 John 8). They were called to remain pure by not welcoming or receiving these false teachers (2 John 7–11). Instead, the community must focus on their mutual love for one other (2 John 4–6).

Unfortunately, the crisis worsened, and the elder wrote his third letter to the fractured community. The elder's opponent Diotrephes was domineering the congregation (3 John 9). As a result, the elder could no longer address the entire church, and he could only write to his disciple

[1]See the discussion of authorship in the last chapter.
[2]There is a debate on the sequence of the letters. Brown, *Epistles of John*, 14–35.

Gaius (3 John 4).[3] Regrettably, modern readers do not know the outcome of this conflict. However, the letters to the churches in Revelation 2–3 may describe how the various churches in the region of Asia Minor (modern-day western Turkey) responded to these letters and lived out their faith.

What Were the Letters of John All About?

The Importance of Jesus

First John is the longest of the three letters. We might think of it as the first commentary on the Fourth Gospel because it clarifies central theological interpretations of the Gospel, especially concerning understanding Jesus and Christian ethics (1 John 5:13). Second and Third John give insight into the reaction of the community to these issues.

Like the Fourth Gospel, 1 John emphasizes Jesus as the ultimate revelation of God.[4] He was the one sent by God into the world (1 John 4:9–10). Jesus revealed that "God is light" (1 John 1:5),

The seven churches of Revelation and other significant places.

Carl N. Toney

Curetes Street in Ephesus.

[3]For the ways that John the elder responded to false ideas, see Marshall, "Orthodoxy and Heresy in Earlier Christianity," 9. On the relationship between the elder and Diotrephes, see Barrett, *Church, Ministry and Sacraments*, 46, 82.

[4]Painter, *1, 2, and 3 John*, 94.

1 JOHN

- Prologue: The Word of Life (1:1–4)
- Living in the Light (1:5–3:10)
  - God Is Light So Walk in the Light (1:5–2:2)
  - The Command to Love (2:3–11)
  - Resist the World (2:12–17)
  - Warning against Antichrists (2:18–27)
  - God's Children Versus the Devil's Children (2:28–3:10)
- Living by Loving One Another (3:11–5:12)
  - Command to Love One Another (3:11–24)
  - Test the Spirit of Truth Versus Deceit (4:1–6)
  - God Is Love, So Love One Another (4:7–5:4a)
  - Faith Overcomes the World (5:4b–12)
- Epilogue: Call to Remain in the Life (5:13–21)

contrasting the darkness of the world. And believers were called to "walk" (*peripateō*) in the light, meaning they were called to a life of discipleship and "fellowship" (*koinōnia*) with God and believers (1 John 1:6–7). Those in the light had been cleansed from sin and followed the command to love their brothers and sisters (1 John 2:7–11). They were challenged to hate the world and not submit to the desires of the flesh (1 John 2:15–17). In addition, because Jesus revealed that "God is love" (1 John 4:8, 4:16), believers were obligated to love one another (1 John 4:11).

Jesus's humanity was stressed as his coming in the "flesh" (*sarx*, 1 John 4:2–3, 5:6; cf. 2 John 7). His ministry was tangibly experienced as "seen with our eyes," "touched with our hands," and "heard" (1 John 1:1–3). His baptism and crucifixion were described as him coming "by water and blood" (1 John 5:6). For 1 John, Jesus's humanity was essential because it was tied with his salvific death for people (1 John 2:2, 3:16, 4:10).

God's abiding presence with believers is also important in 1 John. God "abides" (*menō*)[5] with those who "confess" (*homologeō*) Jesus (1 John 2:23–23, 4:15), and Jesus's presence gives eternal life (1 John 2:24–25). However, the elder emphasized that this confession must be the right kind of confession. First, a person must believe that Jesus is the Messiah (1 John 2:22, 2:23, 5:1, 5:5; cf. 2 John 9). Second, a person must affirm Jesus's full humanity (1 John 4:2). Third, believers must confess that Jesus is the Son of God (1 John 4:15, 5:5, 5:10, 5:13; cf. 1 John 3:8, 5:12, 5:20). Like the Fourth Gospel, this letter stresses Jesus's unique relationship with God as his "only begotten" (*monogenēs*) Son (1 John 4:9; cf. John 3:16), and

[5]See comments on "abide" (*menō*) below.

2 JOHN

- Letter Greeting the Elect Lady and Her Children (vv. 1-3)
- Love One Another (vv. 4-6)
- Reject the Antichrists (vv. 7-11)
- Letter's Conclusion (vv. 12-13)

believers are called "children" (*tekna*) of God (1 John 3:1, 3:2, 3:10, 5:2; cf. John 1:12, 11:52).[6] It is through Jesus that God's eternal life is granted to believers (1 John 5:10–12).

Overcoming Sin

Another focus of 1 John is dealing with "sin" (*hamartia*, *hamartanō*, 1 John 1:10, 2:1, 3:6, 3:8, 3:9; 5:16, 5:18). Jesus's blood cleanses people from sin (1 John 1:7). His death demonstrated God's love and is an "atoning sacrifice" (*hilasmos*) for the whole world (1 John 2:2, 4:10).[7] Those who sin are children of the devil (1 John 3:8), but the Son exerts his authority by destroying the devil's work (1 John 3:8). Jesus's death frees people from sin and makes believers children of God (1 John 2:12–14, 5:1). God's children are promised that they will overcome the world (1 John 5:4–5). His children also walk in God's light (1 John 1:7). Although sinners abide in death (1 John 3:14), Jesus gives his followers life (1 John 4:19, 5:13).

John the elder held up the ideal that believers who abide in Christ and are born of God should not sin (1 John 3:6, 3:9, 5:18). The elder hoped this ideal would encourage believers to avoid sinning (1 John 4:10, 4:14). This ideal that believers should be sinless (1 John 3:1–10) stands in contrast with the reality that everyone sins (1 John 1:1–2:2), and anyone who claims to be sinless is delusional (1 John 1:8). Believers must regularly confess their sins to be forgiven and purified (1 John 1:7–10, 2:1, 5:16–17).

Carl N. Toney

Circular monument in Domitian Square with the Temple of Domitian in the background. Ephesus. (89-90 CE)

First John may also be distinguishing between two kinds of sin—unintentional sin versus intentional sin (Lev. 4:2, 4:13, 5:14, 5:17; Num. 15:29–30). One view is that unintentional sin can be forgiven (1 John 5:16–17; cf. 1 John 1:79–2:2) but intentional sin cannot (1 John 5:18, 3:1–10). A true believer should never intentionally sin (1 John 5:18). Another view is that 1 John may have specific sins in mind that are unforgivable, like idolatry

[6] God was willing to sacrifice his only Son like Abraham was willing to sacrifice Isaac (Gen. 22:2, 22:12, 22:16; cf. Heb. 11:17). Brown, *Epistles of John*, 516–17, 551.

[7] The New Testament draws upon the *hilaskomai* word family to speak of Jesus's atoning sacrifice (Rom. 3:25; Heb. 2:17, 9:5; 1 John 2:2, 4:10). See comments in the footnote on Romans 3:25 in Chapter Ten.

Political agora and terracotta freshwater pipes in Ephesus.

(1 John 5:21), denying Jesus as the Christ (1 John 2:22), or denying the atoning sacrifice (1 John 4:10). Most likely, 1 John presents a person's susceptibility to sin in relationship to how well a person abides in Christ. Those who fully abide in Christ will not be susceptible to sin (1 John 3:1–10, 5:18), but those who abide less with Christ will sin and need forgiveness (1 John 1:7–2:2, 5:16–17). The more believers abide in Christ, the less they will sin.[8]

The Ethic of Love

The command to "love one another" is central to Johannine ethics. This command is based on the new command Jesus gave his disciples in the Gospel (John 13:34–35, 15:12, 15:17). Love was so essential for the community that the command is mentioned seven times in these letters (1 John 3:11, 3:14, 3:23, 4:7, 4:11, 4:12; 2 John 5).[9]

Notably, John the elder affectionately called his audience "beloved" (*agapētoi*, 1 John 2:7, 3:2, 3:21, 4:1, 4:7, 4:11; cf. 3 John 1, 2, 5, 11). This expression of endearment connected the community to the ideal beloved disciple in the Fourth Gospel (John 13:23, 19:26–27, 20:3–10, 21:1–14, 21:20–24). It also identified John's community with Israel as God's beloved (Jer. 6:26, 31:20; Pss. 60:7, 108:7, 127:2; cf. Rom. 1:7). This reminded the community that because God first loved them, they should embody God's love by loving each other (e.g., 1 John 4:11; cf. John 13:34, 15:12, 15:17).[10]

---

[8] Painter, *1, 2, and 3 John*, 102–3.

[9] Painter, 265–66.

[10] Brown, *Epistles of John*, 264.

3 JOHN

- Letter Greeting Gaius (vv. 1-2)
- Praise for Hospitality (vv. 3-8)
- Diotrephes Is Condemned, while Demetrius Is Praised (vv. 9-12)
- Letter's Conclusion (vv. 13-15)

According to John, they were to love each other as a family—as children, brothers and sisters, and fathers (1 John 2:9–11)—and as fellow children of God (1 John 3:1). Those who did not love their brothers and sisters abided in death (1 John 3:14). A lack of love indicated that they were not God's children but were the devil's children (1 John 3:12, 3:15). Being children of the devil identified them with those who tried to kill Jesus (John 8:39–44) and Judas, whom the devil entered when he betrayed Jesus (John 13:2, 13:27; cf. John 6:70–71). Further, when they hated their brothers or sisters, they were like Cain, whose hatred led to the murder of his brother (1 John 3:12, 3:15; Gen. 4:1–16).[11]

Believers only love because God first loved them (1 John 4:10, 4:19). God's love is demonstrated by sending his Son (1 John 4:10, 4:14, 4:19) and by giving his Spirit (1 John 4:13). Because God loved the community, they ought to love each other, and his love was made "complete" (*teleioō*) in the community (1 John 4:11–12).[12] Believers are begotten as children of "God [who] is love" (1 John 4:8, 4:16). By nature, the true children of a loving God will display his love. Through love for others, believers grow in their knowledge of their Father. Further, knowing God is necessary for loving one another (1 John 4:7), and loving others is necessary for knowing God (1 John 4:8).

In some ways, the Johannine love command sounds like the love command found elsewhere in the New Testament (Matt. 22:36–40; Mark 12:28–31; Luke 10:25–28; cf. Rom. 13:9; Gal. 5:14). This tradition extends the command in the Jewish scriptures to love one's neighbor (Lev. 19:18) to all people, as illustrated in the parable of the good Samaritan (Luke 10:29–37). This love is even extended to include one's enemies (Matt. 5:44).

However, for the Johannine community, this command was given a narrower scope. The command to "love *one another* [*allēlous*]" (1 John 3:11—emphasis added) focused on John's community (cf. John 13:34, 15:16–17). Believers were urged not to love the world (1 John 2:15–16), which hated them (1 John 3:13). Instead, they were called to love each other because they had passed from death to life (1 John 3:14). Their love for one another included a willingness to lay down their lives for other believers, as well as tangibly helping other community members in need (1 John 3:16–17).[13] Their love for one another should not be abstract, and the community was urged to "love, not in word or speech, but in truth and

[11] Brown, *Epistles of John*, 468–71.

[12] Recall from our discussion about James that language of "completion, perfection" describes something living up to its full potential.

[13] Brown, *Epistles of John*, 271–73.

action" (1 John 3:18). This love for each other marked John's community as distinctively living under the reign of God.

The Importance of Hospitality

Related to the command to love one another is the importance of hospitality. Hospitality may be understood in terms of the community "abiding" (*menō*) in God (1 John 2:6, 2:10, 2:14, 2:17, 2:19, 2:24, 2:27–28, 3:6, 3:9, 3:14, 3:15, 3:17, 3:24, 4:12, 4:13, 4:15–16; 2 John 2, 9).[14] God abides in those who properly confess Jesus as the Son of God (1 John 2:27, 4:13–16), and those who love other believers abide in God (1 John 2:6, 2:10, 4:16). Those who abide in God share fellowship with one another. This may be drawing upon the true vine image in the Fourth Gospel (John 15:1–6) as well as Jesus's language of wishing his disciples to be "one" as he and the Father are "one" (John 17:11, 17:21–22).

First John highlights how mutual "fellowship" (*koinōnia*, 1 John 1:3, 1:6–7), especially in the sense of sharing something in common, expresses hospitality. Believers may share material goods, such as when they help the poor (1 John 3:17). Sharing also includes sharing common spiritual benefits, such as sharing a common Spirit (1 John 3:24). Believers benefit from their common fellowship with the Father

Carl N. Toney

Library of Celsus in Ephesus (built ca. 110-35 CE).

[14]"Abide" (*menō*) is used to describe the believer in God (1 John 2:6, 3:24, 4:13, 4:15, 4:16), the believer in Jesus (1 John 2:27, 2:28, 3:6; cf. John 6:56), the believer in Jesus and the Father (1 John 2:24), and God in the believer (1 John 3:24, 4:12, 4:13, 4:15, 4:16). Brown, 259–60.

REVELATION

- **Prologue (1:1–20)**
- **Letters to Seven Churches (2:1–3:22)**
- **First Apocalyptic Cycle (4:1–11:19)**
  - God and the Lamb Enthroned (4:1–5:14)
  - Seven Seals (6:1–8:1)
  - Seven Trumpets and Two Witnesses (8:2–11:19)
- **Second Apocalyptic Cycle (12:1–22:9)**
  - Seven Signs including the Dragon, Woman, and Beasts (12:1–14:20)
  - Seven Bowls (15:1–16:21)
  - The Fate of Babylon (17:1–19:10)
  - Victory over God's Enemies (19:11–21:8)
  - The New Jerusalem (21:9–22:7)
- **Epilogue (22:8–21)**

and Son (1 John 1:3, 1:6) and fellowship with each other (1 John 1:7). This fellowship with God and other believers allows the community to share the positive characteristics of God as they love one another.

Second John 7–11 warns against fellowship with those not holding proper beliefs because this leads to "sharing" (*koinōneō*) their evil deeds (2 John 11). Third John 5–10 encourages hospitality toward faithful believers and chastises those who will not welcome them. Because people share the traits of those they fellowship with, it is important to only love and fellowship with fellow believers, not the world. The letters of John encourage a healthy community of believers. While these letters addressed internal threats to the church, the final book of the Bible, Revelation, helped the church face external threats from society. It is to that book we now turn.

How to Read Revelation

Let's be honest—Revelation is weird and confusing. It cannot be easy to figure out how to apply the work to the present context. Some readers approach Revelation as a **preterist**, understanding the book as primarily directed toward its first-century context with most predictions already being fulfilled. A second approach, the **historicist**, reads the work as offering predictions over the entire history of the church, from the first century until the time when Jesus comes again. Third, an **idealist** sees the book as speaking to greater principles about the conflict between good and evil before the final return of Christ. Finally, a **futurist** considers the book to focus on the last days of the church. For many readers, taking a combination of these approaches is most helpful.

The work consists of a variety of genres. Notably, the first chapters include letters addressed to churches in Asia Minor, which situates the message in its first-century context. Since it addressed a persecuted church, some suggest it was composed in response to Nero's persecution of Roman Christians (64 CE) or after the fall of Jerusalem under Vespasian and Titus (70 CE). However, early Christian writers dated the composition during the end of Domitian's reign (ca. 95–96 CE; Eusebius, *Hist. eccl.* 3.18.3, 5.8.6). This is confirmed by the work if **Domitian** is the eighth king mentioned in Revelation 17:9–11.[15]

Public Domain

Fresco depicting scenes from Revelation. Osogovo Monastery. Macedonia.

This work also labels itself as a "prophecy" (Rev. 22:7–19; cf. Rev. 1:3, 10:11, 19:10), and Revelation is full of allusions to prophetic material, especially Ezekiel and Daniel. The focus on prophecy in Revelation is not on foretelling—that is, predicting the future. Instead, its focus is upon "forth-telling," meaning it provides God's perspective and guidance about events, whether they occur in the past, present, or future. This divine perspective offers insight into godly living in the present.

Equally important is the title the "Apocalypse of Jesus" (Rev. 1:1, 22:6).[16] **Apocalypse** means "revelation" or "unveiling." In the Jewish scriptures, Daniel 7–12 is apocalyptic literature.[17] As an apocalypse, Revelation presents a highly symbolic vision mediated by a heavenly being to a human that reveals the future and/or the spiritual reality behind our physical reality. Revelation is an apocalypse that reveals God's actions in human history and demonstrates that God is in control. As an apocalypse, Revelation inspires hope and calls for a response to live according to God's standards.[18] Additionally, as an apocalypse, Revelation is full of wild and confusing imagery. This is because John was invited to "Write in a book what you see" (Rev. 1:11). As a book overflowing

[15] The following are the eight emperors in Revelation 17: (1) Augustus (27 BCE–14 CE), (2) Tiberius (14–37 CE), (3) Gaius Caligula (37–41 CE), (4) Claudius (41–54 CE), (5) Nero (54–68 CE), [Galba-Otho-Vitellius (68–69 CE)], (6) Vespasian (69–79 CE), (7) Titus (79–81 CE), and (8) Domitian (81–96 CE). Galba, Otho, and Vitellius are not part of the eight since their reigns did not last because Vespasian came back to Rome from Israel to claim his rule as the sixth emperor.

[16] Aune, *Revelation*, 1:lxxvii.

[17] Other Jewish scriptures that exhibit the features of the apocalyptic genre include Isaiah 24–27, 56–66, Zechariah 9–14, and Joel 2–3. Noncanonical apocalyptic Jewish writings include 1 Enoch, 2 Enoch, 2 Baruch, 3 Baruch, 4 Ezra, the Apocalypse of Abraham, the Testament of Abraham, and the Testament of Levi 2–5.

[18] Collins, "Toward the Morphology of a Genre," 9; Collins, "Early Christian Apocalypticism," 7.

Temple in Laodicea in the second cent. CE. The church in Laodicea was challenged for being lukewarm but promised to co-rule with Christ if they repented (Rev. 3:14-22).

with stunning visuals, Revelation invites us to embrace its imagery, visualize what we read, and use our imaginations.[19]

God's Sovereignty versus the Empire

We opened this book with the question, "Who is in charge?" During the time of the New Testament, Roman rule made it apparent that Rome was in charge. However, from the Gospel of Matthew to Revelation, the New Testament authors have made the counterclaim that God is truly in charge. Of all the works in the New Testament, Revelation makes the strongest critique of Roman rule.

Revelation begins and ends by affirming the sovereignty of God. The opening verses describe God as the "Alpha and the Omega," the one "who is and who was and who is to come," and the "Almighty" (Rev. 1:8). Similarly, the work ends describing Jesus as the "Alpha and Omega," "first and last," and "beginning and end" (Rev. 22:13). These related descriptions of God and Jesus reinforce their divine rule over creation. When John's gaze shifts toward heaven, he sees an opening vision of God's rule. God and Jesus as a lamb appear enthroned and being worshiped at the center of heaven (Rev. 4:1–5:14). This throne is referenced thirty-four times, and the vision provides the foundation for God's authority to judge and redeem throughout the entire work.

In contrast to the vision of the lamb, halfway through the work John presented a vision of a dragon, who represents the **devil** as the heavenly challenger to God's rule (Rev. 12:1–17). The devil was also known

[19] For a reading that encourages the imagination, see McKnight and Matchett, *Revelation for the Rest of Us*.

as Satan, whose name means "adversary" or "accuser" (Job 1–2; 1 Chron. 21:1; Zech. 3). Readers of the New Testament first encounter Satan being defeated by Jesus during his wilderness temptations (Mark 1:12–13; Matt. 4:1–11; Luke 4:1–13). Jesus also defeated his minions whenever he exorcised demons (e.g., Mark 1:21–28). Throughout the New Testament, the devil is the believer's enemy (e.g., Eph. 6:11; Heb. 2:14; James 4:7; 1 Pet. 5:8).

In Revelation, the devil is portrayed as a dragon to recall images from Jewish scriptures of the serpent in the Garden of Eden (Gen. 3:1–19) and the sea monster leviathan (Job 3:8, 41:1; Pss. 74:14, 104:26; Isa. 27:1). In the vision, the dragon fails its attempt to consume a pregnant woman's child (Rev. 12:1–6, 12:13–17). The child—who is the Messiah—is taken to God's heavenly throne (cf. Pss. 2, 110). The woman—who represents either Mary, Israel, or the church—flees to the safety of the wilderness. The dragon also leads a failed heavenly coup (Rev. 12:4). When he is defeated, he and his angels are cast out of heaven (Rev. 12:7–9), and he raises a rebellion against God's people through the earthly power of Rome (Rev. 13:1–2). However, this rebellion will not succeed, and the devil and his followers will ultimately be defeated by the end of the work (Rev. 20:7–10).

The Roman Empire is portrayed as the earthly embodiment of Satan's rebellious rule. The emperor (Rev. 13:1–10) and priests (Rev. 13:11–18) are described as vicious beasts. The **mark of the beast** is 666, calculated according to the principles of gematria. The letters spelling "Nero Caesar" add up to 666.[20] Those who received this mark of the emperor did so to show their loyalty to the empire (Rev. 13:18; cf. Rev. 14:9–11, 16:2, 19:20, 20:4). In contrast to those receiving the mark of the beast, believers will have their names written in the book of life (Rev. 13:7–10). The power of Rome was both alluring and destructive, as illustrated by the image of being a prostitute like Babylon (Rev. 17:1–6, 17:15–16, 18:3). The empire demanded undivided loyalty (Rev. 13:17, 18:11–13). It ignored the suffering of the innocent and perpetuated violence against the righteous (Rev. 13:7, 18:24). Rome represented a society that stood against God and claimed his power and authority (Rev. 13:5–6).

Illustration of the Mark of the Beast in the *Elizabeth Day McCormick Apocalypse*. University of Chicago Library. (1650)

However, Rome would face God's judgment for its injustice and aligning itself with the devil's rebellion against God's rule (Rev. 19:11–21, 20:7–15). God remained in control of the historical process that would usher in the return of Christ, the overthrowing of evil, and the sovereign reign of God over all creation. Knowing that God is in control offered the church hope, challenged believers not to be tempted by Roman power or influence, and compelled them to worship God. Believers were called to live ethical lives, following

[20] Gematria is when the numerical value is assigned to a word or phrase by adding the value of the letters. Using the following values: *w* = 6; *n* = 50; *s* = 60; *q* = 100; and *r* = 200, we get 666 from the transliteration of the Hebrew *qsr nrwn* when we add 360 (*qsr*) plus 306 (*nrwn*). The variant reading of 616 reflects the alternative transliteration of *qsr nrw* when we add 360 (*qsr*) plus 256 (*nrw*).

The reconstructed altar to Zeus in Pergamum. Pergamon Museum, Berlin. The church of Pergamum was promised a new name if they repented (Rev. 2:12-17).

the example of Christ who died but was vindicated. In the end, Revelation reminds everyone that God is in charge.

The Judgment of God

The promises of God's ultimate defeat of evil and his presence with his people are the foundation for the final exhortation for believers to remain faithful (Rev. 22:6–21). God's judgment of the world is vividly portrayed throughout Revelation with the seven seals (Rev. 6:1–8:1), seven trumpets (Rev. 8:2–11:19), and seven bowls (Rev. 15:1–23). The first four seals are known as the four horsemen of the apocalypse—conquest, war, famine, and death (Rev. 6:1–8; cf. Zech. 1, 6). The fifth seal gives voice to the martyrs pleading for vindication (Rev. 6:9–11). The sixth seal returns to judgment with the world cataclysmically undone through earthquakes, a darkened sun, a bloody moon, and the stars falling from the sky (Rev. 6:12–17).

The seventh seal (Rev. 8:1) leads to the blowing of the seven trumpets (Rev. 8:2–11:19).[21] The first four trumpets echo the plagues of Egypt, reminding the audience that the purpose of God's judgment is the deliverance of God's people (Rev. 8:6–13; Exod. 7:8–13:16; cf. Pss. 78:43–52, 105:27–36; Amos 4:6–13). The fifth trumpet causes the plague of locusts (Joel 1:6, 2:1–5, 2:10) led by the angel whose two names means "death" ("Abaddon" in Hebrew; cf. Job 26:6, 28:22) and "destruction" ("Apollyon" in Greek). With the sixth trumpet, four angels wipe out a third of humanity (Rev. 9:13–21). The seventh trumpet announces the impending triumph of God (Rev. 11:15–19). After this scene, Revelation seems to reset its timeline as it tells of the conflict between the dragon and the hosts of heaven (Rev. 12:1–18).

Remains of an ancient portico in Thyatira in modern Turkey (fourth cent. CE). The church in Thyatira was praised for its deeds but chastised for its tolerance of sin (Rev. 2:18-29).

[21]The trumpets signify divine anger (e.g., Caesar, *Civ.* 3.105; Lucan 1.578; Sib. Or. 8.239), the day of the Lord (e.g., Amos 5:18–20; Zech. 9:14; Zeph. 1:14–16; 4 Ezra 6.23), and the return of Christ (e.g., Matt. 24:31; 1 Cor. 15:52; 1 Thess. 4:16; Did. 16:6). Aune, *Revelation*, 2:519.

Violence in Scripture

The Jewish scriptures are full of violent stories. In order to liberate Israel, God struck Egypt with deadly plagues (Exod. 7–11), killed the firstborn Egyptian infants (Exod. 12:29–32), and destroyed Pharoah's army (Exod. 14:1–31). Joshua and Judges tell stories of the conquest of the land (e.g., Josh. 10:40–43, 11:20–23). Israel was commanded to annihilate the Canaanites (Deut. 20:16–18) and Amalekites (1 Sam. 15:1–7). These stories contrast Jesus's teachings about non-retaliation (Matt. 5:38–42; Luke 6:29–39), enemy love (Matt. 5:43–48; Luke 6:27–36), his general rejection of violence (Matt. 26:52; Luke 9:51–56), and his willingness to die on the cross (Mark 15:21–32; Matt. 26:32–44; Luke 23:26–43; John 19:16–27).

The New Testament also has violent texts. Some have interpreted Jesus's exorcising the legion of demons (Mark 5:9–13; Luke 8:30–33), teachings about future judgment (e.g., Matt. 5:30, 10:28, 13:37–43, 21:33–46, 25:31–46), cursing the fig tree (Mark 11:20–25; Matt. 21:18–22), temple actions (Mark 11:15–19; Matt. 21:12–17; Luke 19:45–48), and command to purchase a sword (Luke 22:36) as violent. In the days of the early church, Ananias and Sapphira were killed by the Holy Spirit (Acts 5:1–11). Revelation includes God striking the earth with plagues reminiscent of the exodus (Rev. 6:1–8:1, 8:2–11:19, 15:1–23). Jesus is also cast as a divine warrior, leading the armies of heaven (Rev. 19:1–21). And the work ends with God's enemies either being completely destroyed or eternally punished in the lake of fire (Rev. 20:7–15).

Public Domain

The First Seal of Apocalypse and the White Rider of War illustrated in the *Tolkovy Apocalypse*, Moscow. (seventeenth cent. CE)

So, what do we do with the stories of violence in Scripture?[22] Some consider any form of divine-sanctioned violence as permittable and even praiseworthy.[23] Others would say that if God is just and holy, then we must assume that these actions are done according to his character.[24] When God destroys or commands his people to destroy his enemies, it is the correct response to human sin. Jesus's death offers payment for sin, but those who reject God's grace are subject to the final judgment in Revelation. Others contextualize the violence within ancient times, arguing that it was necessary to form and protect the nation of Israel. So, some forms of violence may be permitted when it comes to self-defense or protecting others. Others trace an arc of redemption from the stories of Israel to the time of Jesus, who ultimately

[22]This paragraph is based on Webb and Oeste's five-category grid: (1) The traditional "plus" sees no ethical problems because God is morally free to do anything he wants. (2) The traditional view understands these texts as difficult because God must act within his holy and just character. (3) The "realigned" traditional view traces a redemptive movement toward Jesus's ethic. (4) The antitraditional view sees violent texts as inaccurate, human representations of God in contrast to Jesus's full revelation. (5) The antitraditional "plus" perceives the God of these texts as unredeemable. Webb and Oeste, *Bloody, Brutal, and Barbaric?*, 20. Alternatively, Trimm provides four categories: (1) God is not good. (2) The Jewish scriptures are not faithful records. (3) The stories are not genocide. (4) The violence was situationally permitted. Trimm, *Destruction of the Canaanites*.

[23]Beale, *Morality of God*.

[24]Longman and Reid, *God Is a Warrior*.

revealed God's character.[25] Some would say that Jesus could teach a nonviolent ethic because he relied upon the justice of God.[26] Still others consider Jesus's nonviolent ethic in critiquing violent texts, revealing them as flawed, human misrepresentations of God's will.[27] For others, the Bible is a violent religious text and should be critiqued.[28]

In the end, readers of both the Jewish scriptures and the New Testament must wrestle with violent texts. Thankfully, modern interpreters are given a variety of options for making sense of the violence in the biblical text. More importantly, we can use the Bible to help us make ethical decisions as we encounter violence in our world.

The final series of seven in Revelation are the bowls of wrath (Rev. 16:5–23; cf. Isa. 51:17–23). Unlike the trumpets, the full judgment of God is meted out with the bowls, and there is no longer a "one third" qualifier. The first five bowls—skin diseases, the bloody sea, bloody rivers, the scorching sun, and darkness—echo the plagues of Egypt (Rev. 16:5–11). The sixth bowl dries up the Euphrates River to prepare for the defeat of the armies from around the world at Armageddon (Rev. 16:12–16).[29] This scene echoes the parting of the Red Sea and the destruction of Pharoah's army by its waters. The final bowl causes a great earthquake and the defeat of Rome (Rev. 16:17–21).

Following the bowls of wrath is a description of the complete ruin of Rome (Rev. 17:1–19:10) and a vision of Christ riding in judgment on a great white horse (Rev. 19:11–21). God's enemies will receive their final judgment when thrown into the lake of fire. These enemies include the beast who represents Rome, the false prophet representing the priests of the imperial cult of Rome (Rev. 19:19–20), Satan (Rev. 20:10), Death, Hades (Rev. 20:14), and anyone who opposes God (Rev. 20:15). This final judgment of God proves he is in ultimate control. Just as the Roman Empire did not last and underwent God's judgment, so all empires of all ages that stand against God's people face judgment. Whatever evil and suffering the church may face, it can be reassured by the final victory of God at the end of Revelation.

Suffering and Hope

Revelation is full of stories of God's people suffering, including the 144,000 martyrs (Rev. 7:1–17, 14:1–5), the two witnesses who were killed (Rev. 11:1–14), the woman chased by the dragon (Rev. 12:1–6, 12:13–17), the saints whom the first beast made war against (Rev. 13:7–8), and those not worshiping the image of the first beast whom the second beast killed (Rev. 13:11–18).

God's sovereignty is meant to reassure those suffering because they know that the power of their enemies will not last (Rev. 13:10, 14:12). Yet if God is in control, then why does he permit or tolerate this suffering?[30] First, we can distinguish between the unjust suffering caused by Satan and his earthly agents

[25] Webb and Oeste, *Bloody, Brutal, and Barbaric?*

[26] Volf, *Exclusion and Embrace.*

[27] Seibert, *Violence of Scripture.*

[28] This position is often taken up by the New Atheists. Anyone believing in biblical inspiration would not hold a position that rejects the Bible in its entirety.

[29] Some Christian traditions read this as a final great battle near the "mountain of Megiddo" (Heb. *har megiddo*), and the location is debated. It is possibly in northern Israel near the city of Megiddo, which was strategic for defending Israel from invasions (1 Kings 9:15). The Valley of Megiddo is an ancient battleground, including where King Josiah died (2 Kings 23:29–30; 2 Chron. 35:22).

[30] Caird, *Revelation*, 81–83.

like Rome versus the just punishments of God. Second, Revelation falls in the same vein as the Jewish scriptures that portray God justly punishing the wicked while also disciplining his children (e.g., Gen. 6–8; Exod. 7–11; Zech. 6:1–8; Ezek. 14:21; Lev. 26:18–28). Third, trials and suffering can have redemptive elements that refine the faith of believers and punish unbelievers. Finally, God uses the suffering of believers as he used Christ's suffering as part of his triumph over the powers of evil when he transforms that defeat into victory.[31]

Jesus's death and resurrection are examples for believers who are suffering. Just as Satan was defeated by the cross (Rev. 5:5–10), those who persecute the church, including the Roman Empire, are defeating themselves through their oppression. Oppression results in the vindication of God's people and God's judgment of the oppressors (Rev. 8:2–11:19). Believers who suffer will share in Christ's victory over evil and death (Rev. 5:6, 15:2, 17:14). According to Revelation, the anti-God society of Rome would eventually be judged (Rev. 17:1–19:21). There will be a coming day of "wrath" (Rev. 6:12–16). At the end of Revelation, those who endure suffering are victorious and given a place in the new heaven and earth (Rev. 21:9–22:5), while the oppressors and the faithless are thrown into the lake of fire (Rev. 21:7–8).

Carl N. Toney

The church at Smyrna was praised for its steadfastness during persecution (Rev. 2:8-11).

[31] Beale, *Revelation*, 172–73.

These ruins of Sardis include the temple to Artemis and the acropolis. The church in Sardis was called to repentance for being spiritually dead and given the promise of eternal life (Rev. 3:1-6).

Revelation casts a grand vision where believers do not merely endure but actually conquer the forces of evil through their suffering. "The Lamb's followers are to recapitulate the model of his ironic victory in their own lives; by enduring through tribulation, they reign in the invisible kingdom of the Messiah."[32] This future victory gives believers hope in the present. Revelation reminds its audience that God's judgment over their enemies is imminent, final, absolute, and severe. The work peels back the earthly reality of Roman rule to reveal the true reign of God. Considering this insight, the audience is challenged to choose the church instead of the empire.

The Worship of God

Because God is in charge, he is worthy of worship. Throughout Revelation, people and heavenly beings continually "worship" (*proskyneō*) God and Christ (Rev. 4:10, 5:14, 7:11, 11:1, 11:16, 14:7, 15:4, 19:4, 19:10, 22:8). God is worthy of this worship because he accomplishes his purposes of judgment and salvation (Rev. 1:6, 4:11, 5:11–13, 11:17, 19:1, 19:5, 19:7).

However, Satan and the empire also demand worship. Thus, people must decide whether to worship God or the empire. This contrast is portrayed by the proper worship of God and the lamb (Rev. 4–5) versus the improper worship of Satan and the beast (Rev. 12–14). While God and Christ should be

[32] Beale, *Revelation*, 171.

glorified (Rev. 1:6, 4:9, 4:11, 5:12, 5:13, 7:12, 15:4, 21:11, 21:23), Rome was condemned for glorifying itself (Rev. 18:7). Although people were encouraged to worship God (Rev. 1:6, 4:11, 5:11–13, 19:1, 19:5, 19:7, 11:17), those who improperly worshiped demons (Rev. 9:20), the dragon (Rev. 13:4), and the beast (Rev. 13:4, 13:8, 13:12, 13:15, 14:9, 14:11, 16:2, 19:20, 20:4) were judged by God.

The worship of God is portrayed through numerous hymns in Revelation, functioning like an ongoing Greek chorus (Rev. 1:4–6, 4:8, 4:11, 5:9–14, 7:10–12, 11:15–18, 12:10–12, 15:3–4, 16:5–7, 19:1–8). As part of worship, God and Christ receive glory (Rev. 1:6, 4:9, 4:11, 5:12, 5:13, 7:12, 15:4, 21:11, 21:23). God is glorified for his just judgment (Rev. 11:13, 14:7, 15:8) and the salvation of his people (Rev. 19:1, 19:7). Jesus is also worthy of worship because his death established God's rule (Rev. 5:5, 5:9–10). By the end of Revelation, he will destroy those armies who opposed God's rule as the rider on the white horse (Rev. 19:17–21). After this, the kings of the earth and nations will submit to God (Rev. 21:23) by bringing their glory into the New Jerusalem (Rev. 21:24, 21:26).

The New Creation

God's sovereignty is ultimately established over a renewed creation. Revelation starts with God's courtroom in heaven (Rev. 4:1–5:14) and concludes with this court joining the earth as the New Jerusalem descends to earth (Rev. 21:1–22:5). In this New Jerusalem, there was a Jewish expectation for a new temple to be built either by God (Ezek. 40–48; cf. 1 En. 90.28–29; 2 Bar. 31.5–32.4) or by people (11QTemple 29.3–10; 4Q174 3.2–7).[33] However, the New Jerusalem in Revelation does not have a temple (Rev. 21:22). Instead, the presence of God and the lamb among their people embodies the new temple (Rev. 21:22–27).

Before the new creation, there is a thousand-year period called the **millennium** where Satan is locked in an abyss and Christ reigns (Rev. 20:1–6). These verses greatly divide readers, and interpreters can be grouped into three categories. **Premillennialists** believe Jesus will return before this reign (Irenaeus). **Postmillennialists** think that he comes at the end (Eusebius). **Amillennialists** argue that Satan's binding is figurative, and this millennial period symbolically began with Jesus's death and resurrection (Augustine). After the millennium is complete, Satan will be released from imprisonment. He will deceive the nations and gather them for battle against God's people. However, God will defeat Satan and his armies (Rev. 20:7–9; cf. Ezek. 38–39).

Revelation ends with a vision of creation restored (Rev. 21:1–22:11; cf. Isa. 65:17, 66:22). The work engages a conversation with Jewish texts that expected either the restoration of creation (2 Bar. 32.6, 57.2; 2 Esd. 7:75; Jub. 1:29; 1 En. 45.3–5; cf. 1 Cor. 7:31; Rom. 8:18–22) or its replacement (1 En. 72.1, 83.3–5, 91.15–16; cf. 2 Pet. 3:10–13). This new creation is free from those powers opposed to God—human empires, Satan, Death, and Hades (the place of the dead).[34]

In this new creation, there is a new heaven and new earth, which recapitulates and returns the world to the Garden of Eden (Gen. 1–2). The heavenly river in Revelation (Rev. 22:1) recalls the rivers in Eden (Gen. 2:10). The tree of life (Rev. 22:2) reminds us of the tree of life in Eden (Gen. 2:9). The removal of

---

[33] The temple, as the center of Judaism's worship, held a prominent place. Both Philo (*Spec. Laws* 1.85–96; *Moses* 2.101–8, 117–35) and Josephus (*J.W.* 5.212–18; *Ant.* 3.123, 179–87) deemed the temple as symbolic of the universe. Some texts may imply or describe the existence of a heavenly temple (Isa. 6:1; Ps. 150:1; 1 En. 14; T. Levi 5.1; 4QShirShabb; 11QShirShabb); Aune, *Revelation*, 1:1190–91.

[34] Death and Hades are thrown into the lake of fire at the end of Revelation because there will be no more death, or need for a place for the dead, in the new heaven and earth.

This relief from Ephesus portrays Nike, the goddess of victory (second cent. CE). The church in Ephesus was praised for its good deeds but was challenged for being loveless (Rev. 2:1-7).

the curse (Rev. 22:3) reverses the curses from Gen. 3:16–19. God's people are portrayed in a renewed fellowship with him (Rev. 21:3–4, 22–26, 22:3–5), which undoes the exile of humanity from the garden (Gen. 3:8, 3:18–24). From a canonical perspective, Genesis and Revelation create an Edenic bookend to the whole Bible. Revelation ends with this fitting reminder that a good God rules over his restored creation.[35]

Who's in charge? Who's really in charge? When we read the New Testament from Matthew to Revelation, the answer seems clear.

God is in charge.

Key Terms and People

Amillennialists: those that argue that the thousand-year reign symbolically began with Jesus's death and resurrection

Apocalypse: meaning "unveiling" because it "reveals" the future and/or spiritual realities to promote ethical living based on the hope that God is in control

[35] For those wishing to engage further on the study of the New Testament, see Martin and Toney, *New Testament Foundations.*

Domitian: the Roman emperor whose persecution of the church prompted the writing of Revelation
Futurist interpretation: Revelation predicts the last days of the church
Historicist interpretation: Revelation makes predictions over the entire history of the church
Idealist interpretation: Revelation conveys principles about the conflict between good and evil before the final return of Christ
John the elder: the author of 1–3 John
John the seer: the author of Revelation
Mark of the beast: 666, which refers to "Nero Caesar"
Millennium: the thousand-year reign of Jesus proceeding the new heaven and earth
Postmillennialists: those who think Jesus comes at the end of his thousand-year reign
Premillennialists: those who believe Jesus will return before his thousand-year reign
Preterist interpretation: Revelation is primarily directed toward its first-century context with most predictions already being fulfilled
Satan/devil: the name means "adversary," or accuser"; he is presented as God's heavenly enemy who stands behind Roman power; after his final defeat, he is thrown into the lake of fire

Conversation Starters

1. What are some similar themes between John's letters and the Fourth Gospel?
2. How do believers overcome sin according to 1 John?
3. How would you describe love according to John's letters? How is this similar and distinct from commands to love found elsewhere in the New Testament?
4. How did the Johannine letters understand fellowship and hospitality?
5. How have you been taught to read Revelation? Why is reading Revelation in light of its first-century context important?
6. How does Revelation describe God's sovereignty? How does this relate to the judgment of God? How does God's sovereignty and judgment give hope to those suffering?
7. What is your perspective on violent passages in Scripture? How does this relate to the judgment of God and the love of God? What do you think Jesus teaches about violence?
8. Why is God worthy of worship?
9. How do the new heaven and new earth reflect a restored creation?
10. How can reading Revelation and the New Testament help remind us that God is in charge?

FOR FURTHER READING

Johannine Letters

Brown, Raymond. *The Epistles of John: Translated, with Introduction, Notes, and Commentary.* AYB 30. Yale University Press, 2008.

Lieu, Judith. *I, II & III John: A Commentary.* New Testament Library. Westminster John Knox, 2008.

Marshall, I. Howard. *The Epistles of John*. NICNT. Eerdmans, 1978.

Myers, Alicia D. *Reading John and 1, 2, 3 John*. RNT. Smyth & Helwys, 2019.

Thompson, Marianne Meye. *1–3 John*. The IVP New Testament Commentary Series. InterVarsity Press, 1992.

Revelation

Blount, Brian K. *Revelation: A Commentary*. Westminster John Knox, 2009.

deSilva, David A. *Discovering Revelation: Content, Interpretation, Reception*. Eerdmans, 2021.

González, Catherine Gunsalus, and Justo L. González. *Revelation*. Westminster Bible Companion. Westminster John Knox, 1997.

Gorman, Michael J. *Reading Revelation Responsibly: Uncivil Worship and Witness—Following the Lamb into the New Creation*. Cascade, 2011.

Keener, Craig. *Revelation: From Biblical Text . . . to Contemporary Life*. NIV Application Commentary. Zondervan, 2000.

Koester, Craig R. *Revelation: A New Translation with Introduction and Commentary*. Edited by John J. Collins. 2nd ed. AYB 38A. Yale University Press, 2014.

Kovacs, Judith, Christopher Rowland, and Rebekah Callow. *Revelation: The Apocalypse to Jesus Christ*. John Wiley & Sons, 2007.

McKnight, Scot, and Cody Matchett. *Revelation for the Rest of Us: A Prophetic Call to Follow Jesus as a Dissident Disciple*. Zondervan, 2023.

BIBLIOGRAPHY

Achtemeier, Paul. *1 Peter: A Commentary on First Peter*. Hermeneia. Fortress, 1996.

Adams, Edward. *The Earliest Christian Meeting Places: Almost Exclusively Houses?* Rev. ed. The Library of New Testament Studies 450. T&T Clark, 2016.

Allison, Dale, Jr. *Constructing Jesus: Memory, Imagination, History*. Baker Academic, 2010.

Argyle, Aubrey W. "Greek Among the Jews of Palestine in New Testament Times." *New Testament Studies* 20 (1973): 87–89.

Ashton, John. *Understanding the Fourth Gospel*. 2nd ed. Oxford University Press, 1991.

Aune, David E. "A Note on Jesus' Messianic Consciousness and 11Q Melchizedek." *Evangelical Quarterly* 45 (1973): 161–65.

———. *Revelation*. 3 vols. Word Biblical Commentary 52A–52C. Word Books, 1998.

———. "The Problem of the Messianic Secret." *Novum Testamentum* 11 (1969): 1–31.

Bacon, Benjamin W. *Studies in Matthew*. H. Holt, 1930.

Barclay, John. *Jews in the Mediterranean Diaspora*. University of California Press, 1996.

———. *Paul and the Gift*. Eerdmans, 2015.

Barker, Glenn, William Lane, and J. Ramsey Michaels. *The New Testament Speaks*. Harper & Row, 1969.

Barnett, Paul W. "Opposition in Corinth." *Journal for the Study of the New Testament* 22 (1984): 3–17.

———. "Tentmaking." In *Dictionary of Paul and His Letters*. Edited by Gerald F. Hawthorne, Ralph P. Martin, and Daniel G. Reid, 925–27. InterVarsity Press, 1993.

———. *The Second Epistle to the Corinthians*. New International Commentary on the New Testament. Eerdmans, 1997.

Barrett, Charles K. *A Critical and Exegetical Commentary on the Acts of the Apostles*. 2 vols. International Critical Commentary 34. T&T Clark, 1994–1998.

———. *Church, Ministry and Sacraments in the New Testament*. Eerdmans, 1985.

———. *The Gospel According to St. John: An Introduction with Commentary and Notes on the Greek Text*. 2nd ed. Westminster John Knox, 1978.

———. *The Holy Spirit and the Gospel Tradition*. SPCK, 1966.

———. "Titus." In *Neotestamentica et Semitica. Studies in Honour of Matthew Black*, edited by E. Earle Ellis and Max Wilcox, 1–14. T&T Clark, 1969.

Bartchy, S. Scott. "Slaves and Slavery in the Roman World." In *The World of the New Testament*, edited by Joel Green and Lee Martin McDonald, 169–78. Baker, 2013.

———. Μᾶλλον Χρῆσαι: First-Century Slavery and the Interpretation of 1 Corinthians 7:21. Society of Biblical Literature Dissertation Series 11. Scholars Press, 1973.

Barth, Gerhard. "Matthew's Understanding of the Law." In *Tradition and Interpretation in Matthew*, edited by Gerhard Barth, Günther Bornkamm, and Heinz J. Held, 58–164. Westminster John Knox, 1963.

Barth, Markus. *Ephesians: Introduction, Translation, and Commentary*. 2 vols. Anchor Yale Bible 34–34A. Doubleday, 1974.

Bates, Matthew. *Gospel Allegiance: What Faith in Jesus Misses for Salvation*. Brazos, 2019.

Bauckham, Richard. *2 Peter, Jude*. Word Biblical Commentary 50. Word Books, 1983.

———. *Jesus and the God of Israel*. Eerdmans, 2008.

Beale, Gregory K. *The Book of Revelation: A Commentary on the Greek Text*. New International Greek Testament Commentary. Eerdmans, 1999.

———. *The Morality of God in the Old Testament*. Christian Answers to Hard Questions. P&R, 2013.

Beare, Francis W. *A Commentary on the Epistle to the Philippians*. 3rd ed. Black's New Testament Commentary. Black, 1974.

———. *The First Epistle of Peter*. 2nd ed. B. Blackwell, 1958.

Beasley-Murray, George R. *Baptism in the New Testament*. St. Martin's, 1963.

———. *John*. Word Biblical Commentary 36. Word Books, 1999.

———. *The Book of Revelation*. New Century Bible. Eerdmans, 1981.

Best, Ernest. *1 Peter*. New Century Bible. Eerdmans, 1982.

Betz, Hans Dieter. *Galatians: A Commentary on Paul's Letter to the Churches in Galatia*. Hermeneia. Fortress, 1979.

Bird, Michael. *7 Things I Wish Every Christian Knew*. Zondervan, 2021.

———. *Colossians and Philemon*. New Covenant Commentary Series 12. Cascade, 2009.

Bock, Darrell. *Proclamation from Prophecy and Pattern: Lucan Old Testament Christology*. Journal for the Study of the New Testament Supplement Series 12. JSOT Press, 1987.

Bowman, John. "The Term 'Gospel' and Its Cognates in the Palestinian Syriac." In *New Testament Essays: Studies in Memory of Thomas Walter Manson*, edited by Angus J. B. Higgins, 54–67. Manchester University Press, 1959.

Bradley, Keith R. *Slaves and Masters in the Roman Empire: A Study in Social Control*. Latomus, 1984.

Brown, Raymond. *An Introduction to the New Testament*. Doubleday, 1997.

———. *The Epistles of John: Translated, with Introduction, Notes, and Commentary*. Anchor Yale Bible 30. Yale University Press, 2008.

———. *The Gospel According to John*. 2 vols. Anchor Yale Bible 29–29A. Doubleday, 1966.

———. "The Paraclete in the Fourth Gospel." *New Testament Studies* 13 (1966): 113–32.

Brown, Schuyler. *Apostasy and Perseverance in the Theology of Luke*. Pontifical Biblical Institute, 1969.

Bruce, Frederick Fyvie. *1 & 2 Thessalonians*. Word Biblical Commentary 45. Word Books, 1982.

———. *New Testament History*. Doubleday, 1969.

———. *The Epistle to the Hebrews*. Rev. ed. New International Commentary on the New Testament. Eerdmans, 1990.

———. *The Epistles to the Colossians, to Philemon, and to the Ephesians*. New International Commentary on the New Testament. Eerdmans, 1984.

———. *The Speeches in the Acts of the Apostles*. Eerdmans, 1990.

Bultmann, Rudolf. *The Gospel of John: A Commentary*. Westminster John Knox, 1971.

———. *The History of the Synoptic Tradition*. Translated by John Marsh. Rev. ed. Harper & Row, 1968.

———. "Theology of the New Testament." Translated by Kendrick Grobel. Charles Scribner's Sons, 1951.

———. "ΔΙΚΑΙΟΣΥΝΗ ΘΕΟΥ." *Journal of Biblical Literature* 83 (1964): 12–16.

Burridge, Richard A. *What Are the Gospels?* 2nd ed. Cambridge University Press, 1992.

Cadbury, Henry J. "Commentary on the Preface of Luke." In *The Beginnings of Christianity: The Acts of the Apostles*, edited by Frederick J. Foakes-Jackson and Kirsopp Lake, 489–510. Baker, 1979.

———. "Roman Law and the Trial of Paul." In *Beginnings of Christianity*, edited by Kirsopp Lake and Henry J. Cadbury, Vol. 5. Macmillan, 1920.

———. *The Beginnings of Christianity*. 5 vols. Macmillan, 1933.

———. *The Style and Literary Method of Luke, Part 1: The Diction of Luke and Acts*. Harvard University Press, 1919.

Caird, George B. *A Commentary on the Revelation of St. John the Divine*. Harvard New Testament Commentary. Harper & Row, 1966.

———. *Paul's Letters from Prison*. Oxford University Press, 1976.

Campbell, Douglas. "Romans 1:17—A *Crux Interpretum* for the ΠΙΣΤΙΣ ΧΡΙΣΤΟΥ Dispute." *Journal of Biblical Literature* 113 (1994): 265–85.

———. *The Deliverance of God: An Apocalyptic Reading of Justification in Paul*. Eerdmans, 2009.

Campbell, R. Alastair. "Identifying the Faithful Sayings in the Pastoral Epistles." *Journal for the Study of the New Testament* 16 (1994): 73–86.

Carson, Donald A. *Exegetical Fallacies*. Baker, 1984.

Chadwick, Henry. "St. Peter and St. Paul in Rome: The Problem of the *Memoria Apostolorum Ad Catacumbas*." *Journal of Theological Studies* 8 (1957): 31–52.

Charlesworth, James H. *Old Testament Pseudepigrapha*. 2 vols. Yale University Press, 1983.

Coggan, Frederick D. "A Note on Ephesians 2:14." *Expository Times* 53 (1941): 242.

Collins, Adela Yarbro. "Introduction: Early Christian Apocalypticism." In *Early Christian Apocalypticism*, edited by Adela Yarbro Collins, 1–12. Semeia 36. Scholars Press, 1986.

Collins, John J. "Introduction: Toward the Morphology of a Genre." In *Apocalypse: The Morphology of a Genre*, edited by John J. Collins, 1–20. Semeia 14. Scholars Press, 1979.

———. *The Scepter and the Star*. Doubleday, 1995.

Conzelmann, Hans. *The Theology of Saint Luke*. Translated by Geoffrey Buswell. Faber and Faber, 1960.

Cousar, Charles B. *Reading Galatians, Philippians, and 1 Thessalonians: A Literary and Theological Commentary*. Reading the New Testament. Smyth & Helwys, 2001.

Creed, John Martin. *The Gospel According to St. Luke; the Greek Text with Introduction, Notes, and Indices*. Macmillan, 1930.

Crossley, James, and Chris Keith, eds. *The Next Quest for the Historical Jesus*. Eerdmans, 2024.

Cullmann, Oscar. *Peter: Disciple, Apostle, Martyr: A Historical and Theological Study*. Translated by Floyd Filson. Westminster John Knox, 1962.

———. *The Christology of the New Testament*. Westminster John Knox, 1959.

Dalton, William J. *Christ's Proclamation to the Spirits: A Study of 1 Peter 3:18—4:6*. 2nd ed. Editrice Pontifico Isituto Biblico, 1989.

Danker, Frederick W. *Benefactor: Epigraphic Study of a* Greco-Roman *and New Testament Semantic Field*. Clayton, 1982.

———. *Jesus and the New Age: A Commentary on St Luke's Gospel*. Rev. and exp. ed. Fortress, 1988.

Davies, William D., and Dale Allison Jr. *A Critical and Exegetical Commentary on the Gospel According to Saint Matthew*. 3 vols. *International Critical Commentary*. T&T Clark, 1988–1991.

deSilva, David A. *Honor, Patronage, Kinship, & Purity: Unlocking New Testament Culture*. 2nd ed. InterVarsity Press, 2022.

———. "Paul and the Stoa: A Comparison" 38 (1995): 549–64.

Dibelius, Martin. *From Tradition to Gospel*. Translated by Bertram Lee Woolf. James Clarke, 1971.

Dibelius, Martin, and Hans Conzelmann. *The Pastoral Epistles: A Commentary on the Pastoral Epistles*. Translated by Philip Buttolph and Adela Yarbro. Hermeneia. Fortress, 1972.

Dibelius, Martin, and Heinrich Greeven. *James: A Commentary on the Epistle of James*. Translated by Michael William. Rev. ed. Hermeneia. Fortress, 1976.

Dodd, Charles H. "Ephesians." In *Abingdon Bible Commentary*, edited by Frederick C. Eiselen, Edwin Lewis, and David G. Downey, 1250–62. Abingdon, 1929.

Donaldson, T. "Proselytes or 'Righteous Gentiles'? The Status of Gentiles in Eschatological Pilgrimage Patterns of Thought." *Journal for the Study of the Pseudepigrapha* 7 (1990): 3–27.

LeDonne, Anthony. *Historical Jesus: What Can We Know and How Can We Know It?* Eerdmans, 2011.

Downs, David J. "Paul's Collection and the Book of Acts Revisited." *New Testament Studies* 52 (2006): 50–70.

———. *The Offering of the Gentiles: Paul's Collection for Jerusalem in Its Chronological, Cultural, and Cultic Contexts*. Wissenschaftliche Untersuchungen zum Neuen Testament II/248. Mohr Siebeck, 2008.

Dunn, James D. G. *Christology in the Making: A New Testament Inquiry into the Origins of the Doctrine of the Incarnation*. 2nd ed. Eerdmans, 1996.

———. *Did the First Christians Worship Jesus?* Westminster John Knox, 2010.

———. "Once More, ΠΙΣΤΙΣ ΧΡΙΣΤΟΥ." Society of Biblical Literature Seminar Papers 30 (1991): 730–44.

———. *Romans*. 2 vols. Word Biblical Commentary 38A–38B. Word Books, 1988.

———. *The Epistle to the Galatians*. Black's New Testament Commentary. Hendrickson, 1993.

———. *The Epistles to the Colossians and to Philemon: A Commentary on the Greek Text*. New International Greek Testament Commentary. Eerdmans, 1996.

———. "The New Perspective on Paul." *Bulletin of the John Rylands University Library of Manchester* 65 (1983): 95–122.

———. *The New Perspective on Paul*. Eerdmans, 2008.

———. "Yet Once More—'The Works of the Law': A Response." In *The New Perspective on Paul*. 2nd ed., 213–26. Eerdmans, 2008.

Dupont, Jacques. "The Salvation of the Gentiles and the Theological Significance of Acts." *The Salvation of the Gentiles: Essays on the Acts of the Apostles* 6 (1979): 11–33.

———. *The Sources of the Acts of the Apostles*. Translated by Kathleen Pond. Herder and Herder, 1964.

Easton, Burton Scott. *The Pastoral Epistles: Introduction, Translation, Commentary and Word Studies*. SCM Press, 1948.

Ehrhardt, Arnold. "The Construction and Purpose of the Acts of the Apostles." *Studia Theologica* 12 (1958): 45–79.

Elledge, Casey D. *Life after Death in Early Judaism*. Wissenschaftliche Untersuchungen zum Neuen Testament II/208. Mohr Siebeck, 2006.

Elliott, John H. *1 Peter: A New Translation with Introduction and Commentary*. Anchor Yale Bible 37B. Yale University Press, 2008.

———. "Ministry and Church Order in the New Testament: A Traditio-Historical Analysis (1 Pt. 5,1–5 and Par.)." *Catholic Biblical Quarterly* 32 (1970): 367–91.

Ellis, E. Earle. "The Authorship of the Pastorals." In *Paul and His Recent Interpreters*, 49–57. Eerdmans, 1961.

Engberg-Pedersen, Troels. *Paul & the Stoics*. T&T Clark, 2000.

Enns, Peter. *The Bible Tells Me So: Why Defending Scripture Has Made Us Unable to Read It*. Hodder & Stoughton, 2020.

Esler, Phil. *Community and Gospel in* Luke-Acts*: The Social and Political Motivations of Lucan Theology*. Society for New Testament Studies Monograph Series 57. Cambridge University Press, 1987.

Evans, Craig. "Jesus' Actions in the Temple: Cleansing or Portent of Destruction?" *Catholic Biblical Quarterly* 51 (1989): 237–70.

Farmer, William. *The Synoptic Problem: A Critical Analysis*. 2nd ed. Mercer University Press, 1976.

Farrer, Austin. "On Dispensing with Q." In *Studies in the Gospels*, 55–86. Blackwell, 1955.

Fee, Gordon D. *Paul's Letter to the Philippians*. New International Commentary on the New Testament. Eerdmans, 1995.

———. *The First Epistle to the Corinthians*. New International Commentary on the New Testament. Eerdmans, 1987.

Fee, Gordon D., and Douglas K. Stuart. *How to Read the Bible for All Its Worth*. 4th rev. ed. Zondervan, 2014.

Ferguson, John. *The Religions of the Roman Empire*. Thames & Hudson, 1970.

Findley, Moses I. *Ancient Slavery and Modern Ideology*. Chatto and Windus, 1980.

Fitzgerald, John, ed. *Friendship, Flattery, and Frankness of Speech: Studies on Friendship in the New Testament World*. Brill, 1996.

Fitzmyer, Joseph. "Further Light on Melchizedek from Qumran Cave 11." *Journal of Biblical Literature* 86 (1967): 25–41.

———. *The Acts of the Apostles: A New Translation with Introduction and Commentary*. Anchor Yale Bible 31. Yale University Press, 2008.

———. *The Gospel According to Luke*. 2 vols. Anchor Yale Bible 28–28A. Yale University Press, 2008.

———. *The One Who Is to Come*. Eerdmans, 2007.

Florentino, Martínez García, and Eibert J. C. Tigchelaar, eds. *The Dead Sea Scrolls: Study Edition*. 2 vols. Eerdmans, 1997.

Foschini, Bernard. *Those Who Are Baptized for the Dead." I Cor 15:29: An Exegetical Historical Dissertation*. Heffernan, 1951.

Foster, Paul. *Colossians*. Black's New Testament Commentary. Bloomsbury Academic, 2016.

Fotopoulos, John. *Food Offered to Idols in Roman Corinth*. Wissenschaftliche Untersuchungen zum Neuen Testament II/151. Mohr Siebeck, 2003.

France, Richard T. "Chronological Aspects of 'Gospel Harmonization.'" *Vox Evangelica* 16 (1986): 43–54.

———. *The Gospel of Mark: A Commentary on the Greek Text*. New International Greek Testament Commentary. Eerdmans, 2002.

Franklin, Eric. *Christ the Lord: A Study in the Purpose and Theology of Luke-Acts*. Westminster John Knox, 1975.

Fuller, Reginald H. *The Mission and Achievement of Jesus*. SCM Press, 1954.

Gaventa, Beverly. *From Darkness to Light*. Fortress, 1986.

Gerhardsson, Birger. *Memory and Manuscript: Oral Tradition and Written Transmission*. C. W. K. Gleerup, 1961.

Glahn, Sandra. *Nobody's Mother: Artemis of the Ephesians in Antiquity and the New Testament*. IVP Academic, 2023.

Gooch, Peter. *Dangerous Food: 1 Cor 8–10 in Its Context*. Studies in Christianity and Judaism 5. Wilfrid Laurier University Press, 1993.

Goodacre, Mark. *The Case against Q*. Trinity Press International, 2002.

Goulder, Michael D. "Is Q a Juggernaut?" *Journal of Biblical Literature* 115 (1996): 667–81.

Grasso, Kevin. "A Linguistic Analysis of πίστις Χριστοῦ: The Case for the Third View." *Journal for the Study of the New Testament* 43 (2020): 108–44.

Graves, David E. "What Is the Madder with Lydia's Purple? A Reexamination of the Purpurarii in Thyatira and Philippi." *Near East Archaeological Society Bulletin* 62 (2017): 3–29.

Grayston, K., and G. Herden. "The Authorship of the Pastorals in the Light of Statistical Linguistics." *New Testament Studies* 6 (1959): 1–15.

Green, Michael. *2 Peter Reconsidered*. Tyndale New Testament Lecture. Tyndale, 1961.

Green, Joel. *Theology of the Gospel of Luke*. Cambridge University Press, 1995.

Grenfell, Bernard P., and Arthur S. Hunt. *The Oxyrhynchus Papyri*. London: Egypt Exploration Fund, 1898.

Guelich, Robert A. *Mark 1–8:26*. Word Biblical Commentary 34A. Word Books, 1989.

Gundry, Robert H. *The Use of the Old Testament in St. Matthew's Gospel*. Brill, 1967.

Gupta, Nijay K. *The Affections of Christ: Love at the Heart of Paul's Theology*. Eerdmans, 2025.

———. *Paul and the Language of Faith*. Eerdmans, 2020.

Hadidian, D. Y. "Palestinian Pictures in the Epistle of James." *Expository Times* 63 (1951): 227–28.

Hagner, Donald A. *Matthew*. 2 vols. Word Biblical Commentary 32A–32B. Word Books, 1993–1995.

Harnack, Adolf von. "Probabilia über die Addresse und den Verfasser des Hebräerbriefes." *Zeitschrift für die neutestamentliche Wissenschaft und die Kunde der älteren Kirche* 1 (1900): 16–41.

Harris, J. Rendel, and Vacher Burch. *Testimonies*. Vol. 2. Cambridge University Press, 1916.

Harris, Murray J. *The Second Epistle to the Corinthians: A Commentary on the Greek Text*. New International Greek Testament Commentary. Eerdmans, 2005.

Harrison, James. *Paul's Language of Grace in its* Graeco-Roman *Context*. Wissenschaftliche Untersuchungen zum Neuen Testament II/172. Mohr Siebeck, 2003.

Hawthorne, Gerald F., and Ralph P. Martin. *Philippians*. Rev. and exp. ed. Word Biblical Commentary 43. Thomas Nelson, 2004.

Hays, Richard. *The Faith of Christ*. 2nd ed. Eerdmans, 2002.

Hedrick, Charles. "Paul's Conversion/Call: A Comparative Analysis of the Three Reports in Acts." *Journal of Biblical Literature* 100 (1981): 415–32.

Hengel, Martin. *Christ and Power*. Translated by Everett Kalin. Fortress, 1971.

———. *Jews, Greeks and Barbarians*. Translated by John Bowden. Fortress, 1980.

———. *Judaism and Hellenism*. Translated by John Bowden. Fortress, 1974.

———. *The Johannine Question*. Translated by John Bowden. Trinity Press International, 1989.

Hering, James P. *The Colossian and Ephesian* Haustafeln *in Theological Context: An Analysis of Their Origins, Relationship, and Message*. Peter Lang, 2007.

Hewitt, Thomas. *The Epistle to the Hebrews: An Introduction and Commentary*. Tyndale New Testament Commentaries 15. Eerdmans, 1960.

Hezser, Catherine. *Jewish Literacy in Roman Palestine*. Texts and Studies in Ancient Judaism 81. Mohr Siebeck, 2001.

Hobart, William K. *The Medical Language of St. Luke*. Baker, 1956.

Hock, Ronald F. *The Social Context of Paul's Ministry: Tentmaking and Apostleship*. Fortress, 1980.

Hoehner, Harold W. *Herod Antipas*. Cambridge University Press, 1972.

Holmes, Michael, ed. *Apostolic Fathers*. Baker, 1999.

Hooker, Morna. "The Bible and the Believer: A. S. Peake Memorial Lecture 1978." *Epworth Review* 6 (1979): 77–89.

———. "Πίστις Χριστοῦ." *New Testament Studies* 35 (1989): 321–42.

Hoskyns, Edwyn. *The Fourth Gospel*. 2nd ed. Faber and Faber, 1947.

Houlden, J. L. "Christ and Church in Ephesians." *Studia Evangelica* 6 = *Texte und Untersuchungen* 112 (1973): 267–73.

Hughes, Philip. *A Commentary on the Epistle to the Hebrews*. Eerdmans, 1977.

Hurtado, Larry. *Lord Jesus Christ: Devotion to Jesus in Earliest Christianity*. Eerdmans, 2003.

Irons, Charles Lee. *The Righteousness of God*. Wissenschaftliche Untersuchungen zum Neuen Testament II/386. Mohr Siebeck, 2015.

Jensen, Morten Hørning. *Herod Antipas in Galilee: The Literary and Archaeological Sources*. Wissenschaftliche Untersuchungen zum Neuen Testament II/215. Mohr Siebeck, 2006.

Jeremias, Joachim. *Jesus' Promise to the Nations*. Translated by S. H. Hooke. Studies in Biblical Theology 24. SCM Press, 1958.

———. "The Gentile World in the Thought of Jesus" *Society for New Testament Studies Bulletin* 1–3 (1950–52): 18–28.

Jewett, Robert. *Letters to Pilgrims*. Pilgrim, 1981.

———. *Paul's Anthropological Terms*. Arbeiten zur Geschichte des antiken Judentums und des Urchristentums 10. Brill, 1971.

———. *Romans: A Commentary*. Hermeneia. Fortress, 2006.

———. "The Agitators and the Galatian Congregation." *New Testament Studies* 17 (1970): 198–212.

Johnson, Luke Timothy. *Sharing Possessions: Mandate and Symbol of Faith*. Fortress, 1981.

———. *The Acts of the Apostles*. Sacra Pagina 5. Liturgical Press, 2006.

———. *The Canonical Paul*. 2 vols. Eerdmans, 2020–2021.

———. *The First and Second Letters to Timothy: A New Translation with Introduction and Commentary*. Anchor Yale Bible 35A. Yale University Press, 2008.

———. "The Letter of James." In *The New Interpreters Bible: General Articles & Introduction, Commentary, & Reflections for Each Book of the Bible*, 12:473–500. Abingdon, 1994–2004.

———. *The Letter of James: A New Translation with Introduction and Commentary*. Anchor Yale Bible 37A. Yale University Press, 2008.

———. *The Literary Function of Possession in Luke-Acts*. SBL Press, 1977.

———. *The Writings of the New Testament: An Interpretation*. 2nd ed. Fortress, 2010.

Johnson, Marshall D. *The Purpose of the Biblical Genealogies*. Society for New Testament Studies Monograph Series 8. Cambridge University Press, 1969.

Johnston, George. *The Spirit-Paraclete in the Gospel of John*. Society for New Testament Studies Monograph Series 12. Cambridge University Press, 1970.

Kähler, Martin. *The So-Called Historical Jesus and the Historic Biblical Christ*. Translated by Carl E. Braaten. Fortress, 1964.

Karris, Robert. "Romans 14:1—15:13 and the Occasion of Romans." In *The Romans Debate*, edited by Karl Donfried, Rev. ed., 65–84. Hendrickson, 1991.

———. "The Background and Significance of the Polemic of the Pastoral Epistles." *Journal of Biblical Literature* 92 (1973): 549–64.

Käsemann, Ernst. *Commentary on Romans*. Translated by Geoffrey W. Bromiley. Eerdmans, 1980.

———. "'The Righteousness of God' in Paul." In *New Testament Questions of Today*, 168–82. Fortress, 1969.

Keith, Chris, and Anthony LeDonne, eds. *Jesus, Criteria, and the Demise of Authenticity*. T&T Clark, 2014.

Kelly, John N. D. *Early Christian Creeds*. 3rd ed. McKay Co, 1972.

———. *Epistles of Peter and Jude*. Black's New Testament Commentary. Continuum International, 1990.

———. *The Pastoral Epistles*. Black's New Testament Commentary 14. Hendrickson, 1993.

Kennedy, George. *New Testament Interpretation through Rhetorical Criticism*. University of North Carolina Press, 1982.

Kim, Seyoon. *The Origin of Paul's Gospel*. 2nd ed. Eerdmans, 1981.

Klauck, Hans-Josef. *Ancient Letters and the New Testament: A Guide to Context and Exegesis*. Baylor University Press, 2006.

———. "Compilation of Letters in Cicero's Correspondence." In *Early Christianity and Classical Culture: Comparative Studies in Honor of Abraham Malherbe*, edited by John T. Fitzgerald, Thomas H. Olbricht, and L. Michael White, 131–55. Brill, 2003.

Kloppenborg, John. *Christ's Associations: Connecting and Belonging in the Ancient City*. Yale University Press, 2019.

Knight, George W., III. *The Faithful Sayings in the Pastoral Letters*. Baker Biblical Monograph. Baker, 1979.

Konstan, David. *Friendship in the Classical World*. Cambridge University Press, 1997.

Kümmel, Werner Georg. *Introduction to the New Testament*. Translated by Paul Feine. Rev. ed. Abingdon, 1975.

Kysar, Robert. *The Fourth Evangelist and His Gospel: An Examination of Contemporary Scholarship*. Augsburg, 1975.

Lampe, Geoffrey W. H. "The Holy Spirit in the Writings of St. Luke." In *Studies in the Gospels: Essays in Memory of R. H. Lightfoot*, edited by Dennis E. Nineham, 159–200. Blackwell, 1955.

Lampe, Peter. *From Paul to Valentinus: Christians at Rome in the First Two Centuries*. Translated by Michael Steinhauser and Marshall Johnson. Fortress, 2003.

Lane, William L. *The Gospel of Mark*. New International Commentary on the New Testament. Eerdmans, 1974.

Latz, Andrew B. "A Short Note toward a Theology of Abiding in John's Gospel." *Journal for Theological Interpretation* 4 (2010): 161–68.

Lehrmann, Richard. *Epître à Philémon*. Labor et Fides, 1978.

Levenson, Jon D. *Resurrection and the Restoration of Israel: The Ultimate Victory of the God of Life*. Yale University Press, 2006.

Lewis, Clive Staples. *The Four Loves*. Geoffrey Bles, 1960.

Lietzmann, Hans. *Mass and Lord's Supper: A Study in the History of the Liturgy*. Brill, 1979.

Lightfoot, Joseph. *Saint Paul's Epistle to the Galatians*. 10th ed. Macmillan, 1890.

Lincoln, Andrew T. *Ephesians*. Word Biblical Commentary 42. Word Books, 1990.

Lockett, Darian. *Letters from the Pillar Apostles*. Pickwick, 2017.

Lohse, Eduard. *Colossians and Philemon; a Commentary on the Epistles to the Colossians and to Philemon*. Hermeneia. Fortress, 1971.

Long, Fredrick. *Ancient Rhetoric and Paul's Apology: The Compositional Unity of 2 Corinthians*. Society for New Testament Studies Monograph Series 131. Cambridge University Press, 2004.

Long, Thomas G. *Hebrews*. Interpretation. Westminster John Knox, 1997.

Longenecker, Bruce. "Good News to the Poor: Jesus, Paul, and Jerusalem." In *Jesus and Paul Reconnected: Fresh Pathways into an Old Debate*, edited by Todd D. Still, 58–63. Eerdmans, 2007.

Longman, Tremper, III, and Daniel G. Reid. *God Is a Warrior*. Studies in Old Testament Biblical Theology. Zondervan, 1995.

MacRae, George. "Whom in Heaven Must Receive Until the Time." *Interpretation* 27 (1973): 151–65.

Malherbe, Abraham. *Ancient Epistolary Theorists*. Society of Biblical Literature Monograph Series 19. Scholars Press, 1988.

———. *Paul and the Popular Philosophers*. Fortress, 1989.

———. *The Letters to the Thessalonians: A New Translation with Introduction and Commentary*. Anchor Yale Bible 32B. Yale University Press, 2008.

Manson, Thomas W. "The Johannine Logos Doctrine." In *On Paul and John: Some Selected Theological Themes*, 136–60. SCM Press, 1963.

Manson, William. *The Epistle to the Hebrews: An Historical and Theological Reconsideration*. Hodder & Stoughton, 1951.

Marco, Angelus A. *The Tomb of Saint Peter*. Supplements to Novum Testamentum 8. Brill, 1964.

Marshall, I. Howard. *Biblical Inspiration*. 1st ed. Eerdmans, 1983.

———. *Last Supper and Lord's Supper*. Eerdmans, 1980.

———. *Luke: Historian and Theologian*. Zondervan, 1970.

———. "Orthodoxy and Heresy in Earlier Christianity." *Themelios* 2 (1976): 5–14.

———. *The Gospel of Luke: A Commentary on the Greek Text*. New International Greek Commentary. Paternoster, 1978.

Marshall, I. Howard, and Philip Towner. *A Critical and Exegetical Commentary on the Pastoral Epistles*. International Critical Commentary. 1999.

Martin, Dale. *Slavery as Salvation: The Metaphor of Slavery in Pauline Christianity*. Yale University Press, 1990.

Martin, Ralph P. *2 Corinthians*. Rev. ed. Word Biblical Commentary 40. Zondervan, 2014.

———. *A Hymn of Christ Philippians 2:5–11 in Recent Interpretation & in the Setting of Early Christian Worship*. 3rd ed. InterVarsity Press, 1997.

———. "Salvation and Discipleship in the Gospel of Luke." *Interpretation* 30 (1976): 366–80.

———. "The Setting of 2 Corinthians." *Tyndale Bulletin* 37 (1986): 3–19.

———. "The Theology of Jude, 1 Peter, and 2 Peter." In *The Theology of the Letters of James, Peter, and Jude*, edited by Andrew Chester and Ralph P. Martin, 63–163. Cambridge University Press, 1994.

Martin, Ralph P., and Carl N. Toney. *New Testament Foundations: An Introduction for Students*. Wipf & Stock, 2018.

Martyn, J. Louis. *Galatians: A New Translation with Introduction and Commentary*. Anchor Yale Bible 33A. Yale University Press, 2008.

Marxsen, Willi. *Introduction to the New Testament: An Approach to Its Problems*. Fortress, 1968.

———. *Mark the Evangelist: Studies on the Redaction History of the Gospel*. Abingdon, 1969.

Matson, David. "'Eating and Drinking Whatever They Provide' (Luke 10:5–7): Luke's Household Mission of the Seventy(-Two) in Light of the Philip Esler/E. P. Sanders Debate." *Perspectives in Religious Studies* 42 (2015): 371–89.

———. *Household Conversion Narratives in Acts: Pattern and Interpretation*. Journal for the Study of the New Testament Supplement Series 123. Sheffield Academic, 1996.

McCaulley, Esau. *Reading While Black: African American Biblical Interpretation as an Exercise in Hope*. IVP Academic, 2020.

McHugh, John. *The Mother of Jesus in the New Testament*. Doubleday, 1975.

McKnight, Scot. *The King Jesus Gospel: Original Good News Revisited*. Rev. ed. Zondervan, 2016.

McKnight, Scot, and Cody Matchett. *Revelation for the Rest of Us: A Prophetic Call to Follow Jesus as a Dissident Disciple*. Zondervan, 2023.

McPherson, Miles. *The Third Option: Hope for a Racially Divided Nation*. Howard, 2020.

Meeks, Wayne. *The First Urban Christians: The Social World of the Apostle Paul*. 2nd ed. Yale University Press, 2003.

Meier, John. *A Marginal Jew: The Roots of the Problem and the Person*. Vol. 1. Doubleday, 1991.

———. *A Marginal Jew: Probing the Authenticity of the Parables*. Vol. 5. Doubleday, 2016.

Merrill, Elmer T. *Essays in Early Christian History*. Macmillan, 1924.

Mettinger, Tryggve N. D. *The Riddle of Resurrection: "Dying and Rising Gods" in the Ancient Near East*. Coniectanea Biblica Old Testament Series 50. Almqvist & Wiksell International, 2001.

Meyer, Marvin, and Wolf-Peter Funk, eds. *Nag Hammadi Scriptures*. HarperOne, 2008.

Michaels, J. Ramsey. *1 Peter*. Word Biblical Commentary 49. Word Books, 1988.

Mitchell, Margaret. *Paul and the Rhetoric of Reconciliation: An Exegetical Investigation of the Language and Composition of 1 Corinthians*. Westminster John Knox, 1993.

Mitton, C. Leslie. *The Epistle to the Ephesians: Its Authorship, Origin and Purpose*. Clarendon, 1951.

Moloney, Francis J. *The Gospel of John*. Sacra Pagina 4. Liturgical Press, 1998.

Montefiore, Claude G., and Herbert Loewe. *A Rabbinic Anthology*. Schocken Books, 1974.

Moo, Douglas J. *The Epistle to the Romans*. 2nd ed. New International Commentary on the New Testament. Eerdmans, 2018.

Moule, Charles F. D. *The Birth of the New Testament*. 3rd ed. Adam & Charles Black, 1981.

———. "The Nature and Purpose of 1 Peter." *New Testament Studies* 3 (1956): 1–11.

Mounce, Robert H. *The Book of Revelation*. New International Commentary on the New Testament. Eerdmans, 1997.

Munck, Johannes. *Paul and the Salvation of Mankind*. Translated by Frank Clarke. SCM Press, 1959.

Murphy-O'Connor, Jerome. *Paul: A Critical Life*. Oxford University Press, 1997.

———. *St. Paul's Corinth*. Rev. ed. Michael Glazier, 1990.

Neyrey, Jerome H. *2 Peter, Jude: A New Translation with Introduction and Commentary*. Anchor Yale Bible 37C. Yale University Press, 2008.

O'Brien, Peter T. *Colossians, Philemon*. Word Biblical Commentary 44. Word Books, 1982.

———. "Thanksgiving and the Gospel in Paul." *New Testament Studies* 21 (1974): 151–52.

Osiek, Carolyn, Margaret Y. MacDonald, and Janet H. Tulloch. *A Woman's Place: House Churches in Earliest Christianity*. Fortress, 2006.

Painter, John. *1, 2, and 3 John*. Sacra Pagina 18. Liturgical Press, 2002.

Parsons, Mikeal C. *The Departure of Jesus in* Luke-Acts. Journal for the Study of the New Testament Supplement Series 21. Sheffield Academic, 1987.

Pennington, Jonathan T. *Heaven and Earth in the Gospel of Matthew*. Supplements to Novum Testamentum 126. Brill, 2007.

Porter, Stanley, and Andrew Pitts. "Πίστις with a Preposition and Genitive Modifier: Lexical, Semantic, and Syntactic Considerations in the Πίστις Χριστοῦ Discussion." In *The Faith of Jesus Christ: Exegetical, Biblical, and Theological Studies*, edited by Michael Bird and Preston Sprinkle, 33–53. Hendrickson, 2009.

Powell, Evan. *The Myth of the Lost Gospel*. Symposium, 2006.

Powell, Mark Allan. "The Magi as Kings: An Adventure in Reader-Response Criticism." *Catholic Biblical Quarterly* 62 (2000): 459–80.

———. "The Magi as Wise Men: Re-Examining a Basic Supposition." *New Testament Studies* 46 (2000): 1–20.

Quinn, Jerome D. *The Letter to Titus: A New Translation with Notes and Commentary and An Introduction to Titus, I and II Timothy, The Pastoral Epistles*. Anchor Yale Bible 35. Yale University Press, 2008.

Ramsay, William. *A Historical Commentary on St. Paul's Epistle to the Galatians*. 2nd ed. Hodder & Stoughton, 1890.

———. *Luke the Physician and Other Studies in the History of Religion*. Hodder & Stoughton, 1908.

———. *The Church in the Roman Empire before A.D. 170*. G. P. Putnam's Sons, 1892.

Rapske, Brian. *The Book of Acts and Paul in Roman Custody*. The Book of Acts in Its First Century Setting 3. Eerdmans, 1994.

Rawlinson, Alfred E. J. *St. Mark: With Introduction, Commentary, and Additional Notes*. 6th ed. Westminster Commentaries. Methuen, 1925.

Reasoner, Mark. *Strong and Weak: Romans 14.1–15.13 in Context*. Society for New Testament Studies Monograph Series 103. Cambridge University Press, 1999.

Reicke, Bo. *The Epistles of James, Peter, and Jude*. 1st ed. Anchor Yale Bible 37. Doubleday, 1964.

———. *The Gospel of Luke*. Translated by Ross Mackenzie. SPCK, 1965.

———. "The Historical Setting of Colossians." *Review and Expositor* 70 (1973): 429–32.

———. "The Risen Lord and His Church: The Theology of Acts." *Interpretation* 13 (1959): 157–69.

Reimer, Ivoni Richter. *Women in the Acts of the Apostles: Feminist Liberation Perspective*. Translated by Linda Maloney. Fortress, 1995.

Richards, E. Randolph. *Paul and* First-Century *Letter Writing: Secretaries, Composition, and Collection*. InterVarsity Press, 2004.

Riesner, Rainer. *Paul's Early Period*. Eerdmans, 1998.

Rindge, Matthew. *Jesus's Parable of the Rich Fool. Luke 12:13–34 among Ancient Conversations on Death and Possessions*. SBL Press, 2011.

Robinson, John A. T. *Redating the New Testament*. Westminster John Knox, 1976.

Rodríguez, Rafael. *If You Call Yourself a Jew: Reappraising Paul's Letter to the Romans*. Wipf & Stock, 2015.

Ropes, James. *A Critical and Exegetical Commentary on the Epistle of St. James.* International Critical Commentary. T&T Clark, 1916.

Russell, R. "Eschatology and Ethics in 1 Peter." *Evangelical Quarterly* 47 (1975): 78–84.

Saller, Robert P. *Personal Patronage under the Early Empire*. Cambridge University Press, 1982.

Sampley, J. Paul. "The Weak and the Strong: Paul's Careful and Crafty Rhetorical Strategy in Romans 14.1–15.13." In *The Social World of the First Christians: Essays in Honor of Wayne A. Meeks*, edited by L. Michael White and O. Larry Yarbough, 40–52. Fortress, 1995.

Sanday, William, and Arthur Headlam. *A Critical and Exegetical Commentary on the Epistle to the Romans*. 5th ed. International Critical Commentary 32. T&T Clark, 1902.

Sanders, E. P. *Jesus and Judaism*. SCM Press, 1985.

———. *Paul and Palestinian Judaism: A Comparison of Patterns of Religion*. Fortress, 1977.

———. *Paul, the Law and the Jewish People*. Fortress, 1983.

Scherman, Nosson, and Yitzchak Zev Scherman. *The Illustrated Haggadah*. Mesorah, 2018.

Schneemelcher, Wilhelm, and Robert McL. Wilson, eds. *New Testament Apocrypha*. Rev. ed. 2 vols. Westminster John Knox, 2003.

Scroggs, Robin. *The New Testament and Homosexuality: Contextual Background for Contemporary Debate.* Fortress, 1983.

Seibert, Eric. *The Violence of Scripture: Overcoming the Old Testament's Troubling Legacy*. Fortress, 2012.

Selwyn, Edward G. *The First Epistle of St. Peter: The Greek Text*. 2nd ed. Macmillan, 1958.

———. "The Persecutions in 1 Peter." *SLATS Bulletin* 1–3 (1950): 39–50.

Sevenster, Jan N. *How Much Greek Could the First Jewish Christians Have Known?* Brill, 1968.

———. *Paul and Seneca*. Brill, 1961.

———. *The Roots of Pagan Anti-Semitism in the Ancient World*. Brill, 1975.

Sidebottom, E. M. *James, Jude, 2 Peter*. New Century Bible Commentary. Eerdmans, 1982.

Slaten, A. Wakefield. "The Qualitative Use of Νόμος in the Pauline Epistles." *American Journal of Theology* 23 (1919): 213–18.

Smalley, Stephen. "The Delay of the Parousia." *Journal of Biblical Literature* 83 (1964): 41–56.

———. *Thunder and Love: John's Revelation and John's Community*. Word, 1994.

Sprinkle, Preston. "Πίστις Χριστοῦ as an Eschatological Event." In *The Faith of Jesus Christ: Exegetical, Biblical, and Theological Studies*, edited by Michael Bird and Preston Sprinkle, 165–84. Hendrickson, 2009.

Stanglin, Keith D. *The Letter and Spirit of Biblical Interpretation: From the Early Church to Modern Practice.* Baker Academic, 2018.

Stauffer, Ethelbert. "The Critique of Paganism in I Peter 1:18." In *Neotestamentica et Semitica: Studies in Honour of Matthew Black*, edited by E. Earle Ellis, Max E. Wilcox, and Matthew Black, 129–42. T&T Clark, 1969.

Stendahl, Krister. "The Apostle Paul and the Introspective Conscience of the West." *Paul among Jews and Gentiles* 56 (1963): 199–215.

———. *The School of St. Matthew*. C. W. K. Gleerup, 1954.

Stonehouse, Ned. *The Witness of Matthew and Mark to Christ*. Presbyterian Guardian, 1944.

Stowers, Stanley K. *Diatribe and Paul's Letter to the Romans*. Society of Biblical Literature Dissertation Series 57. Scholars Press, 1981.

———. "Paul on the Use and Abuse of Reason." In *Greeks, Romans, and Christians: Essays in Honor of Abraham Malherbe*, edited by David Balch, Everett Ferguson, and Wayne Meeks, 253–86. Fortress, 1990.

Stronstad, Roger. *The Charismatic Theology of St. Luke*. Hendrickson, 1984.

Talbert, Charles. "II Peter and the Delay of the Parousia." *Vigiliae Christianae* 20 (1966) 137–45.

———. *Reading Acts: A Literary and Theological Commentary on the Acts of the Apostles*. Rev. ed. Reading the New Testament. Smyth & Helwys, 2005.

———. *What Is a Gospel?* Fortress, 1977.

Tannehill, Robert. "The Mission of Jesus According to Luke." In *Jesus in Nazareth*, edited by Erich Grässer and Walther Eltester, 51–75. Walter de Gruyter, 1972.

Taylor, Vincent. *The Gospels: A Short Introduction*. Epworth, 1945.

Theissen, Gerd. *The Social Setting of Pauline Christianity*. Fortress, 1982.

Theissen, Matthew. *Jesus and the Forces of Death. The Gospels' Portrayal of Ritual Impurity within* First-Century *Judaism*. Baker Academic, 2020.

Thiering, Barbara E. "*Mebaqqer* and *Episkopos* in the Light of the Temple Scroll." *Journal of Biblical Literature* 100 (1981): 59–74.

Thiselton, Anthony C. *The First Epistle to the Corinthians: A Commentary on the Greek Text*. New International Greek Testament Commentary. Eerdmans, 2000.

Thompson, Marianne Meye. *The God of the Gospel of John*. Eerdmans, 2001.

———. "The Gospel According to John." In *The Cambridge Companion to the Gospels*, edited by Stephen Barton, 182–200. Cambridge University Press, 2006.

———. *The Incarnate Word: Perspectives on Jesus in the Fourth Gospel*. Hendrickson, 1993.

———. *The Promise of the Father: Jesus and God in the New Testament*. Westminster John Knox, 2000.

Thorsteinsson, Runar. *Roman Christianity and Roman Stoicism: A Comparative Study of Ancient Morality*. Oxford University Press, 2010.

Tobin, Thomas. *Paul's Rhetoric in Its Contexts: The Arguments of Romans*. Hendrickson, 2004.

Toney, Carl N. "Excursus: Resurrection in 2 Corinthians." In *2 Corinthians*, edited by Ralph P. Martin, Rev. ed., 250–56. Word Biblical Commentary 40. Zondervan, 2014.

———. "Excursus: The Composition of 2 Corinthians (1985–2007)." In *2 Corinthians*, edited by Ralph P. Martin, Rev. ed., 50–63. Word Biblical Commentary 40. Zondervan, 2014.

———. "Paul in Acts." In *Issues in Luke-Acts: Selected Essays*, edited by Sean Adams and Michael Pahl, 239–61. Gorgias Handbooks 26. Gorgias, 2012.

———. *Paul's Inclusive Ethic: Resolving Community Conflicts and Promoting Mission in Romans 14–15*. Wissenschaftliche Untersuchungen zum Neuen Testament II /252. Mohr Siebeck, 2008.

———. *Ruining Christmas—Rediscovering Jesus*. Cascade, 2021.

Towner, Philip H. *1–2 Timothy & Titus*. The IVP New Testament Commentary Series 14. InterVarsity Press, 1994.

———. *The Letters to Timothy and Titus*. New International Commentary on the New Testament. Eerdmans, 2006.

Trimm, Charlie. *The Destruction of the Canaanites: God, Genocide, and Biblical Interpretation*. Eerdmans, 2022.

VanderKam, James. *The Dead Sea Scrolls Today*. Eerdmans, 1994.

Vanhoye, Albert. *Our Priest Is Christ: The Doctrine of the Epistle to the Hebrews*. P. I. B., 1977.

Vielhauer, Philipp. "On the 'Paulinism' of Acts." Edited by Leander E. Keck, J. Louis Martyn, Wm. C. Robinson Jr., and Victor P. Furnish. *Studies in* Luke-Acts*: Essays Presented in Honor of Paul Schubert* 10 (1966): 33–50.

Volf, Miroslav. *Exclusion and Embrace: A Theological Exploration of Identity, Otherness, and Reconciliation*. Abingdon, 1996.

Watson, Francis. "By Faith (of Christ): An Exegetical Dilemma and Its Scriptural Solution." In *The Faith of Jesus Christ: Exegetical, Biblical, and Theological Studies*, edited by Michael Bird and Preston Sprinkle, 147–63. Hendrickson, 2009.

Webb, William J. *Slaves, Women & Homosexuals: Exploring the Hermeneutics of Cultural Analysis*. InterVarsity Press, 2001.

Webb, William J., and Gordon K. Oeste. *Bloody, Brutal, and Barbaric?: Wrestling with Troubling War Texts*. IVP Academic, 2019.

Wedderburn, Alexander J. M. "Paul's Collection: Chronology and History." *New Testament Studies* 48 (2002): 95–110.

Weeden, Theodore J. *Mark—Traditions in Conflict*. Fortress, 1971.

Weisser, Sharon. "Philo's Terapeutae and Essenes: A Precedent for the Exceptional Condemnation of Slavery in Gregory of Nyssa." In *The Quest for a Common Humanity: Human Dignity and Otherness in the Religious Traditions of the Mediterranean*, edited by Katell Berthelot and Matthias Morgenstern, 289–310. Studies in the History of Religions 134. Brill, 2011.

Westerholm, Stephen. *Perspectives Old and New on Paul: The "Lutheran" Paul and His Critics*. Eerdmans, 2003.

———. "Torah, Nomos, and Law: A Question of Meaning." *Studies in Religion* 15 (1986): 327–36.

Westermann, William L. *The Slave System of Greek and Roman Antiquity*. American Philosophical Society, 1955.

Wheeler, Sondra E. *Wealth as Peril and Obligation: The New Testament on Possessions*. Eerdmans, 1995.

White, L. Michael. "Urban Development and Social Change in Imperial Ephesos." In *Ephesos Metropolis of Asia: An Interdisciplinary Approach to Its Archaeology, Religion, and Culture*, edited by Helmut Koester, 27–79. Harvard Theological Studies 41. Trinity Press International, 1995.

Wilson, Stephen G. *The Gentiles and the Gentile Mission in* Luke-Acts. Cambridge University Press, 1973.

Wink, Walter. *Naming the Powers: The Language of Power in the New Testament*. Fortress, 1984.

Winter, Bruce. "Acts and Food Shortages." In *The Book of Acts in Its* Graeco-Roman *Setting*, edited by David W. J. Gill and Conrad Gempf, 59–78. Eerdmans, 1994.

———. *Roman Wives, Roman Widows: The Appearance of New Women and the Pauline Communities*. Eerdmans, 2003.

Wire, Antoinette C. *The Corinthian Women Prophets: A Reconstruction through Paul's Rhetoric*. Fortress, 1990.

Wise, Michael, Martin Abegg Jr., and Edward Cook. *Dead Sea Scrolls: A New Translation*. HarperCollins, 1996.

Witherington, Ben, III. *Conflict and Community in Corinth: A Socio-Rhetorical Commentary on 1 and 2 Corinthians*. Eerdmans, 1995.

———. *Matthew*. Smyth & Helwys Bible Commentary. Smyth & Helwys, 2006.

———. *New Testament Rhetoric: An Introductory Guide to the Art of Persuasion in and of the New Testament*. Wipf & Stock, 2009.

———. *The Letters to Philemon, the Colossians, and the Ephesians: A Socio-Rhetorical Commentary on the Captivity Epistles*. Eerdmans, 2007.

Wrede, William. *The Messianic Secret*. Translated by James C. G. Grieg. James Clark & Company, 1971.

Wright, Nicholas Thomas. *The Climax of the Covenant: Christ and the Law in Pauline Theology*. Fortress, 1992.

———. *Jesus and the Victory of God*. Fortress, 1996.

———. *Paul and the Faithfulness of God*. Fortress, 2013.

———. *Scripture and the Authority of God: How to Read the Bible Today*. Rev. and exp. ed. HarperOne, 2011.

———. *Surprised by Scripture: Engaging Contemporary Issues*. HarperOne, 2014.

———. *The Resurrection of the Son of God*. Fortress, 2003.

Wright, Nicholas Thomas, and Michael Bird. *The New Testament in Its World: An Introduction to the History, Literature, and Theology of the First Christians*. Zondervan, 2019.

Yancey, George. *Beyond Racial Gridlock: Embracing Mutual Responsibility*. InterVarsity Press, 2009.

SUBJECT INDEX

H

I

J

K

L